Table of Contents

IRELAND

National Development Plan
2000-2006

BAILE ÁTHA CLIATH
ARNA FHOILSIÚ AG OIFIG AN tSOLÁTHAIR
Le ceannach díreach ón
OIFIG DHÍOLTA FOILSEACHÁN RIALTAIS,
TEACH SUN ALLIANCE, SRÁID THEACH LAIGHEAN, BAILE ÁTHA CLIATH 2,
nó tríd an bpost ó
FOILSEACHÁIN RIALTAIS, AN RANNÓG POST-TRÁCHTA,
4 - 5 BÓTHAR FHEARCHAIR, BAILE ÁTHA CLIATH 2,
(Teil: 01 - 6476834/35/36/37; Fax: 01 - 4752760)
nó trí aon díoltóir leabhar.

───────

DUBLIN
PUBLISHED BY THE STATIONERY OFFICE
To be purchased directly from the
GOVERNMENT PUBLICATIONS SALE OFFICE,
SUN ALLIANCE HOUSE, MOLESWORTH STREET, DUBLIN 2,
or by mail order from
GOVERNMENT PUBLICATIONS, POSTAL TRADE SECTION,
4 - 5 HARCOURT ROAD, DUBLIN 2,
(Tel: 01 - 6476834/35/36/37; Fax: 01 - 4752760)
or through any bookseller.

───────

(Pn. 7780)   £15.00   €19.05

Foreword by the Minster for Finance, Mr Charlie McCreevy T.D.

The National Development Plan (2000-2006) has been framed after the most extensive consultation process, including with the Social Partners and regional interests. It reflects the broad consensus in the consultation process as to the future development needs of the country.

The Plan will lay the foundation for Ireland's continuing economic and social development into the next Millennium. It sets out an ambitious and coherent development strategy supported by a fully quantified multi-annual investment commitment in the key areas of infrastructural development, education and training, the productive sector and the promotion of social inclusion. The Plan also contains a commitment and accompanying framework for the promotion of more balanced regional development.

The vision of the National Development Plan is to ensure that Ireland will remain competitive in the global international marketplace and that the fruits of our economic success will be shared more equally at regional level and throughout society. The Government will seek in the implementation of the Plan to ensure that this vision is realised.

Executive Summary

Introduction

The National Development Plan (2000-2006) (NDP) will involve an investment of £40.588 billion[1] in 1999 prices over the period 2000-2006 of Public, EU and Private funds. This publicly funded element (including EU and Public Private Partnership sources) of the investment will be matched by an estimated £6.4 billion of private investment. The £40.588 billion is broken down as follows with the 1999 base figure shown for comparative purposes.

Heading[2]	2000-2006 £ billion	Annual Average £ billion	1999 Base £ billion	% Increase
Economic and Social Infrastructure	20.948	2.992	1.931	54.9
Employment and Human Resources	10.952	1.565	1.560	0.3
Productive Sector	8.588	1.227	1.054	16.4
Peace Programme	100	20*	20	—
Total	**40.588**	**5.798**	**4.565**	**27.1**

*Peace only relates to 2000-2004

Regional Allocations

The annual investment in the Plan is broken down by Region in line with the designation of Ireland into two Regions — Southern and Eastern Region (S&E Region) and Border, Midland and Western Region (BMW Region) — for Structural Fund purposes. The breakdown of the overall Plan expenditure on a regional basis is as follows:

	£ billion	Per Capita £
S&E Region	27.274	10,250
BMW Region	13.314	13,793
Total	**40.588**	**11,193**

General Strategy

This new National Development Plan is designed to underpin the development of a dynamic competitive economy over the period 2000-2006. It aims to build on the unprecedented economic progress of recent years and to strengthen the foundations for further strong and

---

[1] All figures in this Executive Summary are in IR£; figures in the various Chapters of the Plan are primarily in EURO to meet EU requirements.

[2] Expenditure under the Regional Operational Programmes is grouped as appropriate under each Heading.

sustainable progress in the years ahead. Unlike its two predecessors, this is not a Plan primarily designed to draw down EU Structural and Cohesion Funds. Whilst these Funds will continue to perform a valuable, albeit, declining role as a source of funding, this Plan is based first and foremost on an assessment of the development needs of the country.

The central challenge which is addressed in this National Development Plan is the implementation of public policies which will increase the capacity of Ireland's economy to maintain strong and sustainable output and employment growth. It must prepare the economy for the competitive challenges arising from new and rapidly changing domestic and international economic conditions. In doing this, it will help to ensure that Ireland's recent economic progress is consolidated and built on in a sustainable way.

Crucial associated challenges are the better distribution of the fruits of economic growth both regionally and throughout society and an appropriate balance between the environment and development. The Plan strategy will be complemented by appropriate policies in non-Plan areas of public policy.

Specific Objectives and Strategies

The following national objectives will underpin the strategy for the National Development Plan (NDP) 2000-2006.

- continuing sustainable national economic and employment growth;
- consolidating and improving Ireland's international competitiveness;
- fostering balanced Regional Development;
- promoting Social Inclusion.

The key elements of the strategy to meet these objectives are:

- continuation of the stability orientated macroeconomic policies of recent years;
- a major investment programme in Economic and Social Infrastructure;
- a commitment to a better regional distribution of public and private investment;
- the promotion of education and employment training policies attuned to the needs of the labour market and a special focus on those most at risk of unemployment;
- a multi-faceted approach to the promotion of Social Inclusion, including targeted interventions aimed at areas and groups affected by poverty and social exclusion throughout the community.

Background to NDP 2000-2006

The recent economic transformation has resulted in a vastly changed environment for the preparation of this Plan as compared to that which obtained in 1994. Notwithstanding the investment in Infrastructure under the current Plan, it is clear that Ireland has a significant infrastructural deficit which threatens to inhibit achievement of our economic and employment potential. In the area of human capital, the prospective slowing down in the expansion of the labour force and skills shortage in key areas are emerging as constraints on further economic and employment growth.

The pressure on the country's physical and human resource infrastructure is compounded by lack of sufficient regional balance in our economic development. The infrastructure in large urban areas, especially the Dublin region, is under pressure from the upsurge in commercial and business activity and the increasing population in these areas to serve this activity. By contrast rural and smaller urban areas have lagged behind. In the overall there has been continuing divergence between the economic performances of the S&E and BMW Regions.

Not all sectors of society have, however, benefited from the economic transformation. Unacceptable levels of poverty and social exclusion continue to exist in both urban and rural areas.

Economic and Budgetary Framework

An essential pre-condition for the major level of investment proposed in Plan 2000-2006 is the continuation of stable macroeconomic and budgetary policies. The Government is committed to this fundamental policy position. The fruits of these policies have delivered a level of resources which will allow the Plan investment to be funded notwithstanding the fall in EU Structural and Cohesion Fund receipts over the period. Accordingly, the annual allocations and ultimately the overall NDP commitment, will have to be kept to a level that respects the public expenditure ceilings set by Government, takes account of wider budgetary priorities and accords with the requirements of economic stability.

In the context of making prudent provision for future costs the Government's medium term Budgetary strategy also contains provision for pre-funding against some of the likely additional costs as a result of the prospective ageing profile of the population. Provision for such future contingencies is as important a part of planning as other elements of the NDP.

Flexibility in Plan Implementation

The priorities and multi-annual allocations in the Plan reflect the current assessment of the situation. Over the period of a 7 year Plan priorities may change in line with economic and social circumstances. Implementation of the Plan will be monitored and there will be flexibility to switch resources if necessary.

Balanced Regional Development

More balanced Regional Development is a fundamental objective of the Plan. This commitment is not simply about policies to develop regions of the State which are lagging behind. It also encompasses policies to ease the pressure on urban infrastructure, to tackle urban and rural poverty and, over the long term, to better integrate Physical and Economic Planning through more effective land use in particular.

The objective of balanced Regional Development will be implemented in the Plan in the following way.

- Infrastructural investment in the Operational Programmes especially Roads, Public Transport and Environmental Services investment;

- The promotion over the period of the Plan of a small number of additional regional Gateways (urban growth centres) to complement the existing Gateways and to drive development throughout both Regions — A National Spatial Strategy is to be completed within two years, which will include identification of a small number of additional regional Gateways (urban growth centres) to be promoted over the period of the Plan;

- A commitment to spread the benefits of growth to other smaller urban and rural areas in the regions;

- The inclusion for the first time in a National Development Plan of two Regional Operational Programmes targeted particularly at local infrastructure, the local productive sector and the promotion of social inclusion; the two Regional Operational Programmes will be managed by the two new recently established Regional Assemblies;

- Consistent with the new Regional Aid Guidelines positive discrimination in favour of regions lagging behind in relation to support for new enterprise and the Productive Sector in general.

The general strategy for balanced Regional Development is set out in Chapter 3.

The Southern and Eastern Region and the Border, Midland and Western Region face a number of key and distinctive challenges which will be addressed in the Plan. These can be summarised as follows:

S&E Region

- Consolidate and build on the Region's recent economic performance, especially regarding employment and reductions in long-term unemployment thereby maintaining the Region's key role in national economic competitiveness;

- Address urban congestion and general bottlenecks to growth in Dublin and other urban centres particularly as regards economic and social infrastructure and human resources;

- Further develop counter-balances to Dublin, relieving pressure on the capital and its hinterland, and distributing growth more widely throughout the Region;

- Support the further development of agriculture, agribusiness and the seafood sector;

- Promote social inclusion in deprived urban and rural areas; and

- Maintain a viable rural economy.

BMW Region

- Increase the potential of the Region to act as a counterbalance to the S&E Region, especially Dublin, and pursue more balanced growth within the Region;

- Increase the presence in the Region of the key drivers of sustainable economic growth, notably in the productive sector;

- Improve the quality of the Region's economic and social infrastructure and human resources;

- Build on the Region's natural resource base, especially in the areas of agriculture, tourism, the seafood sector and rural enterprise; and

- Promote rural and urban social inclusion.

The indicative allocations of planned investment between the two Regions is set out in the following table:

Indicative breakdown of NDP planned expenditure (2000-2006) by Region

Programme	S&E Region (£ million)	BMW Region (£ million)	Total (£ million)
Economic and Social Infrastructure	12,918	4,692	17,610
Employment and Human Resources	7,054	2,834	9,893
Productive Investment	2,856	1,653	4,509
S&E Regional Programme	2,986	—	2,986
BMW Regional Programme	—	2,084	2,084
CAP Accompanying Measures	1,456	1,949	3,405
Peace	—	100	100
All Programmes	**27,274**	**13,313**	**40,588**

Social Inclusion

The Plan responds to the National Employment Action Plan employment process as developed in the framework of the EU Co-ordinating Employment Strategy and will also involve a major integrated approach to promoting social inclusion. A key element of the overall strategy is the continuation of sustainable economic growth to promote jobs. There will also be substantial investment in education and training, childcare and recreational infrastructure and investment in people through lifelong learning and skills development, community development and family services. The objective is that employment is opened up to all sectors of society as this is the best way to counter poverty and social exclusion. However, the Plan also recognises that ensuring the correct overall economic environment for job creation is not sufficient on its own to alleviate poverty in areas and groups throughout the community. Targeted interventions are therefore provided for, primarily in the Regional Operational Programmes, to deal with these problems. In total some £15 billion is provided in the Plan directly to promote Social Inclusion. Chapter 10 of the Plan gives an overview of the NDP measures to promote Social Inclusion.

Rural Development

The NDP gives effect to the policy set out in the recent White Paper on Rural Development. In total some £6.7 billion will be expended on measures which will support Rural Development. An overview of the NDP provision on Rural Development is provided in Chapter 11 of the Plan.

Structure of the National Development Plan 2000-2006

The National Development Plan comprises three National or Inter-regional Operational Programmes, two Regional Operational Programmes and a separate Operational Programme for the PEACE Programme which operates in the border counties and in Northern Ireland. In addition to the Structural Funds cofunded programmes, there will be a separate national programme for the Common Agricultural Policy (CAP) rural development cofunded accompanying measures. The Inter-regional Operational Programmes are as follows:

- **Economic and Social Infrastructure (Chapter 4)**

- **Employment and Human Resources (Chapter 5)**

- **Productive Sector (Chapter 6)**

Economic and Social Infrastructure

The total investment (2000-2006) under the Economic and Social Infrastructure Operational Programme will be £17.6 billion. This investment will be broken down between the two regions as follows:

	£ billion	Per Capita
S&E Region	12.9	4,855
BMW Region	4.7	4,861
State	17.6	4,856

The breakdown of the Economic and Social Infrastructure Programme by sector will be as follows:

Category	Total allocation for 2000-2006 period (£ million)
National Roads	4,700
Public Transport	2,234
Water and Waste Water	2,495
Coastal Protection	35
Energy	146
Social and *Affordable* Housing	6,000
Health Capital	2,000
Total	17,610

Roads Investment

National Primary Roads: The development strategy for national primary roads will include:

- the development in their entirety by 2006 of the following routes to motorway/improved dual carriageway standard

    - Dublin to Border (M1);

    - Galway to Dublin (N4/N6);

    - Cork to Dublin (N8);

    - Limerick to Dublin (N7);

    - Waterford to Dublin (N9) (road type and route to be further evaluated).

There will be further major improvements on other[3] national primary routes including

- routes to the North-West: N2 (Dublin/Monaghan/Omagh/Derry, Letterkeny), N3 (Dublin/Belturbet/Enniskillen/Derry), N4 (Kinnegad to Sligo), N13-N15 (Sligo/Donegal/Lifford/Letterkenny/Derry), N16 (Sligo/Blacklion/Enniskillen/Dungannon/Larne);

---

[3] Internal Northern Ireland connecting routes are indicated where appropriate.

- the Western Corridor from Sligo through Limerick to Rosslare (N17, N18, N24 and N25) N5 (Castlebar/Longford), N26 (Ballina/Foxford);

- other roads in South and East: N11 (Rosslare/Dublin), N20 (Limerick/Cork), N21 (Tralee/Limerick), N22 (Tralee/Killarney/Cork), N28 (Cork/Ringaskiddy), N30 (Enniscorthy/New Ross);

- completion of the M50 and Dublin Port Access Tunnel.

National Secondary Roads: Among the National Secondary Roads to be improved are:

- Letterkenny/Dungloe/Donegal (N56), Ballisadare/Ballina/Westport/Clifden/Galway (N59), Athlone/Boyle (N61), Moate/Stradbally (N80), and Mullingar/Birr (N52), in the BMW Region;

- Birr/Nenagh (N52), Tralee/Listowel/Limerick (N69), Tralee/Dingle (N86), Tralee/Caherciveen/Kenmare (N70), Killarney/Bantry/Bandon/Cork (N71), Stradbally/Bunclody (N80), Tallaght/Blessington (N81), and Ennis/Ennistymon (N85) in the S&E Region.

Public Transport

The key elements of the public transport provision are:

Greater Dublin Area

- Implementation of the light rail network (LUAS)

- Major short-term investment in suburban rail including:

  - the phased purchase of 46 additional DART cars and 58 diesel railcars;

  - upgrading of the Greystones to Arklow line;

  - linking Heuston and Connolly stations to permit the Kildare Arrow service to run through to Connolly;

  - quadrupling of track between Hazelhatch and Sallins to separate long distance and suburban services;

  - provision of new stations at Intel, Lucan North and South and Ashington;

  - resignalling of Howth to Barrow Street.

- A substantial enhancement and expansion of the bus service, including:

  - the expansion of the bus network, including the provision of orbital and local routes to complement the existing largely radial network;

  - the phased purchase of 275 additional buses to increase passenger capacity and meet the development requirements of the network;

  - an ongoing bus replacement and equipment renewal programme;

  - the provision of five new Quality Bus Corridors (QBCs), the enhancement of the existing QBCs and the introduction of other bus priority measures;

  - Promotion of transport integration through the provision of additional park and ride facilities and the introduction of integrated public transport ticketing;

- Implementation of traffic management measures (including measures to respond to the needs of mobility impaired and disabled people) and additional cycling facilities.

There is also a substantial contingency provision to meet the cost of implementing the recommendations of the strategic rail study and the underground section of LUAS. The strategic rail study will be completed by end 1999 and is examining a range of options for the longer term development of the suburban rail network. A public private partnership approach to the implementation of both light rail and rail projects will be used where appropriate.

This investment programme will be complemented by a demand management strategy which will be developed by the Dublin Transportation Office during 2000 and implemented thereafter.

Regional Public Transport

There will be a major investment in Public Transport outside Dublin comprising the following main elements:

- Implementation of the Railway Safety Programme;
- Significant investment in mainline rail renewal;
- Public transport development in the Greater Cork Area, Limerick, Galway and Waterford;
- Regional bus improvements;
- Accessibility improvements to existing public transport infrastructure and facilities;
- Bus Éireann ongoing fleet replacement and re-equipment;
- Pilot measures for rural public transport to encourage local or community-based initiatives to provide bus services in rural areas.

Accessibility

The Government is committed to improving accessibility to public transport for mobility impaired persons and people with disabilities. New and upgraded bus and rail stations, light rail vehicles, new suburban railcars and new urban buses will be fully accessible. New implementation structures will be put in place.

Infrastructure Delivery

The Government is fully committed to ensuring that its proposals for economic infrastructure in the Plan are implemented within the Plan period. In mid-1999 the Government established a Cabinet Committee on Infrastructural Development, including Public Private Partnership. This Committee is chaired by An Taoiseach and includes An Tánaiste, the Minister for Finance, the Minister for the Environment and Local Government, the Minister for Public Enterprise, the Minister for Justice, Equality and Law Reform and the Attorney General. The Cabinet Committee, supported by a Cross-Departmental Team of officials, has a number of objectives:

- to monitor and oversee at a high level the delivery of key infrastructure projects;
- to promote measures and Best Practice Guidelines which will support the acceleration of programme and project delivery;
- to promote appropriate institutional, administrative, legal and regulatory reforms to avoid unnecessary delays in the delivery of infrastructure projects;

- to devise and implement a communications strategy to raise public awareness of the economic and social benefits of rapid implementation of the infrastructure programme;

- to support the development and implementation of the Public Private Partnership Framework.

The Cabinet Committee is focusing initially on transport, notably the core inter-urban road network and the Dublin Transport Package. The National Development Plan will involve an unprecedented expansion in and acceleration of investment in transport infrastructure, including in the area of public transport. As indicated above, the Cabinet Committee has an objective of promoting appropriate institutional reform, including the area of public transport; if deemed necessary the Government will show no hesitation in putting in place structures which will meet the public's needs in this area.

Water and Waste Water

The investment under this heading will provide for:

- the construction of all the outstanding schemes required under the EU Urban Waste Water Treatment Directive, including Dublin and Cork, and also major schemes in Swords, Waterford, Limerick, Sligo, Westport and Letterkenny;

- investment in water supply focused on extending treatment and distribution capacity in the major urban areas and on conservation of water through leakage detection and mains rehabilitation and replacement;

- further extending the lake and river catchment protection programme over the Plan period; the investment will also include funding for the development of systems to monitor the effects of the implementation of waste water treatment infrastructure and other pollution abatement measures;

- water and sewerage services for development of land for housing and commercial use and support for tourism priority areas;

- meet in full the requirements of the Urban Waste Water Directive in relation to the provision of secondary treatment in urban areas by end 2005.

This investment will be supplemented by an investment of £420 million for Rural Water Services under the Regional Operational Programmes.

Coastal Protection

Coastal erosion is a serious threat to some public infrastructure, tourist amenities and areas of ecological importance. The Plan provision will strategically address urgent coastal erosion problems in a prioritised way.

Energy

Market failure among smaller energy users will require complementary programmes and measures to encourage energy efficiency. This has implications for Regional Development which will inform the distribution of Plan investment in this area. The NDP provision will:

- promote energy efficiency through information and education programmes;

- promote research and development in energy efficiency and CO_2 abatement;

15

- promote alternative energy;
- improve the energy efficiency of the pre-1980 housing stock and Government and Local Authority Buildings.

Social Affordable Housing and Health Capital

Unlike its two predecessors this National Development Plan includes Social Housing and Health Capital. The priorities for investment in housing under the Plan will be:

- to provide the necessary infrastructural investment to facilitate the overall level of housing output required to meet current and anticipated levels of demand in a planned, coherent fashion;
- to increase social housing output to meet rising need;
- to continue the drive to improve the physical condition of the social housing stock.

In specific terms the Plan will lead to:

- An additional 35,500 local authority housing units.
- An increase in the output of the voluntary housing sector from the current level of 500 to 4,000 units per year.
- An increase to 2,000 units per year under the local authority affordable housing scheme and shared ownership schemes.

In relation to Health Capital the investment priorities will be:

- to provide facilities for persons with an intellectual disability;
- to develop a range of facilities for the elderly;
- to address major unmet needs in the provision of modern accommodation for the mentally ill and the physically disabled;
- to provide a comprehensive, quality and accessible acute hospital infrastructure;
- to address child care needs;
- to remedy deficiencies in the network of health centres;
- to maximise the potential of information and communication technology (ICT) in the health care sector.

Employment and Human Resources

A total provision of just under £10 billion is proposed for investment in the Employment and Human Resources Operational Programme broken down as follows between the two Regions:

	£ billion	Per Capita £
S&E Region	7.1	2,651
BMW Region	2.8	2,936
State	9.9	2,729

The priorities for the Employment and Human Resource Development Operational Programme will reflect those of the National Employment Action Plan and will be organised under four Sub-Programmes to reflect the four pillars of the EU employment guidelines: *Employability, Entrepreneurship, Adaptability and Equal Opportunities.* The allocation is broken down as follows between the four pillars:

Pillar	2000-2006 Allocation (£ million)
Employability	4,631
Entrepreneurship	413
Adaptability	4,647
Equality	202
Total	**9,893**

Employability

The Employability Sub-Programme will comprise a combination of Social Inclusion measures in the education sector and labour market integration and training measures. The Social Inclusion measures targeted at disadvantaged people will include:

- Early Education;
- School Completion;
- Early Literacy;
- Third Level Access Programme;
- Traveller Education;
- Career Guidance.

Among the Labour market measures will be:

- Active Measures for the Long-term Unemployed and Socially Excluded;
- An Action Programme for Unemployed;
- Early School Leavers progression to employment;
- Skills and Sectoral Training for the Unemployed and Redundant Workers.

Entrepreneurship

The Entrepreneurship Sub-Programme will comprise:

- Management Training for SMEs and
- The Social Economy Scheme.

Adaptability

Under the Adaptability heading there will be measures for:

- Lifelong Learning including a Back to Education Initiative to complement the early interventions under the Employability Pillar;
- Skills Development;

- Apprenticeship/Traineeship;
- Sectoral Training;
- Improvement of the Quality of Education and Training Provision;
- Back-to-Work Schemes including a new family service approach to enhance the capacity of disadvantaged families to improve their circumstances.

Equality

The childcare provision of £250 million in the Regional Operational Programmes will account for the bulk of expenditure on equality. Provision of £200 million is also being made in the Employment and Human Resources OP for measures which will include:

- Training for Employment for People with Disabilities;
- Refugee Language Training;
- Promotion and Monitoring of Equal Opportunities.

Education and Training Capital

A provision of £1.62 billion, is being made for educational and training infrastructure in facilities, new equipment and information technology. In particular, investment at third level in R&D and in the technological sector will provide higher education relevant to the needs of the modern economy. This will be an important element in assisting the Regional Development strategy in the Plan.

Productive Sector

The third national or interregional programme will cover the Productive Sector. Total Plan expenditure of £4.5 billion is proposed, broken down between the two Regions as follows:

	£ billion	Per Capita £
S&E Region	2.8	1,073
BMW Region	1.7	1,713
State	4.5	1,243

Excluding the CAP accompanying measures which are the subject of a separate programme, the Productive Sector Programme investment will be allocated as follows:

Category	2000-2006 Allocation (£ million)
RTDI	1,946
Industry	1,903
Marketing	337
Agricultural Development	278
Fisheries	45
Total	4,509

The strategy for the productive investment programme will be:

- to provide selective support for FDI particularly in the BMW region; this strategy will be facilitated by the higher level of regional state aids permissible in the BMW Region. There is a commitment in the Plan that IDA Ireland will seek to ensure that over the Plan period, at least 50% of all new jobs from greenfield projects will be in the BMW Region;

- to provide an integrated response to the needs of all indigenous firms across all sectors through, where appropriate, the implementation of business development plans by the development agencies;

- to address in a targeted way the specific needs of the food industry;

- to strengthen the marketing capacity of Irish firms;

- to promote marketing of the island of Ireland as a tourist destination;

- to support tourism investment in areas that have lagged behind in terms of market share;

- to improve agricultural structures at farm level through selective supports;

- to support the modernisation of the fishing fleet.

There will be a major accelerated increase in Research, Technological Development and Innovation (RTDI) investment with the objectives:

- to strengthen the capacity of Irish third level institutions and other research establishments to conduct research relevant to the needs of the Irish economy;

- to strengthen the capacity of Irish firms to assimilate the results of R&D into their products and processes, and

- to provide support for sectoral research in agriculture, food, marine and the environment.

CAP Accompanying Measures

A separate programme will be implemented for CAP rural development accompanying measures. A total £3.4 billion is provided under this heading which will be expended on:

- Rural Environment Protection Scheme (REPS);

- Early Retirement Scheme;

- Compensatory Allowances;

- Forestry Measures.

Regional Operational Programmes (Chapters 7 and 8)

Both the S&E Region and the BMW Region will benefit from the substantial investment under the Inter-regional Operational Programmes. The investment in economic infrastructure will facilitate further sustainable economic growth in both Regions. It will also relieve existing infrastructural bottlenecks especially in the S&E Region. In the BMW Region the Inter-regional Programmes on Infrastructure and the Productive Sector will assist in the overall objective of greater convergence of the economic performance of that Region.

Investment under the two regional Operational Programmes will complement investment in the Inter-regional Programmes as part of an integrated strategy designed to promote balanced regional development. Their focus will be primarily on the development of local infrastructure, local enterprise development and on promoting social inclusion. The overall provision for each Regional OP is as follows:

	S&E Region £ million	BMW Region £ million
Regional Infrastructure	1,812	1,525
Social Inclusion	837	221
Productive Investment	336	338
Total	**2,985**	**2,084**
Overall Expenditure Per Capita £	**1,122**	**2,159**

The regional infrastructural investment will include:

- Non National Roads;
- Rural Water;
- Waste Management;
- Urban and Village Renewal;
- Communications and lead business;
- Seaports and Regional Airports;
- Culture, Sport and Recreation.

In the productive sector there will be investment in:

- Micro Enterprises;
- Tourism;
- Fisheries;
- Forestry;
- Rural Development.

The Social Inclusion measures will include:

- Childcare;
- Equality;
- Community Development/Family Support;
- Countering involvement in crime and drug abuse;
- Youth Services;
- Services to the unemployed.

The provision for childcare represents a major new initiative in this area. The allocation will be expended on increasing the supply and quality of childcare facilities, particularly on the provision of infrastructure in disadvantaged communities, increasing the number of childcare places and on encouraging private providers.

PEACE Operational Programme/Co-operation With Northern Ireland

A separate Operational Programme will be established to draw down over the years 2000-2005 the £80 million of Structural Funds being made available for the PEACE Programme in the Border counties.

The framework for co-operation with Northern Ireland is set out in Chapter 9. Apart from the PEACE Programme and the Ireland/Northern Ireland Interreg Community Initiative, this Chapter sets out the other key areas for co-operation between the two administrations. Particular stress is laid on the areas for co-operation referred to in the Belfast (Good Friday) Agreement 1998.

Proposals for EU Co-Financing

The total amount of Structural and Cohesion Funds available to Ireland over the period of NDP (2000-2006) is approximately £3 billion. The proposals for Structural and Cohesion Fund co-financing are as follows in summary form:

	Structural Funds Contribution £ million	Cohesion Funds Contribution £ million
Economic and Social Infrastructure	568	454
Productive Sector	335	—
Employment and Human Resources	661	—
Regional OPs	846	—
PEACE OP	83	—

In broad terms the proposed apportionment of the Structural Funds allocation is based on the prioritisation of Plan expenditure by sector and the desire to provide for a substantial level of Structural Funds in the Regional Programmes. The Regional breakdown of the Structural Funds allocation is fully consistent with the outcome of the Agenda 2000 negotiations. The actual allocation of the Structural Funds to priorities will be a matter for negotiation with the European Commission in the context of agreeing a Community Support Framework for Ireland.

Provision is also included for expenditure of approximately £47 million in TENs (Trans European Networks) funding under the Economic and Social Infrastructure Programme.

In addition, to the Structural Funds cofinancing the EU will cofinance £1.7 billion of the £3.4 billion CAP Accompanying Rural Development Programme under FEOGA Guarantee.

Community Initiatives

Ireland's share of the next round of Community Initiatives is £131 million and it is expected that Initiatives will operate in Ireland in the following areas:

- Ireland/Northern Ireland Interreg
- Ireland/Wales Interreg
- Transnational Programme in Spatial Planning
- URBAN
- EQUAL
- LEADER

Public Private Partnerships

Provision is included for £1.85 billion of Public Private Partnership (PPP) funding. An indicative allocation of PPP funding across the main sectors is as follows:

	PPP Funding £ million
Roads	1,000
Public Transport	300
Waste Management	450
Water Services	100

This is a **minimum target** for PPPs in the Plan. Precise designation of projects or parts of projects for PPP purposes will be decided as the Plan is implemented. The objective is maximum usage of PPPs consistent with the principles of efficiency and best value for money. The provision of £1.85 billion for PPP funding does not reflect the total level of PPP activity under the Plan, as arrangements for public private partnerships without private capital investment will be used in a number of areas covered by the Plan.

General Issues

Consultation

There has been intensive consultation in the formulation of the Plan. This has included submissions from and meetings with the Social Partners, the Regional Authorities and the Western Development Commission. Two studies were undertaken by Fitzpatrick Associates on investment priorities in the S&E and BMW Regions respectively. The Minister for Finance also met with delegations from the recently established Regional Assemblies to brief them on the Plan. A major study "National Investment Priorities for the Period 2000-2006" was undertaken by the ESRI on behalf of the Government. Consultation has also taken place with the European Commission.

Impact on Poverty

The promotion of social inclusion is a key NDP objective. More generally the NDP investment proposed will have a positive effect on employment prospects thereby assisting in the fight against poverty. This will be augmented by specific measures to promote social inclusion notably in the area of educational disadvantage, access to housing, local and community development, family services and childcare etc.

Impact on Gender Policy

Both men and women will benefit from the investment in all the Operational Programmes. Particular potential exists under the education and training measures in the Employment and Human Resources Development OP through mainstreaming of equal opportunities to assist men and women to compete on the same lines for the same types of employment. Moreover, the substantial provisions for childcare under the Regional OPs will facilitate people with family responsibilities to avail of employment and training opportunities.

Impact on the Environment

The Plan has also been subject to pilot eco-audit and the outcome is set out in Appendix 4 to the Plan. The increased investment in economic and social infrastructure such as water and waste management will facilitate compliance with EU Environmental Directives and Policy. The investment in public transport will also have a positive impact on the environment as will sectoral investments such as forestry, REPs etc.

Impact on Rural Areas

The Plan gives effect in specific areas to the policy framework in the White Paper on Rural Development. As agreed by Government in relation to the White Paper on Rural Development, administrative procedures will be introduced for all Departments to ensure that policy makers are aware of the likely impact of all proposals on rural communities. The operation of these procedures will contribute significantly to integrating the strategy for the economic and social development of rural areas with the objectives and principles of other policy initiatives and, in particular, of the National Anti Poverty Strategy.

Monitoring/Administration Arrangements

Provision will be made for Social Partner and Regional Assembly membership of all the OP Monitoring Committees including the Regional Operational Programmes. The Regional Assemblies will be the managing authority for their respective Operational Programmes and will chair and will provide the secretariat for the Monitoring Committees for these Programmes. This is a major new departure in devolution of management of operational programmes as on previous occasions all operational programmes have been managed centrally. The Plan will also provide for the principle of the inclusion of regional representatives on project selection boards, where appropriate, for measures under the Regional Operational Programmes. Mainstreaming of poverty, gender, environmental and rural proofing will be promoted in the implementation and monitoring arrangements.

1 Economic Background to the National Development Plan

Introduction

1.1 This new National Development Plan has been framed against a very different economic background to that of its predecessor in 1993. While its overall ambition — to enable the economy to develop along a path of strong, sustainable growth — may be little changed, the challenges to be faced in achieving this ambition in the future are new. These new challenges spring from the greatly altered economic and budgetary background which now obtains.

1.2 These changes to the economic background to this Plan compared with the Plan covering the period 1994-99 are many but they include the following:

- The previous Plan had to be consistent with enabling Ireland to qualify for Economic and Monetary Union. EMU began last January with Ireland as a founder member and today the challenge is to enable Ireland to avail of the opportunities and meet the demands which the single currency will bring.

- The previous Plan had to address widespread unemployment. Today Ireland is experiencing almost full employment and the challenge is to deal with emerging labour shortages and the cost pressures which a tight labour market entails.

- The previous Plan was prepared against a background of budget deficits and was concerned with ensuring that Ireland achieved sufficient budgetary stability to fulfil the fiscal conditions for membership of EMU. Today we have a substantial budget surplus and significant budget surpluses are envisaged over the period of this Plan. This is entirely appropriate in the context of strong economic growth and relatively favourable demographic conditions. The challenge for budgetary policy now is to provide for the public investment needs of a strongly growing economy while avoiding adding unduly to inflationary pressures which could undermine the achievement of sustainable growth.

- The previous Plan, in attempting to deal with the social consequences of high unemployment, sought to enhance social cohesion, primarily by providing a framework for the maximum sustainable increase in employment. Today the need to provide strong employment growth for an increasing labour force remains — but the new Plan must promote social inclusion on a much wider plane.

- The previous Plan emphasised the need for sustainable national development and the need to promote balanced regional development. These considerations still obtain — but today balanced regional development is also a necessity if the economy's full capacity for development is to be utilised.

- The previous Plan was framed against a background of limited expectations. The new plan must be drafted against a background of high, and in some respects, unrealistic expectations but it must at the same time prepare the economy for the competitive challenges arising from new and rapidly changing international economic conditions.

Economic Developments in Ireland 1994-99

1.3   Ireland's economic progress in recent years has exceeded the targets set in the last NDP by a wide margin. GNP growth averaged about 7.5% *per annum* in real terms. This was much higher than the 3.5% annual GNP growth envisaged in the 1994-99 National Development Plan.

1.4   One of the most encouraging aspects of Ireland's economic performance over this period is that unlike earlier periods of expansion, output growth was extremely employment-intensive. The numbers at work grew by over 370,00. While the labour force grew strongly, the unemployment rate fell from over 15% in 1993 to about 6% in early 1999.

1.5   There was also substantial progress in raising income per head in Ireland towards the EU average. By 1998 Ireland's GDP per head had reached parity with the EU average. On the more appropriate measure for Ireland, GNP per head , it represented 88% of the EU average compared with 79% in 1994.

1.6   All components of GNP have contributed to the strong output growth. Private consumption has grown rapidly since 1993. This was due primarily to higher real disposable incomes and higher employment, although a fall in the savings ratio made some contribution. More recently, lower interest rates have supported consumer confidence.

1.7   Lower interest rates also supported an expansion in investment. Fixed investment grew by a remarkable annual rate of 17% per annum between 1994-1998. Investment in machinery and equipment has grown rapidly since 1993 reflecting the strong expansion in manufacturing industry. Much of this expansion has been in high technology industries. This has resulted in strong demand for commercial construction. Allied to demographic changes that have resulted in high demand for housing, this has contributed to overall growth in building and construction investment of over 14% *per annum* since 1993. Public investment also expanded rapidly, with an average annual increase of 11%.

1.8   The world economy performed well over the Plan period with reasonable growth in Ireland's trading partners. Thanks to an improvement in competitiveness and higher industrial capacity Ireland made substantial gains in export market share. Exports grew at an annual average rate of over 16% since 1993. Demand for industrial inputs, along with buoyant domestic consumption in the last two years, has contributed to strong growth in imports. In spite of this Ireland's trade balance and wider balance of payments have been in substantial surplus during the Plan period.

Labour Market Trends

1.9   Tackling unemployment, particularly long-term unemployment, was identified as the main priority in the Community Support Framework, 1994-1999. In 1993, Ireland had one of the highest unemployment rates in the EU. Since the 1980s Ireland had suffered from both high unemployment and emigration. With strong labour force growth expected, generating sufficient employment to reduce unemployment was seen as a significant challenge. Employment gains of about 12-14,000, or 1.75% *per annum* were expected.

1.10   These employment targets were easily surpassed with employment growing by about 370,000 in the last five years, an annual average increase of about 5%. On a International Labour Organisation (ILO) basis, unemployment has fallen by about 125,000 since 1993. As a result the unemployment rate is now about 6% — well below the EU average. Long term unemployment has also fallen dramatically, and now represents less than 3% of the work force.

1.11   This progress was achieved against a background of very strong labour force growth. Positive demographic factors, increased labour force participation — particularly by women — and net immigration have enabled the labour force to grow rapidly. Over the period of the Plan the work force grew by over 250,000. The population boom of the 1970's resulted in an increasing young work force in the 1990's. Moreover, as a result of enhanced investment in education and training over the last 20 years the new cohorts of entrants to the labour force were more highly educated than their predecessors. As a result, the work force was well suited to respond to the needs of the expanding manufacturing and services sectors.

Budgetary Developments

1.12   The need to address the burden of Government debt which was identified as a priority in the 1988-1993 National Development Plan, was given further impetus by the Maastricht Treaty convergence criteria for participation in EMU. Adherence to these criteria was a central concern of the 1994-99 Plan. The Maastricht budgetary criteria required that the General Government deficit should remain below 3% of GDP and that the general Government debt should be no more than 60% of GDP or be falling towards that level at a satisfactory rate. Ireland's performance over the period was more than sufficient to meet these conditions.

1.13   In 1993 the General Government deficit was 2.3% of GDP and the debt/GDP ratio was 93.1%. The deficit fell between 1994 and 1996, while the budget has been in surplus for the last two years. As a result the Government debt fell to 56% of GDP in 1998.

Prices, Earnings and Costs

1.14   Maintaining moderate inflation and competitiveness were key concerns of the 1994-99 Plan. Once again, these target were achieved. Inflation, as measured by the consumer price index, has averaged 2.1% since 1994 with a high of 2.5% in 1995 and a low of 1.5% in 1997. Inflation was remarkably moderate and stable, particularly given the buoyancy of demand.

1.15   There were a number of reasons for this inflation performance. Domestically, price developments were underpinned by successive National Agreements which delivered modest labour cost increases. Given the open nature of the Irish economy, price developments are particularly sensitive to international price trends and exchange rate movements. International prices have remained relatively stable during the 1994-99 Plan period although exchange rate developments contributed to inflationary pressures in 1997 and early 1998. As a result inflation rose to a peak of 3.2% in August 1998 but subsequently moderated.

Reasons for Success

1.16   A number of factors contributed to the strong performance of the economy during the Plan period. The most important was the stable macro economic background of low inflation, moderate wage developments and prudent budgetary policies. The Social Partnership model has been an integral part of this framework. The four agreements between the Trade Unions, Employers, Farmers and the Government — and since 1996 Community and Voluntary Sector — have helped to restore Ireland's cost competitiveness. This generated confidence in economic policy and boosted business activity and productivity, resulting in high levels of investment and job creation. This in turn has delivered a turnaround in the public finances facilitating tax reform and increased expenditure on public services. A continuation of this successful social partnership model can play an important role in sustaining Ireland's competitiveness in today's global economy.

1.17   Apart from macrecoeconomic factors the following combination of structural factors have also been important:

- Ireland's high birth rate in the 1970s has led to large increases in the working-age population in the 1990s.

- Combined with falls in unemployment, and modest increases in the number of people reaching 65 years of age, these positive demographic developments have led to a large fall in Ireland's dependency ratio. This falling dependency ratio alone explains a part of the rise in per capita incomes.

- Investment in education over a long period has improved the average educational levels of the workforce.

- High levels, by historic standards, of public investment in physical and human capital, undertaken with the help of substantial EU Structural and Cohesion funding, improved the stock of public infrastructure.

- For most of this period relatively low interest rates have encouraged strong private sector investment.

- There has been a positive environment for business including a falling tax burden on both employees and companies.

Economic Outlook 2000-2006

1.18   This new National Development Plan is set against a background of record economic and employment growth. However, there is now increasing evidence that supply-side constraints may inhibit growth unless they are tackled.

1.19   Significant congestion is evident in many of our towns and cities. House price inflation has increased reflecting the initial weak supply response to a sharp rise in the demand for housing. Tensions are also evident in the labour market with skills shortages in a number of areas. Unless addressed, these pressures will undermine competitiveness and the economy's capacity to realise its growth potential. Tackling these problems — in many ways problems of success — therefore requires a different strategy to previous National Development Plans.

1.20   The National Economic and Social Council(NESC) is finalising a Strategy Report which will set out a vision for Ireland in the next decade reflecting recent economic and social progress and the challenges which must now be faced. The report recognises that the foundations for a successful society are a dynamic economy, and an inclusive society, incorporating a commitment to social justice, based on consistent economic development that is socially and environmentally sustainable, which responds especially to the constantly evolving requirements of international competitiveness, understood as the necessary condition of continuing economic and social success. As well as economic and social inclusion, the NESC strategy places a particular emphasis on adaptation to change, the Information Society, Lifelong Learning and balanced regional development. The NDP has a central role to play in the realisation of this vision, and the investment provided for is consistent with, and essential to, the implementation of these shared economic and social goals at the beginning of the new century.

Policy Environment in Economic and Monetary Union

1.21 Maintaining competitiveness and sustaining economic stability poses a particular challenge in the new policy environment of EMU. Responsibility for monetary policy has been transferred to the European Central Bank (ECB). This new framework reinforces the need to remain competitive. The option of adjusting exchange rates to offset short-term losses in competitiveness is now no longer available. Economic instability and competitiveness losses will have significant implications for employment performance.

1.22 EMU requires greater flexibility in the economy as a whole. To maintain employment growth cost developments including, prices and wages must be more responsive to changing economic conditions. More than ever the Irish economy requires open and well functioning markets for products, services, capital and labour. Fostering and promoting competition, where possible, is essential to maximise productivity and improve competitiveness. This will help to improve the economy's overall potential growth rate and help to lower unemployment.

1.23 Fiscal policy must seek to influence economic activity — offsetting excess demand in periods of strong growth and supporting growth in less favourable times. The stabilisation function of fiscal policy in a small open economy can be limited. However, it is clear that running significant surpluses during periods of strong growth is a necessary condition for a prudent budgetary policy. As detailed in Ireland's *Stability Programme 1999-2001*, budgetary surpluses will be maintained for as long as growth remains favourable. This approach to Budgetary policy underpins this National Development Plan.

1.24 This approach to budgetary policy is consistent with the terms of the Stability and Growth Pact (SGP). The Pact states that budget positions should be close to balance or in surplus in normal economic conditions to enable Member States to keep their general Government deficit below the Maastricht reference value of 3 per cent of GDP even in unfavourable economic conditions. Ireland is currently experiencing economic conditions which are significantly better than normal and in these circumstances it is entirely appropriate that we should be operating a significant Budget surplus. On the basis of projected economic growth of the order of 5 per cent and the maintenance of prudent fiscal policies, the budgetary outlook is for continued surpluses of the order of 3 per cent of GDP over the period of the plan.

Making provision for the longer term

1.25 At present, Ireland is benefiting from a relatively favourable demographic position. There is one person aged 65 or over for every five persons of working age. Demographic projections indicate that by the middle of the next century there will be one pensioner for every two persons of working age. As a result, it is expected that the ratio of both Social Welfare and Public Service pensioners to persons at work will increase substantially in the decades ahead. Demand for health services will also rise appreciably, in line with the proportion of older people in our population.

1.26 The Government has decided to begin now to provide resources on a planned basis to secure the pensions in retirement of a progressively ageing population and to this end an annual provision of 1% of GNP will be set aside in future to pre fund part of these prospective costs. The Government has also decided to allocate a tranche of the proceeds of the Telecom Eireann flotation to supplement the annual allocations.

1.27   While this advance provision is a significant step in the direction of securing the Exchequer's ability to continue to maintain and improve public services into the longer term, an annual budgetary allocation of 1% of GNP together with the lump-sum contribution from the Telecom Eireann flotation may meet only about one third of the extra Exchequer costs which demographic change promises over the period to middle of the next century.

1.28   These provisions for pensions will be accommodated within a sustainable overall budgetary strategy which will allow for the significant infrastructural and other developments being provided for in this National Development Plan.

1.29   The central goal of fiscal policy in the period ahead will be to underpin sustainable economic growth, in order to further enhance living standards, increase employment and promote social inclusion on a sustainable basis over the longer term. The aim will be

(1) to maintain the competitiveness of the economy by securing a competitive evolution of wages and costs and continue to enhance public infrastructure;

(2) to ensure continued investor confidence in the Government's management of budgetary policy by running substantial surpluses in order to minimise inflationary pressure while preparing the public finances for the long-term costs of population ageing.

Within these constraints, the Government intends to continue its programme of tax reform while addressing key social and investment needs.

Economic Prospects 2000-2006

1.30   On a reasonable set of assumptions, it is estimated that the Irish economy can sustain annual average growth rates of about 5% over the medium-term. Crucially, this view assumes that existing infrastructural bottlenecks and labour market tensions are tackled. Failure to address these problems will eventually undermine competitiveness. This will lead to below-potential growth and lower employment growth than is required to match the expected increase in labour supply.

1.31   Thus, this National Development Plan is based on the assumption that annual GNP growth will average about 5%. This favourable medium-term economic outlook assumes the continuation of prudent budgetary policy and the maintenance of low and stable inflation. It is also based on a positive outlook for the world economy.

1.32   Social cohesion has played a key part in Ireland's economic performance. Through the social partnership process the fruits of economic growth have been distributed through higher profits and wages, tax reform, higher public investment in physical and human capital and in the development of comprehensive strategies for the reintegration of the socially excluded, in particular the long-term unemployed, into the wider economy. The forthcoming partnership negotiations will play a major part in determining Ireland's ability to continue its current economic performance.

International Outlook

1.33   Given Ireland's openness and dependence on capital inflows, assumptions about economic growth in the world economy are crucial. For the purposes of the medium-term forecast underlying this Plan, it is assumed that the OECD economy grows in line with its potential. This is estimated at between $2\frac{1}{2}$ and $2\frac{3}{4}$% per annum. This assessment does not include a view about the timing of future cyclical events. Over the time frame of the forecast period there will be periods of below and above trend growth.

1.34 Of course, there are many potential economic shocks which could result in international economic developments taking a different course to the one outlined here. However, over the period of the Plan it is assumed that the international economy grows in line with potential. In developing these forecasts the risks that face the international economy are acknowledged. In particular, there are concerns about developments in the US and the prospects of achieving a soft-landing there from the current high rates of growth. The large current account deficit in the US and high equity valuations increase the risk of a sharp deceleration in growth. With Ireland's links with the US this would have an impact on our economic prospects.

Labour Market Developments

1.35 The estimates of Ireland's growth potential at around 5% are, of course, dependent on future labour market prospects. It is estimated that from 1994-1999 the labour force grew by over 3% per annum. The factors behind this rapid increase — favourable demographics, rising participation and net immigration — were discussed earlier. These factors will become less significant over the next decade. The number of Irish births peaked in 1980, leading to a large increase in the natural labour force growth over the following two decades. The lower birth rate since 1980 will gradually reduce the number of labour market entrants in the coming years, although returned emigrants will partially offsetting this. However, net immigration should begin to slow from the recent high levels. Finally, participation rates have increased rapidly during the 1990s reflecting a combination of factors including employment growth and higher educational levels amongst the workforce. Participation rates should continue to rise albeit at a slower pace.

1.36 Taking account of these factors, it is forecast that the labour force will grow by about 2% per annum over the period. This is a slowdown compared to the recent past but is faster than forecasts for the rest of the EU. This illustrates the extent to which Ireland must continue to generate employment, while making efforts to further reduce unemployment. Overall average employment growth of about 2% per annum is expected over the Plan period.

1.37 The priorities identified in the 1999 National Employment Action Plan (NEAP) are important in the context of these labour market projections. The NEAP priorities are:

- Setting a new objective of reducing unemployment to 5% and long-term unemployment to 2% by end year 2000;

- Mobilising labour supply by tapping into potential pools of labour to support sustainable low inflationary growth;

- Enhancing the quality of labour supply through continued investment in education and training and, in particular, through developing a strategic vision for lifelong learning;

- Strengthening the preventative element in employability strategy to minimise the duration of short term unemployment and to prevent the drift into long term unemployment;

- Maintaining the effort to reintegrate those who are currently long term unemployed into the labour force;

- Supporting an increase in female labour force participation and encourage a balanced increase in net inward migration.

31

Labour Productivity

1.38 Output growth per person employed, in conjunction with employment trends, is the second element which makes up growth in GNP. Growth in productivity depends on the volume of private investment in plant and machinery, public infrastructure, changes in the quality of the workforce and the rate of technical progress. It is also influenced by the efficiency with which these various factors are combined and the expected rewards from work and enterprise.

1.39 During the 1990's productivity growth, as measured by GNP per person employed, averaged over 3% per annum. This enabled a substantial increase in both earnings and company profitability. All the various elements outlined above contributed to this: private investment rose dramatically, the public infrastructure was improved, aided by the Structural and Cohesion Funds, while the benefits of many years of investment in education began to pay dividends.

1.40 A large element of the private investment was Foreign Direct Investment particularly from the US. In the 1990s Ireland has attracted a large number of projects in sectors such as Electronics, Computers and Chemicals. The availability of staff with the necessary skills and competitive wage rates was a key factor in the success of Ireland's industrial policy. As a result of the reduction in the pool of available labour and an increase in Irish wage rates maintaining this level of FDI will present a challenge. In overall terms, some slowdown in private investment from the very rapid levels of recent years can be expected.

1.41 Higher public sector investment in this National Development Plan will offset lower growth in private sector investment. This will lead to improvements in the quality of the public infrastructure over the next decade. The projections underlying this Plan assume that fixed investment will expand by almost 7% per annum in volume terms.

1.42 Improvements in the quality of education is a key factor behind growth in productivity. Over the period of the Plan further improvements in the average educational levels of the workforce are expected as less well-educated older workers are replaced by younger better-educated new labour market entrants. Taking account of these factors, productivity growth of about 3% on average per annum can be attained over the period 2000-2006. This compares with an average of about 2% for the EU-15.

1.43 Accordingly, a trend increase in employment of about 2%, and productivity growth of 3% in GNP terms, potential GNP growth of 5% per annum can be attained over the period 2000-2006. This should be seen as the average growth per annum over the period; it implies that growth moderates in the short-run from the existing levels. Supply constraints, most notably in the labour market, are expected to bring this about.

Annual average growth rates for the Plan period are shown in Table 1.1 below.

Table 1.1:   Macroeconomic Projections 2000-2006 (annual averages)

Summary Sheet	2000-2006
	%
Gross Domestic Product (GDP)	5.4
Gross National Product (GNP)	5.0
Consumer Prices	2.0
Employment rate	2.0
Unemployment rate	<5.0

2 National Development Strategy and Priorities for 2000-2006

National Objectives for the 2000-2006

2.1 The following key national objectives will underpin the strategy for the National Development Plan (NDP) 2000-2006:

- continuing sustainable national economic and employment growth;
- consolidating and improving Ireland's international competitiveness;
- fostering balanced regional development;
- promoting social inclusion.

These are the broad national objectives of the NDP which will apply to both the Objective 1 Border, Midland and Western (BMW) region and the Objective 1 region in transition Southern & Eastern (S&E) region. Within the two regions there will be different emphasis as appropriate to meet the different challenges arising in the regions.

Elements of Strategy

2.2 An essential pre-condition for the success and feasibility of the major level of investment proposed in Plan 2000-2006 is the continuation of macro economic and budgetary policies conducive to economic stability. The Government are committed to that fundamental policy position. Accordingly, the annual allocations, and ultimately the overall NDP commitment, will have to be kept to a level that respects the public expenditure ceilings set by Government, takes account of wider budgetary priorities, and accords with the requirements of economic stability. In that context the key elements of the NDP strategy are:

- Continuation of the stability oriented macroeconomic policies of recent years;
- A major investment programme in Economic and social Infrastructure;
- A commitment to a better regional distribution of public and private investment;
- The promotion of education and employment training policies attuned to the needs of the labour market and a special focus on those most at risk of unemployment;
- a multi-faceted approach to the promotion of Social Inclusion, including targetted interventions aimed at urban and rural poverty black spots.

Strengths of the Irish Economy

2.3 The Irish economy has a number of key strengths, notably:

- macroeconomic stability reflected in the Budget surplus, declining debt ratio and low inflation;
- broadly based consensus on economic and social policy;

- growing well-educated labour force;

- favourable demographic structure;

- attractive location for Foreign Direct Investment;

Macroeconomic Stability

2.4 Sound macroeconomic management has given Ireland a very strong fiscal outlook, with continuing budget surpluses and rapidly declining debt levels in prospect. To ensure that this position is maintained over the period of the Plan it is an absolute prerequisite that stability oriented macroeconomic policies continue to be pursued throughout the period. The Government are committed to this fundamental policy position which also involves making prudent provision for longer-term costs.

Social Consensus

2.5 The economy has been very well served by the series of Social Partnership agreements since 1987. These agreements whilst underpinning economic stability have brought real gains to all sectors of society through real increases in income, better public services, more employment and lower poverty levels. The proposals in this National Development Plan reflect the consensus of all the social partners as to the development needs of the economy.

Growing well educated dynamic labour force

2.6 Investment in education and training over the past 30 years are now paying dividends. While there was a heavy drain of educated Irish workers to the US, Britain and elsewhere in Europe during the 1980's and early 1990's this reservoir of skilled labour has been a key asset in attracting high-technology investment to Ireland. The transition in the Irish labour market from relatively poorly educated to well educated is also making a major contribution to increasing the productivity of the labour force as the older less well educated cohorts are replaced by the younger better educated more dynamic labour market entrants. This process is likely to continue for sometime before it reaches stationary equilibrium.

Positive Demographic Structure

2.7 A relatively rapid natural increase in the labour force reflecting high birth rates in previous decades combined with increasing female participation and the mobile nature of Irish labour has facilitated a rapid increase in the Irish labour force to meet increased demand for labour. The growth in the occupied labour force and increase in female participation combined with a relatively low percentage of retired persons in the population has also reduced the dependency ratio and as a consequence the demand on resources. This situation is likely to prevail for at least another 15 years.

Attractive location for Foreign Direct Investment (FDI)

2.8 Ireland possesses a number of characteristics which has made it a particularly attractive location for FDI, especially from the US which is the largest global source of FDI. These include: a reservoir of skilled English speaking labour; unrestricted access to a large European market; a stable macroeconomic environment; business friendly regulatory regimes; an attractive corporate tax regime, and an overall welcoming attitude to foreign investors. Ireland's economic growth over the past decade has been fueled by this foreign owned manufacturing and internationally traded services sector.

Weaknesses

2.9   The Irish economy has a number of weaknesses which need to be addressed and challenges which need to be overcome, if economic and social progress is to be maintained. These include:

- infrastructural deficits, especially in transport and environmental services

- congestion in major urban areas and on main road arteries

- a growth imbalance between and within regions

- housing shortages especially in urban areas

- human resource skills and training needs

- an underdeveloped indigenous industrial sector

- concentrations of deprivation and lack of opportunities in certain areas, both urban and rural

Infrastructural deficits

2.10   While Ireland's income per capita is converging rapidly towards the EU average, the relatively recent nature of that convergence means that the accumulated wealth of the country, in terms of physical infrastructure and accumulated human capital, is considerably lower than that for countries at or above the EU average income levels. The budgetary adjustment programme of the 1980's and early 1990's meant a necessary curtailment of the capital expenditure programme for most of that period, so that by the mid-1990's much of our physical infrastructure was inadequate for our existing needs and is now seriously under strain due to our rapidly growing economy. The level of pressure varies but it is especially a feature of the more densely populated urban areas and of the main national arteries.

2.11   Roads: Roads are the dominant mode of internal transport in Ireland accounting for 90% of freight traffic and 96% of passenger traffic. Despite the investment programme under the 1994-1999. Transport OP the road network is still inadequate by reference to needs and EU standards. Rapid economic growth over recent years has put an even greater strain on this inadequate road infrastructure with serious congestion now a feature of parts of the network. If this congestion is not addressed promptly in a systematic fashion promptly the competitiveness of the economy will be impaired with adverse consequences for growth and employment.

2.12   Public transport: Cities and larger urban areas are the primary engines of growth in modern economies. In order for them to reach their full potential they need to have efficient public transport systems. This is not the case in Ireland especially in the Dublin and surrounding areas. If not addressed, poor public transport infrastructure will become a constraint on growth. Our underdeveloped public transport system, with a consequent over-reliance on private cars, is also contributing to increased pollution which is an issue of concern given our commitment under the Kyoto Protocol.

2.13   Environment: Rapid economic progress has put pressure on our environmental resources, particularly water resources. While substantial investment has been made in water and waste water treatment, considerable investment is still required in order to meet the obligations under

EU Directives in this area. Investment in this area is also a key element in housing and industrial location strategies. Our economic progress has also contributed to increased levels of CO_2 emissions; additional investment combined with other strategies aimed at lowering the CO_2 emissions intensity of growth will be required in order to meet our obligations under the Kyoto Protocol.

2.14 Telecommunications and energy: The deregulation of the telecommunications services and energy sectors means that delivery under these headings will be primarily by the market. However, the market alone may not deliver advanced telecommunication services to rural areas and smaller towns in less developed regions. The lack of these services hinders businesses in these areas exploiting commercial opportunities. Furthermore the market may not take adequate account of the environmental externalities (e.g. CO_2 emissions) associated with energy production and use, or of the energy needs of more remote communities.

Housing Shortage

2.15 The ESRI in their report on "Investment priorities for the period 2000-2006" identified the shortage of affordable housing as a major capacity constraint on the economy. The shortage of housing has the potential to slow down economic growth through its effect on wage demands and labour supply. This potential threat is particularly acute in the major urban centres. The shortage of housing is in part due to a shortage of serviced building land which can be addressed by investment in water and sewage services and a better public transport system. However the market alone will not address the housing needs of all sections of the population. There is a need for additional social housing programmes, targeted at less well-off households.

Unbalanced Regional Development

2.16 The regional distribution of our economic progress has been uneven with rapid growth taking place in the main urban centres, particularly Dublin, Cork, Limerick and Galway. Other regions of the country lacking in urban centres have failed to attract the quantity and quality of investment needed to bring productivity and incomes to levels approaching those in the more prosperous regions. More balanced regional development will benefit the less developed regions, through increased prosperity, and the more developed regions, through reduced congestion. This issue is addressed in more detail in Chapter 3.

Human Resource Constraints

2.17 Growth in the Irish economy is particularly dependent on high technology industries. The availability of skilled labour has been an important determinant of our capacity to attract these industries to locate and expand their operations here. The pool of skilled labour is now considerably diminished and shortages are beginning to emerge in some key occupations. A skills deficit is indirectly manifested in the high proportion of the population of working age which have a relatively low level of educational attainment. It is estimated by the OECD that 50% of the Irish population aged 25-64 years have less than upper secondary education compared to 19% in Germany and 26% in Sweden. If these shortages and deficits and their causal factors are not addressed and the pool of skilled labour replenished the convergence performance of the economy will be difficult to sustain.

Underdeveloped indigenous manufacturing sector

2.18   Manufacturing industry in Ireland is dualistic in nature with a small number of sectors (chemicals, computers and instrument engineering and electrical engineering) accounting for over 50% of manufacturing output (gross value added). Since 1990 real output in these sectors has grown at an annual rate of 15.7% compared to 4.7% for the rest of manufacturing industry. The indigenous sector (i.e. Irish owned) accounts for one third of gross manufacturing output but about 53% of manufacturing employment. Gross output per person engaged in Irish owned manufacturing plants is about 45% of that for workers in foreign owned plants. The average size of plant in terms of persons employed is about 5 times greater in the foreign owned plants. The indigenous sector is characterized by a preponderance of small low productivity firms which are not engaged in the production of high technology products or using high technology processes, which devote very limited resources to research and product development and which are the dominant source of industrial employment in less developed areas. The weaknesses of the indigenous sector is a particular barrier to the convergence of the less developed regions.

Agriculture

2.19   A particular challenge facing the economy is to improve the competitiveness of Irish agriculture in the post Agenda 2000 climate and as we face a new Trade Round where agriculture is likely to feature high on the agenda. Agriculture remains a key sector in the Irish economy and has a particularly important part to play in regional and rural development.

Social exclusion

2.20   The benefits of Ireland's rapid economic progress over the past few years are evident in the significant reduction in many of the key indicators of social exclusion. For example, the number of people in consistent poverty has been reduced to 7-10%. By early 1999, overall unemployment had fallen to 5.8% with long-term unemployment dropping to 3%. However, it is clear that not everyone has benefited proportionately from this new-found prosperity — indeed, the disparity between higher income earners and the socially excluded may even have widened. In addition, concentration of poverty may be intensifying in certain areas. Indeed, in many disadvantaged communities, poverty, social deprivation and the effects of marginalisation are becoming, or may already have become, endemic and inter-generational.

2.21   Clearly, the outward manifestation of social exclusion and marginalisation is not limited to financial poverty or living in areas of social deprivation. Not only do disadvantaged people have greater reliance on the State for direct income support and housing, they also suffer from poorer health and lower educational achievement resulting in lower employability. Many marginalised areas are also disproportionately affected by crime and drug abuse, while a disproportionately large percentage of the prison population comes from them. As a result, society suffers in two ways. Firstly, social exclusion imposes additional costs, direct and indirect, on society and reduces the quality of life generally (e.g. crime). Secondly, society is at the loss of the potential contribution — both economic and otherwise- which people who are affected by social exclusion could make to it. Thus, alleviating poverty and building an inclusive society will yield the multiple benefits of reducing the direct cost of social exclusion, of improving the quality of life generally and of allowing people to contribute to the wealth of the nation and share in the benefits of economic and social development.

Sustainable development

2.22 Economic and social development should not be to the detriment of environmental quality. While Ireland has retained a good environment, economic growth and changing lifestyles are placing greater pressure than ever before on environmental quality. The main environmental challenges which must be addressed by the NDP and other policy measures include:

- Halting the decline in the quality of rivers and lakes caused by excessive inputs of nutrients (eutrophication)

- Better management of solid waste

- Meeting our Kyoto commitment to limit the growth of greenhouse gas emissions

- Protecting the urban environment

- Protecting flora and fauna in the countryside and along the coast

2.23 The Plan has been framed taking into account the need for balance between environment and development embodied in the concept of sustainable development. Integration of environmental considerations into other policies is a key means of securing this balance, and environmental considerations associated with development proposals are addressed in the relevant chapters of the Plan. A National Spatial Strategy will be prepared to secure sustainable spatial development over the longer term.

National Priorities and strategy for 2000-2006

2.24 The development strategy to achieve the key national objectives expressed at Paragraph 2.1 will concentrate investment on the following six key priority areas:

- economic infrastructure primarily, roads, public transport and the environment

- employment and human resource development

- productive sector investment

- rural development

- social inclusion

- social capital (housing and health capital)

The investment actions under these priority areas will be delivered through four inter-regional programmes and two regional programmes (details of the strategies to be pursued are given in the chapters dealing with each programme):

- an economic and social infrastructure programme (Chapter 4)

- an employment and human resource development programme (Chapter 5)

- a productive investment programme (Chapter 6)

- a rural development programme for CAP accompanying measures (Chapter 11)

- a regional development programme for the Border, Midland and Western Region (Chapter 7)

- a regional development programme for the Southern and Eastern Region (Chapter 8)

3 Regional Development

Introduction

3.1 As the analysis in Chapter 1 indicates, Ireland has undergone a major economic transformation during the period of the current National Development Plan. This has resulted in unprecedented progress across all key economic indicators, most significantly in the area of sustainable employment creation. All regions of the country have benefited from this transformation as is clearly evidenced by regional economic indicators.

3.2 While the positive impact on national economic and social development is evident, the rapid pace of economic growth, the pattern of development and increasing urbanisation and centralisation of economic activity have raised issues in relation to:

- imbalance between and within regions in the distribution of national economic progress;

- the growth and expansion of the Greater Dublin area, giving rise to problems of congestion and housing shortage;

- rapid growth of major urban centres outside Dublin and their role in driving the development of their hinterlands and providing a counter-balance to Dublin;

- the implications of these trends for smaller towns and villages and rural areas;

- the social, economic and environmental consequences of these trends;

- the role of infrastructural provision in facilitating and promoting development at regional, as well as at national level;

- how the investments needed to underpin sustained economic progress at the national level might, at the same time, more effectively advance balanced regional development;

- the relationship between economic and social planning, physical planning and land use policies.

3.3 The regionalisation arrangements negotiated by Ireland in the context of the Agenda 2000 Agreement resulted in the designation of two Regions in Ireland for Structural Fund purposes (see map at Appendix 3). These Regions are

(a) the Border, Midland and Western (BMW) Region which has retained Objective I status for Structural Funds for the full period to 2006 and

(b) the Southern and Eastern (S&E) Region which will qualify for a six-year phasing-out regime for Objective 1 Structural Funds up to the end of 2005.

3.4 The ESRI Study "National Investment Priorities for the Period 2000-2006" was completed prior to the finalisation of the Agenda 2000 negotiations and did not specifically focus on the two new Regions. The Study did, however, put forward a clear framework for Regional Policy and Spatial Development which has helped inform consideration of these issues in the context of the NDP.

Comparative Regional Analysis

3.5 The two Consultancy Studies on the Development Strategies 2000-2006 for the BMW and S&E Regions respectively have been a valuable input to the national and regional development policies to be pursued under the National Development Plan. The Study produced by the Western Development Commission "Blueprint for Success — a Development Plan for the West 2000-2006" has also been beneficial in terms of its analysis and recommendations. These studies set out in detail the different socio-economic characteristics of the BMW and S&E Regions and a recital of some of the key elements is pertinent to the Regional Development Policy framework set out in this Plan.

Population Structure

3.6 There is significant variation in population across the two Regions as illustrated by Table 3.1 below. This difference is reflected in the profile of populations of towns and cities in each Region. While the S&E Region is characterised by a predominantly urban population concentrated in a small number of large urban centres, the BMW Region has a much more dispersed population living mainly in small towns and rural areas.

Table 3.1:   Demographic Statistics

	State	BMW Region	S&E Region
Population (000's) % Total	3,626	27%	73%
Area (Sq Km)	68,895	32,481	36,414
Urban : Rural	58% : 42%	32% : 68%	68% : 32%
Pop Density (per Sq Km)	53	30	73
Major Urban Centres	5	1	4
Towns over 10,000	23	7	16
Towns (5,000-10,000)	26	8	18

Source: CSO Census of Population, 1996.

3.7 Population growth in recent years has been concentrated in urban centres. The biggest population growth in the S&E Region has taken place in Dublin and its surrounding towns. In the BMW Region, the strongest growth has been in Galway City. Excluding Galway City, the BMW Region's population growth of 1.1% between 1991 and 1996 has been much slower than the rate of growth for the State of 2.8%.

General Economic Indicators

3.8 The State's improved economic performance has been unevenly distributed between the S&E Region and the BMW Region as is reflected in Table 3.2 below.

Table 3.2:   Gross Value Added (GVA)*

	State	S&E Region	BMW Region
GVA per capita (1996)	100	110	74
% of EU Average GVA	93	102	70
Distribution of Total GVA	100	80%	20%

*GVA at basic prices is the same as GDP at basic prices which is the official measure of economic activity at regional level within the EU.

Source: CSO Regional Accounts, 1996.

3.9 Outside of the headline figures, there are also important regional variations in the composition of GDP. Table 3.3 below sets out the distribution of National GDP by Sector:—

Table 3.3: GDP by Sector

	S&E Region	BMW Region
	%	%
Market and Non-Market Services	81	19
Building, Construction and Manufacturing	81	19
Agriculture, Forestry and Fisheries	65	35

Source: CSO Regional Accounts, 1996.

Employment and Earnings

3.10 There are also significant regional variations in employment, skills and qualifications and earnings across the two Regions as shown in Table 3.4 below.

Table 3.4: Labour Force Statistics

	State	S&E Region	BMW Region
National Labour Force	100%	75.6%	24.4%
Employment Ratio*	61%	62.0%	58.3%
Unemployment Rate	7.8%	7.6%	8.3%
Third Level Qualifications**	17%	19%	12%
Average Earnings (£)	16,171	16,941	12,941

*Number employed/people of working age [15-64 years]
**As a% of the population aged 15 and over.
Source: Quarterly National Household Survey, Q2, 1998.

3.11 The distribution of the labour force and employment largely reflects the distribution of population across the two Regions. However, there are significant differences in average GVA per capita and in average earnings. There is also a greater concentration of graduates in the S&E Region. These outcomes are, in part, due to the fact that the larger production units, higher technological sectors and third level institutions are concentrated in Dublin and the existing larger urban centres which are primarily in the S&E Region. Moreover, larger agricultural units producing higher value added goods are more concentrated in the S&E Region.

Disadvantaged Areas

3.12 Notwithstanding the economic progress of recent years, pockets of poverty and disadvantage are evident throughout both Regions. The findings of the National Anti-Poverty Strategy identified marginalised communities in urban and inner-city areas particularly in Dublin, Cork and Limerick and high concentrations of low income groups (particularly the long-term unemployed and lone parents) in public housing estates. The Anti-Poverty Strategy also identified marginalised rural communities throughout the country. While these are more prevalent in the BMW Region, the S&E Regional Development Strategy Report also identified specific remote and disadvantaged areas in that Region. Additional analysis of socio-economic differences between the two Regions is set out in the chapters on the Operational Programmes.

Key Challenges

3.13 A general assessment of the comparative position in both Regions shows the distinctive development challenges in each Region. Whilst both Regions are generally well-advanced as

41

regards trained and skilled work forces, the S&E Region scores heavily on industry and services, especially in the crucial technological and back-up Research, Development, Technology and Innovation (RTDI) sectors. The S&E Region is also better endowed in terms of third-level educational institutions and graduates. In contrast, the physical infrastructure in the S&E Region is under considerably more pressure than the BMW Region but the quality of the infrastructure in the latter Region is comparatively poor. Finally, the BMW Region enjoys a better quality environment but because of the overall attractiveness of large urban centres to the modern population, as evidenced by their growth, it may be less desirable than the S&E Region as a location in which to work and live.

3.14 Arising from this analysis, the key challenges facing the S&E and BMW Regions over the period of the Plan could be summarised as follows:

S&E Region

- Consolidate and build on the Region's recent economic performance, especially regarding employment and reductions in long-term unemployment, thereby maintaining the Region's key role in national economic competitiveness.

- Address urban congestion and general bottlenecks to growth, particularly as regards economic and social infrastructure and human resources;

- Further develop counter-balances to Dublin, relieving pressure on the capital and its hinterland, and distributing growth more widely throughout the Region;

- Support the further development of agriculture, agri-business and the seafood sector;

- Promote social inclusion in deprived urban and rural areas; and

- Maintain a viable rural economy.

BMW Region

- Increase the potential of the Region to act as a counterbalance to the S&E Region, especially Dublin, and pursue more balanced growth within the region;

- Increase the presence in the Region of the key drivers of sustainable economic growth, notably in the productive sector;

- Improve the quality of the Region's economic and social infrastructure and human resources;

- Build on the Region's natural resource base especially in the areas of agriculture, tourism, the seafood sector and rural enterprise; and

- Promote rural and urban social inclusion.

The Role of Gateways in Development

3.15 The key determinants of sustained economic performance both nationally and at regional level are:

- ease of access to domestic and foreign markets;

- a modern telecommunications network;

- back-up research and technology infrastructure which is accessible to enterprises in all sectors;

- a well-developed educational system;

- a highly qualified and skilled work force;

- high quality physical infrastructure, including inter-urban transport and energy transmission systems;

- an adequate supply of housing;

- a good overall quality of life;

- a high quality and sustainable environment.

3.16   The areas that are best endowed with these characteristics are generally the larger urban centres which also serve as development Gateways. These are centres which have a strategic location relative to the surrounding territory, possess good social and economic infrastructure and support services and have the potential to open up their zones of influence to further development by providing transport links with contiguous zones. The common attribute of Gateways is that they are the centres which are strategically placed to drive growth in their zones of influence, generating a dynamic of development which embraces the complementarity between city, town, village and country. The analyses of both the ESRI and the Regional Studies confirm the pivotal importance of such Gateways to the economic performance of the surrounding smaller towns and rural hinterlands.

3.17   Ireland has seen accelerated development of Gateways in recent years. Dublin is a national gateway serving the whole country with Cork, Limerick/Shannon, Galway and Waterford acting as regional Gateways for extensive parts of the country. The notable feature of the evolution of such Gateways in Ireland is that all but one (Galway) are in the S&E Region. Critical mass is a key consideration in the evolution of such Gateways, along with location and access to the wider domestic and international markets.

3.18   There are other emerging urban centres throughout the country which may not yet have all the attributes of regional Gateways — in terms of population size, strategic location, range of skills and services, industrial and manufacturing base — but they are, nevertheless, showing the potential to lift the levels of development in their respective counties/regions. These have a key role to play in more balanced regional development, in terms of ensuring a more even spread of economic growth, utilising resources more effectively and alleviating the pressures on the larger urban centres (whether as locations for business or for residence).

Regional Development Policy

3.19   The Government's objective for regional policy in the NDP is to achieve more balanced regional development in order to reduce the disparities between and within the two Regions and to develop the potential of both to contribute to the greatest possible extent to the continuing prosperity of the country. Policy to secure such development must be advanced in parallel with policies to ensure that this development is sustainable with full regard to the quality of life, social cohesion and conservation of the environment and the natural and cultural heritage.

3.20   A key component of the Government's Regional Development Policy will be to facilitate further development of the existing major Gateways *and* the focused development, as Regional Gateways, of a limited number of strategically-placed centres which are already displaying the potential (i) to achieve strong and sustainable economic growth driven essentially by the interplay of market forces, location and accessibility and (ii) to promote such growth within their zones of influence. The challenge is, therefore, to create the conditions whereby a second tier of larger urban centres can start to act as Regional Gateways, thus spreading economic growth more widely across both Regions. Development of Regional Gateways as a means of wider regional development is a long-term strategy requiring an incremental, planned and consistent approach to investment. However, the approach must also be flexible enough to adapt to changing economic and social conditions.

Gateways Regional Development Strategy

3.21   The choice of locations for development as Regional Gateways must be based on their potential to stimulate growth in the towns, villages and rural areas throughout their zones of influence and on the quality of their transport connections to other parts of the country. By virtue of the role envisaged for them, only a limited number of locations should be selected as Gateways so as to ensure the necessary concentration of resources and investment. The Government endorses the view of the ESRI that the specific designation of a secondary tier of Regional Gateways requires further detailed study in the context of developing a National Spatial Strategy for the country as a whole. Such designation would emerge from the application of the principles and criteria of this strategy.

3.22   Whilst the identification and development of additional Regional Gateways will be a key element of Regional Policy over the period of the Plan, it does not mean that development is to be confined to such centres and their immediate hinterlands. The Gateway approach will help create the critical mass to spur growth in the designated centres and in their wider zones of influence. Within these zones, there will also be a crucial need for a tier of development hubs that are primarily relevant at county or local level. In both Regions, a number of medium-sized towns have emerged, below the level of the Regional Gateway, as major county/local hubs for economic growth, supporting the development of smaller towns and villages and rural areas. These towns have the potential to attract smaller scale foreign direct investment and to develop indigenous industry and services both in their own right and with linkages to enterprises based in the Regional Gateways. Investment in these towns to support their ongoing development as locations for smaller scale industry and enterprise will be a key factor in spreading the benefits of national economic development more widely across the Regions.

3.23   An effective regional policy will also require the full exploitation of the potential of smaller towns and villages and rural areas to ensure that they are attractive as locations for commercial activities giving employment and as places for people to live. Consequently, the Gateways approach to balanced regional development will be complemented by multi-sectoral policies to ensure that these locations benefit from economic growth and that local economic activity in these areas provides sufficient opportunities for local communities to secure gainful employment. In this regard, the development agencies will make full use of the incentives available to them to spread the location of enterprise, especially inward investment, across a wide spread of locations in both Regions. Particular attention will also be paid to rural development in line with the policy in the White Paper on Rural Development published earlier this year. Chapter 11 of the Plan sets out the framework for Rural Development.

3.24   If overall Regional Development Policy is to be successful, it is essential that the existing engines of growth are not impeded by capacity constraints. As such, in fostering national competitiveness and balanced development across both regions and in the more remote areas of the regions, the investment needs of existing large urban centres will have to be comprehensively addressed. In this regard, the constraints emerging in Dublin and, to a less acute extent, in the other large urban centres (i.e. Cork, Limerick, Galway and Waterford) must be urgently tackled on a broad front.

3.25 Dublin and its hinterland is a development hub for the a major part of the S&E Region and also is crucial to the continued prosperity of the national economy. It is currently encountering pressures and capacity constraints in terms of its transport network and labour market. The very significant growth of recent years has, moreover, imposed major social costs in terms of rapidly rising property prices and rents, urban sprawl and travel times, and general environmental degradation. The NDP's investment in infrastructure in greater Dublin will be consistent with the recently published "Strategic Planning Guidelines for the Greater Dublin Area". Similar guidelines are being developed to address the problems in the other larger urban centres

National Spatial Strategy

3.26 In order to bring together all these elements of regional policy and to achieve balanced regional development in accordance with the guiding principles of maintaining economic competitiveness and sustainable development, the Government has mandated the Department of the Environment and Local Government to prepare a National Spatial Strategy which will translate the broad approach to regional development in the Plan into a more detailed blueprint for spatial development over the longer term. In essence, a National Spatial Planning Strategy will take the form of a broad planning strategy for the country at large. It will

- identify broad spatial development patterns for areas and set down indicative policies in relation to the location of industrial development, residential development, rural development and tourism and heritage, and

- develop and present a dynamic conception of the Irish urban system, together with its links to rural areas, which recognises and utilises their economic and social inter-dependence.

In these ways, the strategy will, inter alia, provide the basis for long-term co-ordination and co-operation in policy formulation and decision-making on major investment in infrastructure, including public and private transport infrastructure.

3.27 The National Strategy will draw upon the European Spatial Development Perspective (ESDP), published in May 1999, and will take cognisance of the fundamental goals of European policy, notably:—

- economic and social cohesion

- conservation of natural resources and cultural heritage

- more balanced competitiveness of the European territory,

and the ESDP's policy orientations for spatial development:

- polycentric spatial development[1] and a new urban-rural relationship

- parity of access to infrastructure and knowledge

- wise management of the natural and cultural heritage

---

[1] Polycentric spatial development implies decentralised territorial development with several urban centres of national/regional scale and a large number of dynamic towns and urban clusters well distributed throughout Ireland, including the more peripheral and rural areas.

3.28 The National Spatial Strategy will take full account of the regional development policy framework set out in the NDP especially the pivotal role of Regional Gateways in the development of a region. This issue will be a particular focus of the mid-term review of the NDP in 2003.

3.29 The National Spatial Strategy will be prepared by the Department of the Environment and Local Government, with the full participation of other Government Departments and Agencies. It will take two years to complete and will have a 20 year horizon. Structures will be put in place to ensure that the strategy can be prepared on the basis of facilitating the greatest possible degree of consensus among the social partners and sectoral, regional and other interests. The experience of other countries who have undertaken national spatial planning will be utilised.

Implementation of Regional Policy

3.30 As stated at Paragraph 3.19 the central regional policy objective in the Plan is to achieve balanced regional development in order to reduce the disparities between and within the two regions and to develop the potential of both to contribute to the greatest possible extent to the continuing prosperity of the country. A prerequisite for implementation of the policy is the achievement of the macro-economic objectives on which the Plan is based so that the necessary resources for investment can be made available. It will also require an integrated and flexible approach to the development and implementation of sectoral policies and co-ordinated investment in areas such as transport, education and housing.

3.31 The first steps towards the implementation of the policy can be undertaken before the completion of the National Spatial Strategy. The development of the existing Gateways and larger urban centres — those with some or all of the attributes mentioned in Paragraphs 3.15-3.17 will continue, largely driven by market forces. The subsequent National Spatial Strategy will set out a more detailed framework for this, but, from the outset of the NDP, investment within and between the Regions will take full account of regional development policy. Investment under the various Operational Programmes in the Plan will be consistent with this policy and other Plan objectives.

Operational Programmes

3.32 The broad parameters of NDP investment that will, inter alia, support the objective of balanced regional development are set out in the chapters on the Operational Programmes. The detailed investment plans will be set out in the comprehensive Operational Programmes which will be produced before the end of the year. In brief, investment under the Operational Programmes will contribute to the achievement of the Regional Development Policy in the manner set out in the following paragraphs.

3.33 Economic and Social Infrastructure Substantial investment will take place in both Regions in the provision of modern infrastructure to support sustainable and balanced development. Major investment is planned in roads and other transportation modes in order to facilitate access to domestic and international markets. Investment in environmental services, energy transmission systems and telecommunications will also have a major part to play in ensuring balanced regional development. The NDP recognises that major investment in infrastructure will be needed to facilitate the supply of serviced land required to meet the high level of housing demand predicted. Substantial investment in public transport in Dublin and other larger urban centres will address problems of congestion and facilitate better access for those living in suburban and marginalised communities to education, training and employment opportunities. The investment in mainline rail and provincial bus services will facilitate balanced regional development and help to sustain rural areas. The key role played by Housing, Health and Education Services in the regional distribution of economic development is recognised by the inclusion for the first time of capital expenditure in these areas in the NDP.

3.34   Total expenditure under the Economic and Social Infrastructure Operational Programme will be £17,610 million (€22,360 million) of which £4,861 per capita (€6,172) will be spent in the BMW Region and £4,855 per capita (€6,164) will be spent in the S&E Region.

3.35   Employment and Human Resources   Considerable resources will be expended in each Region over the period of the Plan on education and training programmes. These programmes will include provision for both initial training and re-training. In addition, there will also be substantially increased investment in active employment measures (with a particular focus on the long-term unemployed), in education with a special emphasis on literacy and lifelong learning and in integration/reintegration training for groups wishing to enter the labour force, particularly women, people with disabilities and the socially excluded. In order to support the development of further locations as centres for enterprise investment, the existing third level institutions in the Regions will be encouraged to provide outreach services and distance learning and to make their courses and services more relevant to the needs of industry and services. While the S&E Region is well served by third level institutions, particular attention will be paid to enhancing the quality and range of courses in existing third level institutions in the BMW Region. In both Regions, distance learning will also be assisted so as to promote the development of higher skills levels outside of the main urban centres.

3.36   Total expenditure under the Employment and Human Resources Operational Programme will be £9,894 million (€12,563 million) of which £2,936 per capita (€3,728) will be in the BMW Region and £2,651 per capita (€3,366) will be in the S&E Region.

3.37   Productive Sector   A key objective will be to increase the level of new foreign and indigenous investment in the BMW Region. Under the arrangements for State Aids in the period 2000-2006, grant aid of up to 40% of investment for enterprise will be permissible in this Region as an Objective I Region. Additional aid of up to 15% for SMEs (defined as enterprises of less than 250) will be available. In providing for public investment in both foreign and indigenous industry and services, maximum use will be made by the industrial promotion agencies of the State Aid differentials to encourage more balanced regional development. In particular, IDA Ireland will seek to ensure that, in the period 2000-2006, at least 50% of all new jobs from green-field projects will be in the BMW Region.

3.38   Support will also be given, within permitted State Aids rules, in the S&E Region with particular focus on the less-prosperous sub-regions. The maximum aid rates permissible under the Regional Aid Guidelines for enterprises in the S&E Region as an Objective I Region in Transition are 20% plus 10% for SMEs, although in areas outside of Dublin this reduced rate will only apply from 2003. In addition significant assistance will be given in both Regions under this Operational Programme for Research and Development and aid to the Agriculture sector.

3.39   Direct investment in the Productive Sector will be complemented by a major further programme of decentralisation of State Agencies to the Regions from the Dublin area.

3.40 In total some £4,509 million (€5,725.2 million) will be spent on the Productive Sector of which £1,713 per capita (€2,175) will be in the BMW Region and £1,073 per capita (€1,363) in the S&E Region.

3.41 Regional Operational Programmes A particular focus of both Regional Operational Programmes will be investment in non-national roads to improve transport links from towns and villages to the regional Gateways and the arterial network. There will be a programme of investment in urban and village renewal to make urban areas and smaller towns and villages more attractive locations in which to live and to help develop viable commercial activities. Investment in rural water supply, agriculture, tourism, culture, forestry, fishing, and broader rural development will assist less developed and more remote rural areas. In both regions, there will also be substantial investment to counter social exclusion including targeted childcare facilities, and an area-based approach to local development.

3.42 Total expenditure under both Regional Operational Programes will be £5,070 million (€6,437 million) of which £2,158 per capita (€2,741) will be spent in the BMW Region and £1,122 per capita (€1,425) will be spent in the S&E Region.

Institutional and Monitoring Arrangements

3.43 A key element in the regional policy framework is the implementation and monitoring arrangements to be put in place. The two new Regional Assemblies for the BMW and S&E Regions will play an important role in the administration and monitoring of the Regional Development dimension in the National Development Plan. The Assemblies will comprise nominated locally elected representatives. They will have a Director and an adequate complement of staff to enable them to carry out their functions.

3.44 The Assemblies will be the lead agency for the Regional Operational Programmes. On foot of this function, the Assemblies will chair and will be represented on the Monitoring Committees on expenditure under each of the Regional Operational Programmes. In deciding on the composition of the Regional Operational Programme Monitoring Committees, the Government will ensure adequate representation for the Assemblies. The Monitoring Committees will also have representation from central Government, the Social Partners and Community Groups at local level. The Western Development Commission will be represented on the BMW Regional Operational Programme Monitoring Committee. Departments and State Agencies will play a key role in delivering sub-programmes under the Regional Operational Programmes and it will be necessary for them to display maximum co-operation with, and accountability to, the Regional Assemblies.

3.45 More generally, Departments and State Agencies will have an important role to play in ensuring that the objective of balanced regional development is delivered through their management role in the Inter-regional Operational Programmes. In formulating the Inter-regional Operational Programmes and in overseeing the co-ordinated delivery of these programmes, the managing authorities will have to take full account of the National Development Plan objective of balanced regional development. The Assemblies will be represented on the Inter-regional Operational Programmes Monitoring Committees. This representation recognises the importance to the Regions of investment under the Inter-regional Operational Programmes. The Assemblies will also have the power to monitor the overall operation of the NDP in their Region.

3.46 Apart from their specific Plan-related functions, the Assemblies will also have responsibility for the better co-ordination of public services within their respective regions. On foot of this function, the Assemblies will play an active role in the formulation of the National Spatial Strategy.

4 Economic and Social Infrastructure Operational Programme

Introduction

4.1 The stock of public infrastructure in an economy is a major determinant of its competitiveness and of society's capacity to address some of its major social and environmental needs. This infrastructure encompasses roads, public transport, water services, waste water, solid waste management, telecommunications and energy networks, housing, health and educational capital.

4.2 Infrastructure is a major priority of the Plan because of the urgent need to expand the capital stock in this area both to sustain the level of activity and to enhance the potential of less developed areas. Reflecting the importance of this priority, £17.6 billion (€22.4 billion) is being provided under the Economic and Social Infrastructure Operational Programme in the NDP over the period 2000-2006 for public infrastructure in roads, public transport, water services, environmental protection, energy, housing and health capital. The indicative regional breakdown of this expenditure across the main priorities is shown table 4.1 below.

Table 4.1: Economic and Social Infrastructure Operational Programme — Expenditure 2000-2006

Sub-programme	National (€ million)	BMW Region (€ million)	S&E Region (€ million)
National Roads	5,968	2,176	3,792
Public Transport — Greater Dublin area	2,012		
Regional Public Transport	825	250	575
Environmental protection	3,213	888	2,325
Energy	185	90	95
Housing	7,619	2,057	5,562
Health	2,539	800	1,739
Total	**22,361**	**6,261**	**16,100**
Total per capita	**6,167**	**6,486**	**6,051**

4.3 An additional £1,633 million (€2,073 million) is being provided for educational and training capital under the employment and human resource priority. A further £3,132 million (€3,978 million) is being provided for economic and social infrastructure in the regional programmes broken down as follows: £650 million (€825 million) for waste management, £1,600 million (€2,032 million) for non-national roads, £420 million (€533 million) for rural water, £60 million (€76 million) for ports and airports and £402 million (€510 million) for culture and recreational investment. The total provision for economic and social infrastructure across all programmes is over £22.4 billion (€28.5 billion).

4.4 This is not the full extent of investment in public infrastructure over the period of the plan. The public utility companies, in energy, communications and transport sectors will also be making substantial investment from their own resources.

National Roads

Analysis of the current situation

4.5 Roads are the primary mode of internal transport in Ireland, accounting for 96% of passenger traffic and 90% of freight transport. The national primary road network has an overall length of 2,749 kms, of which 2,478 kms (90%) is 2 lane single carraigeway, 177 kms (6%) is dual carraigeway and 94 kms (3%) is motorway. National secondary roads have a total length of 2,694 kms, of which 2,686 kms is 2 lane road. In addition there are 90,300 kms of regional and local road. While Ireland has a reasonably good road coverage in terms of road density (38 persons per km of road compared to the EU average of 99, and 1.3 km of road per square km of area compared to the EU average of 1.6 km) the quality of the road infrastructure is poor by EU standards. For example about 0.1% of the total road network in Ireland is of motorway standard compared to an EU average of 1.3%.

4.6 At the regional level 52% of national primary roads and 30% of national secondary roads are in the S&E Region. The S&E Region has a higher percentage of quality roads reflecting the higher traffic volumes in the region, both from within the region and from outside it. Despite better quality roads in the S&E Region there is greater congestion in the region and journey times can take longer than in the BMW Region. However the lack of better quality roads serving the BMW Region makes it less attractive to inward investment and acts as a constraint on growth and competitiveness in the region.

4.7 Road travel has grown rapidly in Ireland in recent years. Related to this, there has been significant growth in the number of registered vehicles. The number of private cars has risen by 40% since 1992 and now stands at 1.2 million. However, car ownership rates are still low by European standards: in 1997, there were 454 cars per 1000 population in the EU as a whole; the latest figure for Ireland is 330 per 1000 population (1998). The number of goods vehicles in Ireland has risen by over 35,000 since 1994 and reached 170,866 in 1998. A recent projection of vehicle numbers by the External Evaluator for the Operational Programme for Transport (OPTRANS) suggests that the private car stock could reach 1.9 million by 2011. People are more dependent on car travel and travel longer distances in the BMW Region reflecting the relatively rural nature of the region. For example, in 1996, 9.9% travelled more than 24 kilometres to work or school in the BMW Region compared to 8.3% in the S&E Region.

4.8 The *National Road Needs Study* is a comprehensive assessment of the works required to bring the national road network as a whole up to the necessary standards and to maintain these standards as traffic volumes increase. It sets out a proposed type of roadway for each segment of the network in order to cater for projected traffic flows over the period 2000-2019. The study indicates that, in 1995, 91% of the inter- urban national primary network could meet the minimum level of service which is equivalent to an 80 kph average inter-urban (90 kph dual carriageway) journey speed. An assessment was carried out to determine the likely performance of the network at the end of the current OPTRANS (1999), based on traffic levels projected for 1999. This concluded that 24% of national primary roads and 14% of national secondary roads would be below the specified minimum level of service standard at end 1999. By 2019, two-thirds of the national primary network would, in the absence of investment, fail this standard, with about 37% of the national secondary network also not meeting the minimum specified level of service; the percentage failing to meet the standard would be higher in the S&E Region. There is very strong direct evidence of major congestion in parts of the network where road capacity is seriously deficient.

Strategy for National Roads

4.9 The primary road transport objectives are:

- to improve the reliability of the road transport system by removing bottlenecks, remedying capacity deficiencies and reducing absolute journey times and journey time variance;

- to improve internal road transport infrastructure between regions and within regions, contribute to the competitiveness of the productive sector and foster balanced regional development;

- to facilitate better access to and from the main ports and airports with the main objective of offsetting the negative effects of peripherality;

- to contribute to sustainable transport policies, facilitating continued economic growth and regional development while ensuring a high level of environmental protection;

- to help achieve the objectives of the Government's Road Safety Strategy in relation to the reduction in fatalities and serious injuries caused by road accidents.

4.10 These objectives will be achieved as part of an integrated transport investment programme for the period 2000-2006. The key features of this programme will include:

- a concentrated and focused development strategy for the national primary road network focusing in particular on key national routes;

- improvement of national secondary roads of critical importance for economic development and balanced regional development;

- a high priority to the safety of road users in the design and construction of road projects.

4.11 Total planned investment in national roads to implement this strategy will be £4.4 billion (€5.6 billion) over 2000-2006 of which £1 billion (€1.3 billion) will be in Public Private Partnership (PPP) projects. An indicative £1.58 billion (€2 billion — 36%) will be invested on national roads within the BMW Region and an indicative £2.82 billion (€ 3.6 billion — 64%) in the S&E Region. In addition to the investment in national road construction, £300 million (€380.9 million) will be provided for the management and maintenance of the network of national roads, of which an indicative 46% will be in the BMW Region and 54% in the S&E Region. The annual average investment in national roads represents a real increase of 100% over the 1999 level of expenditure. This reflects the high priority which the Government attaches to accelerating the completion of the network to a standard comparable with that of other EU countries and to a level which meets the needs of the economy.

4.12 National Primary Roads: The development strategy for national primary roads will include:

- the development by 2006 of the following routes in their entirety to motorway/ high quality dual carriageway standard;

- Dublin to Border (M1);

- Galway to Dublin (N4/N6);

- Cork to Dublin (N8);

- Limerick to Dublin (N7);

- Waterford to Dublin (road type and route to be further evaluated).

- further major improvements on other* national primary routes within the State including (see Map in Appendix 3):

  - routes to the North-West: N2 (Dublin/Monaghan/Omagh/Derry), N4 (Kinnegad to Sligo), N13-N15 (Sligo/Donegal/Lifford/Letterkenny/Derry), N16 (Sligo/Blacklion/ Enniskillen/Dungannon/Larne), N3 (Dublin/Belturbet/Enniskillen/Derry);

  - the Western Corridor from Sligo through Limerick to Rosslare (N17, N18, N24 and N25), N5 (Castlebar/Longford), N26 (Ballina/Foxford);

  - other roads in the South and East: N11 (Rosslare/Dublin), N20 (Limerick/Cork), N21 (Tralee/Limerick), N22 (Tralee/Killarney/Cork), N28 (Cork/Ringaskiddy), N30 (Enniscorthy/New Ross);

  - completion of the M50 and Dublin Port Access Tunnel.

4.13   This programme is based on a policy of providing a high quality of service on the national primary network. On major inter-urban routes, the aim will be to achieve a minimum level of service C (equivalent to an average inter-urban speed of 94 kph on a dual carriageway and 105 kph on a motorway) from completion of construction through to 2020 on these routes; a higher level of service will in practice be commonly achieved. In relation to the remainder of the national primary network, it is estimated that the investment planned will result in a minimum level of service D (80 kph on inter-urban journeys) on 90% of the routes involved.

4.14   A feature of the work to be undertaken on national primary roads will be the adoption of an integrated planning approach involving the identification of improvement needs and route selections for substantial sections of the routes rather than focusing solely on the delivery of by-passes of congested centres of population.

4.15   National secondary roads: National secondary roads account for 3% of the network and 11% of total road traffic. They act as medium distance through routes connecting important towns, serving medium to large geographical areas and providing links to the national primary routes to form an homogeneous arterial network. The strategy for national secondary roads will concentrate on routes which are of particular importance to economic and regional development, including links to the strategic corridors, roads serving key ports, airports, tourist areas, industry and multi-purpose roads. The works to be undertaken will include:

- widening, realignment and reconstruction of deficient sections;

- the provision of small by-passes, minor inner relief roads and short span bridges;

- structural improvement measures, including new road pavement and improved drainage;

- capacity improvements, including the addition of climbing lanes or hard shoulders where required and improved vertical and horizontal alignments;

---

*Internal Northern Ireland connecting routes are indicated where appropriate.

- safety improvements including the elimination of accident blackspots and the improvement of the layout of junctions and access points;

- bridge replacement, reconstruction or strengthening to cater for EU weight limits for commercial vehicles.

Among the routes on which improvement works will be carried out are:

- Donegal/Dungloe/Letterkenny (N56), Ballisadare/Ballina/Westport/Clifden/Galway (N59), Athlone/Boyle (N61), Moate/Stradbally (N80), and Mullingar/Birr (N52), in the BMW Region

- Birr/Nenagh (N52), Tralee/Listowel/Limerick (N69), Tralee/Dingle (N86), Tralee/Caherciveen/Kenmare (N70), Killarney/Bantry/Bandon/Cork (N71), Stradbally/Bunclody (N80), Tallaght/Blessington (N81), and Ennis/Ennistymon (N85) in the S&E Region.

4.16   In addition to the investment programme set out above for national roads, the need for the development of new routes to augment those mentioned above will be evaluated over the period of the Plan. Where the need for a new route is established, funding will be provided for the advanced planning and design of the route in the Plan period, with a view to bringing the project to construction in an appropriate time frame.

Transport in the Greater Dublin Area

Analysis of the Current Situation

4.17   Traffic congestion is a serious problem in urban areas, particularly in the Greater Dublin Region. There is a need to reduce the reliance on private cars in the Dublin area and switch to public transport in order to reduce congestion and emissions related problems. Progress has been made in recent years in introducing measures to tackle traffic congestion in the Greater Dublin Area. By end-2000:

- 12 Quality Bus Corridors will be in place;

- the peak hour capacity of the bus network will have been increased by over 40% through measures such as the purchase of 150 additional buses;

- the DART extensions to Greystones and Malahide and the upgrading of the Maynooth line will be completed;

- the peak hour capacity of the DART and suburban rail systems will have been increased by 60%;

- 2,700 park & ride spaces will be in use;

- a substantial part of the M50 will have been constructed and work on the remaining parts will be under way;

- planning and design work will have been carried out on the Port Access Tunnel.

There has however, been considerable slippage in implementing elements of the original Dublin Transport Initiative (DTI) Strategy, especially major infrastructural projects.

4.18 Traffic has grown at a much faster pace than previously forecast because of rapid population growth, increased car ownership and a greater level of economic activity. The Dublin Transportation Office (DTO) has reported that:

- the population of the Greater Dublin Area has grown more rapidly than was projected in the original DTI Strategy. The population level of 1.18m predicted for 2001 was actually exceeded in 1997;

- car ownership rates have substantially exceeded those projected and are steadily pushing towards the European average of 454 per 1000 population. Car ownership in 1997 was 317 per 1000 population, outstripping the original DTI forecast of 288 for the year 2001;

- total passenger numbers through Dublin Airport in 1998 (11.6m) exceeded those originally projected for 2011, while the annual tonnage throughput at Dublin Port (16.1m in 1997) already well exceeded the projected level of 10.7m for 2011.

The DTO has estimated that the 2000-2006 transportation programme will have to cater for between 45,000 and 104,000 additional peak hour trips in the period, compared with a peak hour total of 250,000 in 1997.

4.19 An improved transport system is vital to the economic well-being of the Greater Dublin Area. Traffic congestion is a threat to the economic life of the city, affecting over a quarter of the national population. The Strategic Planning Guidelines for the Greater Dublin Area (comprising Dublin city and the counties of Dun Laoghaire-Rathdown, Fingal, Kildare, Meath, South Dublin and Wicklow) have stressed that the future spatial development of the region must be based around public transport. The ESRI in their report on investment priorities 2000-2006 underlined that public transport investment, on a scale not hitherto contemplated, is now essential in Dublin. DKM Economic Consultants, in their review of transport investment needs, have reinforced the point by noting that the rapid economic growth of recent years has produced a backlog in transport investment and that this is particularly acute in the case of urban public transport. However, achieving the necessary shift from private to public transport will require considerable investment and other measures to provide attractive, frequent and reliable services.

Strategy for Transport in the Greater Dublin Area

4.20 Addressing urban transport needs in the Greater Dublin Area will be a major priority over the 2000-2006 period. An allocation of £1,585 million (€2,012 million) is being provided between 2000 and 2006 for public transport and traffic management and substantial additional resources will also be made available for roads investment. The objectives for this unprecedented level of investment will be:

- to address the projected growth in traffic through a combination of investment in transport infrastructure and facilities and demand management measures;

- to reduce the relative attraction of commuting to work by private car, thereby curtailing congestion and vehicular emissions;

- to increase accessibility for all, particularly mobility impaired and disabled people;

- to better reflect evolving commuter travel patterns by providing for a spatial distribution of public transport which addresses the requirements of the Strategic Planning Guidelines;

- to support sustainable development.

4.21 The strategy for the Greater Dublin Area is to concentrate investment on:

- developing, extending and increasing the capacity of the bus network;

- implementing the light rail network approved by Government in 1998;

- exploiting much more fully the potential for development of the suburban rail network;

- promotion of transport integration through the provision of additional park and ride facilities and the introduction of integrated public transport ticketing and public transport interchange facilities;

- completion of the M50, Dublin Port Access Tunnel and national road projects;

- implementation of non-national road projects of particular relevance to the achievement of DTI Strategy objectives;

- provision of further cycle infrastructure and facilities;

- implementation of traffic management measures (including measures to respond to the needs of mobility impaired and disabled people).

This investment programme will be complemented by a demand management strategy which will be developed by the DTO during 2000 and implemented thereafter.

4.22 Roads: Road projects in the Greater Dublin Area will be catered for under the roads investment provision described earlier. This will include completion by 2003/4 of the Southern Cross Route, South-Eastern Motorway and Dublin Port Access Tunnel projects. Other plans related to the C-Ring include its widening to three lanes, the provision of a second bridge at West Link and freeflow slips at interchanges. Within the C-Ring, the policy is for no significant increase in radial road capacity and any road construction projects to be funded must bring clear benefits (e.g. from the safety or environmental perspectives or to support economic development/ regeneration). The option of an Eastern Motorway is being assessed.

4.23 Light Rail: A capital provision of £430 million (€546 million) is being made for the construction of the surface element of the proposed LUAS light rail network. A reliable estimate for the cost of the underground section will not be available until geo-technical studies have been completed at the end of 1999. A contingency provision of £500 million (€635 million) has been made for this and a longer term rail development programme. A Public Private Partnership (PPP) approach to the implementation of these projects is to be examined and within the overall contingency total of £500 million (€635 million) investment, £300m (€381 million) has been identified as potential PPP investment. The current indicative LUAS timetable provides for the completion of construction of the Tallaght to Connolly line by end 2002 and the Sandyford to St Stephen's Green line by Summer 2003. When fully operational the light rail network is expected to deliver an additional 16,000 trips in the peak hour and will contribute an extra 15% in capacity on the suburban public transport system.

4.24 Dublin Suburban Rail: A provision of £185 million (€235 million) is being made for a short-term suburban rail development programme which will include:

- the phased purchase of 46 additional DART cars and 58 diesel rail cars;

- upgrading of the Greystones to Arklow line;

- linking Heuston and Connolly stations to permit the Kildare Arrow service to run through to Connolly;

- quadrupling of track between Hazelhatch and Sallins to separate long distance and suburban services;

- provision of new stations at Intel, Lucan North and South, Ashington Station improvements and new depot facilities;

- resignalling of Howth to Barrow Street and crossover works to provide slots for 3 additional peak hour services.

4.25 The combination of the infrastructural improvements and the additional rolling stock will increase DART capacity by almost 7,400 places (39%) and suburban rail capacity by 7800 seats (26%) and will allow additional services at peak times and the operation of 8-car trains.

4.26 In addition a number of options for the future development of the suburban rail network are being evaluated from a feasibility and cost perspective. These include:

- a new inland rail link to Navan;

- separation of long distance and commuter rail traffic through the construction of by-pass rail lines: options include a new rail link from the Belfast line through Swords and Dublin Airport to the Western lines and a new rail link east of the current loopline in Dublin city centre;

- quadrupling of existing double lines where feasible;

- provision or enhancement of rail services to the development centres identified by the Strategic Planning Guidelines, including Drogheda, Naas/ Newbridge/Kilcullen, Wicklow, Navan, Athy, Arklow, Kildare and Monasterevin;

- more sophisticated signalling technology to increase track capacity.

The feasibility and costing work should be completed by the end of 1999. As already stated, a contingency provision of £500 million (€635 million) has been made for the implementation of this programme and the underground section of LUAS. Decisions on further investment will be consistent with the land use development strategy as set out in the Strategic Planning Guidelines. In particular, synergy will be sought with the Development Plans of the Planning Authorities in the region.

4.27 Dublin Bus Network Development: £120 million (€152 million) will be provided to increase the capacity and improve the quality, reliability, frequency and speed of bus services in the Dublin region. The investment programme will concentrate on:

- the expansion of the bus network to meet demand, including the provision of orbital and local routes to complement the existing largely radial network;

- the phased purchase of 275 additional buses to increase passenger capacity and meet the development requirements of the network.

The additional buses will increase the bus fleet by 28% and increase capacity by 22,000 extra seats.

4.28 In addition to the above investment programme, an ongoing fleet replacement and equipment renewal programme, costing £100 million (€127 million), will be implemented. This will include the purchase by Dublin Bus of over 500 replacement buses and a reduction of the average age of its fleet from 7 to 6 years. This total investment will be supported by the provision of 5 new Quality Bus Corridors (QBCs), the extension and the enhancement of the existing QBCs and the introduction of other bus priority measures.

4.29 Public Transport Integration: There is a recognised need to improve the integration of public transport services in the Greater Dublin Area, both within and between the different modes. The suburban rail programme, the enhancement of the bus network and the development of LUAS all highlight the importance of ensuring that services are provided in an integrated manner so as to optimise the use of resources and more effectively meet travel demands in the Greater Dublin Area. A £50 million (€63m) integration programme is being provided and will include:

- the provision of 3,700 park and ride spaces at 8 sites, additional to the 2,700 spaces being provided under the current programme;

- the development of public transport nodes and interchange facilities to cater for intra-modal and intermodal transfers;

- the introduction of integrated ticketing.

4.30 Traffic Management: In relation to traffic management, £200 million (€254 million) will be provided to create an appropriate traffic environment to facilitate public transport, improve cycling facilities and improve traffic flow, including:

- provision of additional Quality Bus Corridors;

- provision of park and ride facilities;

- further development of the cycle network;

- improved traffic signalling.

4.31 Demand Management: In addition to measures related to the supply of transport infrastructure, the DTO plans to complete work, by end 2000, on the development of detailed demand management measures, building on relevant initiatives already introduced or under examination, to complement the investment proposed. This will be carried out in the framework of the update of the overall DTI Strategy. Achieving sustainable transport throughout the Greater Dublin Area must involve a wide and shared responsibility. Key players - central and local administration, business organisations, the ports and airport authorities, trade unions, educational interests as well as communities and individuals — must assume a greater onus and initiative in relation to good transport practice. Transport policy in the 2000-2006 period will encourage and support the development of good transport solutions on a partnership basis.

4.32 Delivery of public transport investment and services: The Government are determined that the large level of investment in public transport planned for the Greater Dublin Area will be implemented on time. The Government will also ensure that this greatly enhanced level of investment is reflected in real and tangible improvements for public transport customers. Delivery of investment in the public transport system will be a particular focus of the Cabinet Committee on Infrastructure Development (see paragraphs 4.44 to 4.48 below).

Regional Public Transport

4.33 It is proposed to address regional public transport requirements through investment in mainline rail, improved public transport services in major urban areas and the upgrading of regional bus services. The S&E Region is much more dependent on public transport than the BMW Region reflecting the greater degree of urbanisation in the former. A provision of £650 million (€825 million) is being made for a regional transport programme, of which an indicative £197 million (€250 million) will be in the BMW Region and £453 million (€575 million) in the S& E Region. The programme will have the following elements:

- mainline rail investment in safety and renewal;

- bus and rail development in the Greater Cork Area;

- bus development in Limerick, Galway and Waterford;

- regional bus improvements;

- accessibility improvements to existing public transport infrastructure and facilities;

- Bus Éireann ongoing fleet replacement and re-equipment;

- pilot measures for rural public transport to encourage local or community-based initiatives to provide bus services in rural areas.

4.34 The primary focus of the proposed £50 million (€63 million) investment in the main cities is on the upgrading of urban bus services, including the replacement and expansion of the bus fleet and the introduction of bus priority measures. In Cork it is also proposed to upgrade commuter rail services on the Cobh and Mallow lines. The possible introduction of a commuter rail service between Cork and Midleton and Limerick and Ennis will be evaluated as part of the suburban rail development programme (see paragraph 4.26), for which there is a contingency provision in the Plan. The purpose of these investments is to tackle increased congestion in the cities by improving the quality of public transport services.

4.35 Regional bus investment of £12 million (€15 million) is being provided for services outside the five main cities. In addition to the above programme, Bus Éireann also has an ongoing fleet replacement programme, as well as a requirement for equipment purchase and other investment. This has a capital expenditure requirement of £75 million (€95 million). This overall investment package will provide 450 new buses to upgrade Bus Eireann's rural transport fleet, provide 110 new buses to upgrade Bus Éireann's urban fleets in Cork, Limerick, Galway and Waterford, provide additional railcars and renew track and signalling for Cork suburban rail and develop park and ride sites in Cork.

Pilot Rural Transport Projects

4.36 A provision of £3.5 million (€4.4 million) is proposed for capital support for the development of pilot public transport initiatives in rural areas. The aim will be to encourage local or community-based initiatives to provide bus services in rural areas.

Mainline Rail

4.37 Increasingly the transport of goods and people by rail is viewed as an environmentally friendly and safer alternative to road transport. The mainline rail network in Ireland consists of

2,290 kilometres (1,430 miles) of track, of which 2,030 kms (1,270 miles) are used by scheduled passenger trains. The competitive position of mainline rail services has been substantially eroded over a number of decades partly as a result of inadequate investment in the network infrastructure. The lack of investment has been reflected in slower operating speeds, reduced reliability of journey times and an overall poorer quality of service. By the beginning of the 1990s much of the infrastructure was life-expired and the rolling stock had a high age profile. In the same period there was substantial growth in private car ownership and use. A combination of these two factors resulted in a considerable diminution of the relative competitive position of mainline rail services.

4.38 In recent years the investment needs of the railway have begun to be addressed. Since 1990 mainline rail has benefited from considerable grant assistance from both the EU Cohesion and Structural Funds, and more recently has also received Exchequer support. As a result, the quality of both the infrastructure and services on the Belfast and Cork/Limerick routes is now of a high standard. By end-2000 the Galway, Waterford, Tralee and Sligo routes infrastructure will have been substantially upgraded. However, significant infrastructural deficiencies still remain to be addressed, both from a safety perspective and to improve service quality. The number of passengers using the mainline rail network continues to increase. Over 9.8 million passengers were carried in 1998 — an increase of 10% on the 1997 figure. This followed a 6% increase from 1996 to 1997.

Mainline Rail — Strategy

4.39 The objectives of the mainline rail programme are to upgrade the infrastructure, rolling stock and facilities so as to:

- improve the safety of the network;

- increase the physical capacity of the railway to cater for growing passenger demand;

- improve the quality, speed and reliability of services.

4.40 A provision of £500 million (€635 million) is being allocated for investment. This investment will comprise two principal components:

- completion of the implementation of the Railway Safety Programme 1999 to 2003, as approved by the Government in March 1999;

- a renewal/upgrading programme.

The priorities of the safety investment programme will be:

- the replacement of jointed track on passenger lines with continuous welded rail;

- safety improvements in electrical, signalling and telecommunications infrastructure;

- resignalling of safety-deficient railway terminals;

- renewal of bridges and fencing;

- safety-related remedial works at level crossings.

This infrastructural investment will be complemented by a programme to improve safety management systems. A total expenditure of £350 million (€546 million) is required to complete the implementation of the Railway Safety Programme (1999 to 2003). Before the end of this

Programme, the Government will reconstitute the Railway Safety Task Force to prepare recommendations for a second five year safety programme.

4.41   The £150 million (€190 million) renewal/upgrading programme is designed to build on the firm foundation provided by the 1994 to 1999 investment. It will focus on:

- the provision of new rolling stock;
- upgrading stations;
- renewing railway plant and equipment.

4.42   The overall £500 million (€635 million) mainline rail investment programme will ensure a substantial physical improvement of the network, including:

- the renewal of about 490 kms of jointed track;
- the renewal of signalling and trackwork at Heuston and Limerick terminals;
- the provision of 20 new mainline carriages;
- safety improvements at over 530 level crossings and around 100 bridges and structures.

This investment will:

- improve railway safety;
- cater for projected annual passenger growth of the order of 5-10%;
- permit a maximum speed of 160 kph (100 mph) on the Cork and Belfast lines and 110-145 kph (70 to 90 mph) on the other passenger lines.

Accessibility

4.43   In keeping with the Government's commitment to improving accessibility of public transport for mobility impaired and disabled people, the following measures will be implemented:

- all new and upgraded rail and bus stations financed under this Plan will be accessible to mobility impaired and disabled people;
- all light rail vehicles and suburban railcars financed under this Plan will also be accessible to mobility impaired and disabled people;
- all buses purchased by CIE from 2000 for use on urban services will be low floor;
- a special provision of £10 million (€13 million) will be available to part-finance accessibility improvements to existing public transport infrastructure and facilities;
- each of the CIE operating companies will establish an Accessibility Unit and appoint a full-time Accessibility Officer to provide a focal point for accessibility issues and to review all significant investment proposals from an accessibility perspective;
- the Minister for Public Enterprise will establish a Public Transport Accessibility Committee, including representation from disability bodies, to advise on the accessibility aspects of proposed public transport investment and other public transport accessibility issues.

Transport Infrastructure Delivery

4.44 The Government is fully committed to ensuring that its proposals for economic infrastructure in the Plan are implemented within the Plan period. It is imperative that the overall programme of economic infrastructure in the NDP be completed on time — otherwise, the inadequate state of the country's infrastructure will act as an increasing constraint on economic development. In mid-1999 the Government established a Cabinet Committee on Infrastructural Development, including Public Private Partnership. This Committee is chaired by An Taoiseach and includes the Tanaiste, the Minister for Finance, the Minister for Environment and Local Government, the Minister for Public Enterprise, the Minister for Justice, Equality and Law Reform and the Attorney General. The Committee is being assisted by a Cross-Departmental Team of senior officials.

4.45 The Cabinet Committee will give the necessary momentum to the delivery of infrastructure, focusing initially on the core inter-urban road network and the Dublin transport package. The Committee, supported by the Cross-Departmental Team, has a number of objectives:

- to monitor and oversee at a high level the delivery of key infrastructure projects;

- to promote measures and Best Practice Guidelines which will support the acceleration of programme and project delivery;

- to promote appropriate institutional, administrative, legal and regulatory reforms in order to avoid unnecessary delays in the delivery of infrastructure projects;

- to devise and implement a communications strategy to raise public awareness of the economic and social benefits of rapid implementation of the infrastructure programme;

- to support the development and implementation of the Public Private Partnership Framework.

4.46 The initial focus of the Cabinet Committee has been on transport infrastructure. The Government has already approved the Committee's proposals that the following roads, referred to in Paragraph 4.12 above should be developed in their entirety to motorway/ high quality dual carriageway by 2006 with the objective of a minimum inter-urban speed of 60 mph:—

- Dublin-Belfast (to the Border)

- Cork to Dublin

- Galway to Dublin

- Limerick to Dublin

- Waterford to Dublin (road type and route to be further evaluated)

4.47 The Government also endorsed the Committee's view that the following transport projects for the greater Dublin area should be given priority for implementation:—

- completion of the M50 and Port Access Tunnel;

- completion of LUAS Lines from Tallaght to Connolly by end 2002 and Sandyford to St. Stephen's Green by end 2003;

- enhancement of existing rail and bus services proposed in the DTO Transportation Blueprint 2000-2006;

- implementation of further traffic management and possible demand management strategies on the lines proposed in the DTO Blueprint.

4.48 The NDP will involve an unprecedented expansion in and acceleration of investment in infrastructure, including in the area of public transport. As indicated in Paragraph 4.45 the Cabinet Committee has an objective of promoting appropriate institutional reform in the area of public transport; if deemed necessary the Government will show no hesitation in putting in place structures which will meet the public's needs.

Environmental Services

4.49 The protection of the environment is a key National and EU priority. The management of our water resources and the treatment of waste are key elements in any environmental protection programme. The provision of effective water and waste water infrastructure is essential to meet social, public health and environmental protection needs and is also vital to the availability of new housing and to the development of the industrial and services sectors. Good water and waste water infrastructure will help to attract foreign investment into the country and can underpin marketing Ireland as a clean green country for food and tourism. Eco-efficient economic growth should as far as possible prevent or minimise the generation of solid waste and air pollution. Policies in these regards are now important priorities for Government.

4.50 Almost £3.6 billion (€4.6 billion) is being provided for environmental investment (including water supply, waste water treatment, rural water supply, waste management, coastal protection, and environmental research) in the NDP over the 2000-2006 period. Approximately £2.5 billion (€3.2 billion — 70%) of this will be invested in the S&E Region and £1.1 billion (€1.4 billion — 30%) in the BMW Region. A significant amount of the waste management, water and waste water infrastructure will be undertaken under the Public Private Partnership arrangements, ranging from contracts to: Design & Build; Design, Build & Operate; Design, Build, Operate & Finance contracts. Of the investment of £3.6 billion (€4.6 billion), it is anticipated that projects to the value of £450 million (€571 million) in the waste management sector and £100 million (€127 million) in the water and waste water sector will be implemented through the Public Private Partnership arrangements involving private finance. Considerable private sector funding towards water services investment will also be received from capital contributions where services are provided to non-domestic users from public schemes and from development levies where services are provided to support commercial/industrial or residential development.

Analysis of the Current Situation

4.51 The current state of the environment is dealt with in Chapter 13. The main environmental challenges which must be addressed by the NDP and other policy measures include:

- halting the decline in the quality of rivers and lakes caused by excessive inputs of nutrients (eutrophication);

- meeting the requirements of EU Directives on Water and Waste Water treatment;

- better management of solid waste;

- meeting our Kyoto commitment to limit the growth of greenhouse gas emissions;

- protecting the urban environment;

- protecting flora and fauna in the countryside and along the coast.

Water and Waste Water — analysis of current situation

4.52   Capital investment in water and waste water services over the period of the National Development Plan 1994-1999 amounts to about £960 million (€1,219 million) which is well in excess of the £605m (€768 million) envisaged when the Plan was prepared. This investment has allowed, inter alia, :

- 128 major water and sewerage schemes to be completed in the 1994-1998 period. This facilitated an increase in water treatment capacity of 202,956 cubic metres/day (almost 45 million gallons/day) or the equivalent of providing additional supply to over 812,000 persons. Water storage capacity has increased by 193,500 cubic metres (almost 43 million gallons). In addition, waste water treatment capacity increased by nearly 379,000 population equivalent. A further 35 major schemes are scheduled for completion in 1999;

- waste water treatment and collection infrastructure to be provided in the major river and lake catchments including Loughs Derg, Ree and Leane and rivers Boyne, Suir and Liffey. Particular attention has also been focused on providing phosphorous reduction facilities for the 6 rivers and 4 lakes which were designated in 1994 as sensitive on the basis of their eutrophic condition (including some of the aforementioned);

- the provision of water and sewerage services to open up land for residential development through the Serviced Land Initiative;

- the initiation of planned measures to ensure the provision of adequate supplies of good quality water to rural areas though the Rural Water Programme.

4.53   Many of the visitors to Ireland are principally drawn by active water-based pursuits such as fishing, cruising and sailing. The protection of Ireland's inland waterways has become a priority in recent years as increased pollution from multiple sources has resulted in an increase in slight and moderate pollution of rivers and eutrophication of some of our major lakes. In February, 1999, the EPA published its second national report on urban waste water discharges covering the years 1996 and 1997. The report concluded that at end 1997, 22% of waste water received secondary treatment, representing a 4% increase in the level of secondary treatment since the previous report (1994/1995). Significant progress has already been made in meeting the requirements of the EU Urban Waste Water Treatment Directive. While progress has been made, substantial investment is still required to comply with EU Directives on waste water and water quality and to meet current economic development and housing needs.

4.54   The Environmental Protection Agency (EPA) has identified 155 urban agglomerations, each with a population equivalent of over 2,000 which are required to be provided with waste water treatment in accordance with the Urban Waste Water Treatment Directive. Of these, 116 agglomerations are already or soon will be in compliance. Of the 3 major centres that account for 55% of the discharges nationally, construction is well underway on the Dundalk treatment works, work on the Dublin treatment works will commence in 1999 and on the Cork treatment works next year. A further 36 schemes need completion, of which 13 are in the BMW Region.

4.55   75% of drinking water in Ireland is abstracted from surface waters. Successive EPA reports have highlighted the fundamentally good quality of public drinking water supplies. Substantial investment will have to continue to be made to maintain and improve where necessary the quality of these supplies and to extend the public supply to those areas which have an inadequate supply. The strategy under the NDP will be to provide additional water supply through new treatment works and substantial investment in water conservation measures and to extend public supplies where necessary.

4.56   One result of Ireland's recent economic buoyancy combined with relatively low interest rates has been a significant rise in residential development. With annual gross immigration of 44,000 concentrated in the household formation ages, there has been record levels of house building completions in the last few years. This is putting major pressure on existing water and waste water services and is creating a demand for additional services to support these developments.

Water and Waste Water — Strategy

4.57   Building on the investment that has been made under the previous NDP, £2,495 million (€3,168 million) is being provided over the 2000-2006 period in the Economic and Social Infrastructure Programme for water and waste water treatment. Approximately £1,810 million (€2,298 million — 72.5%) is being provided for the S&E Region and £685 million (€870 million — 27.5%) for the BMW Region. This investment is being provided to:

- meet in full the requirements of the EU Urban Waste Water Treatment Directive in relation to provision of secondary treatment in urban areas by the end of 2005;

- bring the quality of all public and group water supplies up to the Drinking Water Directive standards;

- tackle serious pollution of rivers, and reverse and minimise slight and moderate pollution of rivers and eutrophication of lakes;

- strengthen economic infrastructure to facilitate further industrial and other forms of economic development, including residential development;

- protect natural resources which are a basis for growth and competitive advantage in the tourism, food and aquaculture sectors; and

- promote regional development.

4.58   The investment will provide for:

- the construction of all the outstanding schemes required under the EU Urban Waste Water Treatment Directive, including Dublin and Cork, and also major schemes in Swords, Waterford, Limerick, Wicklow, Sligo, Westport and Letterkenny;

- investment in water supply focused on extending treatment and distribution capacity in the major urban areas and on conservation of water through leakage detection and mains rehabilitation and replacement. Investment will be made in replacing of lead piping in public water supply systems, as required, to comply with the new Drinking Water Directive. A national water study which will be completed at the end of 1999 will form the basis for prioritising investment in improving/extending medium/large water supplies, numbering more than 100 throughout the country;

- extending the catchment protection programme to other lake and river catchments over the Plan period; the investment will also include funding for the development of systems to monitor the effects of the implementation of waste water treatment infrastructure and other pollution abatement measures;

- water and sewage services for development of land for housing and commercial use;

- the improvement of the quality of water and waste water infrastructure in small towns and villages below the thresholds in the Urban Waste Water Treatment Directive.

4.59 Water quality problems on group water supplies will be addressed in the Regional Programmes through investment which will be targeted primarily at private group water supplies. The investment will be made in providing new treatment facilities or upgrading existing facilities, and, where appropriate, taking over group supplies by the local authorities. The range of measures to be put in place on a county by county basis will be guided by Strategic Rural Water Plans being drawn up by county councils in conjunction with the group scheme sector. A Rural Water provision of £420 million (€533 million) is being provided for this under the regional programmes.

Coastal Erosion

4.60 Coastal erosion is a serious threat to some public infrastructure, tourist amenities and areas of ecological importance. The objective for the period 2000-2006 will be to address on a prioritised basis urgent coastal erosion problems. The response to particular cases of erosion will be formulated in the context of a national coastal protection strategy, taking account of the need to adopt an environmentally-friendly approach to providing the necessary protection and the need to ensure value for money in the works undertaken. The total expenditure over the period of the NDP will be £35 million (€44 million) , comprised of £30 million (€38 million) for works and an indicative £5 million (€6 million) for research. An estimated £18 million (€23 million) of the funding for works is being provided for the S&E Region, and £12 million (€15 million) for the BMW Region, both of which will be supported by the national research programme.

Waste Management

4.61 Appropriate waste management infrastructure is vital not only for environmental protection reasons, but also for industrial development reasons, where lack of appropriate facilities may hamper development. The recent levels of economic growth have placed a significant strain on existing waste management infrastructure and extensive investment is now required to provide the necessary infrastructure. If this investment does not take place in a timely fashion, future economic development could be jeopardised. This is therefore a key priority infrastructure in the NDP.

4.62 The waste management policy framework is set out in the policy statement 'Changing Our Ways' (1998). The thrust of the Policy Statement is the need for a dramatic reduction in reliance on landfill, in favour of an integrated waste management approach which utilises a range of waste treatment options to deliver ambitious recycling and recovery targets. The Policy Statement suggests that an adequate, national infrastructure is required to facilitate the achievement of the following targets over a fifteen year timescale:

- a diversion of 50% of overall household waste away from landfill;

- a minimum 65% reduction in biodegradable wastes consigned to landfill;

- the development of waste recovery facilities employing environmentally beneficial technologies as an alternative to landfill, including the development of composting and other feasible biological treatment facilities capable of treating up to 300,000 tonnes of biodegradable waste per annum;

- recycling of 35% of municipal waste; and

- rationalisation of municipal waste landfills, leading to an integrated network of some 20 state-of-the-art facilities.

4.63 Local authorities are required under the Waste Management Act, 1996, to prepare waste management plans. A comprehensive waste management planning exercise is now underway at local/regional level, which will, inter alia, identify infrastructural and investment requirements necessary to give effect to this policy approach. Most authorities are currently engaged in the preparation of regional waste management plans, based in many cases on regional strategy studies which addressed the scope for, and made recommendations regarding the provision of integrated waste management infrastructure. In order to give effect to the requirements identified in the plans being prepared, it is estimated that a total of £650 million (€825 million) will be required to provide the necessary infrastructure. An estimated £240 million (€305 million — 37%) will be in the BMW Region and £410 million (€521 million — 63%) in the S&E Region. Public Private Partnership will be used to fund most of this infrastructure. The information emanating from the waste management strategy studies and draft plans indicate that both the BMW Region and the S&E Region are essentially the same in terms of the range of infrastructure required but the scale is larger in the S&E Region because of the larger population. Since waste management planning is carried out at Local Authority and regional level, the investment provisions for waste management is being included in the two regional programmes.

Energy

4.64 The Electricity Regulation Act, which came into force in July, 1999, provides for a limited opening of the electricity market to competition in line with the requirements of the EU Electricity Directive. From 19 February, 2000, approximately 28% of the market (made up of the largest electricity consumers) will be able to choose their supplier. This percentage opening will rise to about 33% in 2003. A number of independent power producers are proceeding with plans to establish new power stations to serve this market segment. It is expected, that with the emerging competitive framework, the investment requirements for power generation will be met by the energy industry. Likewise in the case of gas, the market should be able to cater for the investment needs of the sector.

4.65 In the energy sector, a key priority in the National Development Plan will be to identify those areas of expenditure which will assist Ireland in complying with its obligations under the Kyoto Protocol to the UN Convention on Climate Change. The strategy will be to pursue least cost approaches to achieving more sustainable energy services and systems. There will be a pronounced emphasis on economic instruments such as emissions trading to give incentives to CO_2 emitters and energy users to reduce emissions cost effectively.

4.66 Known and widespread market failure, among smaller energy users especially, will require complementary programmes and measures to encourage energy efficiency. This has implications for regional development which will inform the distribution of Plan investment. This will be of particular importance in the BMW Region. Special efforts will also be necessary to expand the use of renewable energy and to promote the development of technology which contributes to CO_2 abatement. There will also be a special measure to encourage improvements in poorly insulated housing stock.

4.67 A provision of £146 million (€185 million) is being provided to:

- promote energy efficiency through information and education programmes;

- promote research and development in energy efficiency and CO_2 abatement;

- promote alternative energy;

- improve the energy efficiency of the pre-1980 housing stock and Government and Local Authority Buildings.

An estimated 56% of the investment will be in the BMW Region.

4.68 The vast bulk of capital investment in the energy sector over the period to 2006 will take place outside of the provisions provided for in the Plan. The importance of the energy transmission network to the promotion of regional development is recognised. The Government will be concerned, in the context of a more competitive environment for energy supplies, to ensure that energy capacity does not act as a constraint on regional development.

Communications/Electronic Commerce

4.69 The communications/electronic commerce sector is a key input to continued economic development. It provides the basic infrastructure for new information, communications and digital industries and is already altering the modus operandi of traditional industries, the way in which work is organised, the interaction between consumers and business and vice versa. The rollout of this infrastructure to economically and socially disadvantaged regions will provide growth, employment and wealth sharing opportunities. The economic development potential which is dependent on the availability of an advanced information and communications infrastructure and services portfolio is illustrated by the following:

- the share of information industries dependent on advanced communications in the European economy is expected to rise to between 10 and 15% of GDP in the coming years;

- the European Commission estimates that the telecommunications sector itself will account for 6% of GDP by the year 2000; and

- the full availability of advanced communications services in Ireland could lead to the creation of 100,000 jobs by 2010.

4.70 Since the late 1980's the Irish communications sector has gone through the process of market liberalisation to full market opening. In that time, the sector has grown in terms of both choice of services and investment in infrastructure. Since the liberalisation of alternative infrastructure on 1 July, 1997 investment has grown rapidly from approximately £200 million/250 million (€254 million/317 million) p.a. to an estimate for 1998 of approximately £400 million (€508 million) for all market players. This growth has, however, to be viewed in the context of bridging a rapidly expanding gap between Ireland's infrastructure and that of our OECD competitors.

4.71 It is crucial that Ireland should not fall behind in the provision of advanced communications and e-commerce facilities and in the provision of the basic infrastructure capacity necessary to support the development of the Information Society. This has been recognised in several recent reports. There is now evidence that a competitive market alone will not ensure the provision of advanced communications networks and services to the extent required to contribute to national competitiveness and attract inward investment.

4.72   While investment in infrastructure in Ireland has increased following the Government's decision to liberalise the telecommunications market in Ireland, not all areas in the country are attractive for commercial investment in infrastructure. Under the current investment plans of the communications companies, large areas of the midlands will not have access and much of the west coast will not be served. Leitrim will be almost completely devoid of modern information and communications infrastructure and other border counties are poorly served. This deficiency has clear implications for regional development and it will accordingly inform the distribution of Plan investment under this heading.

Communications/Electronic Commerce Strategy

4.73   In order to leverage the benefits of the Information Society and to exploit its potential to contribute to economic development the following objectives are being pursued:

- the development of the Irish communications sector so that its ranks in the top decile of OECD countries in terms of service range, quality availability and price; and

- the establishment of a legal, regulatory and administrative framework which will create a favourable climate for the development of electronic commerce and digital industries.

These objectives will be pursued through a range of Government led actions. The strategy for the development of the communications sector is based on the promotion of a liberalised market, effective competition, with clear regulatory rules backed by independent arbitration through the Office of the Director of Telecommunications Regulation. This must be allied to investment in responsive high calibre, advanced communications infrastructure with a choice of distribution and delivery platforms. It is in the area of promoting the development of advanced communications' infrastructure and services that priming funding can provide the stimulus to close the gap between the development of the information and communications' sector in Ireland and that of the world's most advanced economies.

4.74   A provision of £120 million (€152 million) is being made in the Plan to promote investment in advanced telecommunication in areas where it is clear the market will not deliver sufficient investment, and to support the acceleration of the information society and e-commerce. This investment is being provided in the regional programmes with two thirds of it in the BMW Regional Operational Programme.

Housing

Analysis of current situation

4.75   The inclusion of housing in the National Development Plan for the first time reflects the Government's commitment to addressing the infrastructural deficit in the size of the national housing stock in relation to the growing housing requirements of an expanding and changing population. Failure to address these issues effectively would impose significant costs and constraints upon Ireland's economic growth, competitiveness and social development. The ESRI, in presenting its views on national investment priorities, clearly outlined four public policy priorities in relation to housing: the preparation of a long-term strategic planning framework, increased resources for servicing residential lands, increased resources for public transport and adequate funding for an increased level of social housing provision. In "An Economic Assessment of Recent House Price Developments", Peter Bacon and Associates forecast annual private housing output increasing to 46,000 units by 2003 to satisfy increasing demand, implying total housing output (including social housing) of well in excess of 50,000 units per annum.

4.76 It is estimated that it will be necessary to provide some 500,000 additional new dwellings over the coming ten years to meet demand, over 70% of which will be required in the Southern and Eastern region. In terms of quantifying the housing deficit, Ireland's housing stock per thousand population is the lowest in the EU at *327* housing units per thousand population as compared to 435 per thousand in the UK and a European average in the region of 450 per thousand. It is estimated that the construction of 500,000 dwellings over the next ten years would bring the Irish housing stock to about 395-400 units per thousand population.

4.77 Average household size in Ireland has fallen from 3.28 in 1991 to 3.04 in 1998 and is forecast to converge rapidly to the European average of 2.63. As the average Irish household size converges towards European norms a significant demand for additional housing is created. In addition, the rapid growth in incomes and employment, the significant increase in the number of people in the key household formation age groups, and, particularly, high immigration, have all impacted very significantly on demand for housing. These factors have resulted in demand for housing escalating at an unprecedented rate in recent years and it is likely that this high level of demand will continue for the period of the Plan. The most significant symptom of this increased level of demand, and the inability of the supply response to keep pace, has been rapid increases in house prices and rents over recent years.

4.78 Housing output has responded well to increased demand with record levels of output in each of the last four years. Output in 1998 was over 42,000 units, double the output in 1993. However, as a consequence of this significant increase in output, which must be sustained and further increased, the available stock of zoned and serviced land is being depleted at unprecedented rates and its replacement is now a key priority. The projected requirement of some 500,000 additional dwellings over the next ten years places the need to provide the necessary infrastructure and housing in a planned, sustainable and affordable way in very sharp focus.

4.79 In the five years to the end of 1998, the Border, Midland and Western Region accounted for 27% of housing output. In the short-term, the consolidation of the Dublin metropolitan area and the development of the major centres outside the existing Dublin conurbation as proposed in the Strategic Planning Guidelines for the Dublin and Mid-East Region, will ensure that new housing activity will be concentrated in the Southern and Eastern Region where demand remains very strong. However, the drawing up of the National Spatial Development Strategy will provide the context for longer-term infrastructural and employment investment to stimulate a better geographical balance of population distribution, economic activity and, accordingly, housing output.

Housing Strategy

4.80 The priorities for investment in housing under this Plan will be:

- to provide the necessary infrastructural investment to facilitate the overall level of housing output required to meet the current and anticipated levels of demand in a planned coherent fashion;

- to increase social housing output to meet rising needs;

- to continue the drive to improve the physical condition of our social housing stock.

£6 billion (€7.6 billion) is being provided for social and affordable housing over the period of the Plan, of which £4,675 million (€5,936 million — 78%) will be invested in the Southern and Eastern Region and £1,325 million (€1,682 million — 22%) will be invested in the Border, Midland and Western Region, reflecting the current population distribution and projections of need. In addition, a provision of £385 million (€489 million) will be allocated for the provision of water and waste water services to develop land for housing and commercial use.

4.81   A key housing priority of the National Development Plan will be to increase social housing output in accordance with increased needs. The approach will encompass an increase in the local authority housing programme, the expansion of voluntary housing activity, the provision by local authorities of affordable housing and the continuation of the shared ownership scheme.

4.82   In response to increased need the Plan provides for a multi-annual local authority housing programme to deliver an additional 35,500 units, an average of over 5,000 dwellings per annum over the 2000-2006 period, some 26,000 of which will be in the Southern and Eastern Region and some 9,500 of which will be in the Border, Midland and Western Region. To respond more quickly to needs, the provision will be front-loaded with 5,500 dwellings in each of the first four years. The voluntary housing sector also plays an important role in meeting social housing needs. The Government recognises that the voluntary housing sector has the capacity, with proper support, to increase output from under 500 units in 1998 to 4,000 units of accommodation per year and additional funding and administrative support will be provided to facilitate the sector in achieving this target within the Plan period.

4.83   Under the local authority affordable housing scheme, authorities provide additional new houses which will be offered for sale to eligible purchasers at cost price and, accordingly, at a significant discount from the market value of comparable houses in the area. The necessary funding to facilitate an output of 1,000 units per annum under this scheme will be provided together with the continuation at current levels of 1,000 units per annum of the local authority shared ownership scheme. This offers home ownership in a number of steps to those who cannot afford full ownership in one step in the traditional way.

4.84   Under the terms of the Planning and Development Bill 1999, each planning authority will be obliged to prepare a housing strategy for insertion in their Development Plan to provide for the housing of the existing and future population of the area. The authority will be required to estimate the amount of housing required in this area and may provide that up to 20% of land to be used for residential purposes must be provided for social or affordable housing. Under Section 82 of the Bill, a planning authority may require, as a condition of a grant of permission for residential development, the transfer to the planning authority of the ownership of up to 20% of the land for those purposes at existing use values.

4.85   Significant resources will also be made available under the Plan to local authorities for redevelopment and refurbishment of their housing stock. Resources will be provided for the Remedial Works Scheme which targets the improvement and upgrading of low cost, pre-1960 dwellings and run-down urban estates. Area-based regeneration initiatives to restore the physical fabric of established areas and to support local communities will also be supported, most notably the redevelopment of Ballymun and a number of inner-city flat complexes. Funding is also included for a number of schemes for private house improvements particularly the Disabled Persons and Essential Repairs Grants Schemes and the Task Force on Special Housing Aid for the Elderly. These schemes are targeted at the most vulnerable and those with special needs. Measures will also be taken over the period of the Plan to improve the standard and supply of hostel accommodation for homeless persons. Resettlement programmes will also be introduced to help homeless persons back into independent living with an appropriate range of supported accommodation. Resources will be made available to address the accommodation needs of travellers in the context of the requirements of the Housing (Traveller Accommodation) Act, 1998.

4.86　Achieving a better geographical balance of population distribution and economic activity also forms a key objective of the National Development Plan. The proposed National Spatial Strategy (see Chapter 3) will provide a coherent context for longer-term investment decisions. However, it will be necessary to provide up to 100,000 additional houses (some 75,000 in the Southern and Eastern Region and some 25,000 in the Border, Midland and Western Region) over the period 2000-2001 in advance of finalisation of the Strategy. In the meantime, the Strategic Planning Guidelines for the Dublin and Mid-East regions will provide the basis for the investment required in the area where the imbalance between housing supply and demand has been greatest.

4.87　It is essential to underpin future housing development by integrated infrastructural investment in water, roads, public transport and social and community infrastructure. Housing objectives are fully reflected in public transport planning and investment under the Plan. Proposals for improvement in public transport facilities to locations having scope for growth and a supply of land suitable for development are being given particular attention including enhancement of rail services to Phase One and Two centres identified in the Strategic Regional Guidelines for the Dublin and Mid-East Regions. Public transport improvements will also have regard to measures being taken to open additional serviced land for housing and maximising the potential of higher residential densities in increasing housing supply.

Health Capital

Analysis of current situation

4.88　The ability of a society to create and maintain an environment which supports its people in attaining the highest level of health compatible with their natural endowment is one of the key indicators of the stage of development of a society. Improving the health of the population enhances individual and social capital and thus supports economic and human development both at local community level and for the country as a whole.

4.89　The 1990s, and in particular the period since the publication of the National Health Strategy 1994-1998, *Shaping a Healthier Future,* has been characterised by accelerated progress in strategic planning and policy development in the health services in Ireland. The Health Amendment (No. 3) Act, 1996 requires health boards to adopt service plans and to operate within these plans throughout the year. This binding legislative requirement has given a structure to the review and planning of service delivery. The Health (Eastern Regional Authority) Act which was recently passed by the Dail, is a further step in ensuring that the optimum structure and systems are in place to facilitate best practice in planning a seamless delivery of services to the public.

4.90   This period has also seen the publication and commencement of implementation of a wide range of policies and strategies for different areas of the health service. These policies and strategies have given rise to commitments to, and public expectations of, improved health services. The combination of better planning and an improved physical infrastructure (as envisaged in the NDP) has the potential to give more effective service delivery which should contribute to improved health status.

4.91   Following a period of fiscal restraint in the mid-to-late 1980's, the 1990's have seen a resurgence in public spending on health, which has accelerated in the second half of the decade. Since 1994, there has been a real increase of 7% per annum in voted health expenditure and over the three years 1997-1999 the average annual real increase has been about 10%. Capital investment, particularly in the area of estate maintenance and equipment replacement, suffered from difficulties faced by the Exchequer in the past. The NDP provision for health capital will allow investment in our health infrastructure to be taken to a new level so that we will be in a position to meet the real challenges facing future service provision in the sector.

Health Capital Strategy

4.92   £2 billion (€2.5 billion) is being provided over the Plan period to address the capital needs of the health services; an indicative £602 million (€764 million — 30%) will be provided in the BMW Region and an indicative £1,398 million (€1,775 million — 70%) in the S&E Region. Many of the issues being addressed will be common to both regions. There will be regional differences in emphasis in some programmes since variations in the geo- and socio-demographic profiles of the two regions can affect the intensity of health needs and access to health care. In the BMW Region there will be a particular emphasis on redressing inequities or imbalances which have arisen because of the higher dependency ratio, the lower population density and the less developed transport infrastructure, particularly in the North Western Health Board part of the region. In the S&E Region there will be a particular focus on addressing problems arising in the larger centres of population — in particular, health and personal social service needs related to higher concentrations of problems such as drug (particularly heroin) use, homelessness, family breakdown and child abuse/neglect.

4.93   The priorities for spending the funds will be:

- to provide facilities for persons with an intellectual disability with the aim of ensuring that appropriate services are available as required;

- to develop a range of facilities for the elderly;

- to address major unmet needs in the provision of modern accommodation for the mentally ill and the physically disabled;

- to provide a comprehensive, quality and accessible acute hospital infrastructure;

- to address child care needs;

- to remedy deficiencies in the network of health centres;

- to maximise the potential of information and communication technology (ICT) in the health care sector.

Providing facilities for persons with an intellectual disability

4.94   There are three main elements to the capital programme associated with meeting the needs of people with intellectual disabilities:

- the provision of new facilities from which a broad range of support services, including day, residential and respites services, can be delivered;

- the renovation or replacement of existing facilities, many of which have been in use for over 30 years;

- the provision of alternative accommodation for persons with an intellectual disability currently accommodated in psychiatric hospitals or other inappropriate settings and the renovation of existing facilities which will continue to be used in the medium to long term.

The problems being addressed in both regions are basically the same. However expenditure in BMW Region will take account of the larger concentration of rural and more isolated communities in that region and the ensuing problems in relation to transport to and from services and the distances which multi-disciplinary support staff may have to travel to see clients. In the S&E Region the focus of expenditure will be on alleviating the problems of access resulting from the concentration of persons requiring services in major population centres such as Dublin and Cork.

Facilities for the elderly

4.95   Investment under the Plan will develop a range of facilities for the elderly, including community nursing units which provide a range of services such as extended nursing care, rehabilitation, day care, respite care and care for elderly persons with dementia. On a regional basis, specialist acute assessment, rehabilitation and day hospital units attached to general hospitals need to be further developed to deal with the acute episodes of illness encountered by older people. In addition to the need to provide these services for the increasing number of older people, this investment is a critical element in the strategy to relieve pressures on the acute hospital system. The proportion of elderly persons in the population is higher in the BMW Region than in the S&E Region and this, together with the personal isolation which can result from its lower population density, could necessitate a particular focus in the BMW Region on day care facilities. The supply of public nursing beds (long-stay, respite and convalescent) for older people in the Eastern Health Board area is lower than the norm for other parts of the country and necessitates an emphasis on expenditure in the S&E Region to redress this imbalance.

Accommodation for mentally ill and physically disabled

4.96   Investment will be directed towards the provision of modern accommodation for the mentally ill and the physically disabled. The measures to address needs for the mentally ill will be largely the same in both regions except in the case of child and adolescent psychiatric facilities. These are currently more developed in the S&E Region and there will be a special focus on improving these services in the BMW Region. In relation to the physically disabled, differences in approach between the two regions will (as in the case of intellectual disability) relate mainly to ameliorating the problems of access resulting from low population density in the BMW Region and high population density in the S&E Region (particularly in the larger urban areas). Existing regional assessment facilities are located in the S&E Region. It is a policy priority to redress this imbalance by developing like facilities in the BMW Region.

Provision of acute hospital infrastructure

4.97 Upgrading of acute hospital infrastructure to provide a better and more accessible service will be addressed through investment in estate maintenance (including equipment) and new developments. This is an objective common to both regions. However, the historic tendency to centre the major tertiary hospital services in the Eastern region means that there is now a significant difference of emphasis in terms of the problems to be addressed through acute hospital spending under the NDP. Whereas the emphasis in the S&E Region will be on consolidation and enhancement of facilities, initiatives in the BMW Region will centre on investment aimed at improving access to services in order to address inequities, to the extent that they exist, arising from lower population densities, higher dependency rates and the availability of a narrower range of acute services available. This is in line with the overall objective stated in the Action Plan accompanying the National Health Strategy of "providing within each health board area a self-sufficiency in community and regional specialities". It is also in line with the approach to addressing regional imbalances set out in the Cancer Strategy and the Cardiovascular Strategy.

Child care needs

4.98 The health provision in the Plan for child care needs will be directed in particular to provide high support units for out-of -control non-offending children, to upgrade ordinary child care residential units (which will be the first focus of examination of the Social Services Inspectorate), to provide accommodation for homeless children and others who are disadvantaged, and to establish the information technology infrastructure for a much needed child care database. In view of the policy requirements of developing effective and equitable services throughout the country the approach is generally similar in both regions. However the demand for high support units and for the homelessness initiative is greatest in the larger urban areas of the S&E Region and this will be reflected in the Plan.

Improving health centres

4.99 The Plan provides for investment in the network of health centres required to advance the aims of the Health Strategy in order to ensure that such centres operate effectively and become the local hubs for the delivery of a wide range of community services.

Information and communications technology

4.100 Resources are being provided to maximise the potential of information and communication technology (ICT) to support effective modern management as well as delivering, as far as possible, out-reach services such as hospital diagnostic imaging and laboratory pathology to remote areas through developments in telemedicine.

Impact of Strategy

4.101 The potential impact of the investment in the health sector includes the following:

- **General Hospitals** — Capital developments involving the provision of additional capacity in surgical specialities with lengthy waiting lists (such as orthopaedics, ENT, vascular surgery etc.), will impact positively on waiting lists. Many of the capital projects in acute hospitals involve replacement of outdated or cramped facilities which will provide a more efficient service generally. Investment in step-down facilities (see section on Older People below) will also help reduce waiting lists. The investment will also result in improved rehabilitation facilities. These impacts are common to both regions. A major impact in the BMW Region will be to attain regional self-sufficiency through developing strong regional hospital facilities supplemented by a network of local general hospitals that have the capacity to underpin the overall development of regional specialities with a view to addressing any existing inequities of access. This will reduce considerably the need for people in peripheral areas to travel long distances for treatment and follow-up.

- **Intellectual Disability** — The proposed investment will meet the current identified needs in relation to both waiting lists for services and the need to enhance the level of overall support available to persons with an intellectual disability and their families. The level of respite care, and in particular the level of planned respite care, available to families will be significantly increased. It will also enable the programme to transfer persons with an intellectual disability from psychiatric hospitals and other inappropriate placements to more suitable settings to be completed, and a programme of renovation and replacement of existing facilities to be undertaken. These impacts will in large measure be common to both Regions but in the BMW Region the service attendance and delivery problems associated with low population density will be significantly ameliorated while in the S&E Region the impact will be felt most in reductions in the larger waiting lists which result from higher concentrations of persons in need of services.

- **Physical and Sensory Disability** — The proposed investment will meet the balance of capital spending needs identified by the Review Group on Health and Personal Social Services for People with Physical and Sensory Disabilities in its report, *Towards an Independent Future,* and will have a significant impact on anticipated needs for 2002-2006. In addition, the funding will enable a regional assessment centre to be established in the six health boards (four of which are located in the BMW Region) which do not already have such a facility. Investment in upkeep and refurbishment will improve existing facilities.

- **Mental Health** — Investment will provide a number of additional acute psychiatric units; considerable improvements in the relatively underdeveloped areas of child and adolescent psychiatric facilities (particularly in the BMW Region) and of old age facilities; and additional numbers of community residential facilities, mental health centres, mental health day hospitals and mental health day centres.

- **Community Health** — Investment here will result in a wide geographical spread in both regions of multi-purpose health centres which will be local hubs for the provision of a range of primary care health and personal social services leading to a more comprehensive and integrated service to patients. In terms of dental services the investment will result in a new Regional Oral Surgery and Maxillo-Facial Unit in Dublin, increased provision for orthodontic services, equipment for children's dental services, and the replacement of plant and equipment for water fluoridation. The investment will also result in improved facilities for rehabilitation of drug users particularly in the S&E Region where the greatest concentration of problems exists.

- **Older People** — Additional provision will include extra day hospitals, day care centres, new community nursing units as well as improved capacity in palliative care / hospices. An important impact will be redressing the imbalance in the supply of nursing beds in the Eastern Health Board area in the S&E Region.

- **Child Care** — Investment will provide high support units, better children's residential accommodation, a range of facilities for young homeless people with, for example, drug problems (particularly, though not exclusively in the S&E Region), additional accommodation, and improvements to existing accommodation, for community based social workers, facilities for community based projects designed to strengthen family services, facilities for counselling victims of abuse, comprehensive child care database systems, and financial support to pre-school services for at-risk or disadvantaged children.

- **Information and Communications Technology (ICT)** — The investment in ICT will have a significant impact in providing for:

  - better management information for planning and more effective decision making;

  - more efficient processes in service delivery and administration;

  - faster multifaceted communication with resultant services integration;

  - provision of more information to the public;

  - delivery of services at the most appropriate locations with access to various centres of excellence via telemedicine as required.

The latter will enable hospital diagnostic imaging and laboratory pathology services to reach out to the remotest areas via GPs supported by other health professionals.

Public Private Partnership

Background

4.102 Public Private Partnerships (PPPs) are defined as partnerships between public sector organisations and private sector investors and businesses for the purposes of designing, planning, financing, constructing and/or operating infrastructure projects, particularly projects which are normally provided through traditional procurement mechanisms by the State or other government bodies. The use of output specification, the optimal allocation of risk between the private and public sectors and the objective of value for money for the public sector over the lifetime of a project are at the heart of PPP. PPPs are an important element within the overall investment planned under the National Development Plan 2000-2006, particularly under the Economic and Social Infrastructure Operational Programme.

4.103 The benefits of increased private sector involvement in all stages of development of public capital projects are widely acknowledged. The PPP approach, in its various forms, is now being adopted in many European countries and elsewhere. This approach can not only increase the level of funding available for investment but also can generate benefits for the public sector by allocating risks to those best able to handle them and by generating greater efficiency. The private sector can bring benefits in terms of management, financial and technical skills. The benefits of risk sharing and of increased efficiency through improved exploitation of private sector skills can be captured to differing degrees. PPP mechanisms can include options which are funded directly by the public sector, such as Design and Build, or Design/Build/Operate. However, the greater the degree of private sector involvement, the greater the scope to capture such benefits.

4.104   The private sector already works in fairly close partnership with the public sector in relation to the provision of economic infrastructure in Ireland. The PPP approach has been adopted on a case by case basis to meet specific requirements, such as the Government Offices' decentralisation programme, and the toll bridges in Dublin. In the Partnership 2000 agreement, the Government expressed its support in principle for Public Private Partnership in construction and agreed that a detailed assessment of the scope of private financing mechanisms for public infrastructure and the methodology of identification of suitable projects would be undertaken early in the life of the new Partnership. The Government has decided to adopt a Public Private Partnership approach, on a pilot basis, to public capital projects, with an initial concentration on economic infrastructure projects. The initial priority for the pilot projects is the roads area.

4.105   The pilot projects were selected with a view to the wider adoption of the PPP approach in the context of the National Development Plan. The rolling out of PPP is not intended to await the final completion of the pilots. The experience gained at each stage of developing the pilots is being used for additional projects, whether in the pilot sectors or others, at the same time as the pilots are being implemented. It should also be noted that the pilot projects will largely come on stream in the period covered by the Plan.

PPP Investment in the National Development Plan 2000-2006

4.106   While programmes in relation to the Productive Sector and Employment have always relied on some degree of partnership between the public and private sectors, and this is expected to be strengthened further, PPP funding will be particularly focused on the Economic and Social Infrastructure Programme and Regional Programmes of the NDP 2000-2006. A total of £1.85 billion (€2.35 billion) of PPP-financed developments are proposed for inclusion in Plan of which £1.40 billion (€1.78 billion) is earmarked for the Economic and Social Infrastructure Programme and £450 million (€571 million) for waste management in the Regional Programmes; further PPP investment is also to be included in the Human Resources Programme. This is a **minimum target** for PPPs in the Plan. The objective is maximum usage of PPPs consistent with the principles of efficiency and best value for money. The overall level of investment does not reflect the total level of PPP activity, as arrangements for Public Private Partnerships without a private capital investment element will be used in a number of areas covered by the Programme as outlined in paragraph 4.107 below.

4.107   In the context of NDP funding, PPP investment refers to investment in public capital projects which are privately-financed. The scale of PPP (i.e. privately-financed) investment in Economic Social Infrastructure is summarised in Table 4.2 below. In addition, the provision of £1.67 billion (€2.21 billion) for investment in educational and training infrastructure in the Human Resources sector is to include an element of PPP funding.

Table 4.2:   **PPP investment in Economic and Social Infrastructure**

Priority	NDP Measures	Plan Allocation for PPP Investment € million	PPP Investment as % of Total
Economic Infrastructure	National Roads	1,270	23
	Water Supply	127	9*
	Public Transport — LUAS/ Long-term Suburban Rail	381	60
Regional Programmes	Waste Management	571	69

*This figure represents the PPP funding as a percentage of the estimated water supply component of overall investment in water and sewerage services under the Economic and Social Infrastructure Operational Programme.

Indicative PPP Projects

4.108 Precise designation of projects or parts of projects for PPP purposes will be decided as the Plan is implemented. The appropriate funding structures, including, where appropriate, road user tolls, for projects will be examined and identified as they are developed, bearing in mind the level of funding available and the appropriateness of particular projects for the PPP approach.

4.109 However, within the measures identified as availing of PPP funding, the broad classes of projects for which PPP may be appropriate can be indicated. In the first instance, the pilot projects announced by the Minister for Finance in June 1999 will all be developed within the NDP period of 2000-2006. These include, subject to statutory procedures and negotiations where appropriate:

- a new Western River Crossing in Limerick on the N7;

- the Waterford By-Pass, including a new bridge over the Suir, on the N25;

- the second West Link Bridge on the M50;

- key elements of the Dublin Light Rail (LUAS) project.

In addition, the potential for a PPP to develop the Kilcock-Kinnegad section of the N4 is being actively explored. Projects in education, the solid waste management area, and water supply will be named following further consultations. Indications at this stage are that some of the pilot projects will go to tender within the first year of the NDP period and that the rest should go to tender within the first two years of the NDP period, subject to satisfactory and speedy completion of the necessary statutory procedures and any negotiations.

4.110 Investment which is classified as "PPP investment" does not cover all PPP activity within the NDP. PPP approaches which do not avail of private finance (for which the capital investment is sourced directly from the Exchequer or other public sources) will also be significant in the overall investment programme, particularly in certain sectors. For example, the bulk of investment under the Urban Waste Water Treatment Directive Measure, to total £700 million (€889 million), is expected to be take the form of Design/Build/Operate arrangements. Such PPPs permit the private sector to take full responsibility for the provision of infrastructure and also for the operation or maintenance of the infrastructure over its life span. This can deliver improved value for money over the lifetime of the infrastructure through costs and time savings, and can also contribute to improved services and more efficient management of resources.

Developing the Administrative Framework for PPP

4.111 Effective implementation of PPP requires that the responsible bodies avail of, and where possible develop, the necessary skills to manage this innovative approach. A number of structures have been put in place to facilitate implementation of the PPP approach both within the responsible agencies and Departments through establishment of PPP Units, and in the form of cooperative arrangements. The Government established the Central Public Private Partnership Unit in the Department of Finance at the beginning of 1999, to lead, drive and co-ordinate the process. A PPP Unit was established in the Department of the Environment and Local Government at the same time and a PPP Units was subsequently set up in the Department of Education and Science. A PPP Unit for LUAS will shortly be established in the Department of Public Enterprise.

4.112 Government bodies are also actively seeking support in the form of expertise and advice, through engaging private sector skills in the form of specialist recruitment as well as consultancy.

The PPP Units are also working with and maintaining close contacts with other administrations and international bodies, both bilaterally and through international fora. Steps will also be taken to develop the awareness and skills of the public sector through training and information programmes. The European Commission has been strongly supportive of the principle of PPP's and the possibility of seeking some EU funding to support the technical and administrative aspects of PPP is being examined.

4.113   As well as addressing the areas of staffing, structures and skills, the responsible authorities will also ensure that the legal, administrative and policy framework facilitates the effective use of PPP. This includes ensuring that the legislation in each sector is compatible with the optimum PPP approach for that sector, and putting in place suitable administrative control and direction for the use of PPPs.

Cohesion Fund

4.114   Agenda 2000 provides for the continuation of the Cohesion Fund for the 2000 to 2006 period. Member States whose per capita GNP is less than 90% of the community average will eligible for assistance. A mid-term review of eligibility will be carried out in 2003 based on per capita GNP criterion for the 2000 to 2002 period. This is likely to establish that Ireland's per capita GNP exceeds 90% of the Community average and, in this eventuality, Ireland's eligibility for Cohesion Fund assistance will cease after 2003. Ireland allocation from the Fund for 2000-2003 amounts to £439 million (€557 million).

4.115   It is expected that Fund assistance will be distributed evenly between the transport and environment sectors. More than sufficient potential projects have been identified to absorb the EU aid available. These consist of priority road projects, major waste water projects and a large-scale rail project. Preliminary planning is well advanced on these projects which will facilitate the commencement of construction early in the new funding round.

4.116   The priority on the transport side is to complete the main roads network which are being funded by the Cohesion Fund under the current round. The rail development project under consideration mainly involves completion of track and signaling improvement works on mainline and suburban lines started under the current round. On the environment side, the strategy is to concentrate investment on three major waste water projects required under the Urban Waste Water Treatment Directive viz: Dublin Bay project, Cork Main Drainage (Treatment Works) and Limerick Main Drainage. A solid waste management project may also be included.

Trans-European Network (TENS) Funding

4.117   Ireland is eligible for TENS funding. It is available for road and rail projects on the TENS network. Appropriate projects are being considered to absorb some £47.2 million (€60 million) of TENS funding. The aid rate for TENS projects is about 10%.

Environmental Impact of Economic and Social Infrastruture Programme

Roads

4.118 Roads and road transportation can have adverse environmental effects in terms of emissions, noise, visual intrusion, road accidents, property severance and impacts on residential and shopping/business districts and sensitive areas. Well-designed road improvements do however help reduce emissions, whilst by-passes and relief roads remove traffic from unsuitable areas, and road improvements contribute to improved safety. Many towns situated on national roads have substantial traffic problems, with congestion, traffic encroachment into the main shopping streets and even residential areas, pedestrian/vehicular conflict, and increased road accidents, noise and emissions. The provision of by-passes and relief roads alleviates these problems and make the towns safer, quieter, cleaner and more attractive places in which to live, work and visit.

4.119 The national roads programme will result in the removal of through-traffic from many towns and villages with a consequent improvement in environmental conditions and the quality of life generally in these areas. The elimination of congestion due to through-traffic, and improvement of journey times and traffic conditions, will also have beneficial effects on vehicle emissions. Particular care will be taken in the route selection and design of road projects to minimise the impact on local communities (by, for example, avoiding demolition of houses and preventing severance), to by-pass sensitive areas, and to minimise the impact on flora and fauna and visual intrusion. Effective and early public consultation and careful planning are important in ensuring environmental compatibility. All road projects in the NDP likely to have significant effects on the environment will be subject to a comprehensive Environmental Impact Assessment (EIA) process. It is proposed under the Planning Bill to transfer the role of competent authority in the EIA process in relation to road and other infrastructure projects from the Minister for the Environment and Local Government to An Bord Pleanála.

Public Transport

4.120 The large investment in public transport will have substantial environmental benefits particularly in the Greater Dublin Area. It will encourage a switch to public and non-motorised transport leading to reduced congestion, emissions, noise levels and accidents. There will also be environmental improvements associated with the development of environmental traffic cells, traffic calming and street/suburban village improvement schemes. In addition it is envisaged that transport demand management policy will be increasingly important in ensuring effective, efficient and sustainable use of our transport infrastructure, particularly in the major urban areas. A comprehensive demand management strategy for the Dublin area will be developed for implementation over the time scale of this investment programme.

Environmental Services

4.121 The investment programme in waste water and drinking water is geared towards meeting the requirements of EU Directives in these areas. It will have clear environmental benefits in that less pollutants will be entering rivers, lakes and the sea with positive environmental benefits in terms of cleaner rivers, lakes and beaches. The investment in drinking water in aimed at improving its quality in rural and urban areas. Investment in waste management in the regional programmes will reflect national and EU environmental policy objectives and give practical effect to a waste management philosophy which favours waste prevention and minimisation.

Housing

4.122 The housing investment will be co-ordinated with public transport development and this should have positive environmental benefits. Investment in the improvement of local authority housing stock will improve the energy efficiency of those houses with consequent positive environmental benefits.

Health Capital

4.123 The investment in health capital will have no adverse impact on the environment and will have some positive benefits. The investment will give greater geographic distribution of health services. This will reduce the need to travel long distance for services with positive consequences for the environment. The investment will refurbish existing facilities and this should lead to improvement in the energy efficiency of these facilities.

Gender Impact of Economic and Social Infrastructure Investment

4.124 The significant investment in economic and social infrastructure over the period of the NDP will have considerable benefits for both women and men. In general road investment should be gender neutral allowing for better travel conditions for men and women road users. Recent analysis indicates that proportionately more women than men use public transport to travel to work. On this basis the increased investment in public transport should have a positive impact on women. Similarly, investing in improved accessibility of public transport for the mobility impaired will be of positive benefit to people, including women, travelling with young children on public transport. Investment in environmental services is gender neutral as is investment in energy and coastal protection.

4.125 The investment in housing and health should be particularly beneficial to women. Social housing will address the housing needs of poorer women with children, particularly those without partners. Women are more frequently involved in caring for the elderly, the handicapped, and children who need hospital treatment. The health investment in the NDP will improve the infrastructure in these area making it better for patients and carers.

Impact on Poverty

4.126 The direct impact of roads investment on poverty will be broadly neutral. However roads investment through its positive effects on growth and competitiveness will create employment opportunities for poorer people and will make more resources available for dealing with poverty. Public transport investment will have a positive impact on poverty because poorer people are more heavily reliant of this mode of transport. Investment in, water services, energy, and coastal erosion will have a broadly neutral affect on poverty. Investment in housing and health will have a very positive effect on poverty. Housing investment will make more public housing available for poorer families who cannot afford their own houses. The health expenditure on the handicapped, the elderly, disadvantaged children and the public health services generally will benefit the poorer and disadvantaged sectors of society.

Rural Impact

4.127 It is widely recognised that off-farm employment has a key role to play in maintaining population in rural areas and improving the overall economic welfare of the rural population. The National Roads investment in the NDP will improve accessibility for people in rural areas to jobs in towns and urban centres and makes these towns and urban centres more attractive locations for inward investment thereby increasing the job choices for rural people. The environmental investment programme will help reduce river and lake pollution making the environment more attractive for those living in rural areas and improving the attractiveness of these areas for tourism. The investment in water and water services will also make towns more attractive for inward investment which will benefit those living in the surrounding rural hinterland.

4.128 Investment in telecommunications and energy will be mainly concentrated in more peripheral areas where the market alone is unlikely to provide and this should be of direct benefit to the surrounding rural areas. Finally investment in health care capital will bring health care facilities and services closer to people living in rural areas.

5 Employment & Human Resources Development Operational Programme

Introduction

5.1 People are a country's most important asset. Making full use of this valuable resource requires the adoption of policies which will enable all those who wish to do so to find a job and which will enable people to develop their skills levels so that they can realise their full potential within the ever changing market place. As a result of a comprehensive assessment of the skills attainment of the labour force and the skills requirements of the economy, Plan investment on the Employment and Human Resources Development Operational Programme will amount to £9.9 billion (€12.6 billion).

5.2 Reflecting the EU Employment Guidelines and the National Employment Action Plan (NEAP) investment will take place under four pillars as follows:

Table 5.1:   **Employment and Human Resources Development Operational Programme – Expenditure 2000-2006**

	€ billion		
	National	**S&E Region**	**BMW Region**
Employability	5.9	4.2	1.7
Entrepreneurship	0.5	0.4	0.1
Adaptability	6.0	4.2	1.8
Equal Opportunity	0.26	0.19	0.07
Total Expenditure	12.6	9.0	3.6
Expenditure Per Capita €	3,471	3,378	3,725

In addition to the investment of £0.2 billion (€0.26 billion) on equal opportunities under this priority further investment amounting to £1.06 billion (€1.3 billion) is also provided for under Social Disadvantage in the Programmes for the Development of the Border, Midland and Western (BMW) and Southern and Eastern (S&E) Regions. This includes £250 million (€317.5 million) for the provision of child care facilities. This represents the single biggest specific investment in the Plan under gender mainstreaming in pursuit of the objective of reconciling family and working life and facilitating access for women to education, training and employment. Equal opportunity in the National Plan covers both gender mainstreaming and the elimination of inequalities in order to address national priorities in relation to tackling social exclusion and poverty, and to meet the requirements of the ESF Regulation (Regulation No 1262/1999 of 21 June, 1999 – in particular Articles 1-3) and the General Structural Funds Regulation (Regulation No 1260/1999 of 21 June, 1999 – Article 1) respectively.

Analysis of the Labour Market

5.3 Ireland's recent employment performance has been remarkable when compared with past experience or with current experience elsewhere in the developed world. Table 5.2 shows how the labour market has developed since 1993.

Table 5.2: Labour force, employment and unemployment, April 1993-Winter 1998/99 (000s)

	April 1993	April 1994	April 1995	April 1996	April 1997	2nd quarter 1998[1]	2nd quarter 1999
Labour Force	1,403	1,432	1,459	1,508	1,539	1,621	1,688
Participation rate[2]	52.8%	53.3%	53.6%	54.5%	54.7%	56.5%	57.9%
Employment	1,183	1,221	1,282	1,328	1,380	1,495	1,591
Employment rate[2]	44.5%	45.4%	47.1%	48.0%	49.0%	52.0%	54.5%
Unemployment	220	211	177	179	159	127	97
Unemployment rate	15.7%	14.7%	12.2%	11.9%	10.3%	7.8%	5.7%
Long-term unemployment	125	128	103	103	86	64	42
LTU rate	8.9%	9.0%	7.1%	6.9%	5.6%	3.9%	2.5%

Source: Central Statistics Office, Labour Force Surveys (LFS), 1993-97; Quarterly National Household Survey (QNHS), 2nd quarter 1998 and 2nd quarter 1999

5.4 In the six years up to the second quarter of 1999, the labour force increased by 285,000 (an average of over 3% per annum). Much of this growth has been driven by demographic trends (including the reversal of migration flows) which have seen a large increase in the population of working age. However, as the table shows, rising labour force participation has also played a part, particularly since 1995. Virtually all of this increase relates to women, whose participation rate rose from 38.2% in 1993 to 46% by 2nd quarter of 1999; male participation showed a more modest increase, from 67.9% to 70.2% over the same period.

5.5 Employment grew even more rapidly, by 370,000 (over 5% per annum). This led to an increase in the employment rate, from 44.5% in 1993 to 54.5% by 2nd quarter of 1999. Again, women's employment rate rose particularly rapidly, from 32% to 43.4%. However, the male employment rate, which had been falling previously, also showed a significant increase, from 57% to 66%. As a result, unemployment fell by 123,000, from 220,000 in 1993 to 97,000 by quarter one of 1999, bringing the unemployment rate down from 15.7% to about 6%.

5.6 The youth unemployment rate, although considerably reduced, from 25% in 1994 to 11.1% (2nd Qtr. '99), remains high in comparison to the adult (over 25) rate. In addition, early school leaving remains a concern. The preventative strategy remains key here in the first instance with a gradual extension of its application to longer duration young unemployed people.

Regional Analysis of the Labour Market

5.7 Regional analysis of the employment and unemployment situation Table 5.3 reveals regional differences in the labour force growth, participation and employment rates. Between 1993 and 1998 the labour force grew in the Border, Midland and Western (BMW) Region by 9% compared to almost 18% in the Southern and Eastern (S&E) Region. The female participation rate grew in the BMW Region from 45% to 47% while in the S&E Region it grew from 47% to over 54%. Employment

---

[1] The change from the LFS to QNHS is estimated to have boosted the headline figure for both employment and the labour force by approximately 20,000 as a result of improved identification of part-time jobs held by students and others. In the text, allowance is made for this discontinuity in any comparisons between 1999 and previous years.

[2] Calculated as a proportion of the population of 15 and over.

grew by 58,000 or 19% in the BMW Region while in the S&E Region employment grew by 253,0000 or 29%. The rate of growth in female employment was twice that of male employment in the BMW Region at 28%. In the S&E Region at 40% it was over three times the growth in male employment. The unemployment pattern in both regions was similar, falling from approximately 16% in the BMW Region to just over 8% and from 15.5% in the S&E Region to 7.6%.

Table 5.3:   Regional breakdown of Labour Force, Employment and Unemployment

(000s)	BMW Region		S&E Region		National	
	1993	1998	1993	1998	1993	1998
Population (15-64)						
Female	279.2	305.1	838.1	914.7	1,117.3	1,219.8
Male	296.1	317.9	835.8	911.7	1,131.9	1,229.6
Total Population (15-64)	575.3	623.0	1,673.9	1,826.4	2,249.2	2,449.4
Labour Force						
Female	124.6	144.2	390.5	498.2	515.1	642.4
Male	239.2	252.2	648.8	726.5	888.0	978.7
Total labour force	363.8	396.4	1,039.3	1,224.7	1,403.1	1,621.1
Participation Rate						
Female	44.6%	47.3%	46.6%	54.5%	46.1%	52.7%
Male	80.8%	79.3%	77.6%	79.7%	78.5%	79.6%
Total Participation Rate	63.2%	63.6%	62.1%	67.1%	62.4%	66.1%
Employment						
Female	103.2	132.5	330.5	462.1	433.7	594.6
Male	201.7	230.5	547.7	669.4	749.4	899.9
Total at work	304.9	363.0	878.2	1,131.5	1,183.1	1,494.5
Employment Rate						
Female	37.0%	43.4%	39.4%	50.5%	38.9%	48.7%
Male	68.1%	72.5%	65.5%	73.4%	66.2%	73.2%
Total Employment Rate	53.0%	58.3%	52.5%	62.0%	52.6%	61.0%
Unemployed						
Female	21.4	11.7	60	36.1	81.4	47.8
Male	37.5	21.7	101.1	57.1	138.6	78.8
Total Unemployed	58.9	33.4	161.1	93.2	220.0	126.6
Unemployment Rate						
Female	17.2%	8.1%	15.4%	7.2%	15.8%	7.4%
Male	15.7%	8.6%	15.6%	7.9%	15.6%	8.1%
Total Unemployment Rate	16.2%	8.4%	15.5%	7.6%	15.7%	7.8%
Long-term Unemployment						
Female	10.6	4.2	30.1	13	40.7	17.2
Male	22.6	12.8	62.1	33.5	84.7	46.3
Total Long-term Unemployment	33.2	17.0	92.2	46.5	125.4	63.5
Long-term Unemployment Rate						
Female	8.5%	2.9%	7.7%	2.6%	7.9%	2.7%
Male	9.4%	5.1%	9.6%	4.6%	9.5%	4.7%
Total Long-term Unemployment Rate	9.1%	4.3%	8.9%	3.8%	8.9%	3.9%

Source: CSO LFS 1993 & QNHS Q2 1998

5.8 In both regions long-term unemployment has fallen faster than overall unemployment, indicating a previously unanticipated responsiveness to economic growth and the effectiveness of targeted active labour market programmes. However, there remains a strong structural component to those who remain in long-term unemployment.

Educational Attainment

5.9 The lack of educational attainment remains a critical factor in the risk and persistence of long-term unemployment. At the level of the individual, a wide range of disadvantage can present itself. Table 5.4 sets out educational attainment of the population by region and by gender.

Table 5.4: Educational Attainment

(000s)	BMW Region		S&E Region		National	
	1993	**1997**	**1993**	**1997**	**1993**	**1997**
Population(15 years and over)						
Female	348.7	368.8	1,001.4	1,063.3	1,350.0	1,432.0
Male	354.7	369.3	952.3	1,013.5	1,307.0	1,383.1
Total	703.4	738.1	1,953.7	2,076.8	2,657.1	2,815.1
Primary						
Female	125.7	114.5	297.5	270.5	423.2	385.0
Male	144.0	129.5	287.5	262.5	431.5	392.0
Total	269.7	244.1	585.0	533.0	854.7	777.1
Lower Secondary						
Female	89.1	96.8	248.6	266.7	337.7	363.5
Male	102.1	111.2	270.9	287.2	373.0	398.4
Total	191.2	208.0	519.5	554.0	710.7	762.0
Upper Secondary						
Female	91.8	102.4	301.4	313.4	393.2	415.8
Male	68.3	79.3	232.0	255.3	300.3	334.6
Total	160.1	181.7	533.4	568.7	693.5	750.4
Non-Degree 3rd level						
Female	26.6	34.2	82.2	116.5	108.8	150.7
Male	20.8	27.6	70.8	93.7	91.6	121.3
Total	47.4	61.8	153.0	210.2	200.4	272.0
Degree 3rd level						
Female	14.5	19.0	67.8	87.1	82.3	106.1
Male	18.6	20.4	88	109.0	106.6	129.4
Total	33.1	39.4	155.8	196.1	188.9	235.5
Not Stated						
Female	1.0	1.9	3.9	9.1	4.9	11.0
Male	0.9	1.3	3.1	5.8	4.0	7.1
Total	1.9	3.2	7.0	15.0	8.9	18.1

Source: CSO LFS 1993 and 1997

In 1997 the proportion of the population (15 years of age and over) with education only up to primary level was 27% for the State. Across the two regions the breakdown was 33% for the BMW Region and 26% for the S&E Region. However, between 1993 and 1998 there has been a reduction, nationally of 77,600 or 9% in the number of people with only Primary Education. In the regions the percentage reduction was in the order of 9% for both. The percentage increase of those with Lower Secondary level education was 7% nationally with the regional increases of the same order. The percentage increase between 1993 and 1997 in those with Upper Secondary education was 8% nationally, 13.5% for the BMW Region and 6.6% for the S&E Region. For Non-Degree Third Level the increase was 36% nationally, 30% for the BMW Region and 37% for the S&E Region. The category Degree Third Level showed an increase of 25% nationally, 19% for the BMW Region and 25% for the S&E Region. The overall trend nationally is of an increasingly educated population reflecting, in particular, the availability of free second level education since the 1960s, the young profile of the population and the substantial investment in human resources development in the two previous structural fund programming rounds.

5.10 There are differences between the regions in the level of educational attainment. The proportion of the population with third level qualifications in 1997 at 20% in the S&E Region is ahead of the 14% for the BMW Region. In 1997 the representation of women among the population with lower levels of education (Lower Second Level or Primary Education) was lower in the BMW Region at 47% than in the S&E Region at 49%. 53% of those with third level education in the BMW Region are women while in the S&E Region the figure is 50%. The recent evaluation report of the ESF Evaluation Unit on Equal Opportunities between Men and Women indicates that women constituted 43% of all participants benefiting from ESF supported education and training in 1994-1999.

Sectoral Employment Analysis

5.11 Sectoral analysis of employment shows similar patterns in terms of women's involvement in the sectors but there are significant overall differences between the BMW Region and the S&E Region between the sectors. As can be seen from Table 5.5 there are generally less women than men employed in both regions across sectors but this is less marked in manufacturing and the services. There are, however, more women than men employed in the professional services and other services. The BMW Region's share of the State's Agriculture, Forestry and Fishing employment is 44% while its share of Building and Construction and Manufacturing stands at 29%. Similarly, its share of employment in Market and Non-Market Services stands at 21% compared to the S&E Region's share of 79%.

Table 5.5:   Sector of Employment

(000s)	BMW Region		S&E Region		National	
	1993	**1998**	**1993**	**1998**	**1993**	**1998**
Agriculture, Forestry and Fishing						
Female	5.8	7.4	10.0	8.7	15.8	16.1
Male	56.7	54.4	77.2	71.1	133.9	125.5
Total	62.5	61.8	87.2	79.8	149.7	141.6
Building and Construction						
Female	0.7	0.9	2.8	4.0	3.5	4.9
Male	17.4	24.8	50.5	67.9	67.9	92.7
Total	18.1	25.7	53.3	71.9	71.4	97.6
Other Production Industries						
Female	20.2	27.9	48.3	60.3	68.5	88.2
Male	45.4	58.4	130.4	146.2	175.8	204.6
Total	65.6	86.3	178.7	206.5	244.3	292.8
Commerce, Insurance, Finance and Business Service						
Female	22.4	27.3	84.5	107.3	106.9	134.6
Male	32.4	33.4	114.6	127.6	147.0	161.0
Total	54.8	60.7	199.1	234.9	253.9	295.6
Transport, Communication and Storage						
Female	2.7	2.8	11.5	15.9	14.2	18.7
Male	11.1	11.9	45.0	54.1	56.1	66.0
Total	13.8	14.7	56.5	70	70.3	84.7
Professional Services						
Female	31.2	38.1	105.3	124.6	136.5	162.7
Male	18.2	18.0	60.0	63.5	78.2	81.5
Total	49.4	56.1	165.3	188.1	214.7	244.2
Public Administration and Defence						
Female	5.0	6.8	17.3	21.7	22.3	28.5
Male	11.6	9.1	34.1	37.5	45.7	46.6
Total	16.6	15.9	51.4	59.2	68.0	75.1
Other						
Female	15.1	17.5	51.0	68.6	66.1	86.1
Male	8.7	12.5	36.1	49.9	44.8	62.4
Total	23.8	30.0	87.1	118.5	110.9	148.5
Total						
Female	103.1	128.7	330.7	411.1	433.8	539.8
Male	201.5	222.5	547.9	617.8	749.4	840.3
Total	304.6	351.2	878.6	1,028.9	1,183.2	1,380.1

Source: Fitzpatrick Associates analysis of CSO Data

5.12 The latest available information on earnings from the Census of Industrial Production shows a marginally higher increase in earnings per capita for the BMW Region between 1994 and 1996.

Table 5.6: Industrial Activity — Persons engaged and Wages and Salaries

	BMW Region		S&E Region		Non-attributable to Region		National	
	1994	1996	1994	1996	1994	1996	1994	1996
Number of local units	1,313	1,320	3,412	3,438	80	45	4,805	4,803
Total Persons engaged of which:	57,786	63,075	153,012	169,490	13,875	12,020	224,673	244,585
males	35,318	39,381	105,999	116,354	11,998	10,340	153,315	166,075
females	22,468	23,694	47,013	53,136	1,877	1,680	71,358	78,510
Outside piece workers	1,574	1,650	371	261	0	0	1,945	1,911
Overall totals at work	59,360	64,725	153,383	169,751	13,875	12,020	226,618	246,496
Wages & Salaries (£000s)								
Industrial workers	502,231	579,518	1,558,646	1,774,638	158,960	180,675	2,219,837	2,534,831
Other 'ees	212,744	257,024	878,201	1,099,964	133,154	92,958	1,224,099	1,449,046
Outside piece workers	1,805	1,065	1,250	1,192	0	0	3,055	2,257
Totals	716,780	837,607	2,438,097	2,875,794	292,113	273,633	3,446,991	3,986,134
Wage & Sal per capita £000s	12,075	12,941	15,895	16,941	21,053	22,765	15,342	16,171

Source: CSO Census of Industrial Production

at 7.2% compared to 6.6% for the S&E Region but earnings per capita in the BMW Region still lag significantly behind those in the S&E Region by some 30%.

Early indications for 1999 and the labour force outlook

5.13 The increase in employment and fall in unemployment continued into early 1999. In the QNHS for the second quarter of 1999 employment was shown to have increased by 96,600 over the same period in 1998; the overall unemployment rate had fallen to 5.7%, and the long-term rate had fallen to 2.5%.

5.14 The employment rate has risen to just under 55%, with the female rate reaching over 43% and the male rate rising to 66%. The 1999 estimate of labour force growth assumes that immigration continues at its 1998 level of 23,000, and that participation, after the surge seen in 1997-98, reverts towards the more moderate upward trend seen in the preceding years. With employment continuing to grow strongly, further falls in unemployment are anticipated for the latter part of 1999.

Medium-Term Labour Force Outlook

5.15 The medium term growth of the labour force will depend on a combination of underlying demographic trends and developments in labour force participation. It is anticipated that the expected natural increase in the Labour Force will be augmented by further net immigration and higher Labour Force participation. As outlined in Chapter 1, annual average Labour Force growth of about 2% is assumed over the period of the Plan.

5.16 Irish labour market trends in comparison to recent EU trends are set out in Table 5.7

Table 5.7: Employment Rates Ireland and EU Average

		1985	1990	1998
Men & Women	IRL	51.4	53.5	60.5
	EU 15	59.8	60.5	61.1
Men	IRL	70.2	70.3	73.5
	EU 15	75.0	72.0	71.2
Women	IRL	32.1	36.2	47.4
	EU 15	45.0	47.9	51.1

Source: EU Joint Employment Report 1999-Part 2 The Member States

The labour market in Ireland is changing rapidly in the face of strong increases in employment and the decline in unemployment. On the basis of a continuation of the recent performance in employment, the Irish employment rate will have exceeded the European average rate in 1998. Unemployment rates are at their lowest level in two decades and, at this stage, well below the European average. The target set in the 1998 Action Plan of reducing unemployment to 7% by end year 2000 has already been exceeded.

5.17 As outlined above, Ireland's recent Labour Market performance has been remarkable. While favourable Labour Market conditions are expected over the period of the Plan there are clear structural problems emerging that need to addressed.

5.18 The national stock of human capital needs to be improved further through training and education. As unemployment and long-term unemployment rates continue to fall, Ireland's labour market is experiencing particular pressures, most notably in the high skills sector where there is an emerging imbalance between labour supply and demand. Retention in employment, through up-skilling and retraining of workers, is a major challenge in a highly dynamic business and industry environment. In a tightening labour market, efforts must be made to mobilise potential labour supply through a range of measures ranging from reintegrating the long-term unemployed in addition to encouraging more female participation and helping those suffering from disadvantage to access the labour market.

5.19 The National Anti-Poverty Strategy (NAPS) identifies unemployment, particularly long-term unemployment as a fundamental cause of poverty. While long-term unemployment has fallen even more rapidly than overall unemployment in recent years, there is a strong structural component to those who remain in long-term unemployment. Lack of educational attainment has been identified as a critical factor in the risk and persistence of long-term unemployment. Nearly three quarters of the long-term unemployed have no, or low, levels of educational attainment. Only 19% have attained a Leaving Certificate. Early school leaving still persists and the youth (15-24) unemployment rate, although considerably reduced, from 23.3% in 1994 to 8.5% (2nd Qtr. 1999) remains high by comparison with the adult (>25) rate.

Objectives

5.20 In light of Ireland's current and forecast economic, demographic and labour market situation, the key objectives of the National Development Plan 2000-2006 in relation to the Employment and Human Resources Development Operational Programme will be to:

- promote employment growth in order to provide employment for all those who want employment;

- address skills shortages in the economy;

- promote social inclusion, with particular reference to the reintegration of the socially excluded into the labour force and equal opportunities;

- strive for balanced regional development by addressing the existing and potential education, training and skills needs of each region.

5.21 The priorities identified in the 1999 National Employment Action Plan (NEAP) are seen as important to the consolidation of a successful labour market strategy and to the achievement of these key objectives. The NEAP priorities are:

- Setting a new objective of reducing unemployment to 5% and long-term unemployment to 2% by end year 2000;

- Mobilising labour supply by tapping into potential pools of labour to support sustainable low inflationary growth;

- Enhancing the quality of labour supply through continued investment in education and training and, in particular, through developing a strategic vision for lifelong learning;

- Strengthening the preventative element in employability strategy to minimise the duration of short-term unemployment and to prevent the drift into long-term unemployment;

- Maintaining the effort to reintegrate those who are currently long-term unemployed into the labour force;

- Supporting an increase in female labour force participation and encouraging a balanced increase in net inward migration.

5.22 In respect of education and training, the National Development Plan will facilitate the achievement of the following specific objectives:

- Meeting the particular and diverse needs of specific groups in society, including those experiencing educational disadvantage and those with special educational needs;

- Facilitating the development of a system of lifelong learning, which includes the provision of accessible and flexible routes of progression between different parts of the system and which enables individuals to develop their skills to cope with the challenges of the information society in a situation of changing demands for skills;

- Enhancing the quality of the vocational training and education systems and, in particular, ensuring that the curricula and programmes offered to students at all levels of the system remain relevant, in light of the ongoing and substantial economic and social changes facing the system;

- Providing for flexibility of provision in order to respond meaningfully to individual needs as well as to industry needs and to ensure equality of access particularly for those who are marginalised;

- Linking vocational training and education programmes to the skills needs of the market with a view to ensuring that a sufficient number of skilled persons is available to meet the changing needs of business and industry;

- Ensuring that the education system is equipped to increase its use of information and communications technologies and to meet the rapidly changing information technology skills needs of the economy;

- Ensuring that the education system, especially, at third level, plays its key role in the achievement of the Plan strategy on balanced regional development;

- Providing opportunities so that every individual can attain an adequate level of literacy and numeracy skills;

- Enhancement of the knowledge base of the Irish economy and promoting entrepreneurship and adaptability through capability enhancement in research, science and technology including post graduate training;

- Providing the physical infrastructure, in terms of buildings and equipment, to meet the needs of the education sector.

Strategy

5.23 The 1997 Treaty of Amsterdam put employment at the centre of Europe's policy agenda and provided for co-ordination of national employment initiatives within a European Employment Strategy. At the first ever Jobs Summit in Luxembourg in 1997, the EU leaders agreed on an annual cycle to implement and review the European Employment Strategy. The process takes the form of agreed annual Employment Guidelines, set out under *a four pillar framework of Employability, Entrepreneurship, Adaptability and Equal Opportunities*. Member States give effect to these Guidelines through their National Employment Action Plans (NEAPs).

5.24 Ireland's national strategy for employment and employability-related human resource development is set out in Ireland's NEAP. This was prepared in the context of the European Employment Strategy and recently updated for 1999. The key objective of the NEAP is to bring about effective structural reform of the Irish labour market and to ensure that new employment opportunities are exploited in a sustainable way. The strategy is, at its simplest, two fold. On the one hand, it is a preventive strategy with the aim of helping to prevent people from becoming unemployed, by seeking to ensure that they do not leave the education system without suitable qualifications and, if they do become unemployed, by engaging with them in the early stages of their unemployment and offering them a choice of interventions aimed at minimising their unemployment duration. This preventive strategy also encompasses adaptability, by helping to ensure that those in the labour market are equipped to remain there in the face of rapid change, by way of continued learning and upskilling. On the other hand, the strategy aims to reintegrate those who are already long-term unemployed back into the labour market by equipping them with skills or providing work experience.

5.25 The NEAP strategy will form an integral part of the National Development Plan strategy on employment and human resources development. Having regard to the fact that investment in employability and human resources development tends to gravitate towards those areas with higher population densities and an available pool of skilled workers, the National Development Plan will seek to ensure that human resources needs of less developed regions are met through regionally targeted actions. In particular, the Plan will seek to enhance the labour force pool and skills levels with a view to promoting greater convergence between the BMW Region and the S&E Region in educational and skills attainment and labour force participation rates.

5.26 The measures in the Employment and Human Resources Development Operational Programme will be complemented by the Social Inclusion and Local Development measures in the Regional Operational Programmes. These measures will reflect the Equality and Employability Pillars of the NEAP and EU Employment Guidelines. The Research, Technological Development and Innovation (RTDI) and Indigenous Industry Measures in the Productive Sector Operational Programme will provide further assistance for developing enterprise and adaptability. It will also serve to boost human potential in research, science and technology and strengthen the research capability of third level institutions.

Specific Sectoral Strategies

5.27 The Tourism, Agriculture, Forestry and Seafood Sectors made a significant contribution to employment and economic growth in the period 1994-1999 and they will continue to have the potential to do so in the period of the Plan. A new focus to reflect their changing operational environment will be required in the support being provided for human resource development within these sectors. Due to the nature of the sectors they are uniquely positioned to make a contribution to balanced regional development and, in particular, rural development.

5.28 Over the past ten years, tourism has matured into a major sector of the Irish economy with associated employment now at 127,000 or one in 12 of the work force. The remarkable success of Irish tourism is set to continue and Bord Fáilte estimates well over eight million overseas visitors annually by the year 2006 with tourism employment expected to rise by up to a further 50,000 over the period. This will happen simultaneously with change in visitor demographics, attitudes and lifestyles, combined with greater travel sophistication and experience on the part of both the domestic and foreign tourist. CERT training provision for the tourism industry attracts between 50%-60% female participation rates annually, depending on the particular programme. The male/female output levels on programmes very closely reflect the employment opportunities within tourism. The 1998 CERT Employment Survey (Hotels/Guesthouses and Restaurants) showed the male/female ratio in employment to be 48%:52%, compared to 44%:56% in the 1996 survey. At managerial level, women now account for over 40% of the total employed. During 1999, CERT will be examining participation rates on programmes and developing strategies to improve the gender balance on programmes where an imbalance currently exists. CERT, through its Return to Work Programme, encourages women back into the work force by providing flexibly structured training programmes (to take account of domestic responsibilities) and assistance in securing employment, particularly at local level. In addition, men are encouraged to participate in training programmes in skill areas that have predominantly attracted women, i.e. reception and accommodation.

5.29 The tourism industry will be expected to undertake more responsibility itself for the recruitment, training and development of its work force. The industry needs to adapt its approach to human resource management to take account of the potential now on offer to personnel, entering or already within the industry, for career progression and development as a result of a much expanded, competitively driven industry. The emphasis will be on maintaining quality customer service and competitiveness and continuing to attract more new entrants. Public intervention will be focused on the considerable tourism employment potential amongst socially excluded target groups such as the long-term unemployed, early school leavers, women wishing to return to work, non-nationals and older age groups, as well as offering employment for traditional school leavers. In addition to a more targeted mix of interventions to secure new entrants to the sector, a range of other policy measures are also required, including knowledge transfer programmes, certification of in-house trainers, and entrepreneurship programmes to encourage the industry itself to be more self sustaining in the future as regards human resource development.

5.30 A recent ESRI Study[3] of likely future demand for agricultural training observed that "in agriculture and forestry, education levels remain low" and concluded that "while the demand for training in agriculture may be weakening, the need for it remains great if this important industry is to function effectively and prosper in Ireland". Noting the poor facilities at the colleges and, in particular, the lack of computerisation, the Study commented: "The agricultural training system is a significant component of the national educational and training system which is so vital to Ireland's continued economic success. As such, it is entitled to enjoy the same measure of support for its ongoing activities, and the same level of investment in facilities, as other components of the system". Women make up almost half of all farm labour in Ireland, yet only a small fraction of farm women participate in training and education. The challenges facing the Agriculture, Forestry and Fisheries Sectors are to improve education levels in the sectors, to address skills shortages relating to environmental issues and food safety, as appropriate, to upgrade skills for the development of alternative enterprises and to facilitate the use of new technology and to improve the gender balance in training programmes for the sectors.

Education and training

5.31 The links between economic growth and education have been intensively researched. Indeed the rate of investment in education and training has been identified as one of the primary contributors to our economic development in recent contributions to the study of economic growth. There is a clear consensus that investment in education and training has a very high rate of return and that it accounts for a significant proportion of the observed variation in economic growth rates around the world. Many studies have demonstrated the contribution of the rising educational levels of the labour force to Ireland's economic success. A survey of the largest multinational companies operating in Ireland in 1998 listed *"labour force flexibility"*, *"the educational system"* and *"labour force availability"* among the five most important determinants of competitiveness.

5.32 Improvements in living standards will increasingly depend on the growth of the productivity of the employed labour force; this will depend to a considerable extent, on the development of the skills of the Irish work force through education and training. This is the key underpinning rationale for the continued significant increase in investment in the education and training system both within the context of the National Development Plan and indeed, as part of the overall programme of Government expenditure.

5.33 Whilst comparison of inter-country data on outcomes suggest that Ireland's education system has produced consistently good outcomes, a great deal remains to be achieved if economic and social policy objectives are to be met. Investment in education under the Plan will therefore be concentrated on:

- Prevention of early school leaving;

---

[3] "Likely Demand for Training by New Entrants and Adults in Agriculture, Horticulture and Forestry up to 2010" — ESRI 1999.

- Increasing the retention rate at second level;

- Expanding adult and second chance education and training opportunities;

- Widening access to third level education;

- Improving the funding situation for Research, Technological Development and Innovation (RTDI) — currently the lowest in Europe. (An integrated approach to RTDI including linkages with the education sector is being pursued under the Productive Sector Operational Programme — Chapter 6 refers);

- Establishment and continuous development of a coherent National Qualifications Framework which underpins a strategy of lifelong learning;

- Supporting the requirements of the labour market.

In addition, the Plan recognises the essential need to promote the success of the technological and university sectors in providing the highly educated skilled young persons who are vital to the continued attraction of Foreign Direct Investment (FDI) to Ireland.

5.34 Low educational attainments have been found to increase the risk of becoming unemployed, of entering into long-term unemployment and eventually dropping out of the labour force and becoming impoverished. The Government recognises that, whilst other factors have also to be addressed simultaneously, it is clear that raising the educational attainment of the work force has to be a priority both from the perspective of reducing the equilibrium rate of unemployment and reducing the level of social exclusion. Accordingly, tackling low educational levels and preventing early school leaving will be a key objective of the National Development Plan. Resources devoted to meeting this challenge will have a very high benefit/cost ratio.

Measures

5.35 Training measures for the unemployed and those in employment are included under all four pillars. Measures to address educational needs are included under social disadvantage, lifelong learning and skills under the Employability Pillar and higher level skills under the Adaptability Pillar and equality under the Equality Pillar. The measures have been developed and will be implemented as part of an integrated strategy designed to meet national and regional employment and human resource development needs to 2006.

5.36 The implementing bodies for the Employment and Human Resources Development Operational Programme will, subject to the principles outlined in Chapter 12 on the Implementation of Programmes, include the Department of Education and Science, the Department of Social, Community and Family Affairs, FAS, CERT, Teagasc, BIM and others. Full details of the implementation arrangements will be set out in the Operational Programme and the Programme Complement for Employment and Human Resources Development. Detailed performance indicators for each measure at national and regional level will also be developed and set out in the Programme Complement.

Employability Sub-Programme

5.37 The Employability Sub-Programme will comprise Lifelong Learning measures including Social Inclusion in the education sector and labour market training measures. The labour market training measures are *an Action Programme for Unemployed, Active Measures for the Long-term Unemployed and Socially Excluded, Lifelong Learning (General Training, Back to Education Initiative,*

National Adult Literacy Strategy, Further Education Support Services and *Languages), Early School Leavers Progression, Sectoral Entry Training for Early School Leavers and Long-term Unemployed and Skills Training for Unemployed and Redundant Workers.* The Social Inclusion measures are *Early Education Initiative, School Completion Initiative, Early Literacy Initiative, Traveller Education, School Guidance Service and Third Level Access.*

Action Programme for Unemployed

5.38   FAS will play a major role, in co-operation with relevant Government Departments and education/training institutions, in implementing Guidelines 1 and 2 of the Employment Action Plan. The key innovation of these Guidelines is an explicit strategy of trying to stop the drift into long-term unemployment. This process began in respect of young persons in September 1998 and has been extended more widely in 1999. It will be implemented fully by the end of the year 2000 and will be continued throughout the period of the National Development Plan.

5.39   The process involves the identification by the Department of Social, Community and Family Affairs of persons approaching an unemployment threshold (6 months on the Live Register for young persons, 9 months for older persons) who are referred to FAS for a vocational guidance interview. The interview begins a process of advice and support to the unemployed individual. This includes referral to job vacancies, information on education and labour market options across the full range of providers and referral to such programmes as is desirable. For older persons it also involves referral to Community Employment or subsidised employment. A further option being expanded at present is Job Clubs which provide support in such aspects as preparing for interview, CVs and job search. Experience to-date has been positive. Of those referred in September-December 1998, 79% had left the Live Register by end-May 1999. Where the destination of these leavers was known, 53% had obtained jobs and 33% had entered education/training programmes.

5.40   Despite the continuing overall reduction in unemployment, there will inevitably be some persons who become unemployed and reach the Employment Action Plan thresholds. While it is impossible to predict the numbers concerned exactly, provision is being made for an estimated 50,000 referrals per annum, 35,000 in the S&E Region and 15,000 in the BMW Region. Many of these will be able to obtain employment directly through the advice and information services of FAS, but a proportion will wish to attend training or employment programmes. Provision is made in the Plan for 3,000 young persons and 9,500 older persons to enter such programmes each year, 2,000 young persons and 6,600 older persons in the S&E Region and 1,000 young persons and 2,900 older persons in the BMW Region.

5.41   Planned expenditure on the Action Programme for the Unemployed is £663 million (€841.8 million), £464.1 million (€589.3 million) in the S&E Region and £198.9 million (€252.5 million) in the BMW Region.

National Employment Service

5.42   FAS will provide a National Employment Service to meet the needs of employers, job-seekers and job-changers over the period of the Plan, through its network of over 70 Employment Services Offices supplemented by part-time offices and electronic media. The Employment Service has been strengthened in recent years. It will be further strengthened in 2000, to meet the needs of those referred under the NEAP process. The Service will incorporate the specialist Local Employment Service for the long-term unemployed. It will further develop its ability to cater for the needs of job-seekers by expanding its guidance and counselling services, increasing its use of new information technologies to provide information and advice, and by closely tracking the progress of its clients on a caseload basis. Information technologies, including the Web, will be used to assist employers in notifying and filling vacancies. The Service will also develop its role in identifying the needs of job-seekers for training and advising training providers of such needs.

5.43 Expenditure under this measure will amount to £179 million (€227.3 million), £125.3 million (€159.1 million) in the S&E Region and £53.7 million (€68.2 million) in the BMW Region. Over 120,000 persons are expected to register with FAS each year. Of these, it is estimated 84,000 will be in the S&E Region and 36,000 in the BMW Region.

Active Measures for the Long-term Unemployed and Socially Excluded

5.44 Although their number has fallen, there is a group who have been out of work for long periods and who have difficulty in returning to work. This includes those who are long-term unemployed, on One Parent Family Payment, people with a disability and dependants of the long-term unemployed. They require a range of services and programmes to assist their return to regular employment. In the past, Community Employment has been one of the main programme options for this group and has assisted a significant proportion of them to return to the work force. However, given current and projected labour market conditions, programmes of education and training, and supports to return to 'normal' employment can be preferable in many cases.

5.45 Government is adopting a series of measures to increase provision on these programmes, including increased training provision for the long-term unemployed, increased training allowances for the long-term unemployed, funding for the Back to Education Allowance Scheme and Back to Work Allowance places and improvements to the Vocational Training Opportunities Scheme and the Social Economy. Increased flexibility of training programmes will be introduced to ensure that they meet the particular needs of persons with family responsibilities.

5.46 The aim over the period of the Plan will be to provide increased assistance to the socially-excluded through these types of measures, and consequently to reduce activity on public employment programmes such as Community Employment and the Job Initiative. Specifically, the combined numbers on these programmes are projected to decline from about 40,000 annually in 1999 to 28,000 by 2003.

5.47 Projected expenditure on Active Measures for the Long-term Unemployed is £1,717 million (€2,180 million), £1,202 million (€1,526 million) in the S&E Region and £515 million (€654 million) in the BMW Region. Of the estimated 28,000 Community Employment and Job Initiative participants annually, 19,600 are expected in the S&E Region and 8,400 in the BMW Region.

Social Inclusion Measures in the Education Sector

5.48 The Social Inclusion measures within the education sector include an Early Education Initiative, a School Completion Initiative, Early Literacy, Traveller Education, School Guidance Service and Third Level Access.

5.49 The ESRI ex-ante evaluation identified the first priority for investment in education as being the needs of those whom the system fails. Addressing educational disadvantage requires interventions in the context of a continuum of provision from early childhood through to adulthood, with a strong focus on preventive strategies. This accords with the priorities in Guidelines 7, 8 and 9 of the NEAP which state that the quality of the school system will be improved in order to reduce substantially the number of young people who drop out of the school system early and that special attention will be given to the needs of minorities and other disadvantaged groups in order to promote and facilitate their integration into the labour market.

5.50 The aim of the Early Education Measure is to provide early interventions to encourage long-term education participation, address literacy and numeracy difficulties at an early stage and to prevent subsequent problems giving rise to long-term unemployment, social problems etc. The principal focus will be on families where the parents have a low level of educational attainment and on children with special needs (identified in recent research as greatly benefiting from early specialist education interventions). Funding will be directed at key target groups and provided on a devolved basis and integrated within area-based interventions in the case of areas with significant concentrations of educational disadvantage.

5.51 In the period 2000-2006, it is intended to build on the experiences from the 8-15 year olds early school leaver pilots initiated in 1998 and the Stay-in-School pilot established in 1999. The School Completion initiative will be designed to deal with issues of both concentrated and regionally dispersed disadvantage. It will have four strands — Research and Evaluation Strand, Tracking Strand, School Support Strand and Student Support Strand — which with the development of a primary pupils database will ensure that appropriate arrangements are put in place to facilitate increased retention rates in education and to completion of Leaving Certificate or its equivalent. In that context, one of the basic roles of the Education Welfare Service will be to ensure that services directed at tackling absenteeism and early school leaving are co-ordinated across a wide range of activity. Schools involved in the initiative will be required to operate on a multi-agency basis establishing appropriate cross community links. Studies of educational disadvantage and retention show that many pupils who fit into key target groups are dispersed throughout the system. Key elements of each school's retention plan will be links with feeder primary schools and co-ordination with local agencies.

5.52 The achievement of high literacy skills is central to both general educational attainment and subsequent success. The National Development Plan is providing for a co-ordinated approach to the problem which will significantly improve literacy skills at all age levels. The key elements of the Early Literacy Measure are to:

- Significantly raise public awareness of the importance of reading skills;
- Improve the effectiveness of the school remedial service;
- Improve home/school co-operation on literacy;
- Develop and disseminate materials to support improved literacy standards;
- Implement a proactive approach to preventing literacy difficulties;
- Systematically monitor the progress of individuals

There will also be co-ordination with the adult literacy service. The public awareness and materials development aspects of the measure will form the initial focus of the initiative and will be the principal objective of expenditure in 2000 and 2001.

5.53 The Government is committed to increasing the retention level at post primary to completion of senior cycle and to improving the participation of travellers in the education/training system. The objective is to encourage each traveller child of school-going age to participate in and benefit from the education system and to enable each pupil to develop to his/her full potential and to increase the retention level of traveller pupils to completion of post primary senior cycle and to provide them with further education/training progression options. It is anticipated that not less than 750 pupils will benefit each year from this measure, with approximately 525 in the S&E Region and 225 in the BMW Region.

5.54 The School Completion Initiative and Traveller Education Measure will be supported by the School Guidance Service, which has been a formal feature within second level for more than 30 years, has a major preventative role in helping young people at risk to remain in the formal education system. This service will be complemented by provision for guidance under the Lifelong Learning Measure for young people and adults who have either failed within or been failed by the formal system. The provision of guidance and counselling in second level schools is vital to enable each pupil to gain the maximum benefit from the education system. The aims of the School Guidance Service are to prevent difficulties encountered by students hindering their participation in or benefiting from the education system and to provide guidance regarding further education and third level options. It is anticipated that approximately 560 whole time equivalent Guidance Teachers will be employed as part of this service, in a school year, with approximately 406 in the S&E Region and approximately 154 in the BMW Region.

5.55 Participation in further education, particularly at third level, remains skewed by social classes with the lower social class groupings continuing to be underrepresented. While the factors underlying this phenomenon go beyond the educational system, there is a need for targeted intervention at the transition from second to third level education and at third level itself. Building on the existing arrangements, the development of Third Level Access is necessary to promote the participation of students with disabilities, students from disadvantaged backgrounds and mature "second chance" students.

5.56 The objective of this measure is to facilitate and improve access to the labour market for the beneficiaries whilst improving their long-term employability. It will:

- Meet the specific needs of students with disabilities in terms of equipment and support services;

- Provide financial support to disadvantaged students by way of additional support to the existing maintenance grants scheme;

- Develop outreach initiatives currently undertaken by a number of third-level institutions which involve links with second level schools and community groups and are designed to both assist students to meet the points requirements for the standard CAO entry procedures and to provide complementary special entry arrangements; and

- Expand the provision of particular services, such as counselling and mentoring services, to meet the needs of non-traditional students.

Approximately 10,000 grant holders will receive additional support under this measure, with approximately 6,400 in the S&E Region and approximately 3,600 in the BMW Region.

5.57 The overall provision for Social Inclusion measures in the education sector will amount to £364 million (€462.2 million) with approximately £273 million (€346.6 million) in the S&E Region and approximately £91 million (€115.6 million) in the BMW Region.

Lifelong Learning

5.58   The demands of the global knowledge economy are such that a lifelong learning ethos is needed to underpin long term employability and living standards. Within the framework of the NEAP, a Working Group is being established tasked with developing a strategic framework and defining participation targets for lifelong learning. The strategic framework will be developed within the context of the broad definition of lifelong learning adopted in the 1999 NEAP, which includes all formal and informal learning activity undertaken on an ongoing basis with the aim of improving knowledge, skills and competence.

General Training

5.59   Training activities to support lifelong learning will involve the provision of more open, flexible, opportunities for acquiring skills. These will build on the following components which are already underway:

- Multimedia Learning Centres in Training Centres;
- Training delivered through the Internet;
- Funding of own-time, own-choice, training for those on Community Employment; and
- Accreditation of Prior Learning.

5.60   Lifelong learning for employed persons and the general public during the Plan period will be provided in two principal ways; (a) through the provision of short training courses to employees during normal working time, paid for by their employers, and (b) through the provision of part-time, evening, weekend and open-access courses for the general public. There is an increasing demand for such courses, which are largely self-financing. It is expected that an average annual provision for 30,000 trainees during the period will be required, 22,500 in the S&E Region and 7,500 in the BMW Region.

5.61   Provision for this measure will amount to £11 million (€14 million), £7.7 million (€9.8 million) in the S&E Region and £3.3 million (€4.2 million) in the BMW Region.

Back to Education Initiative

5.62   The OECD Education at a Glance Indicators 1998 show Ireland as lagging significantly behind other countries in terms of the proportion of the population aged 25-64 with less than upper secondary education. The proportion is 50% for Ireland, compared with 18% in Norway, 19% in Germany, 26% in Sweden, and 34% in Denmark. Within the labour force alone, there are 658,700[4] people over 15 with less than upper secondary education. In addition, the International Adult Literacy Survey points to adult participation in continuing education and training in Ireland (22%) also being considerably below the European average of 34%, and the best performer, Sweden at 54%.

5.63   According to the NEAP, 51% of the short-term unemployed, and just under 75% of the long-term unemployed have less than upper secondary education. Improved job prospects in recent years are resulting in participants being attracted out of educational courses into employment prior to completion and attainment of qualifications. For those most marginalised, an immediate return to full-time education or training is not always realistic. In addition,

---

[4] Central Statistics Office Labour Force Survey, 1997

demographic change will make it an imperative to encourage those not at present in the labour force to re-enter employment. A range of factors are therefore converging which highlight the need for much greater flexibility in the delivery and timing of educational provision to enable it to be combined with family responsibilities or employment.

5.64 The Back to Education Initiative (BTEI) involves the merging and continuation of existing levels of provision under Youthreach, Senior Traveller Training Centres, the Vocational Training Opportunity Scheme and Post Leaving Certificate courses, allied to new forms of provision of the courses. It will contribute to meeting the objectives of the NEAP under guidelines 1-9 and 20-22 and is particularly relevant to the preventative strategies in Guidelines 1 and 2.

5.65 The Back to Education Initiative will play a key role both in addressing the needs of those with minimal or no educational qualifications, and providing a re-entry route for those who wish to upgrade their skills in line with emerging needs. Access to information and communications technology training, electronic technician training, language skills, enterprise development, business, tourism, arts and crafts, child care, and a broad range of disciplines within the industry and services sector will form part of the approach as will access to the Junior and Leaving Certificate examinations and other access programmes. Community education opportunities will be expanded and supported as part of the initiative, given the success of this model in reaching very marginalised groups.

5.66 The overall target will be to increase the opportunities for participation in lifelong learning through a significant expansion of part-time options so that by the end of 2006 approximately 50,000 early school leavers and adults will be participating annually in further education. Overall, the number of persons projected to avail of the initiative in the period of the Plan is approximately 320,000 including those pursuing full-time or part-time options, 246,000 in the S&E Region and 74,000 in the BMW Region. Expenditure under this measure will amount to £1,027 million (€1,304 million), £790 million (€1,003.1 million) in the S&E Region and £237 million (€300.9 million) in the BMW Region.

National Adult Literacy Strategy

5.67 The 1995 International Adult Literacy Survey, published in 1997, found that about 25% of the Irish population were found to score at the lowest level (Level 1), performing at best tasks which required the reader to locate a simple piece of information in a text, with no distracting information, and when the structure of the text assists the task. This percentage is the highest in any of the countries surveyed, except for Poland. About 36% of the Swedish respondents scored at the highest levels (Levels 4/5) in the document scale while the corresponding figure in Ireland was about 12%. Ireland's relatively poor performance means that addressing adult literacy levels must be a priority in the Plan. High levels of literacy and numeracy are a prerequisite for participation in a modern knowledge based economy. Literacy not only provides the tools for participation in a functional sense, but is also central to self-image, self-esteem and personal development. Literacy levels of parents can have a key influence on children's participation in schooling, and the ability of parents to support their children's learning. While a key goal under Guidelines 3, 4, 5, 6, 7, 8 and 9 of the NEAP will be to address the literacy skills of the unemployed, and to upgrade the skills of those in employment, the measure will also facilitate free access to learning for other adults with literacy needs, irrespective of labour market status.

5.68   The National Adult Literacy Strategy will promote system development to ensure increased access to literacy, numeracy and basic education for adults whose skills are inadequate for participation in society. The measure aims to provide an integrated service to support access to employment, a return to lifelong learning or empower participants with the basic skills needed to participate in the social and economic life of their communities. Investment under this measure will therefore increase on a phased basis. It will be informed by an Inter-Departmental Working Group on literacy initiatives for the unemployed and will involved interaction with a variety of referral networks on an area basis involving key actors such as FAS, the Local Employment Service, the Area Partnerships, Welfare and Health interests, the Garda and probation services, schools, youth services, etc. Delivery will be flexible and innovative ensuring the service is provided in accessible locations at a range of times. It is proposed to have intensive programmes targeted at those most in need allied with family learning programmes and a small number of demonstration open learning centres and distance learning.

5.69   The National Adult Literacy Strategy will promote a rapid increase in participation, rising to 18,000 annually by the end of the Plan. It is anticipated that approximately 110,000 people will participate in the programme during the period of the Plan, 85,000 in the S&E Region and 25,000 in the BMW Region. Expenditure under this measure will amount to £73.8 million (€93.7 million), £56.8 million (€72 million) in the S&E Region and £17 million (€21.6 million) in the BMW Region.

Further Education Support Services

5.70   If access to lifelong learning is to become a reality, the expansion of education and training provision needs to be accompanied by measures to meet the guidance, counselling and psychological service needs of participants while they are on programmes. Initial progress was made in this area arising from the Mid-Term Review of the Community Support Framework, 1994-1999 when additional funding was provided to facilitate a guidance/counselling and psychological service for early school leavers in Youthreach, Community Training Workshops and Traveller Training Workshops and Traveller Training Centres.

5.71   A Further Education Support measure is proposed to support access to the Back to Education Initiatives and Adult Literacy opportunities through the provision of an adult guidance and counselling service aimed at supporting participants enrolled on programmes in the further education sector. It will also support improved quality through staff and programme development initiatives.

5.72   In relation to guidance, linkages with other agencies will form a vital part of the initiative, particularly at the initial referral and progression stages. The measure will be designed to avoid overlap and duplication with existing services in this area. The development of the guidance service in education will also provide an important contact point for providers in the FAS Employment Services. The development of the service will be advised by an inter-agency working group which will include the National Centre for Guidance in Education, FAS and educational providers. Attention will also need to be directed towards the development of an improved information base on education and training options.

5.73   Plan expenditure under this measure will amount to £35 million (€44.5 million), £27 million (€34.3 million) in the S&E Region and £8 million (€10.2 million) in the BMW Region.

Junior Certificate School Programme (JCSP), Leaving Certificate Applied (LCA) and Leaving Certificate Vocational Programme (LCVP)

5.74   Whilst the above programmes are not being specifically provided for in the Plan, there will be further development within the funding arrangements of the Department's LCA, LCVP and JCSP, which have as their objective the provision of a wider range of subject choices to young people who continue in the education system. At the level of the individual, these programmes contribute to enabling pupils to break the cycle of disadvantage and to avoid the problems of early school leaving, to develop to their full potential and to participate fully as citizens in society, and to maximise benefit from the education system and equip them with the skills necessary for lifelong learning.

Languages

5.75   The promotion of a greater general proficiency in languages has been identified as a key to protecting and enhancing Ireland's competitiveness. At present, French and German are the dominant languages taught in second level schools with very low participation in other languages. In recent years new curricula have been introduced in order to improve the quality of language programmes and the level of student attainment.

5.76   Under the Community Support Framework 1994-1999, a pilot programme on the teaching of European languages in primary schools was introduced. Currently involving 270 schools, it is proposed to significantly increase the number of participating schools. During 1999, the Department of Education and Science initiated work to design a fuller policy on the teaching of languages which have low participation in second-level schools or are not available as part of current syllabi. Arising from this work, it is proposed to promote wider teaching of Italian, Spanish and other languages in post-primary schools.

5.77   Provision for this measure will amount to £22.5 million (€28.6 million). Indicative expenditure between the regions is £14.6 million (€18.5 million) in the S&E Region and £7.9 million (€10 million) in the BMW Region.

Early School Leaver Progression

5.78   The Government has taken a series of measures to try to reduce the extent of early school leaving with the aim that at least 90% of young persons complete second-level education. The Department of Education and Science and FAS have developed a series of programmes to meet the needs of those who leave early. These programmes have been further developed in 1998 and 1999 to include increased foundation-training places, new bridging training programmes for access to higher skills training, advisory supports to assist progression and more flexible part-time and work-based options. A major investment programme in Community Training Workshops is underway, and improved literacy/numeracy provision is being developed. The Plan will continue to develop provision, both at foundation and progression phase, along the lines now being pursued.

5.79   An average of 6,000 early school leavers places per annum will be provided, 4,600 in the S&E Region and 1,400 in the BMW Region. Expenditure under this measure will amount to £203 million, (€257.8 million) £156.3 million (€198.5 million) in the S&E Region and £46.7 million (€59.3 million) in the BMW Region.

Sectoral Entry Training for Early School Leavers and Long-term Unemployed

5.80 Professional craft courses in the tourism sector aimed at school leavers will continue to be provided in partnership with the Department of Education and Science, Institutes of Technology and local Vocational Educational Committees. The Department of Tourism, Sport and Recreation will be reviewing the mode of delivery of elementary certificate courses hitherto provided directly by CERT through a network of permanent and temporary training centres, with the aim of putting in place a system with a higher degree of industry involvement. Over the period of the Plan CERT are expected to contract out an increasing proportion of these and other programmes, and place a new emphasis on research, planning, standards and quality assurance of training provided by and for the industry.

5.81 This measure will provide the core of new entrants to the tourism industry and their career progression and employability will be enhanced through day release programmes and advanced skill programmes provided in a new and enhanced partnership between CERT, other training agencies and the industry. Within the period of the Plan, training and employment initiatives in tourism for the unemployed and the disadvantaged will be intensified through more targeted measures, both in terms of course content and geographical location aimed at:

- women who wish to return to work, either on a full or part-time basis, having gained appropriate skills through tailored and time-flexible training initiatives at local level;

- unemployment blackspots and in areas affected by large scale redundancies;

- non-nationals to enable them to integrate into the work force with competencies in key areas such as languages, hygiene, customer care and technical skills.

5.82 Overall, the target will be to increase the number of trainees at entry level from 4,000 per year at present to an annual average of 6,000, 3,900 in the S&E Region and 2,100 in the BMW Region. This includes approximately 1,700 trainees, 800 in the S&E Region and 900 in the BMW Region who will train in third level institutions. The indicative allocation for Tourism Sectoral Entry Training is £170 million (€215.9 million) inclusive of £80 million (€101.6 million) for third level institutional training.

5.83 An indicative allocation of £59.2 million (€75.2 million) is provided for entry training into agriculture. A basic training for school leavers entering agriculture is essential. In order to compete in the market place the skill and knowledge level of Irish farmers must be improved. The environment, animal welfare, equality, food safety, and the need to diversify the rural economy through development of alternative farm enterprises must also be taken into account. Studies have projected that the numbers of new entrants to farming in the 2000 to 2006 period will be 1,500 per annum, 900 in the S&E Region and 600 in the BMW Region. Appropriate training for all of these new entrants will be provided and will include initiatives to encourage female school leavers to enrol in mainstream courses.

5.84 Total expenditure on Sectoral Entry Training will amount to £229.2 million (€291.1 million), £128.5 million (€163.2 million) in the S&E Region and £100.7 million (€127.9 million) in the BMW Region.

Skills Training for Unemployed and Redundant Workers

5.85 Skills training for young job-seekers, older unemployed persons and those made redundant has been successful in helping them to obtain jobs and employers to meet their needs for skilled recruits. Evaluation by the ESRI has shown that skills training has a significant positive effect on an unemployed person's chances of getting a job. Areas which will be targeted to meet needs include software, computing and electronics.

5.86 The volume of public training provision will reflect the improved labour market situation. Three important types of training will be provided. Firstly, training in key skill areas to meet the needs of Irish industry in close liaison with firms, the development agencies and the Expert Group on Future Skill will continue to be provided. Secondly, provision will be made to assist those threatened with or affected by redundancy due to major factory closures. It is intended that provision will include relatively short training courses for persons still in employment, Job Clubs or similar interventions to help persons seek employment and start-your-own-business training. Thirdly, special programmes will be provided to help women to return to the work force after a break for family reasons. There will be a concerted effort to ensure that women can avail of such programmes by increasing delivery flexibility in the form of part-time and community-based provision.

5.87 Plan expenditure under this measure will amount to £106 million (€134.6 million), £81.6 million (€103.6 million) in the S&E Region and £24.4 million (€31.0 million) in the BMW Region.

Entrepreneurship Sub-Programme

5.88 Measures under the Entrepreneurship Sub-Programme will include *Training for Business and the Social Economy*. The investment in entrepreneurship will be complemented by the substantial investment in RTDI and marketing under the Productive Sector and will help to enhance the competitiveness of Ireland's indigenous industry in the global market.

Training for Business

5.89 Government has indicated in its White Paper on Human Resources, and in the NEAP that enterprises in Ireland need to increase, and better leverage, their investment in Human Resources Development. In the context of Ireland's current labour market, and global competitiveness requirements, investment in human resources can help raise productivity. It can also help to provide workers with the skills and competencies needed to cope with the constantly evolving world of work.

5.90 Recent institutional developments, including the formation of Enterprise Ireland will support the enterprises in developing their human resource capability and skills training. Enterprise Ireland will focus on helping firms build up their internal capacity to develop their human resources as part of their business development. FAS will continue to play a key role in supporting enterprise training, especially in the domestic services sector. In addition, emphasis will be placed on quality assurance measures in terms of the training undertaken and on the deployment of standards such as Excellence Through People. Particular attention will also be paid to gender issues and to maximising the potential of people with disabilities.

5.91 Training policy will place a particular emphasis on SMEs, while at the level of the individual, particular attention will be paid to promoting entrepreneurial and management capability, ensuring the enhancement of progression pathways and the development of transferable skills.

5.92 Plan expenditure under this measure will amount to £200 million (€254 million), £140 million (€177.8 million) in the S&E Region and £60 million (€76.2 million) in the BMW Region. It is estimated that 2,000 businesses will be assisted under the measure, 1,400 in the S&E Region and 600 in the BMW Region.

Social Economy

5.93 The need for this Social Economy Measure arises from the report of a working group representing relevant interests including the social partners. It builds also on the European Commission's White Paper on Growth, Competitiveness and Employment. A National Monitoring Group chaired by the Deptartment of Enterprise, Trade and Employment is being established and FAS is establishing a National Support Unit to monitor and implement the programme.

5.94 The introduction of the Social Economy Scheme will be focused on specific projects that benefit the economic and social development of disadvantaged communities. The intention is that the programme will support imaginative, locally based initiatives in disadvantaged communities which have income-generating potential

5.95 A new social economy scheme will be introduced in 1999 and build up to full capacity by the year 2003. The objective is that by then about 2,500 persons will be employed on the programme at a total cost of about £213 million (€ 270.5 million). As this is a new scheme it is difficult to predict take up but the scheme will seek to target an annual average of 1,700 persons in the S&E Region at a cost of £149 million (€189.2 million) and 800 persons at a cost of £64 million (€81.3 million) in the BMW Region.

Adaptability Sub-Programme

5.96 Resources in respect of adaptability will be concentrated in *Ongoing Sectoral Training, Apprenticeship/Traineeship, Skills Development, Employment Support Services and Quality of Provision Measures.* A key objective will be to encourage "second chance" opportunities in regard to education, training and work.

Ongoing Sectoral Training

5.97 This measure will support training on an ongoing basis in the Tourism, Culture, Gaeltacht Industry, Film Industry, Agriculture and Food, Forestry and Fisheries Sectors. Support will be provided to address skills shortages in these sectors and to address skills needs in SMEs. A key priority will be promoting skills development in less developed regions outside of the major urban areas and rural development. The investment in training will complement the investment in product development in these sectors and rural development generally under the Regional Operational Programmes. There will be increased recourse to tendering for the delivery of training in these sectors.

Tourism

5.98 Support for training within the tourism industry will be provided by promoting additional accredited trainers and by providing a limited range of incentives to SMEs to develop systems, structures and personnel to enhance their human resource capabilities and practices. Building on the success of the Trainers in Industry Measure of the Operational Programme for Tourism, 1994-1999 initiatives targeting key individuals within the career pathway will be commissioned to develop:

- world class human resource management programme, aimed at human resource specialists in the sector to gain exposure to best international practice in the field; and

- trainers in industry/supervisory development/operative certification programmes, placing particular emphasis on the ability of trained trainers to successfully implement programmes of certification for operative staff lacking formal qualifications, to improve productivity and to implement staff development initiatives.

5.99 In the education sector, initial education and training, which consists of full-time craft and day-release programmes, and continuing training, which consists of formal off-the-job training for industry employees on Advanced Craft, Supervisory and Management level programmes, will continue to be provided by CERT in association with eight of the Institutes of Technology in the Technological Sector and the Killybegs Tourism College. Training will also be provided in heritage and cultural product and visitor management for staff working in cultural institutions.

5.100 The aim will be to provide a professional and skilled work force to meet the existing and emerging needs of the sector and thereby to enhance the quality of the tourism product and service. It will contribute to the realisation of the aims and objectives of NEAP Guidelines 8 and 18. Attention will be given to maintaining satisfactory gender balance in existing and future programmes and particular attention will be given to encouraging and facilitating recruitment of women and men to non-traditional areas of work and training. The output of highly skilled graduates/trainees from these programmes will assist the development of the tourism industry in all regions.

5.101 An indicative allocation of £17 million (€21.6 million) is provided for Ongoing Training in Tourism. In the education sector, it is expected that approximately 400 trainees will participate in the programme annually, with approximately 170 in the S&E Region and 230 in the BMW Region.

Culture Training

5.102 Cultural training will provide a combination of off and on- the-job training to enhance human resource capabilities and practices in the industry. A key objective will be to maximise the tourism potential of the cultural sector through the provision of trained personnel capable of adding value and interest to the product. Investment in cultural training will also seek to contribute to balanced regional development.

Gaeltacht Training

5.103 Gaeltacht Training supports will seek to enhance the competitiveness of companies in Gaeltacht areas by using training to encourage the creation of new jobs and by upskilling those in employment to enable them to compete in the changing market place. It will also seek to reduce disadvantage by assisting rural people who are not in the labour force to gain employment.

Film Industry Training

5.104 Arising from an evaluation of the training needs of the Film Industry under the 1994-1999 Industry Operational Programme a national training committee for film and television industry was set up under the aegis of FAS. Current full-time equivalent employment in the industry is more than 4000. The Film Industry Strategic Review Group envisages a four fold increase in film production in Ireland over the next decade. Given this growth potential, it is anticipated that employment could grow to more than 12,000. Technological developments in the industry means that the emphasis on training will be on skills development to keep pace with technological advances. Of key strategic importance will also be training in script development.

5.105 An indicative allocation of £20 million (€25.4 million) is provided to support training in culture, the Gaeltacht and the Film Industries, £4 million (€5.1 million) in the S&E Region and £16 million (€20.3 million) in the BMW Region.

Agriculture

5.106 The aim in relation to agriculture will be to tackle skills shortages relating to environmental issues, animal welfare, food safety, alternative enterprises and new technology. It is planned to deliver short courses to 5,000 to 7,000 adults per year to meet these needs, 3,000-4,200 in the S&E Region and 2,000-2,800 in the BMW Region. Gender mainstreaming will be pursued by providing special courses for rural women and consulting with women's interest groups regarding course content and encouraging adult women to attend mainstream courses.

5.107 All agricultural training programmes are aimed at developing the knowledge and skills required by farmers to cope with change, to develop new enterprises, to adopt modern technology, to meet new consumer demands for food safety and traceability, to generate off-farm income, to cope with lower manpower inputs, to reduce input costs, improve product quality and to achieve these ends using animal friendly methods of production along with preserving and enhancing the environment. Certificate and diploma courses in farming, farm management, agriculture including the horse industry, forestry horticulture, food safety and rural enterprise will be provided under the Plan. Courses will also be aimed at prospective part-time farmers and other rural dwellers

5.108 The low participation by women in courses has major implications for the capacity of the industry to be efficient and to respond to change. Accordingly, a target of enrolling 1,500 women (900 in the S&E Region and 600 in the BMW Region) in courses specially for women has been set. Three target groups have been identified for women's training, School Leavers, Unskilled Women in Farming and Women outside the labour force.

Food Sector

5.109 The actions proposed for training within the food industry take account of the White Paper on Human Resource Development and the NEAP by addressing skill requirements that will enable the industry to adapt to its changing environment. The Plan will support training which will enable relevant personnel to obtain the necessary skills and qualifications and will encourage management to afford ongoing priority to training requirements in the food safety and quality areas. Support will be provided only to training conforming to best international practice. Support will be given to training initiatives which target the development of new customer focused models of work organisation and of national industry led training standards. Public funding will also be provided towards the training of food workers in new technology and towards the training of graduates entering the industry. The supplier development programme — which aims to match the performance of the sector to the needs of the retailer in terms of delivery times etc. — will continue. An indicative allocation of £38.8 million (€49.3 million) is provided to support training in the agriculture and food sectors.

Seafood Sector

5.110 The objective of the training in the seafood sector will be to expand the skills base and increase the availability of trained workers. The training will encompass measures to achieve structures training to support clear career progression in sea fishing, aquaculture and processing. The strategy will involve a significant increase in training for new entrants and will address the low level of training within the sector. The skills deficit will be addressed by fostering a lifelong approach to learning, improving access to training and providing flexible modular courses structured to work based training. Training for the industry will assist in underpinning growth in sustainable jobs and a more balanced geographic distribution of activity. The indicative allocation for this purpose is £10 million (€12.7 million).

Forestry

5.111 It is expected that the private sector will be more involved in training under the new programme. Training for the forestry industry will be directed towards improving the skills of the increasing number of participants in the sector, particularly among farmers, and supporting the expected growth in the scale and diversity of the sector which has an afforestation target of up to 20,000 hectares per annum. Forest establishment, harvesting and marketing will be targeted for training purposes. An indicative allocation of £12 million (€15.2 million) is provided to support forestry training.

5.112 The provision for Ongoing Sectoral Training is £97.8 million (€124.2 million), £44.6 million (€56.6 million) in the S&E Region and £53.2 million (€67.6 million) in the BMW Region.

Apprenticeship/Traineeship

5.113 The Government's White Paper on Human Resources Development 1997 indicated that Traineeships would become the primary vocational skills and pre-labour market entry programme for young labour-market entrants. Traineeships provide a new model of training developed between FAS and employers involving periods of off and on-the-job training.

5.114 The education sector element is delivered through the regionally based Institutes of Technology, including institutes in the lesser developed regions (i.e. Sligo, Dundalk, Athlone and Galway-Mayo Institutes of Technology). The output of skilled crafts persons from the apprenticeship measure, assists economic growth in all regions.

5.115 The traineeship approach is successful because it matches the needs of employers for suitably skilled and qualified recruits with the needs of young persons for systematic skills development. The number of traineeships will rise from 700 at end 1997 through a targeted 1,600 at end 1999 to a figure of 5,000 by the end of the Plan period.

5.116 The rapid growth of the Irish economy has resulted in a rapid increase in the demand for crafts persons, and, in some cases, shortages of qualified persons. Employers, in co-operation with

FAS, have tackled such shortages through large increases in apprentice numbers, recruitment of Irish nationals working abroad and employment of those previously unemployed. The Standards-Based Apprenticeship system, introduced in 1995, has proven successful. There were nearly 17,000 apprentices registered at the end of 1998; the highest number for fifteen years. Further expansion is expected to meet future needs. Total apprenticeship numbers inclusive of those in the education sector are expected to exceed 20,000 on average during the Plan period, 15,400 in the S&E Region and 4,600 in the BMW Region. The Plan will ensure that all such apprentices receive relevant, recognised, training to industry-standards. It will also be making particular efforts to increase participation of non-traditional groups including women and older persons.

5.117 A key element of this measure, run jointly between FAS and the Department of Education and Science, is the provision of off-the-job training in the Institutes of Technology. The apprenticeship system is structured in seven distinct phases of education and training of which phases 4 and 6 are delivered in the institutes. The aims of phases 4 and 6 are to provide all apprentices with the opportunity to learn, practice and develop the basic skills of their trade, to familiarise them with the terminology, tools, materials, equipment and working practices which will form the foundation for their further development and progression. In the education sector, it is expected that approximately 7,000 trainees will participate in the programme annually, with approximately 6,000 in the S&E Region and 1,000 in the BMW Region.

5.118 The aims of the apprenticeship programme is to provide the skilled crafts persons essential to ensure economic growth and enhance the sustainable employment prospects of persons who require training from the apprenticeship system, to secure skilled jobs as well as equipping participants with the skills necessary for lifelong learning. Apprenticeship is a key contributor to the realisation of the objectives/aims of NEAP guideline 8.

5.119 Provision for this measure will amount to £660.5 million (€838.7 million), £515.2 million (€654.2 million) in the S&E Region and £145.3 million (€184.5 million) in the BMW Region.

Skills Needs

5.120 A key policy objective of the Government is growing and improving access to employment through a major drive aimed at raising the skills profile of people through education. In so doing, the Plan will seek to build on the experiences of measures under the 1994-1999 Community Support Framework and will pay particular attention to mainstreaming the outcomes of relevant actions developed in the context of the Community Initiatives, ADAPT and EMPLOYMENT. A key objective of educational strategy in relation to Employability and Adaptability as well as under the Productive Investment Programme is to ensure an adequate supply of high quality output from the PLCs, Institutes of Technology and Universities at sub-degree, degree and post graduate levels, as appropriate. This is seen as essential to maintaining and enhancing Ireland's ability to attract and retain highly mobile international investment in an increasingly knowledge based global economy. It also has the potential to play an important role in achieving balanced regional development. Middle and higher levels skills needs will be addressed through three measures in the National Development Plan, namely, *Middle Level Technician/Higher Technical Business Skills, Undergraduate Skills and Postgraduate Conversion Courses*. The objective of the Department of Education and Science policy is, through a series of targeted investment programmes, to enhance the capacity of colleges and universities to support industry through improved interaction and collaboration with the different sectors of the economy, staff development, investment in infrastructure, research and development facilities, training of graduates in research and development techniques and enterprise skills to strengthen the enterprise base of the economy.

Middle Level Technician/Higher Technical Business Skills

5.121 The objectives of the Middle Level Technician/Higher Technical Business Skills Measure are to:

- enhance industrial competitiveness;

- contribute economic growth and maximise sustainable employment;

by providing initial third level education and training to meet the technical and higher level manpower needs of the economy.

5.122 The measure involves the funding of certificate and diploma courses in the regionally based Institutes of Technology, including institutes in the lesser-developed regions (i.e. Sligo, Letterkenny, Dundalk, Athlone and Galway-Mayo Institutes of Technology). Courses are offered in such areas as engineering, biotechnology, telecommunications, information technology, construction studies, marketing, business studies, accounting/financial services, chemical/pharmaceutical and food technology. It is proposed during the period of the National Development Plan to develop greater linkages with industry, including work placement during courses and joint initiatives to tackle particular skill shortages (e.g. the recent joint education/industry task force established to develop the National Certificates in Computing and Technology, to address the shortage of trained technicians). The provision of part-time/evening course modules and options within the programme will be facilitated, as resources permit, in the context of the promotion of lifelong learning in the IT sector.

5.123 It is anticipated that approximately 30,000 students will participate in the programme annually, 18,000 in the S&E Region and 12,000 in the BMW Region. Provision for this measure will amount to £1,056 million (€1,340.9 million) over the period of the Plan, with £645 million (€819 million) in the S&E Region and £411 million (€522.9 million) in the BMW Region. The measure will address the objectives/priorities of guidelines 8 and 18 of the NEAP.

Undergraduate Skills

5.124 The issue of raising the skills profile of people and of addressing the skills needs of the economy has been identified as a key priority in the Action Programme for the Millennium, Partnership 2000, and in the NEAP (Adaptability Pillar — Guideline 18).

5.125 The key importance of the quality and quantity of graduates coming from the education system at certificate, diploma and degree level in attracting high technology industry has been acknowledged and a significant investment has been made in recent years to ensure that the skills needs identified in the high technology area are met by the availability of high quality graduates.

5.126 These various investment initiatives have resulted in a significant expansion in the number of third level places in the area of information and communications technology. This investment has followed the recommendations of the Expert Group on Future Skills Needs and the National Competitiveness Council which was established as part of the business education and training partnership set up to develop national strategies to tackle the issue of skill needs, labour market needs estimation and education and training for business. The focus of the Expert Group's work to date has been on the technology skill needs of the hardware electronics and software sectors, having regard to the employment growth and future potential growth in these sectors.

5.127 The Undergraduate Skills Measure in the National Development Plan will provide the necessary current funding required to support the additional third level places being provided to meet skill needs and thereby contribute to increasing the adaptability of the work-force.

5.128 Expenditure on this measure is projected to amount to £90.6 million (€115.1 million), £72.5 million (€92.1 million) in the S&E Region and £18.1 million (€23 million) in the BMW Region

Postgraduate Conversion Courses

5.129 The National Competitiveness Council, in its 1999 Report, identified the central position of skills as an essential element of long-term competitiveness and highlighted the need to alleviate pervasive skills shortages in the economy which threaten our capacity to realise our full growth potential. The Expert Group on Future Skills Needs recognised multi-skilling and conversion programmes as a cost-effective and flexible mechanism to address emerging skills needs particularly in the context of the information society.

5.130 A key element in this programme is the inclusion of recruitment opportunities for graduates through a number of initiatives to be co-ordinated on behalf of industry by the Irish Business and Employers Confederation. Under the Plan, this programme will be continued and adapted to meet emerging skills needs in the period. This measure will address the objectives of Guidelines 8 and 18 of the NEAP.

5.131 It is anticipated that approximately 1,500 trainees will participate in the programme in an academic year, with approximately 1,300 in the S&E Region and 200 in the BMW Region. Provision for this measure will amount to £46 million (€58.4 million), £39 million (€49.5 million) in the S&E Region and £7 million (€8.9 million) in the BMW Region.

Quality of Provision

5.132 The capacity of the education and training system to respond to the rapid changes in product and labour markets is critically dependent on the continued development of teachers, lecturers, trainers and investment in physical infrastructure. If the Government's employment and jobs creation objectives are to be realised, the education and training sector has to be supported at a level to enhance its capability to form a dynamic partnership with enterprise and the community it serves. The maintenance and enhancement of the quality of education and training provision will be supported through three measures: *Training of Trainers, Quality Assurance and Education and Training Infrastructure.*

Training of Trainers

5.133 Investment is required in changing course mixes to reflect changing skill needs, improved staff skills and improved certification for educational institutions and FAS. There will also be investment to ensure that trainers and teachers have recognised pedagogical skills and qualifications. The need for such qualification extends beyond instructors to other staff such as training advisers and specialist trainers of people with disabilities and their needs will be addressed. Important elements of this training will be in respect of equality and of persons with disabilities.

5.134 The Training of Trainers Measure for primary and post-primary teachers will be delivered to a large extent through the national network of Education Centres and in conjunction with the Education Partners. The measure will include long and short cycle courses, some of which will lead to formal certification or the accumulation of credits towards an award. Modes of delivery will include conferences/seminars, modular courses, on-the-job training by visiting specialists and outreach training. Needs are identified on the basis of systems needs analysis studies undertaken at both levels of the system, and consultation with educational interests.

5.135 Training of Trainers will be provided for a range of programme areas and priority objectives in special and mainstream education. Priorities identified include revised and restructured curricula with particular emphasis on Information and Communication Technologies (ICTs), pedagogical skills, social inclusion issues, parent and school management needs in the effective management of schools and gender equity modules.

5.136 In an era of rapid technological change the need for skills updating in the technological, scientific and organisational fields is self-evident. The measure will provide additional opportunities to address these needs while also focusing on pedagogical training, teaching evaluation and appraisal and the development of management skills. In response to the broadening of higher education and training opportunities, the measure will also address gender equity and the particular needs of non-traditional student groups, such as students with disabilities, disadvantaged students and mature students. It will provide training for 400 FAS trainers, 280 trainers in the S&E Region and 120 trainers in the BMW Region. It is anticipated that there will be approximately 140,000 trainee days in an academic year, for the primary, post primary and further education sectors, 100,000 in the S&E Region and 40,000 in the BMW Region.

5.137 Expenditure on Training of Trainers will amount to £64 million (€81.3 million), £45 million (€57.2 million) in the S&E Region and £19 million (€24.1 million) in the BMW Region.

Quality Assurance (including Training of Trainers)

5.138 The aim of the Quality Assurance (QA) measure in the third level sector (including Training of Trainers) will be to promote a quality culture across the whole range of activities in third-level institutions, and at the same time addressing societies concern for greater transparency and accountability. Under section 35 of the Universities Act, 1997 universities are obliged to establish procedures for quality assurance aimed at improving the quality of education and related services. Central elements in any system of quality assurance will include self-evaluation, peer review, reporting and external monitoring.

5.139 The Institutes of Technology will also be centrally involved in the development of quality assurance procedures under this measure especially in the context of the unique need of multi-level institutions. The Universities and the National Qualifications Authority will be involved in the management of this measure.

5.140 The establishment of a National Qualifications Framework, which is critical to the delivery of a high quality and efficient market led range of programmes will be a key horizontal objective under the Plan. Funding is being made available for the implementation of the Qualifications (Education and Training) Act 1999. A central objective of the Act is the need to ensure greater partnership, co-operation and cohesion between the education and training sector on the one hand and industry, business and the wider community on the other. The primary purpose of the Act is to put in place a legislative framework which will:

- Establish and develop standards of knowledge, skill or competence;
- Promote the quality of further education and training and higher education and training;
- Provide a system for co-ordinating and comparing education training awards;
- Promote and maintain procedures for access, transfer and progression.

5.141 Provision for this measure will amount to £58 million (€73.7 million), £54 million (€68.6 million) in the S&E Region and £4 million (€5.1 million) in the BMW Region. Included in the overall provision and in the provision for the S&E Region is £35 million in respect of the National Qualifications Framework which will apply horizontally. Under the Training of Trainers element it is expected that there will be approximately 4,000 trainees per annum, 2,850 in the S&E Region and 1,150 in the BMW Region.

Education and Training Infrastructure

5.142 The National Development Plan provision for capital expenditure on education and training infrastructure is £1.624 billion (€2.062 billion). This will cover investment in primary and second level schools, further education centres and third level institutions in the education sector as well as FAS capital stock during the period 2000-2006. Such investment is necessary to ensure that education and training programmes and services meet the changing skills needs of individuals, society and Irish industry. The investment will cover buildings, new machinery and equipment and in the use of information technology. This investment, in new technology in particular, will facilitate continuing education and retraining programmes, the development of new open learning and distance education packages, outreach programmes, access for disadvantaged and non-traditional student and rural and community development. A requirement of all expenditure on premises is that it will take place in a cost-effective manner which will provide a safe and healthy environment and will lead improved access for people with disabilities.

5.143 Capital expenditure on the provision of education and training facilities will amount to £1.62 billion (€2.1 billion), £1.2 billion (€1.5 billion) in the S&E Region and £0.5 billion (€0.6 billion) in the BMW Region. The FAS component of this capital expenditure is £49 million (€62.2 million), £34 million (€43.2 million) in the S&E Region and £15 million (€19 million) in the BMW Region.

Employment Support Services

5.144 The Employment Support Services operated by the Department of Social, Community and Family Affairs have been successful in assisting unemployed people, particularly the long-term unemployed to return directly to the active labour market either by taking up employment or becoming self employed.

5.145 The unique feature of this service is that it is directly linked with and adds value to the direct contact between unemployed people and the Department which arises in the unemployment payments process. An essential feature of the service is that it operates in close co-operation with other relevant organisations, whether statutory or voluntary, which can have a role in addressing the needs of unemployed people, and also with employers and employer organisations.

5.146 The Back to Work Allowance Scheme (BTWAS) and the Back to Education Allowance Scheme (BTEAS) together with the advice and support services provided to unemployed people, form the core of the Employment Support Services. As indicated in Paragraph 5.45, there will be greater linkages between the various active labour market measures. The Employment Support Service will be further developed and adapted as changing labour market conditions and improved information indicate priority areas and groups with special needs requiring more focused attention. The BTWAS and BTEAS are supports for the most disadvantaged in the community — those who are unable without support to re-enter the labour market. These schemes by focusing on these groups will be key elements in the drive to achieve social inclusion.

5.147 A 1995 Evaluation of the BTWAS found that it was having a very positive impact and was playing a significant role in enabling the long-term unemployed to take up a job or become self employed. The primary objectives of the scheme are:

- the activation of long-term unemployed people to leave the Live Register to take up employment opportunities and to break out of the unemployed cycle;

- the integration of long-term unemployed people into employment and self employment.

In 1998, there were over 29,000 places on the scheme, 19,472 employed and 9,962 self employed.

5.148 The purpose of the BTEAS is to encourage unemployed people and other disadvantaged groups to improve their educational qualifications, skills etc. with a view to returning to the jobs market. The programmes are targeted at unemployed people, lone parents and people with disabilities who are in receipt of a qualifying social welfare payment. The scheme covers the following study options:

- Full-time second level course of education at any secondary, community, comprehensive or vocational school leading to a recognised certificate;

- Full time third level approved courses of education, including postgraduate, at any university, third level college or institution;

- A wide range of education, training and development courses, including part-time courses designed to enhance the participant's employment prospects.

The numbers participating in the scheme have increased progressively in recent years. In 1998, there were 3,852 participants while the number expected in 1999 will be of the order of 4,400.

5.149 £950 million (€1,206.3 million) is provided for expenditure on the schemes under this measure, £665 million (€844.4 million) in the S&E Region and £285 million (€361.9 million) in the BMW Region. This will complement the £112 million (€142.2 million) included in the Social Inclusion Provision in the Regional Programmes for Community Development. An annual average of approximately 33,000 long-term unemployed persons are expected to benefit from this measure, 23,000 in the S&E Region and 10,000 in the BMW Region.

Equality Sub-Programme

5.150 Specific measures included under this Sub-Programme will include *Educational Disadvantage Measure, Equal Opportunities Promotion and Monitoring, Refugee Language Support and Vocational Training and Pathways to Employment for People with Disabilities*. The bulk of investment under equal opportunities will be included in the Regional Operational Programmes where some £1.03 billion (€1.3 billion) will be spent on social disadvantage to include child care, youth services, local education and services for the unemployed, community infrastructure and crime prevention etc.

Educational Disadvantage Measure

5.151 A Women's Education Initiative was established in 1998 with assistance under the 1994-1999 Community Support Framework to assist projects to address the current gaps in provision for educationally disadvantaged women. Thirteen projects are being supported to develop models of good practice, to improve provision for educationally disadvantaged women. The aim is that these models will be capable of wider application and will impact on future policy thereby bringing about long-term change in the further education opportunities for educationally disadvantaged women and men.

5.152 The measure will provide for an expansion of such activity, focused not just on the particular needs of women, but also on the needs of educationally disadvantaged men. Funding will be used to seed innovation and learning which will inform future practice, particularly in ensuring effective strategies for those who are most in need. While many of the projects selected will continue to have a single sex focus, there will be scope under the initiative also to test innovative approaches to the development of community education models for other specifically marginalised groups. The aim of the projects selected under this initiative will be to:

- Address gaps in the provision of education and training for specific marginalised groups;
- Build local capacity and test models of community education;
- Develop support structures and provide for accreditation and partnerships between statutory and voluntary agencies;
- Mainstream learning;
- Facilitate progression of marginalised groups and individuals;
- Disseminate learning and share good practice.

5.153 Provision for this measure, will amount to £3.5 million (€4.4 million), £2.5 million (€3.1 million) in the S&E Region and £1 million (€1.3 million) in the BMW Region.

Equal Opportunities Promotion and Monitoring

5.154 Ireland is developing a comprehensive legal framework for addressing inequality under the Employment Equality Act, 1998 and the Equal Status Bill, 1999. Under the new legislation, discrimination both in employment and in the supply of goods and services on grounds of sex, marital status, family status, sexual orientation, religion, age, disability, race and membership of the travelling community will be unlawful. The new equality legislation gives a new emphasis to tackling inequalities including between men and women. The Equality Authority (replacing the Employment Equality Agency) will promote equal opportunities for the target groups covered by the legislation. The Authority will have an investigations arm to secure effective enforcement of the legislation.

5.155 Training and educational institutions will ensure that the participation of both men and women is promoted and facilitated. This will be extended to further develop monitoring systems and gender proofing procedures. Under this measure, a technical assistance budget will be provided to enable the Department of Justice, Equality and Law Reform to support gender mainstreaming of the National Development Plan for the period 2000-2006. Technical assistance will also be provided to the Department of Education and Science to fund a Dedicated Equality Unit to co-ordinate and monitor the process of mainstreaming a gender perspective into all areas of the educational system, a computerised management information system and Higher Education Networks. In particular, action will be undertaken to ensure that disadvantaged women are encouraged to participate in all training programmes. Positive action measures will be taken where necessary. Flexible delivery systems, bridging programmes, guidance and advisory services and staff development methods will be used to promote such participation.

5.156 The Equal Status legislation currently before the Oireachtas provides protection against discrimination on the grounds of gender, marital status, family status, sexual orientation, religion, age, disability, race and membership of the traveller community. Gender desegregated data, as well as data for specific groups such as travellers, people with disabilities, older adults, lone parents etc. has long been recognised as key to national strategies in monitoring progress in facilitating equality of access, outcome and benefit. A computerised management information system will be developed for programmes in the further education sector which are not embraced at present by the post-primary pupil data base. The programmes covered will include VTOS, Youthreach, Senior Traveller Training Centres and Adult Literacy programmes, so that participation patterns of specific groups can be monitored, as well as timely and regular data supplied on overall provision and outcomes. Participant information broken down by sex, age, economic status, subject/module choice, levels of certification, prior educational attainment and literacy levels, and progression, as well as programmatic information on access to supporting services such as child care, guidance and counselling would be an essential part of the approach.

5.157 All third-level institutions are charged with developing an equality policy. Both the Institutes of Technology and the Universities have set up Equality networks for the development and promotion of strategies to encourage equality of access, benefit and outcome for participants in third level education. These networks act as a catalyst in testing innovatory approaches, documenting and sharing good practice, networking providers, information and awareness raising and liaison and collaboration with a range of interests with an equality focus who are outside the third level system. Subject to networking and the collaborative approach outlined, it is proposed to support third level institutions to facilitate access of mature students to third level education. The target group are mature students accessing or participating in third level education other than through the Leaving Certificate route.

5.158 Provision for this measure will amount to £20.1 million (€25.5 million) which will have a horizontal impact across both regions. The Units will be based in the S&E Region.

Vocational Training and Pathways to Employment for People with Disabilities

5.159 In spite of the improved employment situation in recent years, people with disabilities experience difficulties in gaining access to, and remaining in, the labour market. It is estimated that 80% of people with disabilities in Ireland are unemployed. The objective of this measure is to improve the employability of people with disabilities and to mainstream the delivery of vocational training and employment services to them. Activities to be funded include vocational training and pathways to employment for people with disabilities.

5.160   Many of the services which the National Rehabilitation Board (NRB) currently administers for people with disabilities will be restructured in 2000. The overall objective of the restructuring is to integrate services for people with disabilities more fully with the State's general, mainstream services. In the context of this restructuring, responsibility for vocational training and employment of people with disabilities will transfer in 2000 from the Department of Health & Children to the Department of Enterprise, Trade and Employment. Relevant programmes and services administered by the NRB will transfer to FAS. The Department of Enterprise, Trade and Employment and FAS will review existing vocational training programmes and employment programmes for people with disabilities with a view to improving employment opportunities for disabled people and to developing and implementing flexible approaches to training and placement of people with disabilities.

5.161   It is anticipated that an increased number of people with disabilities will participate in training courses at FAS Training Centres. However, FAS will also ask specialist agencies to provide training on a contracted-out basis, drawing on the current expertise in the NGO sector, in particular, in relation to training of people with disabilities. Certification will be provided in respect of training completed, as a platform to progression to higher levels of training, education and employment.

5.162   Placement services for people with disabilities need to be developed to complement the investment in vocational training. A central objective will be to mainstream the delivery of placement services to include people with disabilities. Additional and flexible activities will be explored, including innovative projects which test new approaches to pathways to employment for people with disabilities. It is envisaged that these approaches will be developed in partnership between FAS and the voluntary/private sectors.

5.163   All activities will be targeted at men and women, with equality of access to services a fundamental consideration. Provision for this measure will amount to £175 million (€222.2 million), £122 million (€154.9 million) in the S&E Region and £53 million (€67.3 million) in the BMW Region.

Refugee Language Support Unit

5.164   One of the priorities of NEAP is the promotion of equal opportunities for minority groupings. The significant increase in the number of non-EU nationals acquiring rights to reside in Ireland has given rise to the need to address the language difficulties experienced by refugees to ease their integration into the country.

5.165   In March 1999, the establishment of a dedicated Refugee Language Support Unit under the auspices of Trinity College Dublin, was announced. The objectives of the unit are (a) to ensure that the school going cohort will acquire sufficient competency to enable them to be absorbed into the education system and (b) to provide sufficient competency to those not of school going age to enable them to participate in training programmes, take up employment and to live independently.

5.166   The unit will assess each refugee's language needs using a set of benchmarks to be developed for the purpose and then identify a suitable English language training programme. Each person's progress will be monitored through the system. Expenditure will amount to £3.5 million (€4.4 million), £2.5 million (€3.2 million) in the S&E Region and £1 million (€1.3 million) in the BMW Region.

Impact on Poverty

5.167   The actions provided for under the Employment and Human Resources Development Priority of the Plan are an integrated package of measures which will impact positively on poverty. The measures are all targeted at people and supporting employment. They are specifically aimed at providing people with the necessary education and skills to enable them to acquire, develop and adapt life skills to participate in the labour force and to function in a complex and ever changing modern society and global market place. The key target groups are those who are in poverty or at risk of falling into poverty, namely: early school leavers or those at risk of becoming so, the long-term unemployed, women wishing to return to work, the low skilled and those with literacy difficulties, workers recently made redundant, older age groups, non-nationals and people with disabilities. The Priority objectives and targeting will, combined with the wider spatial focus to delivery of the actions, ensure systematic approach to tackling poverty blackspots whether urban or rural.

Impact on the Environment

5.168   The Employment and Human Resources Development Priority will have a positive impact on the environment directly and indirectly. Many of the actions provided for will have a direct beneficial impact on the physical environment. All buildings benefiting from capital support will be designed and constructed, not simply to meet minimum statutory requirements in regard to planning and the environment, but will be developed in harmony with their environment and the principle of sustainable development.

5.169   Many of the measures provide training and work experience for people by way of community based projects. For example, the Community Employment Scheme and other community training and enterprises often have a direct environmental theme. Works involve activities such as landscaping, minor urban construction works, litter prevention, promotion of recycling and heritage maintenance projects etc.

5.170   Investing in human resource development will result in a better educated and trained population. In addition to the employability aspect of such investment there is the less tangible, but still real, effect of heightened awareness and self confidence. Because people, as producers and consumers of goods, have a significant impact on the environment, awareness raising is crucial to environmental sustainability. People, as they become self-aware as a result of education and training, also become aware of their environment. They are more receptive to information which encourages them to modify their behaviour in a way which will benefit the environment and are in a better position to make informed choices which impact daily on the environment.

Rural Impact

5.171   The sectoral training in tourism, agriculture, forestry and seafood will impact in particular on the skills levels of rural dwellers. The development of specific courses in rural development in the newly established multi-campus Tipperary Rural and Business Development Institute (TRBDI), will facilitate innovative approaches to rural and community development. More generally, the use of information and communication technology and other means to support distance learning will provide greater access to education and training opportunities for people who wish to continue to reside in rural locations. This approach will help to promote employment opportunities within the traditional rural sectors such as agriculture and to develop wider employment opportunities in alternative enterprises in rural areas. Combined with the public investment in infrastructure and the productive sector it should help to reverse the trend of rural decline.

6 The Productive Sector Operational Programme

Introduction

6.1 The Productive Sector includes manufacturing industry, natural resources based industries including agriculture and internationally traded services. Activity in the Sector is essentially the driver of economic growth and as such is relied on to deliver jobs and wealth creation. The Productive Sector, particularly manufacturing and internationally traded services, has excelled in recent years with increases in employment, output and exports against a background of solid improvements in productivity. The challenge ahead is to facilitate the conditions which allow for the further development of an indigenous enterprise culture which recognises the importance of high-tech, high value-added business which has at its heart a deep commitment to the role of research and innovation and recognises the strategic role of marketing in the global economy. NDP investment will aim to ensure that Ireland has a business environment and infrastructure that is as favourable as any other location worldwide and hence capable of attracting the best quality Foreign Direct Investment (FDI) projects. In addition investment will be aimed at improving growth in output and employment in the indigenous sector through enhancing its competitiveness.

6.2 In relation to the natural resource based industries, Agriculture faces a particularly challenging time in the post-Agenda 2000 period. Farmers are likely to witness increasing pressure on their incomes and will require improvements in efficiencies and scale if they are to retain adequate income. There is a need to support the structural transformation of the sector and to assist it in meeting more stringent environmental requirements. Forestry and the seafood industry are particularly important to rural communities and these sectors need support in order to reach their potential. While tourism is expanding very rapidly in the country generally, many areas have yet to capitalise on the opportunities that the industry provides. In addition, current favoured centres/attractions for tourists need to ensure that their infrastructure is sufficient to cope with increasing numbers.

Table 6.1: Productive Sector Operational Programme: Expenditure 2000-2006

	National € million	BMW Region € million	S&E Region € million
Research, Technological Development & Innovation (RTDI)	2,471	663	1,808
Industry (Indigenous & FDI)	2,416	1,092	1,324
Marketing	428	141	287
Agricultural Development	353	170	183
Fisheries	57	33	24
Total Expenditure	**5,725**	**2,099**	**3,626**
Per Capita €	**1,579**	**2,175**	**1,363**

6.3 Support for the Productive Sector in the NDP reflects the specific needs of the sector. These are: Research Technological Development and Innovation (RTDI), Indigenous Industry, Foreign

Direct Investment (FDI), Marketing, Agricultural Development, Forestry and Fisheries/Seafood Industry Development. The food sector is covered under the Industry and Marketing sub-programmes and the RTDI sub-programme covers the whole productive sector. The level of funding, and its composition by region, to be provided under the National Development Plan on the productive sector is set out in Table 6.1.

Analysis

Manufacturing Industry

6.4   Manufacturing industry in Ireland has performed exceptionally well in recent years, for example, from the period 1991 to 1996:

- the numbers employed in manufacturing increased by 30,000 or 13.6%;

- net output increased by 88%;

However, analysis shows that manufacturing industry in Ireland has specific characteristics which are a source of concern and will be addressed in the context of the NDP.

Dualistic Nature of Manufacturing Industry in Ireland

6.5   It is generally accepted that Ireland's impressive manufacturing performance has been driven by its ability to attract large-scale high-tech, high value-added FDI projects. This is an extremely welcome development which has helped spawn Irish owned high-tech industry which has achieved significant successes in e.g. the software and electronics sector. However, Irish-owned industry still has some major structural deficiencies such as scale and low productivity. A dual manufacturing structure has now emerged with high-tech, high value-added industries dominated by foreign ownership, and low-tech, low productivity industry being largely of Irish ownership. This is illustrated in Table 6.2.

Table 6.2:   Ownership of Manufacturing Plants 1987-1996

Ownership	No. of Units		Employees 000		Output (£m)		Exports (%)*	
	1987	1996	1987	1996	1987	1996	1987	1996
Irish	3,935	3,871	106.6	120.2	7,364	12,188	31.9	34
Foreign	795	728	78.4	106.4	8,028	24,108	84.7	89.3
Total	4,730	4,599	183	226.6	15,391	36,296	59.4	70.7

Source: Census of Industrial Production
* gross output exported as a percentage of gross output

6.6   Foreign-owned plants are much bigger in size, averaging 146 employees compared with 31 employees per indigenous plant, and productivity (output per employee) in foreign owned plants is well over double that of indigenous plants. While only 16% of manufacturing units are foreign-owned, they produce two-thirds of the state's manufacturing output. The data confirm the export orientation of foreign-owned firms operating in Ireland — 90% of their total output was exported in 1996 while the equivalent percentage of domestic manufacturing output exported was 34%. The destinations of exports from foreign-owned firms differ from those of Irish-owned firms in that they are directed less to the United Kingdom and more to the rest of the EU.

6.7 Key challenges facing the indigenous sector include lack of scale and low productivity. Related to this lack of scale are issues of accumulated experience, depth of infrastructure and information deficits at firm level. Small or developing firms are not in a position to undertake the strategic analysis to identify their strengths and weaknesses or to take the necessary steps to address these. Key information deficits at firm level relate to R&D and design, knowledge of and access to markets, training and human resource development generally.

Regional Disparities of Manufacturing in Ireland

6.8 When regional data is analysed, a divergence emerges in the spread of high-tech manufacturing between the Southern & Eastern (S&E) Region and the Border, Midland & Western (BMW) Region. Table 6.3 provides a useful illustration.

Table 6.3: High-Tech Manufacturing in Ireland 1996

	BMW Region			S&E Region		
	Irish-owned	Foreign-owned	Total	Irish-owned	Foreign-owned	Total
Units	68	74	142	309	249	558
Employees	2,453	15,861	18,314	10,812	43,095	53,907
Net Output (£000)	113,791	1,334,421	1,448,212	414,686	8,623,349	9,038,034
Net Output per employee(£)	46,400	84,100	79,100	38,400	200,100	167,700
Wages & Salaries (£000)	29,500	237,600	267,000	162,800	808,200	971,000
Wages & Salaries per employee (£)	12,000	15,000	14,600	15,100	18,800	18,000

Source: CSO Census of Industrial Production 1996

6.9 The percentage share of the BMW Region's manufacturing employment in 1996 in the high-tech sector is on a par with that of the S&E Region and the region's growth in this sector over the period 1991 to 1996 was greater than that of the S&E Region (albeit from a small base). While the BMW Region has 27% of all foreign owned high-tech manufacturing employment the region only produces 13.8% of the state's foreign high-tech output. This means that net output per employee in the foreign owned high-tech sector of the S&E Region is over twice that for the BMW Region. This fact is reflected in the higher salaries per employee in the S&E Region where a pay premium of 25% is evident.

6.10 The conclusion therefore is that while the BMW Region's manufacturing presence has increased in recent years, it appears that the most productive firms within the most productive and profitable sectors have a larger presence, on a per capita basis, in the S&E Region. Another point also of relevance is that the high-tech sector in the BMW Region is heavily concentrated in the larger urban centres, especially Galway, and this is an important issue to be addressed within the BMW Region.

Services

6.11 The services sector is now the dominant sector of economic activity in all developed economies, including Ireland, and four out of every five new jobs are generated in this sector. Services accounted for 63% of national employment in 1996. The BMW Region has a disproportionately lower level of services GVA output and employment but recent growth in the BMW Region has outstripped that in the S&E Region. Regional analysis of the services sector highlights one significant difference between the BMW and S&E Regions, namely the presence of highly productive internationally traded services almost exclusively in the latter region.

6.12   The greater Dublin area has been a major beneficiary of the growth in internationally traded services. The growth in the financial services area has been concentrated mainly in the ISFC in Dublin while the expansion in data processing, software development and teleservice centres has also been concentrated in the Dublin area, although Cork, Limerick and Waterford have experienced growth in these sectors. Overseas investment has been the major factor in the expansion of financial services and data processing but indigenous firms have been to the fore in growing the software sector, undoubtedly assisted by the close presence of some of the world's biggest software businesses. It is a dynamic sector demanding a high commitment to research and development and is characterised by high rates of new business formation and rapid initial expansion, and many newer Irish owned firms are world leaders in their respective fields.

6.13   Within the BMW Region, expansions in internationally traded services that have occurred have tended to cluster in the Galway area. Effectively, the services sector growth in the BMW Region over recent years is derived from the region's economic buoyancy and not from any targeted initiatives, such as that which underpinned the IFSC in Dublin.

Tourism

6.14   Over the past 10 years with the help of substantial support under two EU Operational Programmes for Tourism, visitor numbers to Ireland have doubled to 5.7m and foreign exchange earnings have tripled to £2.3 billion for 1998. Regional breakdowns up to 1996 are included in Table 6.4 and show that the BMW Region has seen a slippage in its market share of national tourism revenue over this growth period.

Table 6.4:   Overseas Tourism Revenue by Region: 1986, 1991 & 1996

Year	S&E Region	BMW Region	National	National Growth
1986: £m % of total	321 74%	115 26%	436	
1991: £m % of total	646 75%	210 25%	856	1986-1991: 96.3%
1996: £m % of total	1,114 77%	337 23%	1,451	1991-1996: 69.5%

6.15   The emergence of Dublin as Europe's most popular city breaks destination, facilitated by the intense competition in airline travel particularly from the UK, is the primary reason for stronger tourism growth in the S&E Region. This market is particularly lucrative as it operates on a year-round basis. By contrast, the market for more traditional tourist destinations — many of which are in the BMW Region — is generally very seasonal.

6.16   The current spatial spread of tourism is a major problem not just for the nation as a whole but also within the two regions. There is a recognition within the industry of significant untapped potential in many counties which to date are largely ignored by tourists while it is generally accepted that the infrastructure of those centres which have been successful in attracting tourists is in need of investment to protect their product.

6.17   As international tourism expenditure is forecast to grow by close to 6% per annum in real terms over the next decade, further considerable growth in market share by Ireland is achievable and appropriate investment decisions have the potential to deliver substantial gains for regions which have not yet benefited from this industry. Traditionally, because of the diversified nature of the Irish tourism sector and the proliferation of small firms, the level of industry investment in marketing has been low. As the industry matures, there is an increasing recognition on its part of the importance of international marketing activity and the scope for co-operation in destination campaigns. While the industry has begun investing substantial funds in the marketing of its own individual products, there remains a need for public investment to underwrite broad based destination or niche marketing programmes of sufficient scale to have the necessary impact in Ireland's key international markets.

6.18   As the economy continues to grow, the potential of the domestic tourist market is also expanding. In particular, regions outside the main urban centres should be seeking to exploit the fact that they have a ready-made market in the shape of a larger, younger and wealthier workforce that places an increasingly higher value on leisure time.

6.19   Employment in the areas of agriculture, forestry and the seafood industry are of critical importance in the rural areas of each of the regions.

Agriculture

6.20   While the importance of primary agriculture to the economy has reduced in recent years, in line with the trend in all industrialised countries, agriculture remains more important to the Irish economy than it is to 13 of the other 14 Member States, and its contribution to GDP is twice the EU average. Agriculture provides the raw materials for Ireland's growing food industry. In 1998, the agri-food sector (including agriculture, food, drinks and tobacco) accounted for 11.5% of GDP, 11.8% of employment, and 10.2% of Irish exports. Because of its low import content, the agri-food sector is estimated to account for 33% of Ireland's net foreign earnings from trade.

6.21   Analysis of the agriculture sector shows that there is a major divergence between the BMW and S&E Regions. In 1996, farmers and agricultural workers as a percentage of the workforce in the BMW Region at 14.9% was significantly higher than that of the S&E Region at 7.1%. Agriculturally the BMW Region is much less productive than the S&E Region. Only about 25% of farms in the region are based on soils with a wide use range, compared with 70% in the S&E Region. The BMW Region contains 41% of the total agricultural area used for farming but has 52% of farms in the country.

6.22   The future for Irish agricultural policy is, of course, largely determined and constrained by the requirements of the Common Agricultural Policy and international agreements. The recent satisfactory outcome of the Agenda 2000 negotiations sets the framework within which the agricultural industry will develop in the immediate future. That framework is built around:

(a)   the importance of improving the competitiveness of the European agricultural and agri-food sectors on internal and world markets; and

(b)   the recognition of the need for an integrated rural policy, including the environment to accompany the reform process.

125

6.23 The agricultural sector faces an ever increasing level of trade liberalisation. This will require a series of actions to prepare the sector to adapt to the very competitive environment that lies ahead. In this regard the issues of scale, productivity, quality and, in particular, the environment will be of ever increasing importance.

Food

6.24 The Food sector has performed well in recent years; and in its recent report, the Food Industry Development Group acknowledged the significant improvements under the 1994-1999 Food Sub-Programme but points to issues that still remain. These include the limited progress along the value-added chain, scale-related difficulties and the need for continuing emphasis on food safety and quality. The Beef Task Force followed up on that report by identifying specific issues warranting attention in the beef sector. The Minister for Agriculture, Food and Rural Development recently appointed the Agri-Food 2010 committee to develop a strategy for Irish agriculture and food over the next decade. The committee is expected to report next year.

Forestry

6.25 Until the late 1980s, the country was heavily reliant on public forestry to achieve afforestation objectives. However, in the early 1990s the level of afforestation expanded dramatically boosted by greatly increased private and particularly farmer forestry. In the period 1994-99 the forestry sector achieved additional planting of over 100,000 hectares, increased wood production by 2 million cubic metres and created 1,600 jobs in planting and harvesting.

6.26 The industry offers considerable scope for expansion given the very low level of afforestation in Ireland with only 9% (up from 7% in 1993) of land used for this purpose compared to an EU average of more than 30%. The development of forestry, on a certain scale and in a particular manner, can contribute to national, economic and social well-being on a sustainable basis compatible with the protection of the environment. For instance, afforestation has the potential to convey substantial environmental benefit to society by ultimately reducing CO_2 emissions.

6.27 Both regions have broadly the same percentage of afforestation with the levels of planting peaking around 1995/1996 in both regions. The downturn in afforestation since 1996 has been largely attributed to the increased participation of farmers in the REPS scheme and a closer synchronisation of policies in this area is required.

Seafood Sector

6.28 At a national level, annual sales of marine food are worth over £330m with 90% of output exported. The marine fishing, aquaculture, processing and ancillary sectors employ 16,000 people directly and an additional 9,000 people indirectly in supporting sectors. Including family dependants, nearly 60,000 people rely on the fishing industry.

6.29 Fishing and its associated industry is predominantly concentrated in the BMW Region. The BMW Region contains the major national fishing ports of Killybegs, together with Rossavaeal and Greencastle. The industry has an important role in sub-regional distribution of economic activity and employment. In particular it sustains remote coastal communities, including island and Gaeltacht areas, where there are few economic alternatives. Donegal is especially reliant on the industry. The county has 40% of vessels over 100 tonnes and Killybegs is home to a modern ocean-going pelagic fleet. Rossaveal and Greencastle are predominantly involved in whitefish. In-shore fishing of whitefish and shellfish occurs on a smaller scale, but is also important for sustaining communities and employment along the coast. It has the further advantage of providing additional part-time or seasonal employment that combines well with other economic activities such as tourism and small-scale farming. Aquaculture production (fin fish & shellfish) is a vitally important economic activity in the West & Northwest.

6.30   The S&E Region's main fishing ports are Castletownbere, Dingle, Dunmore East and Howth. In-shore fishing of whitefish, prawns and shellfish is important to the region. The intensive production of oysters and mussels is of major importance in the south and south-west while trout and salmon farms are also located throughout the region.

6.31   Marine landings have continued to grow in volume and value terms. National policy will continue to balance the objectives and parameters of EU Common Fisheries Policy with the potential to develop the sector in coastal regions where alternative work opportunities are few. Aquaculture production in both regions has significant further potential for sustainable development.

Objectives

6.32   In light of the analysis provided in the previous section, the key objective of the NDP in relation to the Productive Sector Operational Programme is increased productivity throughout the sector in an environmentally sustainable way. This objective will be achieved in the NDP through:

- Ensuring that the favourable business environment for manufacturing and services in Ireland is maintained and enhanced;

- Building the RTDI capacity of the country;

- Improving the growth in output of the indigenous sector through enhancing its productivity and capability and through the encouragement of increased participation of indigenous enterprises in the fastest growing, knowledge-based industries;

- Promoting the location of high value-added FDI in regions which have previously not been successful in attracting FDI (particularly the BMW Region);

- Maximising the potential of the food industry through attention to competitiveness and market orientation and by providing for quality and food safety assurance at all stages of the food chain and to respond to changing consumer requirements;

- Improving Irish agricultural structures in order to increase the competitiveness of the sector in preparation for the next WTO round and to recognise the need for an integrated rural development policy;

- Ensuring sustainable agricultural development in harmony with the environment;

- Creating a sustainable, competitive, quality driven seafood industry which will maximise its contribution to exports;

- Developing forestry to a scale and in a manner which maximises its contribution to national, economic and social well-being on a sustainable basis and which is compatible with the protection of the environment;

- Investment in marketing capability in order to increase the export growth of indigenous enterprises particularly from the BMW Region;

- Continued development of the tourism industry with special focus on exploiting the untapped potential of tourism in many counties through increased marketing.

Strategy

6.33 The broad strategy aimed at achieving the objectives for the Productive Sector Operational Programme will be delivered by investment throughout the NDP and not just under this operational programme. Achievements of the objectives for the Productive Sector during the Plan period will be contingent on timely implementation of the Economic and Social Infrastructure priorities. In this regard, it should be noted that the productive sector will directly benefit from large scale investment under Economic & Social Infrastructure which will remove bottlenecks and ease up pressures on distribution, and that the perceived tightening of the labour market will be addressed by investment under Employment and Human Resources.

6.34 Under this operational programme, six specific areas have been highlighted for investment. These are: Research Technological Development and Innovation (RTDI), Industry, Marketing, Agricultural Development, Forestry and Fisheries Development.

Research, Technological Development & Innovation (RTDI)

Rationale for Investing in RTDI

6.35 The Government accepts that there is a strong link between investment in the research and innovation base of the economy and sustained economic growth. In recognition of the evolution of the 'knowledge-based' economy where intellect and innovation will determine competitive advantage and in recognition of the fact that it is the accumulation of 'knowledge capital' that will facilitate the evolution of the 'knowledge-based' economy, the Government is committed to significant investment in RTDI. Against this background, NDP investment will:

- develop intellectual infrastructure to "root" overseas companies here through more extensive use of research based in Ireland;

- persuade and encourage companies to develop their own research activities;

- develop a world class research environment in our higher education institutions and State research institutions, and

- ensure a vibrant and dynamic pool of high quality, technically literate graduates from the graduate to postdoctoral levels to service the needs of these companies and to start their own companies.

6.36 In addition to the above, investment in RTDI in areas such as agriculture/food, and marine will also have a major impact on sustainability and innovation. In the interest of ensuring that development is of a sustainable nature, investment in the area of environmental RTDI is entirely appropriate.

6.37 In light of the high priority granted to RTDI in the context of the NDP, the Government has agreed to an overall allocation of £1.95 billion (€2.47 billion) over the period 2000-2006. It is intended, where appropriate, that a suitable process will be established whereby all sectors can compete on an even basis for a share of the overall monies allocated to RTDI. However, in the interim, indicative allocations[1] across different areas have been signalled, as set out below;

Table 6.5:   Indicative Allocations of RTDI Expenditure 2000-2006

Research, Technological Development & Innovation			
	National € million	BMW Region € million	S&E Region € million
Industry	1,506	417	1,089
Education & Science	698	150	548
Agriculture/Food (incl UnaG)	171	70	101
Marine	64	18	46
Environment	32	9	23
Total	**2,471**	**664**	**1,807**

RTDI Strategy

6.38 The new programme will aim to invest substantially in the RTDI base of the country, as a means of enhancing innovation and competitiveness by:

- Strengthening the research capability in the third-level and state research institutes, in particular to meet the RTDI and skills needs of the economy;

- Strengthening the supports available to research students and to researchers in third-level and state institutes in order to encourage students into careers as researchers;

- Increasing the quantity and quality of the RTDI linkages between institutions and companies;

- Helping firms to develop innovative products, services and processes;

- Increasing the number of companies performing effective R&D in Ireland;

- Increasing the scale of RTDI investment by companies in Ireland;

- Encouraging firms to access and exploit R&D and technology from international sources;

- embedding the culture of R&D in SME's through upskilling the RTI capability of employees via training in RTDI Management and other appropriate training courses;

- Providing substantial public investment in niche technologies;

- Promoting balanced regional development while at the same time, having due regard to the excellence of proposals funded (mainly on a competitive basis).

RTDI and Education

6.39 Research is a core element of the mission of higher education. The extent to which higher education institutions are engaged in research and development activities has a key role in

---

[1] the regional basis for these allocations are also indicative

determining the status and the quality of these institutions and the contribution which they make to economic and social development.

6.40 A significant provision of £550 million (€698 million) has been allocated in the NDP towards RTDI in the Education sector. The level of investment will facilitate a major capital investment programme to develop the R&D physical infrastructure of the third-level institutions in line with national strategic priorities. The increased funding of R&D in the education sector will boost human potential in research, science and technology and will strengthen the research and science capability of our higher education institutions. This will in turn facilitate collaborative efforts with industry to ensure an R&D culture in all sectors of the economy.

6.41 The additional investment being provided in the NDP will build upon the existing initiatives to continue and develop the innovative Programme for Research in Third Level Institutions 1999-2001 which involves a system of competitive bidding, between the third level institutions, for research programmes to support national strategic objectives that are consistent with the stated research strategies of the institutions. The strengthening of graduate enterprise programmes and of higher education-industry links will also be a priority. The investment will also allow for the development of schemes of post-graduate and post-doctoral supports for researchers and will facilitate the expansion of peer reviewed project basic research. Inter-institutional co-operation will also be targeted to ensure critical mass at national level in key areas. Similarly, strategies will be developed to ensure that researchers are afforded the opportunity to work alongside top-class researchers and are fully engaged in quality research activities.

RTDI and Industry

6.42 A provision of £381 million (€484 million) for RTDI in Industry will be aimed at delivering the following:

- to embed an R&D culture into firms which already have a technological capability. This measure will be targeted at high potential start-ups and companies which will pursue strategic R& D projects;

- to support the R&D/technology requirements of the 3,000 + companies who do not perform R&D at present and particularly to increase the number of companies doing R& D for the first time. It will also provide support for innovation management training and technical skills.

6.43 Investment in RTDI in certain areas of manufacturing and the agri-food sector, will help them to become more innovative and competitive as they face greater global market pressures.

RTDI Collaboration Networks

6.44 The promotion of greater collaboration within and between the RTI "supply" side (colleges, research organisations and Agencies) and the demand side of industry has benefits for partners as well as the development of national capability in general. An amount of £210 million (€267 million) has been allocated to the promotion of collaboration networks.

6.45 It is intended that a programme of large scale projects, based on a Call for Proposals to industry will be established. These projects may involve collaboration of firms or business associations, with third level colleges or research institutes or any combination of these. The programme would be suited to both large firms, with existing R&D capabilities and networks of smaller firms (e.g. software).

6.46 This programme will be designed to achieve a scaling up of R&D for the firms involved and at the same time spin-off expertise and potential applications into industry from third level colleges/institutes or other firms. International networks will be developed in order to meet the "technology intelligence needs" companies through a "technology watch" mechanism.

RTDI Infrastructure

6.47 With the objective of repositioning Irish industry higher up the economic value chain and prioritising Ireland's R&D investment into areas with the greatest potential, the Irish Council for Science, Technology and Innovation (ICSTI) recently produced the Technology Foresight Ireland Report which makes a number of specific recommendations in relation to Ireland's future RTI infrastructure. These recommendations are the basis for the following courses of action during the NDP.

- A Technology Foresight Fund will be established totalling £560 million (€711 million) over seven years to support RTDI projects in key technologies strategic to long-term sectoral and national development. The objectives of these projects will be to provide internationally competitive world class RTDI, and to signal Ireland as an attractive location in which to perform RTDI. The projects will be implemented on a partnership basis (involving industry, the public sector and research community). The Technology Foresight Fund will be operated on the basis of the selection of projects following a competitive assessment process. It would not be appropriate to pre-judge the outcome of this process as allocations will depend on the quality of the responses from the regions. However the strong emphasis attached in the Plan to balanced regional development will be a factor in determining allocations.

- The development of Regional Innovation Systems, at a cost of £17.5 million (€22 million), in order to encourage regions to bring together elements of the innovation system into the region (industry, colleges, institutes, agencies, financial institutions) in order to build strategies related to local industrial or research strengths. Funding will be available for both the preparation and the implementation of regional innovation plans. It is envisaged that proposals would incorporate regional technology parks or other forms of networks.

- Resources amounting to £17.5 million (€22 million) will be directed into Human Infrastructure in RTDI reflecting the need to build up the scientific, engineering and technical capabilities of the Irish workforce in the expectation that industry will increasingly demand high level skills and in particular R&D expertise. Development on a continuous ongoing basis of the innovation capability of the workforce in companies will also be a priority under this measure.

RTDI and the Natural Resource-Based Industries

Agriculture/Food Sector

6.48 An indicative amount of £128 million (€163 million) has been allocated to RTDI in the agriculture/food sector. At primary production level, Teagasc will concentrate RTDI on achieving competitive and sustainable agriculture, and exploring rural viability potential for smaller farmers.

Other institutes will also be invited to participate in collaborative projects where they identify gaps in the research process.

6.49 Public funding of RTDI in the agriculture/food sector will assist three complementary facets — institutional (or public) research, in-company research, and technology transfer. The support measures will enhance the innovative capability of the industry and will assist in ensuring that development is underscored by attention to food safety and quality issues. The public research initiative will add critical mass to near-market product and process development and, in the context of food safety/quality, will play a crucial role in assuring consumer protection. The in-company initiative will support product/process development by SMEs but, in the case of large companies, will limit public funding to those, which demonstrate a clear long-term commitment to innovation and research. The technology transfer initiative will provide funding for the uptake by the food industry of institutional R&D and will help to maximise the relevance of that research to the market.

Fisheries & Forestry

6.50 An indicative amount of £50 million (€64 million) has been allocated to RTDI for fisheries and forestry. These are sectors which are particularly important to rural communities and therefore an appropriate spend on RTDI in these areas is required to develop these traditional industries.

Fisheries/Marine

6.51 The allocation towards RTDI in the marine sector will assist the following sectors:

- marine food sector through supporting sea fisheries, aquaculture, seaweed development and value-added processing;

- marine environment through supporting research, monitoring, assessment and management to meet both existing needs and the increased pressure on the living and non-living resource which will accompany a growing marine economic sector;

- water-based tourism and leisure sector through supporting the future development of the sector to ensure long term resource quality, capacity and economic benefit;

- marine technology sector through developing new and innovative engineering technologies and products, with particular emphasis on the integration of Information & Communications Technology (ICT) with marine resource development.

6.52 It is intended that funding will be provided for:

- enhanced research vessel capabilities to cover outer Shelf activities;

- upgrade of marine laboratories to provide an infrastructural platform to support ongoing research;

- establishment of a Marine RTDI Fund to support project based R&D in targeted areas.

Forestry

6.53 In the forestry sector RTDI expenditure will continue to support the research and development priorities outlined in "Growing for the Future", the Strategic Plan for the Development of the Forestry Sector, published in 1996. The emphasis will be on:

- ensuring that the forestry industry remains viable, internationally competitive and environmentally compatible within the context of sustainable development; and

132

- developing further 'state-of-the-art' competence and a critical mass of forest research capacity in Ireland to encourage both innovation and market enhancement.

6.54 The expenditure will be geared towards the priorities of improvements in product development and marketing, better knowledge of environmental issues, communications and information technology, farm forestry and socio-economic issues. It is intended that COFORD (National Council for Forest Research and Development) will continue to co-ordinate research activity and transfer technology and information.

RTDI and the Environment

6.55 An indicative amount of £20 million (€25 million) has been allocated to an Environmental Research Programme. Environmental Research will be concerned in particular with the need to measure the impact of economic development, as well as contributing to sustainable development of natural resources using the highest environmental standards. The environmental research programme will complement research work which will be carried out in other sectors and programmes (e.g. Marine, Forestry, Agriculture) and will act as a focus for integration of environmental concerns in other policy sectors.

6.56 Projects may involve the establishment of networks for data gathering and exchange and the setting up of long term monitoring sites for data gathering particularly for emissions and air quality assessments and studies. It is intended that Environmental Research expenditure will provide for applied or demonstration type activities leading to the development of systems, models, instruments and techniques as well as contributing data and information to assist policy and decision making.

6.57 In addition to the expenditure referred to above, an amount of £5 million (€6 million) is earmarked for the possible establishment of a National Environmental Research Unit or centre of excellence (possibly incorporated into the Environmental Protection Agency (EPA)). This would allow for a more structured approach to research than at present, and would provide stronger environmental support across the new CSF.

6.58 Priority programmes for the centre would include:

- integrated environmental assessment;

- environmental management systems;

- information systems development;

- air pollution and acidification;

- waste prevention and management guidance.

Industry (Indigenous & FDI)

6.59 Successive administrations over recent years have facilitated the creation of a positive business environment for industry in Ireland which is attracting an increasing level of private investment. Government policy is therefore that support for the tradable sector of the economy should be limited to measures designed to overcome identified market failures, which have the capacity to significantly impair further growth and expansion of the enterprise sector, particularly in less developed regions. Nevertheless targeted aid consistent with the EU's State Aid Guidelines (see below) will be necessary under the Plan to consolidate and further develop Ireland's industrial sector. The Government is confident that the new aid levels will be strongly supportive of its policy of strong regional development and more spatially balanced economic growth. An amount of £1.9 billion (€2.4 billion) has been allocated in the Plan to Industry with £973 million (€1,236 million) for measures aimed at assisting Indigenous Industry and £930 million (€1,181 million) for measures aimed at promoting FDI.

EU State Aid Guidelines

A key concern of the EU Commission in producing the new guidelines was to reduce the amount of overall state aid given out by Governments in the EU (leading to harmful bidding contests for mobile investment) and to encourage a genuine concentration of permitted aid in disadvantage regions, objectively measured. Under the new Guidelines, Ireland moves from being a single "A" region for State Aid purposes to being composed of an "A" region (comprising the Border Midland & Western Region) and 5 "C" regions which consist of the five regional authorities under the Southern & Eastern Region. The limits which have now been agreed with the Commission based on an assessment of objective economic indicators in respect of each of the regions, are as follows:

"A" Region:
Border, Midland & Western 40% plus up to 15% for SMEs

"C" Regions:
South-East	*20% plus up to 10% for SMEs*
South-West	*20% plus up to 10% for SMEs*
Mid-West	*20% plus up to 10% for SMEs*
Mid-East	*18% plus up to 10% for SMEs*
Dublin	*17.5% plus up to 10% for SMEs*

While the Dublin region becomes subject to the new limit from January 2000, the permitted aid ceiling for the other four "C" regions will be gradually reduced to reach the new limits, which will be effective from 2003.

Indigenous Industry

6.60   While there has been a strong recovery in and development of indigenous industry in the 1990s, the analysis earlier highlighted that domestic enterprises still face a number of growth and competitiveness issues which need to be addressed. The strategy underpinning NDP investment in indigenous industry will be aimed at addressing the following:

- limited export growth outside the UK market;

- continued reliance on many traditional products;

- proliferation of small-scale operations;

- insufficient spending on human resources;

- insufficient investment in RTDI;

- an uneven spatial spread of industrial activity.

6.61 Resolution of these issues involves addressing the key constraints at firm level of scale, productivity, profitability, export levels, innovation and human resource development through a series of measures outlined below.

(i) Strategy Assessment and Formulation

6.62 The objective here is to provide support for in-company strategy planning which will allow companies to review their operations and formulate plans for future growth. Financial support in the form of strategy and feasibility grants and access to experienced advice in the form of mentors as well as the financial incentives to develop other forms of capability is proposed under this measure. An allocation of £57 million (€72 million) has been provided.

(ii) Production and Operations

6.63 The objective of this measure is to enhance the competitiveness of indigenous industry by providing support to increase output, reduce costs and rationalise supply logistics. With regard to capacity expansion, this will be achieved by capital and employment grants and/or, where appropriate, repayable supports e.g. equity. On the capability building side, measures such as World Class Manufacturing will also be used to increase productivity. In addition, to address the emerging needs arising from developments in the area of e-commerce, selective infrastructural supports will be made available to build the capabilities of SMEs in this area. The development of logistics as a key capability will be supported through the National Institute of Transport and Logistics. An allocation of £267 million (€339 million) has been provided for this measure.

(iii) Human Resources

6.64 The development of management and employee skills is a critical requirement for any modern competitive business. This is a particularly critical issue given the current severe skills shortages in some sectors, particularly IT which is acting as a brake in the development of Irish industry.

6.65 The emphasis will be on assisting companies in developing high quality management, highly skilled staff and effective business systems and foster and nurture enterpreneurship by appropriate encouragement and supports. This will be achieved by encouraging and supporting management development training, staff training, particularly in priority areas, and the adoption of human resource development best practice policies by companies.

6.66 A major initiative will be undertaken to encourage indigenous companies, especially SMEs, to adopt IT and e-commerce as intrinsic tools of business. In addition, enterpreneurship and management capability will be encouraged, especially in high-technology and other high-growth sectors, through enterprise development training and advice workshops. An allocation of £200 million (€254 million) is provided (Chapter 5, Paragraphs 5.89-5.92).

(iv) Finance

6.67 The development of a seed and venture capital fund industry in Ireland, supported with funding from the EU, has been one of the most significant improvements in finance for indigenous industry over the past few years. A vibrant venture capital market is a key element in business development with the private sector being the primary source of equity for companies. If the indigenous sector is to continue to grow and prosper it depends on a continual flow of good high potential start up and development companies. To ensure this happens it is vital to consolidate and build on the success achieved over the last few years by continuing to provide support through the Seed and Venture Funds mechanism. Side by side with this the development agencies will, in limited circumstances, supplement the support provided by these funds through the provision of grants, equity investments, and other forms of repayable supports. An overall allocation of £226 million (€287 million) is provided.

(v) Regional Networks

6.68 Improving the access infrastructure, developing enterprise support systems and building regional networks are key elements to achieving balanced regional development. Enterprise support will involve the development of a network of centres in partnership with companies, colleges and communities to ensure that start up companies have access to incubator space. This is especially important in helping to induce and attract new technology start ups.

6.69 The availability of dedicated expertise in areas of product development, process improvement and related areas will contribute to the growth of clusters of companies in particular localities. To assist company competitiveness in the regions it is proposed to develop regional networks of companies. This involves:

- joint marketing of projects with assistance from Agencies' overseas offices;

- learning networks building on the experiences of learning clusters in West Dublin;

- regional innovation networks which will link colleges and companies around an agenda of developing generic RTDI skills and capabilities.

An allocation of £85 million (€108 million) has been provided.

Food Sector

6.70 An allocation of £120 million (€152 million) is provided for capital investment in the food sector which will be largely directed towards implementing the recommendations of the Food Industry Development Group and the Beef Task Force. This allocation will also cater for investment in the livestock marketing sector.

6.71 At primary slaughtering and processing level, the beef sector will receive priority. Allied to proposed rationalisation within the sector, public funding will be provided towards the modernisation of plant and equipment. This will be an important contribution to increased efficiency and will assist this vital sector in its efforts to recover/gain markets. Support will also be provided for other initiatives in the food sector designed to improve competitiveness and/or enhance safety and quality at primary level — e.g. modernisation in the poultry sector, improved storage in the horticultural and cereals sectors. Apart from these areas, the focus of support will be on added value and, in particular, on the high value prepared consumer foods and food ingredients sectors. These sectors present the best growth opportunities and the intended public funding support will assist them to avail of these and to address scale-related difficulties which inhibit competitiveness and market access

Fish Processing Sector

6.72 The investment strategy for the fish processing, amounting to £25 million (€32 million), will support the accelerated development of seafood processing enterprises to create a competitive value-added capability of scale at national and international level. The key objective is to maximise the value of the seafood supply side (catching and aquaculture) and to develop new products, technology and scale in the processing sector.

Assistance for Gaeltacht Areas

6.73 Gaeltacht areas are almost entirely in remote and rural parts of the country and funding towards the development of industry in these areas is consistent with the priority in the Plan afforded to balanced regional development. An amount of £193 million (€245 million) has been allocated towards this measure and it will be aimed at increasing the competitiveness of existing Gaeltacht industry, thereby enabling the industries already in operation not only to survive, but to change and position themselves further along the added value chain. Within the overall allocation of £193 million (€245 million), there is a specific provision of £30 million (€38 million) in respect of the film industry.

Foreign Direct Investment (FDI)

6.74 It was noted earlier that a primary focus of our industrial policy over recent years has been to win, in competition with other countries, the highest possible share of quality inward investment in targeted manufacturing and internationally traded services sectors. A key element of Ireland's economic success has been the relatively large amount of inward investment the country has been able to attract particularly in rapidly expanding high technology products. However, it is also clear that a disproportionate share of these FDI projects are in the S&E Region and in the main urban centres. Consequently the strategy underpinning NDP investment will be driven by:

- a strong emphasis on attracting high value-added FDI projects to the BMW Region and the weaker areas in the S&E Region in line with a policy of balanced regional development.

In parallel with this specific policy, the strategy will aim to:

- increase the value and sustainability of overseas companies in Ireland and secure their future in Ireland; and

- identify and develop activities and sectors that will attract high quality inward investment.

6.75 An amount of £930 million (€1,181 million) will be allocated towards FDI with 44% of this seven-year allocation being directed to the BMW Region. This percentage is well in excess of the population share of 27% and towards the second half of the period of the NDP, resources directed to the BMW Region will actually exceed those in the S&E Region as suitable regional locations will by then have benefited from sufficient infrastructural investment at this stage.

6.76 It is proposed during the period of the National Plan to focus support for inward investment activities in three main areas (i) Regional Development, (ii) Embedding the Existing Base of Companies and (iii) Sectoral Development. Incentive schemes will be appropriately tailored, subject to EU regional and horizontal aid guidelines, to implement objectives in these three key areas.

(i) Regional Development

6.77 There will be a comprehensive approach to securing the regional distribution of inward investment, beginning with an assessment of the attributes of regions and towns — their location, infrastructure and skills — driving improvements where necessary and matching regions with the most appropriate industries or sectors of industries. This will require a strong co-operative approach between the industrial development agencies, the local authorities, local communities, Government Departments and infrastructure/service providers.

6.78 Because existing overseas companies located in Ireland are relatively immobile with respect to expansions and new investment, the large bulk of the contribution to regional development will have to come from new green field activities. The aim is to deliver more than half of all new jobs from future green field projects into the BMW Region. The regional development strategy for FDI will be consistent with the Regional Development Policy set out in Chapter 3. In this context, there will be a special focus on gateway towns which will be catalysts for overall regional growth. An allocation of £565 million (€717 million) is provided for this measure.

(ii) Embedding Existing Companies

6.79 The industrial development agencies will increasingly work with the existing base of foreign companies in Ireland to ensure that they become more embedded in the Irish economy and that they are constantly moving up the value chain in terms of their Irish operations. This attention to embeddedness and quality will also result in a greater emphasis on the quality of jobs created in new projects attracted to Ireland.

6.80 The embedding programme will involve the agencies working closely with local management of overseas companies to secure a wider corporate mandate and to become a vital part of the corporate value chain, thus helping to ensure the long term survival and growth of the company in Ireland. Irish subsidiaries can improve their strategic position within the parent corporation by becoming a reference site or centre of excellence for any function or product. This measure will concentrate on persuading Irish subsidiaries to add strategic functions such as R&D, technical support, software development, logistics and shared services in Ireland in an effort to carve out as much autonomy for the Irish operation as possible and to so structure it within the overall group that it becomes virtually indispensable to the parent. An allocation of £305 million (€387 million) has been provided for this measure.

(iii) Sectoral Development

6.81 The Sectoral Development Programme will focus on identifying and developing activities and sectors that are high growth, high technology and strategically important to meet the country's development needs and have the right characteristics to allow Ireland to compete successfully for inward investment. With technology developing at a faster pace than ever, it is essential that Ireland continues to attract leading edge international companies in strategic sectors such as information and communications technology, biotechnology etc. An allocation of £60 million (€76 million) has been provided for this measure.

6.82 Electronic Commerce is driving fundamental changes in business and will be a significant and strategic area of industrial development opportunities in coming years. The attraction of leading edge international E-Commerce business is an essential plank in the Government's intention to make Ireland an international hub for E-Commerce. Such strategic projects have the potential for generating technological spillovers and long-term competitive advantage in the wider economy.

6.83 The intention is to encourage developments in E-Commerce in selected regional locations, in line with the evolution in site location of teleservices, software and shared services projects. A key issue being addressed in the NDP in order to make this a reality is the provision of broadband capability in regional locations.

Marketing

6.84 The Government recognises that public investment in marketing is appropriate to assisting the indigenous enterprise sector and can assist in promoting balanced regional development. As in the case of research, certain types of marketing have public good characteristics (e.g. marketing Ireland as a tourist destination) which justifies public support on economic grounds. Consequently the Government has agreed to an allocation of £337 million (€428 million) for Marketing with £187 million (€237 million) allocated to marketing across all sectors and £150 million (€191 million) specifically earmarked for Tourism Marketing.

6.85 The strategy underpinning NDP investment in marketing will be driven by:

- increasing the level of exports in the indigenous sector — with an emphasis on SMEs and market diversification;

- assisting the marketing function of firms disadvantaged by their peripheral location;

- assisting sectors that have yet to fully embrace marketing;

- promoting Ireland as a world-class tourist location and specific marketing of activity-based holidays with a view to regional development.

Sectoral Marketing

6.86 Under this measure, resources will be directed to marketing in industry, the food sector and to fisheries and forestry sector. Specific measures will have to comply with EU State Aid rules which prohibit export aid.

Industry Marketing

6.87 An allocation of £128 million (€163 million) will go towards support for marketing capability in industry. This level of marketing support will be focussed towards SMEs (small and medium enterprises) as they often fail to undertake market development on their own due to lack of expertise, financial resources and the perceived risks involved. The development of marketing capability in SMEs will be a high priority and supports will be directed to the following:

- Market Information/Research including market trends, competition, logistics, market strategy options, product development and design upgrading of skills;

- Sectoral and Company Promotional Activities including trade fairs, advertising, literature and public relations;

- Internationalisation including market development personnel, training (customer care skills, language skills etc.), overseas offices, strategic alliances/partnerships, acquisition and sourcing.

6.88 The growth sectors for indigenous SMEs include:

- Software (including E-Commerce);

- Medical Devices and Technology;

- Electronic Sub-Supply;

- Precision Engineering;

- Process Control and Instrumentation;

- Environmental Technology; and

- Other International Services including Education and Consultancy.

6.89 Target markets include Europe, North America and selected Asian markets. As recognised by the National Competitiveness Council the launch of the Euro and the completion of the single market provides a significant opportunity for SMEs to further diversify their trading activities into core EU markets. A new proactive policy to grow foreign earnings in the Asia/Pacific region will be implemented as decided by Government.

6.90 The development agencies' overseas office network are critical in assisting the indigenous sector overcome their constraints, diversify exports and break into new markets.

Food Sector

6.91 An amount of £48 million (€61 million) is being provided for marketing in the food sector. It is intended that this will be used to focus on those sectors offering the greatest growth potential. It is equally important, however, that key sectors vulnerable to severe competitive pressures are assisted. The support initiatives will cover general promotional/marketing work but will also seek to enhance companies' own marketing development capabilities. These initiatives will cover two strands:

- the promotional, market research, trade/consumer programmes undertaken by An Bord Bia; and

- company specific measures which may include market entry/expansion grants for small firms in the consumer foods and food ingredients' areas.

Seafood Sector

6.92 An amount of £6 million (€8 million) will go towards marketing in the marine sector. The aim here will be to capitalise on the buoyant international seafood market for quality, value-added fish products by developing vital supply chain linkages with distributors and retailers. In line with this strategy the following priority areas will be pursued:

- increasing domestic per capita consumption and unit value of product sold;

- development of markets for non-quota aquaculture species;

- targeted market research and promotional trade consumer programmes;

- development of the marketing capabilities of seafood companies;

- address competitive pressures for the sector.

6.93 The seafood marketing programme which will include company specific measures will be directly undertaken by BIM, co-operating and co-ordinating in a strategic alliance as necessary with Bord Bia in generic food promotion and trade activities overseas.

Tourism Marketing

6.94   The key marketing objectives in tourism over the next seven years are to: increase tourism revenue and per diem visitor yield, and to help industry achieve a wider seasonal and regional distribution of tourist business thereby contributing to sustainable development goals.

6.95   The strategy to achieve the objectives outlined above is:

- to market Ireland internationally on an all-Ireland basis as a tourism destination; and

- international marketing of niche special interest products;

- a series of training and product development measures to ensure maximum effectiveness.

6.96   The Marketing Sub-Programme consists of two measures, a Destination Marketing Measure and a Niche Marketing Measure, to be funded from Ireland's first ever Multi-Annual Tourism Marketing Fund. The main purpose of this Fund is to finance the promotion and marketing internationally of Ireland as a tourism destination. The Fund will incorporate a public/private partnership arrangement and will ensure adequate funding, from public and industry sources, for destination marketing over the period of the Plan.

Destination Marketing

6.97   Funding in this area will be directed towards T.V./Radio/Press/Print advertising, development of INTERNET sites, direct marketing, trade and media promotions and production of tourism promotional material. While the U.S. has grown fastest of the major markets since 1993, some of the other markets such as Australia, the Netherlands, Italy and Scandinavia have performed significantly better than France, Germany or even Britain. Support is needed to develop a niche for Ireland in these newer markets which would broaden Ireland's geographic market spread and alternate its dependence on more traditional markets.

6.98   In overseas marketing, *Tourism Brand Ireland* has been the major vehicle and has played a pivotal role not only in refining tourism promotion but also in developing public/private and North/South partnerships within the tourism industry. While the projection and rollout of the brand is well underway, there is a continuous need to track and review its performance over the initial years, make appropriate adjustments and support its further evolution. There is also a need to encourage more widespread adoption and use of the brand by all elements of the tourism industry.

Niche Marketing

6.99   Special interest products (such as golf, cruising, conference visitors, angling, marine tourism, walking, gardens, and the teaching of English as a foreign language) are particularly important in developing a sustainable tourism industry as such market niches deliver higher yield visitors, are more inclined to benefit wider geographical areas and are environmentally friendly. Support will be provided for the branding and marketing of special interest products, with priority given to those that incorporate an industry partnership approach to development. In addition, smaller and less developed niche businesses will be encouraged to improve marketing capabilities (e.g. walking, cycling) while better developed sectors (e.g. golf, cruising, English as a foreign language) will be supported by targeting new markets and segments.

6.100   Small operators, including B&Bs and other small accommodation providers, who are of central importance to the Irish tourism product and facilitate wide regional spread, lack the marketing skills necessary to compete internationally. Target support will be provided to develop the marketing capabilities of this sector and to help them develop appropriate branding and marketing initiatives.

Fisheries/Seafood Industry Development

6.101   The strategic objective for the period of the NDP will be to maximise the value of output by increasing quality and efficiency at each point of the distribution chain, thus ensuring a sustainable future for the Irish fishing industry as a whole and its contribution to the well-being of the coastal communities. Investment strategies will provide a strong internationally competitive seafood sector which will make a significant contribution to sustainable employment and balanced regional growth. To this end, funding for the seafood industry will be provided across different Operational Programmes. Apart from this measure, support for the seafood sector as a whole will be covered under

- the indigenous sector (fish processing), RTDI and Marketing sub-programmes of this Operational Programme

- the Regional Operational Programmes which contain the funding for fishery harbours infrastructure and aquaculture, and

- the Employment and Human Resources Operational Programme (training)

6.102   Under the Fisheries Development measure of the Productive Sector Operational Programme, funding amounting to £45 million (€57 million) will be provided primarily to meet the strategic objective of enhanced safety, quality and competitiveness of the fleet. There will be a particular focus on the continued modernisation of the whitefish fleet within the framework of the Community fleet development guidelines. The revitalisation of the inshore fleet will be addressed. The whitefish fleet provides most of the employment in the catching sector with the inshore fleet accounting for the employment of 3,700 people, building on current reinvestment strategies for the whitefish fleet will be key to improved safety, efficiency and competitiveness and ensure that employment is maintained. Strategic initiatives will critically focus on enhancing the handling, storage and presentation of raw material so as to maximise the value which is generated from the catching sector. In line with EU requirements, measures to adjust fleet capacity to fleet targets will continue during this Programme.

6.103   In the peripheral coastal communities there are still particular challenges to overcome and the challenge of restructuring and diversification will be addressed through supporting new sustainable activities, increasing efficiency, supporting innovation and skills development. Investment strategies will build on achievements to date under the EU PESCA Community Initiative.

Agricultural Development

6.104   The strategy for improving structures in the agriculture, food and related rural development areas in the National Development Plan will reflect in particular, the new EU Council Regulation on Support for Rural Development agreed under Agenda 2000. Accordingly, eight strategic areas have been highlighted for attention:

- improving agricultural structures at farm level;

142

- improving breeding, animal welfare, hygiene and quality;

- focusing on quality and food safety at processing level and assisting the further development of the food industry;

- developing non-surplus products;

- developing rural services and rural enterprise support;

- continuing direct income support for farmers in designated disadvantaged areas;

- improving the environment at farm level; and

- continuing to provide back up research, advice and training in the agriculture, food and rural development areas.

6.105 The above strategies will be taken on board in the context of a number of Programmes under the NDP. The Productive Sector Operational Programme with an allocation of £278 million (€353 million) for Agriculture Development will address the following strategies and measures.

- *Improving Agricultural Structures through the operation of a Scheme of Installation Aid for Young Farmers*

6.106 This measure is aimed towards maintaining as many viable farms as possible by encouraging the take-over of farms by the younger generation. These younger farmers are better able to adapt to the increasing challenge of competitiveness on the agriculture side in the face of production constraints on many products and the need on many farms to earn adequate off-farm income to supplement agricultural income. Additional benefits are likely to accrue as younger farmers are more likely to rear families and contribute to economic growth and employment by increasing productivity, acquiring new skills as appropriate and securing part-time employment outside the farm.

- *Improving Product Quality with an emphasis on cattle and equine breeding, animal welfare and dairy hygiene and cereal grain quality*

6.107 The promotion of quality output along with measures aimed at improving consumer assurance and environment friendly production systems will be essential elements in securing the development of an efficient competitive and modern agriculture. On the production side, it is proposed to operate measures which will improve breeding, animal welfare and general hygiene conditions for animals and also enhance grain quality and safety. These measures are important in the context of securing consumer confidence and they also help to achieve competitiveness as markets are increasingly geared towards quality products

- *Improving the Environment by operating a Farm Waste Management Scheme*

6.108 Agenda 2000 emphasises the more prominent role to be given to agri-environment instruments to support the sustainable development of rural areas and to respond to society's increasing demand for environmental services. Member States are, accordingly, obliged to offer farmers environmental programmes of aid and also they must ensure that all EU funded measures are operated in accordance with acknowledged good agricultural practices in relation to the environment.

6.109 Over 70% of the land area of Ireland is devoted to agriculture and forestry. The Irish landscape, a prized public good, is in large part a by-product of our agricultural systems. Pastures, arable areas, forests and farm hedgerows are vital wildlife habitats and key constituents of our unique landscape, which is one of the most valuable resources of our tourism industry. As pasture is the dominant feature of our agriculture, the promotion of good grazing practice is fundamentally important.

6.110 The main thrust of this agri-environment policy will be the continued importance of the Rural Environment Protection Scheme (REPS) and this is dealt with in Chapter 11. However, under this sub-programme, funding will be provided for a Scheme for Management of Farm Waste.

- *Providing Back-Up Advisory Services to Farmers through Teagasc's revamped Farm Viability and Rural Enterprise Services*

6.111 As already indicated, the strategies proposed in this sub-programme relate to:

- improving farm structures;

- promoting quality production and processing;

- achieving high environmental standards.

6.112 Little progress in any of these areas can be achieved without a formal research, advisory and training structure being put in place to ensure farmers have the best information available to them in a period of substantial change for farmers, processors and consumers as EU policy continues to move towards greater trade liberalisation. Funding of the research and training functions is dealt with in the RTDI sub-programme and the Employment & Human Resources OP, respectively.

6.113 In relation to advisory services, Teagasc have set down 5 objectives for their revamped advisory service:

- to encourage and support farm families who are having viability problems through their new Rural Viability Advisory Programme;

- to promote the development of on-farm Discussion Groups as the method of technology transfer to largely full-time farmers;

- to provide planning and advisory services to ensure that farming systems are sustainable particularly in relation to improved fertiliser use, management of animal manure, grazing and other practices;

- to ensure through their Food Safety and Quality Assurance Programme that farmers have the knowledge and skills necessary to meet the standards necessary of food safety and quality assurance schemes;

- the establishment of Rural Information Centres where farmers and other rural dwellers can have available to them state-of-the-art computer facilities with access to Internet and Intranet sites.

Impact on Poverty

6.114 The key element in the eradication of poverty is the creation of employment. Expenditure under the Productive Sector Operational Programme will be aimed at maintaining growth through securing a favourable business environment and enhancing the enterprise culture. More specifically the objective of promoting industrial development on a more regionally balanced basis will encourage the economic development of lagging behind regions. This will assist in the creation and retention of employment.

Impact on Equality

6.115   It is the policy of the Government that the increased employment opportunities on foot of investment in the Productive Sector are open to all and that, in particular, female involvement in the workplace, especially in management positions, continues to grow. The economy's potential to maintain its strong growth rate is intrinsically linked to the need for greater participation of women in the productive sector. Developments within the productive sector such as the advent of technology to allow for people to work from home and the emergence of e-commerce will support flexible working hours which may be of particular benefit to women. In implementing various support measures across sectors, particular attention will be paid to ensuring that women will be given the opportunity to compete for support.

Impact on the Environment

6.116   The Government recognises that there is considerable challenge in ensuring that the greater level of activity in the productive sector of the economy does not have a detrimental effect on the environment. Consequently, all expenditure decisions will be dependent on the actions that follow being consistent with the goal of maintaining the environment.

6.117   Manufacturing industry support will be linked to firms' commitments to environmentally friendly production and adequate waste management practises. In relation to agriculture, the proposed Farm Waste Management Scheme will enhance the environment by providing farmers with necessary animal housing and waste storage facilities. The direct support for environmental research will assist in monitoring and achieving environmental objectives. In the tourism sector, the future success of the industry in Ireland will effectively be inter-dependent on its ability to manage its growth on an eco-friendly basis.

6.118   The forestry sector in particular can also make a specific contribution to the environmental quality. If properly managed it can have a positive effect on the environment at local level and at national level has an important role to play in achieving Ireland's CO_2 targets under the Kyoto protocol. Protection of the environment is a basic principal of the forestry programme. A National Forestry Standard is being developed, which is essentially a Code of Best Practice, embracing forestry guidelines and criteria for sustainable forest management.

6.119   The Operational Programme will be subject to eco-audit (see Appendix 4) as required by Government policy.

Rural Impact

6.120   All Investment in the NDP is underpinned by the stated objective of balanced regional development, which of course, will be beneficial to rural areas. The problems faced by rural areas will be tackled through a concerted investment package in the transport and educational infrastructure and under the Productive Sector Operational Programme there will be:

- increased emphasis on attracting high quality, value-added FDI to the regions; and
- a high priority afforded to agriculture, and other natural resource based industries which are of critical importance to rural communities.

145

7 Border, Midland and Western Regional Operational Programme

Introduction

7.1 Expenditure under the Border, Midland and Western (BMW) Regional Operational Programme will be as shown in Table 7.1 below:

Table 7.1:   Regional Operational Programme
Expenditure 2000-2006

Sub-programme	BMW Region € million
Local Infrastructure	1,936.3
Productive Investment	429.1
Social Inclusion	280.2
Total Expenditure	2,645.6
Expenditure per Capita €	2,741

Overview of BMW Region

7.2   A general socio-economic overview of the BMW Region is contained in Chapter 3 and, at a sectoral level, in the chapters on the Inter-regional Operational Programmes. The Region is characterised by:

- A workforce which is generally well trained and skilled;

- A good base for enterprise development based on natural resources;

- A relatively high quality environment;

- A lack of congestion generally resulting in less pressure on the physical infrastructure.

Countering this, however, the Region has:

- a weak urban structure, generally poor physical infrastructure and, with the exception of the eastern part of the Region, a lack of efficient access to the main cities and ports;

- a limited industrial or services base with GVA across all sectors lower than the national average;

- poor agricultural land and weak agricultural structures;

- few R&D oriented companies and a relatively small share of national third-level infrastructure;

- the largest proportion of those citizens who would be classified as rural poor.

Objectives for BMW Region

7.3 The major objectives for the BMW Region over the period of the Plan, as set out in Chapter 3, are as follows:

- Increase the potential of the Region to act as a counter-balance to the Southern and Eastern (S&E) Region, especially Dublin, and pursue more balanced and diversified growth within the Region;

- Increase the presence in the Region of the key drivers of sustainable economic growth, notably in the productive sector;

- Improve the quality of the Region's economic and social infrastructure and human resources skillbase;

- Build on the Region's natural resource base especially in the areas of agriculture, tourism, fisheries, aquaculture and rural enterprise;

- Promote rural and urban social inclusion.

Impact of Inter-Regional Operational Programmes

7.4 The three Inter-regional Operational Programmes will make a major contribution to the achievement of these objectives. The **Economic and Social Infrastructure Operational Programme** will improve the transport links within the Region and between it and the rest of the country. This will reduce the peripherality of the Region and also enable it to take greater advantage of 'spill-over' effects from the growth of the S&E Region. The **Employment and Human Resources Development Operational Programme** will provide significant investment in the Region for education, training, skills development, lifelong learning and other schemes designed to support the maximum involvement of the Region's population in economic activity. The **Productive Sector Operational Programme**, utilising the Region's Objective 1 status which allows the use of comparatively better rates of incentives to business, will assist the Region in promoting foreign direct investment and the development of indigenous small and medium sized enterprises. In addition, the substantial EU and national expenditure under the Feoga Guarantee and CAP Rural Development Programme will significantly benefit farm incomes in rural areas while the Peace Programme will provide £100 million (€127 million) for socio economic development of Border areas. Expenditure in the Region under the Inter-regional Operational Programmes, the CAP Rural Development Programme and the Peace Programme is as follows:

Table 7.2: Inter-regional Operational Programmes Expenditure 2000-2006 — BMW Region

Inter-regional Operational Programmes	€ million
Economic and Social Infrastructure	5,957.6
Productive Sector	2,100.1
Employment and Human Resources Development	3,601.0
CAP Rural Development	2,474.7
Peace	127.0
Total	14,260.4
Expenditure per Capita €	14,774.8

148

Operational Programme for the BMW Region

7.5   The Regional Operational Programmes for the BMW Region is designed to complement the three inter-regional programmes by focusing primarily on local investment instruments which, in addition to their benefits locally, will help ensure that assistance under the Inter-regional Operational Programmes deliver maximum impact. Thus, for example, investment in local infrastructure can complement efforts to attract more industry under the Inter-regional Productive Sector Operational Programmes. More generally, the investment under the BMW Regional Operational Programmes will assist the achievement of the overall objectives for the Region in relation to the indigenous sector, rural development and the promotion of social inclusion.

7.6   The Regional Operational Programme is broken down into three sub-programmes, namely, Local Infrastructure, Productive Investment and Social Inclusion. The following is an outline of these sub-programmes. As with the other Operational Programmes, fuller details will be given in the separate Operational Programme for the Region to be produced later this year.

Local Infrastructure Sub-Programme

7.7   This sub-programme will consist of measures in respect of Non-national Roads, Rural Water, Waste Management, Urban and Village Renewal, E-Commerce, Seaports, Regional Airports, and Culture, Recreation and Sports. Expenditure within the Region on each of these measures is shown in Table 7.3 below:

Table 7.3:   Local Infrastructure Sub-programme Measures Expenditure 2000-2006

Measures	€ million
Non National Roads	891.4
Rural Water	373.3
Waste Management	304.7
Urban and Village Renewal	39.4
E-Commerce	106.7
Seaports	12.7
Regional Airports	10.1
Culture, Recreation and Sports	198.1
Total	**1,936.4**

7.8   Non-National Roads Measure: This Measure will involve expenditure additional to the £1,746 million (€2,217 million)to be invested in National Roads in the BMW Region over the period of the Plan under the Economic and Social Infrastructure Operational Programme. This latter investment will significantly improve the quality of National primary and secondary roads in the Region.

7.9   Total planned expenditure on Non-National Roads under the BMW Regional Operational Programmes is as follows:

Table 7.4:   Expenditure on Non-National Roads 2000-2006

BMW Region	€ million
Non-National Roads Restoration and Improvement	679.3
Non-National Roads Maintenance	212.1
Total	**891.4**

7.10 Non-national roads account for 94% of the total national road network and carry over 62% of total road traffic. The BMW Region accounts for 40,516 kms of the 90,303 kms of non-national roads in the country or 45% of the non-national road network. Given the predominantly rural character of the BMW Region, non-national roads play a very important role in its economic and social life. These roads are the means by which communities living outside the larger urban centres can access these centres, which are often key employment centres for them. They are also crucial to the efforts of such communities, especially smaller towns, to diversify their economic bases by attracting new enterprises in industry and services. As was emphasised in the White Paper on Rural Development, ready and easy access to Gateways and to arterial roads and, thus, to domestic and international markets, is vital if such diversification is to be achieved. Furthermore, because of the importance of agriculture, tourism, aquaculture and fisheries (commercial and recreational) as sources of income and employment in the BMW Region, a good non-national road network has an essential role to play in rural development in the Region.

7.11 Since 1995 a concerted effort has been made to improve the quality of non-national roads in the region under the Roads Restoration Programme and a sum of £198 million (€251.4 million) has been invested by the Exchequer in the resurfacing and reconstruction of such roads. By end 1999 it is expected that the amount of the network requiring reconstruction will be reduced to 26% and the amount requiring resurfacing will be reduced to 7.6% of the non-national road network in the Region. During the period of the Plan, this remaining work will be completed.

7.12 In recognition of the key importance of non-national roads in the Region, a sum of £535 million (€679.3 million) or 46% of the overall allocation for the State is being allocated to this Region in the NDP for the improvement of non-national roads. This amount will be supplemented by an amount of £167 million (€212.1 million) for the maintenance of this road network representing 42% of the overall national allocation. The key objectives of this expenditure will be:

- to complete the present Restoration Programme for non-national roads by 2005;

- to assist all road authorities in the Region to further improve the non-national road network in a manner that supports the economic and social development of the Region.

7.13 Rural Water Measure: Total planned expenditure on this Measure is £294 million (€373.3 million).

7.14 A particular problem in the BMW Region is the poor quality of drinking water. In the Region, only about 50% of the households are connected to the public mains. The remaining households are served either by group water schemes or individual wells. The highest density of private group schemes (63%) lies in the BMW Region. These schemes pose the greatest problems in terms of water quality — the Environmental Protection Agency's 1997 Report on drinking water quality showed that about 40% of supplies in the Region provide poor water quality and are in breach of the standards set in the EU Drinking Water Directive. Better quality water is required, not alone for public health and quality of life reasons, but also to strengthen the infrastructural base of the areas concerned. The priority attached to improving the quality of rural water supply as a matter of urgency is reflected in the provision for the BMW Region of £294 million (€373.3 million) which is 70% of the overall national provision for Rural Water.

7.15 Waste Management Measure: Total planned expenditure on this Measure is £240 million (€304.7 million).

7.16 The General policy framework for this area is set out at Paragraphs 4.61 to 4.63 of Chapter 4. Appropriate waste management infrastructure is vital not only for environmental protection reasons, but also for industrial development reasons, where lack of appropriate facilities can hamper development. Recent economic growth has placed a significant strain on existing waste management infrastructure. The development of an integrated waste management strategy which utilises a range of waste treatment options, including waste reduction, recycling and recovery, is essential if Ireland's current over reliance on landfill is to be alleviated and appropriate waste management facilities are to be put in place. This is a problem which faces both the BMW and the S&E Region although the scale is somewhat greater in the S&E Region due to population size and density.

7.17 A comprehensive waste management planning exercise is now underway at local/regional level, which will, inter alia, identify infrastructural and investment requirements necessary to give effect to give effect to policy in this area.

7.18 Urban and Village Renewal Measure: Total planned expenditure on this Measure is £31 million (€39.4 million).

7.19 Expenditure under this measure will complement investment under the Inter-regional Economic and Social Infrastructure Operational Programme especially in the areas of Social Housing and Environmental Services.

7.20 The quality of the urban and rural village landscape can contribute significantly to increasing the attractiveness of these locations as places to live and work and can, in general, very much enhance the quality of life. Consequently, improving the fabric of the built environment can advance social and economic development. Moreover, a high quality built environment, particularly where it encompasses elements of Irish architecture and heritage, can support the development of tourism.

7.21 With the exception of the city of Galway and a small number of other significant urban centres and medium-sized towns, the settlement pattern of the BMW Region is essentially one of small towns and villages. The Urban and Village Renewal measure in the Region will improve the visual amenity of towns and villages, thereby complementing other efforts to make the Region a more pleasant place in which to work and live. In appropriate areas, it will complement the Town Renewal Scheme, and, along with supporting the implementation of Integrated Area Plans in Galway City, will assist other towns in their endeavours to promote urban renewal with a specific emphasis on the most disadvantaged areas. It will also promote the conservation of the architectural heritage.

7.22 Investment in urban and village renewal will be implemented by the appropriate Local Authorities. Each Local Authority will be required, with the involvement of local communities, to draw up a framework action plan to be undertaken during the currency of the National Development Plan and these will form the basis of the more detailed plans to be drawn up for the specific projects to be funded each year. Projects will have to be designed to a high level, promote environmentally-sustainable development and, where possible, provide innovative solutions to urban and village renewal.

7.23 E-Commerce Measure: Planned expenditure on E-Commerce is £84 million (€106.7 million).

7.24   The general policy framework for this area is set out at Paragraphs 4.70 to 4.74 of Chapter 4. Available access to advanced information and communications infrastructure means that physical location no longer needs to be a determining factor in relation to access to work and employment. Investment in this infrastructure can, therefore, yield major benefits for the BMW region, in particular, for the more remote areas and rural communities in the Region. Moreover, it opens up significant opportunities for decentralisation. However, the corollary of this is that a failure to invest in such communications in the BMW Region will put the Region at risk of falling further behind the S&E Region in terms of socio-economic development and an increasing divergence in the quality of life between the two regions as more public services become available via the Internet and other forms of electronic communication. Reflecting the importance of high quality communications networks to future economic development and the need for public investment to stimulate greater private sector participation, particularly in the BMW Region, 70% of the national allocation under this measure will be expended in the Region.

7.25   Funding under this Measure will be utilised to leverage and accelerate private sector investment in competitive advanced information and communication infrastructure and services which will enhance the potential for the development of e-commerce facilities and to enable the provision of public services electronically including education, virtual libraries and welfare and health services.

7.26   Seaports Measure: Planned expenditure on this Measure to support the ongoing development of ports is £10 million (€12.7 million).

7.27   As Ireland's main markets are the UK and continental Europe, the geographic and commercial imperatives have dictated that the country's main ports are located in the S&E Region. While there are 7 regional ports in the BMW Region, the main ones being Galway, Greenore, Dundalk and Drogheda, the total combined cargo throughput in 1998 for these ports amounted to only 5% of the national total. However, all of these ports play a critical role in the local and regional economies, supporting local industry and providing a sustainable transport mode for imports and exports.

7.28   Regional Airports Measure: Total planned expenditure on this Measure is £8 million (€10.2 million).

7.29   Ease of access to scheduled air services can play a significant role in attracting foreign direct investment to a particular locality. The major airline traffic into and out of Ireland goes through the national airports of Dublin, Cork and Shannon. It is vital, therefore, that the transport links, especially road links to these airports, are improved and this will be a focus of investment under the Economic and Social Infrastructure Operational Programme.

7.30   Regional airports play a role in improving access to more remote areas of the country particularly for business interests and tourists. Within the BMW Region, the contribution of the four regional airports (Donegal, Galway, Knock and Sligo) to improving tourism and business access to the Region can be enhanced by upgrading of the existing infrastructure.

7.31   Culture, Recreation and Sports Measure: Total planned expenditure on this Measure is £156 million (€198.1 million).

7.32 The quality of the cultural, social and recreational infrastructure has a significant role to play in enhancing the attractiveness of a Region, as a place to live, visit, work or establish an enterprise. Thus, the provision of high quality cultural, recreational and sports facilities will be an important element in the drive to strengthen population structure and promote development throughout the BMW Region.

7.33 In prosperous and populous communities, many sporting and recreational facilities will be supplied by the market or by the communities themselves through voluntary efforts. However, in many areas of the BMW Region, this is not possible. Consequently, public sector involvement will be necessary to assist in the provision of such facilities.

7.34 In the areas of cultural, heritage and parks facilities, an extensive range of infrastructure has been put in place over a number of years and these facilities now offer increased opportunities for leisure and recreational activity. They also deliver significant benefits in terms of providing major tourism attractions within their localities. This infrastructure will be developed and expanded over the period of the Plan. In relation to heritage site investment nationally, there will be a greater focus on the BMW Region. In addition, resources will be provided to support the development of the inland waterways as a major recreational resource and the development of angling facilities in the Region.

7.35 Funding under the Measure will be available to:

- assist local authorities in the provision of multi-purpose sport and recreational facilities; particularly in areas which lack them, and to up-grade existing facilities;

- encourage voluntary groups to provide multi-sport and recreation facilities where no such facilities currently exist. (Local authorities and the Irish Sport Council will be involved to ensure that such facilities are community-focused and part of a local integrated plan);

- facilitate further development of the arts and cultural infrastructure though the provision of grant aid for new regional/city/county projects, redevelopment of existing facilities and support for community projects so as to improve access and encourage greater participation in the Arts;

- consolidate the heritage site infrastructure by improving facilities, access and information and encouraging cross-thematic linkages with other heritage and cultural attractions so as to enhance their capacity as both recreational and tourism attractions;

- improve accessibility to and to augment the facilities available within the national parks and nature reserves while conserving the natural environment;

- further develop the Shannon navigation and the Shannon/Erne waterway by improving facilities at existing locations and adding new destinations to cater for increased usage of the system;

- continue to restore, improve and develop the canals to attract new visitors and provide a catalyst for regeneration in less developed areas;

- provide for improvements in recreational angling facilities including stock and habitat improvements.

Productive Investment Sub-Programme

7.36 This sub-Programme will consist of measures in the areas of Tourism, Micro-enterprises, Rural Development, Forestry and Fisheries, Acquaculture and Harbours, as shown in Table 7.5 below.

Table 7.5:   Productive Investment Sub-programme Measures Expenditure 2000-2006

Measures	€ million
Tourism	74.9
Micro-enterprises	68.3
Rural Development	119.4
Forestry	60.9
Fisheries, Harbours and Aquaculture Development and Gaeltacht/Islands	105.5
Total	**429.0**

7.37   Tourism: Total planned expenditure on Tourism is £59 million (€74.9 million).

7.38   Tourism has the potential to deliver significant benefits to the BMW Region as a whole. In particular, it offers opportunities for off-farm income in coastal and rural areas. While areas such as Galway City, Connemara and parts of Donegal benefit significantly from tourism, other areas of the Region have yet fully to realise the potential of their scenic attractions and relatively unspoilt environment. The upper-Shannon basin, though increasingly popular, is still in a developing mode. Areas such as East-Connaught and the Midlands and Border counties are still essentially in the undeveloped category. Moreover, much of the North-West of the Region has considerable untapped tourism potential. The underdevelopment of the Region's tourism potential is evidenced by the fact that:

- about 25% of all tourism activity in Ireland is centred in or around Dublin; and

- of the remaining 75%, a major portion of it is centred in the S&E Region which contains many of the country's major tourist attractions.

7.39   The BMW Region currently lacks a sufficient endowment of the necessary infrastructure, particularly well-presented attractors and visitor facilities to attract and retain tourists, which is essential if it is to maximise its potential in this regard. Moreover, much of the available tourism product base is too narrow, being overly dependent on very specific activities such as angling which, while a major contributor to tourism in their respective areas, are insufficiently linked with other attractions and activities to promote more broadly-based and off-season tourism. These deficiencies need to be addressed, not only for the benefit of the Region itself but, also, for the country for a whole.

7.40   The BMW Region is particularly suited to special-interest holidays involving a combination of outdoor pursuits including cycling, walking, angling and marine and water sports which are a particular niche target market for the tourism industry in Ireland generally. A broadening of the product base combining special-interest activities and clustering of visitor attractions has the potential to generate greater revenue from the available resources and to attract further investment. There is also potential to develop facilities for conferences and short-stay breaks which have had a major impact on extending the length of the tourism season in the S&E Region.

7.41   Given the appropriate presentation and promotion of its lack of congestion, remoteness and dramatic scenery, the Region presents significant opportunities for development as a tourist destination. Exploiting this potential will not only benefit the Region directly, but it will also help alleviate increasing congestion at the more popular tourist attractions. Moreover, increasing the volume of tourists and spreading them more widely across the country, will help retain the integrity and quality of the product which Ireland offers as a tourist destination.

7.42 Against this background, a sum of £45 million (€57.1 million) will be expended in the Region on the following measures:

- developing major tourist attractions and clusters of attractions and facilities (in cooperation with Local Authorities, the Regional Tourism Authorities and other agencies, support will be provided for suitable proposals to build up tourism attractions);

- developing special-interest products (the aim will be to increase the Region's share of the expanding niche market by providing assistance for walking routes, cycling routes, riding trails, facilities for people with disabilities, health tourism and tourist information offices);

- continuing support for tourism and the environment (the overall objective is to tackle those problems which threaten the sustainablility of tourism, including litter control, congestion, traffic/visitor management and visitor flows to the islands).

7.43 Measures 1 and 2 will be directed at the underdeveloped areas of the Region including the midlands, west and north-west of the Region while Measure 3 will be directed at the more developed areas. The more developed areas will also gain from a share in the national benefits of destination marketing provided for under the Productive Sector Operational Programmes in the Plan. Moreover, the investment in roads and transport infrastructure under both the Inter-regional and the Regional Operational Programmes will significantly improve access to the more remote areas of the BMW Region which has, to date, been a key constraint on their tourism development.

7.44 Outside of these general measures, there will be a specific focus on the water-based tourism and leisure sector so as to bring development of the sector from its current embryonic state into line with the rest of the tourism and leisure sector. Access infrastructure and integrated product development have been identified as requiring a particular investment effort. Within the total allocation for Tourism in the BMW Regional Operational Programmes, an amount of £14 million (€17.8 million) has been set aside for access infrastructure for marine and water based tourism facilities and £10 million (€12.7 million) for ongoing development of angling and related tourism.

7.45 **Micro-enterprises Measure:** Total planned expenditure on Micro-enterprises is £54 million (€68.3 million).

7.46 The thirty-five City and County Enterprise Boards, which cover the entire country, are responsible for the promotion of local development, principally through the provision of a comprehensive range of business supports, comprising advice, financial assistance and management training, to micro-enterprises (10 employees or less). The Boards provide a pivotal role in assisting start-up business and the development of micro-enterprise to bring them to the stage where they have sufficient mass to access and avail of the services of Enterprise Ireland. The Boards are also engaged in the fostering of an enterprise culture, entailing the formulation of enterprise plans for their areas and the inculcation of a spirit of enterprise in second-level schools and colleges by means of participative project development modules. The Boards assisted the creation of 15,500 jobs in manufacturing, tourism and local services in the period 1994 to 1998.

7.47 Much of the BMW Region is outside of the locations which primarily benefit from FDI. The Region is comprised of areas which do not have a sufficient local market or the necessary access to larger markets to support larger-scale businesses. Moreover, many micro-enterprises in the Region are disadvantaged due to over reliance on traditional but declining industry. There is also a lack of awareness of the opportunities associated with new digital technology and electronic communications which can contribute extensively to the socio-economic development of remote areas. As such, the Micro-enterprise Measure is particularly relevant to the BMW Region where enterprise tends to be on a smaller scale and where there is a requirement for support for the development of local services. The local base of the County Enterprise Boards, who will be responsible for the delivery of this Measure, also means that the projects supported tend to be more appropriate and relevant to their social and economic environment which is a key consideration in the drive for sustainable economic development in the Region.

7.48 The Boards will continue to support the development of micro-enterprise and entrepreneurship over the period of the Plan although there will be some changes in structure and in the nature of support provided:

- In pursuance of the Government's Policy on the Integration of Local Government and Local Development, the Boards' activities will be more closely aligned with the Local Authorities whereby the Chief Executive of each Board will be appointed by the Local Authority, which will also ratify nominations of the Directors. Moreover, to provide a single focus for small business, the local support and development function for small business will be centralised in the Enterprise Boards whose plans will be consistent with, and form an integral part of, the broader social and economic development plans which will be prepared by the proposed City/County Development Boards;

- There will be a progressive shift from the current measures of providing direct financial assistance to the softer forms of support such as advice, mentoring and management development and increasing recourse will be had by the Boards to refundable assistance (repayable grants/equity);

- Specially tailored packages will be designed to extend an enterprise culture to first level schools and to support the participation of women in business.

7.49 Within the BMW Region specifically, there will be a particular emphasis on the promoting the benefits of e-commerce and communications technology (see Paragraphs 7.23 to 7.25 above). This will enhance competitiveness and help provide good and enduring employment, particularly in fast-growing micro-enterprises for which direct financial assistance will continue to be available.

7.50 Rural Development Measure: Reflecting the particular priority problems facing the BMW Region in this area, the total planned expenditure on this Measure is £94 million (€119.4 million).

7.51 The White Paper on Rural Development which was published in mid-1999 set out the approach which the Government proposes to adopt in support of rural development. Chapter 11 sets out in detail the Rural Development Strategy in the National Development Plan.

7.52 Rural Development has particular relevance for the BMW Region because of the nature of the population spread and the prominence of the agricultural sector. More than half of the farms in the country are located within the Region and virtually all of its land is classified as either 'most severely handicapped' or 'less severely handicapped'. The result is a weak farm structure which, combined with continuing poor market conditions for agricultural products, has meant that many rural communities in the BMW Region have not shared fully in the recent success of the economy.

Many farmers in the Region are faced with viability difficulties and, of necessity, are turning to off-farm employment as an additional source of income.

7.53 Substantial assistance for rural areas in the BMW Region will be delivered via the CAP Rural Development Programme viz REPS, Early Retirement and Compensatory Allowances. Moreover, training across all areas which is the key to improving the employability of people and the social and economic development of rural communities is covered under the Employment and Human Resources Development Operational Programme. The specific Rural Development Measure under the Regional Operational Programme will address the objectives of the BMW Region in the following ways:

- Investment by the Western Investment Fund operated by the Western Development Commission in certain designated areas;

- provision of support for policy research, rural services, and rural development programmes including rural tourism;

- support for diversification and the development of non-surplus products in the horticulture, potatoes and organic sectors along with alternative enterprises such as equine production.

7.54 The investment in rural tourism and in community development under the Rural Development Measure will dovetail with investment in related areas so as to maximise the overall benefits to rural communities.

7.55 **Forestry Measure:** Reflecting the major potential of forestry in the BMW Region, the total planned expenditure on this Measure is £48 million (€61 million) out of an overall national provision of £80 million (€101.6 million).

7.56 Substantially more investment — £375 million (€476.2 million) on forestry in the Region will be undertaken under the CAP Rural Development Programme (see Chapter 11).

7.57 Forestry has a particular relevance to the BMW Region because it provides significant opportunities for the economic development of marginal land in less-populated locations and for the generation of non-farm sources of income. Forests also provide a valuable recreational facility for local communities and contribute to the tourism infrastructure. About 50% of the State's total forest area lies in the BMW Region and it is planned to raise this percentage over the period of the Plan.

7.58 The focus for the sub-programme in the Region will be on the following areas:

- forest roads (forest owners will be assisted in improving access for plantation development, maintenance, fire protection, and efficient timber extraction);

- harvesting (investment in cost-efficient harvesting equipment will be encouraged; forestry contracting companies will be targeted);

- reconstruction (assistance will be given to forest owners for the re-establishment of plantations damaged by fire, wind blow, disease or other natural causes);

- education/awareness/publicity (its is intended that this measure will encourage public awareness of and greater involvement in the overall afforestation effort and related activities);

- downstream development supports (investment in this area will comprehend aid to associations, studies and pilot projects, nurseries, forest inventory and the promotion of wood-based Irish furniture);

- woodland improvement (assistance will be given to encourage the improvement of neglected or low quality broadleaf and coniferous woodland; it is also intended to complement economic and social development through the provision of urban or amenity woodland).

7.59 Fishery Harbours, Aquaculture Development & Gaeltacht/Islands Measure: Planned expenditure on this Measure is £83 million (€105.5 million) under the BMW Regional Operational Programme is as follows:

Table 7.6: **Expenditure on Fishery Harbours, Aquaculture Development & Gaeltacht/Islands Measures 2000-2006**

Measures	€ million
Fishery Harbours	38.1
Aquaculture Development	20.3
Gaeltacht/Islands	47.1
Total	**105.5**

7.60 The fishing and aquaculture sector is a key source of income in the BMW Region. The Region has many small coastal and island communities where there are few other employment opportunities because of geographic and economic factors, such as, distance from the major centres of economic activity, sparse population and poor agricultural land and structures. These remote communities are unlikely to benefit significantly from the spin-off effects of growth in the larger urban centres, are incapable of sustaining a farming livelihood and find it difficult to attract sustainable manufacturing or service industry.

7.61 If the economic well-being of such communities is to be protected and improved, there is a need to develop existing fishery harbour infrastructure and aquaculture activities in these areas beyond primary production and establish facilities for the production of higher value fish products. With an increased raw material supply base, a vibrant on-shore sector can be developed with primary processing units clustered around fishery harbours and secondary consumer seafood processing facilities located in those rural towns and communities of greatest economic need. The ongoing development of the seafood industry will benefit from investment in the road network, in that it will facilitate quicker access for producers to the industry's major markets both nationally and internationally. The development of coastal and island harbour facilities will also help alleviate some of the isolation felt in island communities by enhancing the quality of the transport infrastructure and improving access for such communities to available employment, social and education opportunities. In addition, an improved coastal harbour infrastructure will provide opportunities for the development of marine-related tourism and other activities.

7.62 Ongoing support for the acquaculture industry is vital to building on the momentum achieved between 1994 and 1999 in maintaining and enhancing aquaculture production in the West and North-West. Continued investment will aid the competitiveness of the industry in domestic and international markets by achieving critical mass in production to yield scale economies. This will contribute to the economic regeneration and development of rural communities.

7.63 The potential of the seafood industry, particularly in the balanced development of the BMW Region, has yet to be fully realised. This measure will provide £83.1 million (€105.5 million) for the following initiatives to:

- tackle infrastructure deficiencies in the major harbours in the Region and in the smaller harbours and piers dotted throughout the Region which support aquaculture, in-shore fishing and related recreational and tourism activity. Particular priority will be given to the development of berthage facilities and ancillary infrastructure at strategic ports including Killybegs, Rossaveal, Greencastle and Burtonport;

- provide related on-shore facilities (e.g. ice plants, processing facilities auction halls and gear storage facilities) to ensure prompt, efficient and hygienic handling, storage and sale of catch and to support value added economic activity right through the supply chain;

- support the ongoing development and enlargement of the aquaculture industry in particular intensive and extensive production, diversification into new species, infrastructure and technological development and environmental sustainability;

- provide appropriate infrastructure so as to enable island communities gain access to the mainland for social employment and education purposes and to support island tourism.

Social Inclusion Sub-Programme

7.64 This Sub-programme will consist of measures in the areas of Childcare, Equality, Community Development and Family Support, Crime Prevention, Youth Services and Services to the Unemployed. Total planned expenditure within the Region under the sub-programme will amount to £220.7 million (€280.2 million) over the period of the Plan.

Table 7.7:   Social Inclusion Sub-programme Measures Expenditure 2000-2006

Measures	€ million
Childcare	87.6
Equality	7.8
Community Development/Family Support	61.4
Crime Prevention	27.2
Youth Services	57.1
Services to the Unemployed	39.0
Total	**280.1**

7.65 The Plan strategy for achieving greater social inclusion, which is a key objective of the NDP, is set out in Chapter 10 which also outlines the various contributions, direct and indirect, which the Interregional and Regional Operational Programmes will make towards this end. The focus and thrust of the Social Inclusion Sub-programme in the Regional Operational Programmes will be determined by the nature and extent of the problem of social exclusion as it manifests itself in the respective regions.

7.66 Poverty and disadvantage is a nationwide problem which is not spatially delimited within any particular type of area, whether it be rural areas, villages, towns or cities. However, there are areas of extreme deprivation in the BMW Region which suffer from the effects of cumulative disadvantage. Significant pockets of deprivation can be found in the larger urban centres especially in Galway, Dundalk and Drogheda. Moreover, areas of rural disadvantage, characterised by sustained outward migration, educational disadvantage and a lack of employment opportunities, are also heavily concentrated in the Region. These are principally located in the Donegal Gaeltacht, the Connemara Gaeltacht, Mayo and Inishowen.

7.67 The problem of rural deprivation in the Region is exemplified by the low incomes in rural areas and the difficulties people living there have in accessing education, health and social services. In education, the educational attainments of all age cohorts are lower than their counterparts in the S&E Region — in particular, 36% of the population have only a primary-level qualification compared to 27% in the S&E Region. As regards health and social services, the Health Boards in the region have high dependency ratios and physical difficulties in providing these services as a result of low population density, remote communities and difficult terrain with poor access infrastructure.

7.68 The measures in the Inter-regional operational programme and in the other sub-programmes of this operational programme will help to alleviate social disadvantage in the Region by improving access to services, education, training and employment, and supporting economic activity in remote communities. Measures in respect of Forestry, Fisheries and Rural Development are particularly relevant to the BMW Region and this is reflected in the intensity of investment in these measures in the BMW Regional Operational Programmes. These measures will contribute to the alleviation of poverty and disadvantage within the Region by providing opportunities for employment and additional income for people living in the more remote rural and coastal communities, particularly those engaged in subsistance farming. Investment in transport infrastructure, in particular, non-national roads and the harbour infrastructure, will facilitate access for rural, coastal and island communities to a wider range of education, training and employment opportunities in the larger towns and urban centres within the Region. It will also open up the Region, to a much greater degree, for tourism and micro-enterprise development and provide increased opportunities for social and recreational interaction for those living in isolated areas.

7.69 While rural poverty is a key concern for the BMW Region, there are also areas of deprivation in the larger urban centres and towns. People living in these areas suffer from the same problems as those living in disadvantaged city-centre areas within the S&E Region, in that, they are more likely to suffer from low levels of self-esteem, early school leaving/youth unemployment, poor family support, substance abuse and high levels of crime. Moreover, the communities in which these people live do not generally have the type of community or social support structures which tend to be characteristic of rural communities.

7.70 In view of the geographic spread and disparate nature of the groups that suffer from social deprivation in the BMW Region, there is a clear need for a series of specific measures aimed at targeted groups so as to facilitate their participation in the prosperity which the Plan will generate. Consequently, there will be a focus within the Social Inclusion Sub-programme in the BMW Region on alleviating social exclusion in the larger urban areas and towns where cohesive targeted programmes can have their greatest effect.

7.71 In the implementation of the measures under this sub-programme in the BMW Region, there will be a particular focus on the following:

- Childcare, Equality and Community Development/Family Support, to facilitate participation in education, training and employment opportunities, to promote equality and to support parents, particularly women in combining work and family responsibilities;

- Youth Services to support the personal and social development of young people living in disadvantaged areas in urban and rural areas who are at risk;

- Services for the Unemployed, in particular, outreach services to support those who may never have worked and lack the capacity to access available education, training and employment opportunities, and support for those wishing to start up in self-employment in both urban and rural areas.

7.72 A Senior Officials Inter-Departmental Working Group on the Implementation of Social Inclusion Measures in the NDP is currently examining how greater co-ordination in the delivery of these measures can be achieved at local level. The recommendations of the working group in relation to an integrated approach will be reflected in the detailed arrangements to be set out in the Operational Programmes. In this regard, it is envisaged that the County and City Development Boards (CDBs), which are to be set up by 1 January, 2000, will have a key role to play in co-ordinating local delivery of social inclusion measures.

Impact on Equality

7.73 All measures under the BMW Regional Operational Programme aim to optimise the spread of socio-economic development throughout the Region irrespective of gender. However, there are measures under the BMW Regional Operational Programme which will be particularly beneficial to women. Under the Social Inclusion Sub-Programme investment for the provision of improved and more diverse childcare facilities will enable more single parents, particularly women to enter or re-enter the workforce and take up second chance education/training opportunities. Moreover, there are a range of measures which aim to address ineqality among other marginalised groups including, prisoners and drug-users. The training and education initiatives will be particualrly targeted at the long-term unemployed and people living in disadvantaged communities which include travellers and people with disabilities.

7.74 There is also a specific measure on gender equality with the objective of promoting greater sharing of family responsibilities, gender proofing of personnel practices, upskilling of women and facilitating entepreneurship and career development among women. Improvements in the socio-economic performance of the Region will increase the demand for labour creating additional opportunities for those seeking to enter or re-enter the workforce, many of whom are women. Improvements in the telecommunications network and support for e-commerce will allow for the introduction of more flexible work practices which can facilitate the combining of family and work commitments.

Impact on Poverty

7.75 The targeted social inclusion measures under the BMW Regional Operational Programme will play a key role in alleviating poverty and promoting social inclusion. Supports for the provision of early intervention services for disadvantaged youth, for the development of childcare facilities enabling more women to re-enter the labour force, and for the training and education of prisoners are designed to enhance the employability of the most marginalised and disadvantaged in society. Funding will also be provided for various community development and family services initiatives which will enable those living in disadvantaged areas to participate in local development, training and education projects and enterprise and employment opportunities.

Impact on the Environment

7.76 Sustainable development and environmental preservation is of great importance to the BMW Region. A generally unspoilt natural environment is one of the Region's greatest assets particularly in relation to tourism. The tourism measures under the BMW Regional Operational Programme will tackle threats to the environment which also undermine the sustainability of tourism such as litter, congestion, traffic/visitor management and visitor flows to the islands.

7.77 Some 40% of water supplies in the Region provide poor water quality and are in breach of the standards set in the EU Drinking Water Directive. Investment in local infrastructure such as rural water will, therefore, have a positive effect on the environment, as will the Urban and Village Renewal Measure. The development of the forestry industry under the BMW Regional Operational Programme will also have beneficial environmental effects by improving the visual environment at local level and helping Ireland achieve its CO_2 targets under the Kyoto protocol.

Rural Impact

7.78 The Rural Development Measure in the BMW Regional Operational Programme will provide support for the development of rural services, rural enterprise and the development of non-surplus agricutural products. The provision of high quality recreational facilities in rural areas under the Culture, Recreation and Sports Measure will make these areas more attractive as places to live and work. The Small Towns Renewal Scheme under the Village and Urban Renewal Measure will have a complementary effect by augmenting the aesthetic qualities of rural towns and villages. Development of the forestry industry under the BMW Regional Operational Programme will provide alternative opportunities for economic development in rural areas characterised by marginal land. Similarly, increased support for major fishery harbours as well as smaller landing places and the development of the aquaculture industry, which is an important source of income in the BMW Region, will aid remote coastal and island communities with few alternative sources of income. Investment in raising water quality under the Rural Water Measure will improve the quality of life and the health of people living in such areas. Improvements in the standard of non-national roads, as provided for under the BMW Regional Operational Programme will also have a positive effect on the rural economy and dispersed rural communities by making rural towns and villages more accessible, for social and economic purposes, thus facilitating more balanced distribution of economic activity throughout the Region.

8 Southern and Eastern Regional Operational Programme

Introduction

8.1 Expenditure under the Southern and Eastern (S&E) Regional Operational Programme will be as follows:

Table 8.1:   Expenditure 2000-2006

Sub-programmes	S&E Region € million
Local Infrastructure	2,302
Productive Investment	427
Social Inclusion	1,063
Total Expenditure	**3,792**
Expenditure per Capita €	**1,425**

Overview of the S&E Region

8.2 The S&E Region is generally characterised by:

- a relatively well-qualified and skilled workforce;

- extensive training and educational facilities, in particular a strong network of third-level institutions;

- a strong base of industry and services, yielding high per capita Gross Value Added (GVA);

- generally good agricultural land and a relatively strong agri-food sector;

- a strong and vibrant urban network, parts of which have achieved, or are close to reaching, a critical mass in terms of self-generating economic activity; and

- a relatively well-developed infrastructure, including inter-urban transport systems and access to import/export gateways.

8.3 These positive elements are accompanied, however, by significant pockets of social exclusion and deprivation in all urban centres and in remote rural areas. There are also major problems regarding congestion and capacity constraints arising from an overstretched infrastructure. Moreover, there are other parts of the Region which lag behind in terms of infrastructure and industry/services base.

Objectives for the S&E Region

8.4 As outlined in Chapter 3, the primary objectives for the S&E Region over the term of the Plan are as follows:

- consolidate and build on its recent economic performance;

- further develop counter-balances to Dublin;

- address urban congestion and bottlenecks to growth through targeted investment in infrastructure and human capital;

- facilitate more balanced economic growth across the Region;

- support the further development of agriculture and agri-business, tourism and fisheries and aquaculture development;

- promote social inclusion in deprived urban and rural areas; and

- maintain a viable rural economy.

Impact of Inter-Regional Operational Programmes

8.5 Many of these objectives will be realised primarily through investment via the Inter-regional Operational Programmes, the key elements of which are set out in earlier chapters of the Plan. In particular, the Region will benefit from the following:

- Investment in national roads, public transport and environmental services;

- Targeted and sub-regionally differentiated assistance for the productive sector;

- Implementation of a multi-faceted approach in education, training and skills with a particular focus on the ongoing employability of individuals and on areas lagging behind in terms of sustainable development.

Table 8.2: Inter-regional Operational Programmes Expenditure 2000-2006 — S&E Region

Inter-regional Operational Programmes	€ million
Economic and Social Infrastructure	16,402.5
Productive Sector	3,630.2
Employment and Human Resources	8,961.1
CAP Rural Development	1,848.7
Total	**30,842.5**
Expenditure per Capita €	**11,591.3**

Operational Programme for S&E Region

8.6 The S&E Regional Operational Programme will reinforce and complement the impact of the Inter-regional Operational Programmes through the following Sub-programmes:

- Local infrastructure measures, notably non-national roads, rural water supply, local harbours and fishing ports and cultural, sports and recreation facilities;

- Development of local enterprise, tourism and indigenous sectors (agriculture, forestry, fisheries and aquaculture); and

- A comprehensive series of social inclusion measures to address disadvantage, deprivation and exclusion.

In line with the other Operational Programmes in the Plan, the Operational Programmes for the S&E Region will be fully elaborated at a later date.

164

Local Infrastructure Sub-Programme

8.7 This sub-programme will comprise Measures in respect of Non-national Roads, Rural Water, Waste Management, Urban and Village Renewal, E-Commerce, Seaports, Regional Airports, and Culture, Recreation and Sports.

Table 8.3:   Local Infrastructure Sub-programme Measures Expenditure 2000-2006

Measures	€ million
Non National Roads	1,140.2
Rural Water	160
Waste Management	520.6
Urban and Village Renewal	91.4
E-Commerce	45.7
Seaports	45.7
Regional Airports	3.8
Culture, Recreation and Sports	294.6
Total	**2,302**

8.8   Non-National Roads Measure: Total planned expenditure on this Measure is £898 million (€ 1,140.2 million) as follows:

Table 8.4:   Non-National Roads Expenditure 2000-2006

S&E Region	€ million
Non-National Roads Restoration and upgrading	844.4
Non-National Roads Maintenance	295.9
Total	**1,140.3**

This provision of almost £900 million (€1,140 million) is additional to the £2,944 million (€3,738 million) which is to be invested in National Roads in the Region under the Economic and Social Infrastructure Inter-regional Operational Programme.

8.9   Non-national roads account for 94% of the total national road network and carry over 62% of total road traffic. The S&E Region accounts for 49,787 kms of the 90,303 kms of non-national roads in the State or 55% of the Non-national road network. These roads serve as an indispensable complement to National roads, affording access to the larger urban centres and the ports and airports in the region. They are vital to local enterprises, agriculture, forestry and tourism, as well as having a valuable social and community function. Moreover, Non-national roads in urban areas are of crucial importance in terms of the future development of cities and towns in the Region.

8.10   The planned investment in the non-national roads network will significantly improve access from the more remote areas of the Region to the strategic national road network and the ports and airports which link Ireland with the wider European economy. Thus, it will underpin other elements of the Operational Programme, especially tourism, the development of indigenous sectors, rural development and the promotion of social inclusion. In this way, it will make a significant contribution to spreading the benefits of the Plan more widely across the Region as a whole.

8.11 Despite the progress made to date in improving the quality of non-national roads in the S&E Region through the Restoration Programme launched in 1995, it is estimated that, by the end of 1999, almost 25% of the network will still require reconstruction and that up to 17% will require surface restoration. £665 million (€844 million) of the provision for non-national roads in the S&E Region will be devoted to completing by 2005 the Restoration Programme and to improvement measures targeted at those parts of the network which have the greatest potential impact on economic activity and jobs. The balance of about £233 million (€296 million) will be used to provide grant assistance to local authorities in the Region for road maintenance to preserve the investment and work to date on the network.

8.12   Rural Water Measure: Total planned expenditure on this Measure is £126 million (€160 million).

8.13 This allocation will be spent on the following schemes:

• water supply and sewerage services in small towns and villages;

• upgrading quality-deficient group water schemes and installing new group schemes;

• upgrading private individual water supplies to houses where an alternative public or group supply is not available.

8.14 While, compared to the BMW Region, a higher proportion of households in the S&E Region has access to mains water supply and sewage facilities, there are a significant number of individual private schemes in the rural parts of the Region, including those surrounding the main urban centres. For the remoter rural areas in the Region, the same considerations apply about quality of water as in the BMW Region. However, in rural areas close to urban centres, strong economic growth has created additional environmental pressures, particularly as regards ground water supplies, and these need to be addressed. The Rural Water Measure in the S&E Region is designed to respond to these differing requirements.

8.15 The improvement in water quality arising from the proposed investment in rural water will deliver benefits to rural communities within the Region, whether in remote areas or in the vicinity of urban centres. It will improve the quality of life of people living in these areas and allow for increased development and expansion of the resident population while protecting the environment.

8.16   Waste Management Measure: Total planned expenditure on this Measure is £410 million (€520.6 million).

8.17 The overall policy framework for this area is set out at Paragraphs 4.61 to 4.63 of Chapter 4. Appropriate waste management infrastructure is crucial both to the protection of the environment and to future industrial development. Recent levels of economic growth have placed a big strain on existing waste management infrastructure in the S&E Region and significant investment is now required in order both to cope with this pressure and to accommodate future growth. To this end, a comprehensive planning exercise is now underway at local/regional level, inter alia, to identify and quantify these requirements.

8.18   Urban and Village Renewal Measure: Total planned expenditure on this Measure is £72 million (€91.4 million).

8.19   In contrast with the more-sparsely populated BMW Region, the most economically and environmentally blighted areas in the S&E Region are in large urban centres, usually centre-city areas or areas of extensive social housing in deprived suburbs. Although these cities and larger towns are significant employment centres as well as locations for leading-edge enterprises, the more deprived areas do not attract these activities. Consequently, a particular focus of the programme of Urban and Village Renewal in the S&E Region will be to rejuvenate the social and economic fabric of cities and larger towns, in particular the disadvantaged areas within them. In appropriate areas, the Programme will complement the implementation of Integrated Area Plans and the Town Renewal Scheme which will commence operation in 2000. One of the objects of the Measure will be to encourage social and economic development at local level in partnership with local communities. The economic and social renewal of the Dublin Docklands Area in accordance with the Master Plan for the area will also be supported. This Measure will also provide assistance for the conservation of the architectural heritage.

8.20   As in the case of the BMW Region, investment in urban and village renewal will be implemented by the appropriate Local Authorities and the same requirements will apply. In particular, the framework plans prepared by Local Authorities will, inter alia, require that funding is not spread over too many projects and that the projects themselves are designed to a high level, will promote environmentally sustainable development and, where possible, provide innovative solutions to urban and village renewal. Funding will also be conditional on the involvement of local communities.

8.21   The improvement of the built environment in urban areas will enhance their attractiveness as places to live and work and open up economic opportunities to those living there. Public expenditure on urban and village renewal generally will support tourism development, particularly in remote rural areas and will create a foundation for future private sector investment. Moreover, the involvement of local communities in project development will foster local pride and ensure that this Measure meets the particular needs of each community.

8.22   E-Commerce Measure: Total planned expenditure on this Measure is £36 million (€45.7 million).

8.23   The overall policy framework for this area is set out at Paragraphs 4.69 to 4.74 of Chapter 4. Under the current investment plans of the communications companies, parts of the S&E Region will not be served by advanced communication. The absence of such facilities can deprive the communities concerned of the economic advantages which the availability of advanced communications can offer outside investors with resultant adverse effects for balanced regional development. It can also be a hindrance to decentralisation and deter the inward migration of skilled workers and enterprise wishing to relocate from more congested areas. Funding under this Measure will be utilised to leverage and accelerate private sector investment in competitive advanced information and communication infrastructure and services and to enable the electronic provision of public services, including education services, virtual libraries, welfare and health services.

8.24   Seaports Measure: Total planned expenditure on this Measure is £36 million (€45.7 million).

8.25 Given the open nature of the Irish economy and Ireland's peripheral location, the availability of adequate seaport facilities is essential for the transport of Ireland's exports to international markets. All of Ireland's major international ports are located in the S&E Region. There are seven State Port Companies in the Region, namely, Cork, Dublin, Dun Laoghaire, Foynes, New Ross, Shannon Estuary and Waterford, which handle over 90% of national seaborne trade. These Companies will fund their investment costs from their own resources in conformity with their legal obligation to conduct business and investment cost-effectively and efficiently in the interests of the competitiveness of the national economy. In addition, the Region contains another major port, Rosslare, which is managed by Iarnród Éireann, the State transport company.

8.26 Outside of the key strategic ports, there are nine regional ports in the S&E Region which provide a local economic focus, supporting local suppliers and industry. These ports are Arklow, Baltimore and Skibbereen, Bantry Bay, Dingle, Kinsale, Tralee and Fenit, Wicklow, Wexford and Youghal. Investment in these regional ports will be market-driven in terms of response to actual market needs and non-displacement of existing seaborne trade. Consequently, capacity/infrastructural investments will only be undertaken where there is a clear economic rationale and where there are no lower cost alternatives based on existing facilities. Within this framework, the Government proposes to fund the following actions to address the problems of regional seaports:

- *New Infrastructure:* Additional infrastructure will be provided where deficiencies have been forecast;

- *Upgrade Existing Infrastructure:* Projects will be supported to maintain and enhance the existing port infrastructure (e.g. capital dredging works, berth deepening, quay wall construction);

- *Improvement of Capacity Utilisation:* The utilisation of existing assets will be increased through the use of technologies such as port user networks and advanced cargo management systems;

- *Intermodal Connections:* Support for projects linking seaports with road and rail networks so as to enhance port access for local industry.

8.27 The implementation of these measures will address capacity deficiencies in regional ports in the S&E Region which could otherwise inhibit growth and will also maximise the efficient use of existing assets. Planned improvements in the roads network under the NDP will complement the investment proposed by affording better access to ports. The development of ports will also provide opportunities for the development of marine tourism and water-based activities and improve access for coastal and island communities in a manner which will contribute towards a more balanced geographical distribution of economic activity in the region.

8.28 Regional Airports Measure: Total planned expenditure on this Measure is £3 million (€3.8 million).

8.29 The S&E Region is very well served with three international airports, Dublin, Cork and Shannon. Transport, especially road links to these airports, will be a focus of the investment under the Economic and Social Infrastructure Operational Programme. In addition, the two regional airports in the S&E Region, Kerry and Waterford, are strategically placed at opposite ends of the southern part of the region. As such, both have a role in improving tourism and business access. This role will be enhanced by the proposed infrastructural investment under this measure.

8.30   Culture, Recreation and Sports Measure: Total planned expenditure on this Measure is £232 million (€294.6 million).

8.31   As in the case of the BMW Region, the quality of the cultural, social and recreational infrastructure has a significant role to play in the social and economic development of cities, towns, villages and rural areas. In the S&E Region, the basic requirements of many such areas in these respects have been met, often by voluntary effort. However, there are places where the infrastructure is deficient or lacking altogether. In these areas, the public sector will have to take the lead in a targeted way but support will be also be given to voluntary bodies and, where appropriate, the commercial private sector where they take the lead role.

8.32   An amount of over £59 million (€74.9 million) will be expended in the S&E Region under this Measure on the following actions:

- support for the development of multi-purpose sport and recreational facilities by local authorities in association, where appropriate, with private sector partners, utilising, where practicable, existing public facilities including swimming pools, football/hurling pitches, sports halls, golf courses and related ancillary facilities;

- support to voluntary groups towards the development costs of larger multi-sport facilities, as part of a local integrated plan for sport and recreation approved by the local authority and the Irish Sport Council, in areas where no such facilities exist.

8.33   The balance of £173 million (€219.7 million) will be spent on a variety of measures in the areas of culture, sport and recreation. In relation to culture, grant aid will be provided for new infrastructure, refurbishment/redevelopment of existing facilities and community-based projects all of which will improve access to and encourage greater community involvement in cultural activities. As regards recreation facilities, a focus for the S&E Region over the period of the Plan will be to improve facilities and infrastructure in the lower Shannon basin and in the Barrow navigation area, including the canals, to attract and cater for an increasing number of waterway users. Furthermore, in recognition of the role of inland fisheries and sea angling as major recreational activities, funding is being provided to develop the sports and recreation potential of the angling resource.

8.34   In addition, extra funding will be provided for National and Heritage Parks, Nature Reserves and National Monuments to consolidate and conserve the significant heritage infrastructure that is already in place and to extend the range of cultural and recreational facilities available. Particular attention will be given to encouraging linkages between heritage and cultural attractions under the Cultural Development Incentives Scheme and to developing cooperation between the public and private sectors in this context.

Productive Investment Sub-programme

8.35   This sub-programme will comprise measures to promote Tourism, Micro-enterprises, Rural Development, Forestry, and Fishery Harbours, Aquaculture Development and Gaeltacht/ Islands.

Table 8.5: Productive Investment Sub-programme Measures Expenditure 2000-2006

Measures	€ Million
Tourism	95.2
Micro-enterprises	122.1
Rural Development	99
Forestry	40.6
Fishery Harbours, Aquaculture Development & Gaeltacht/Islands	69.7
Total	**426.6**

8.36 Tourism Measure: Total planned expenditure on this Measure is £75 million (€95.2 million).

8.37 Tourism offers particular opportunities for promoting balanced regional development and providing a supplement to part-time agricultural and fishing earnings in many rural and coastal communities. The key difference between the S&E and BMW Regions is that the former is more developed in tourism terms as evidenced by the facts that:

- about 25% of all tourism activity in Ireland is centred in or around Dublin; and

- of the remaining 75%, a major portion of it is centred in the S&E Region which contains many of the country's major tourist attractions.

Thus, the S&E Region is already well placed to benefit from further increases in tourist numbers to Ireland.

8.38 Nevertheless, tourism in the Region has two related challenges to meet. The first is that of developing a better sub-regional spread for the industry in the interests both of alleviating pressure on congested urban areas and major tourism centres and of distributing the benefits more widely. The second is that of lengthening the tourist season and increasing the number of bed nights spent by individual tourists, particularly in areas outside of the main urban centres and the major tourism attractors.

8.39 By facilitating access to less-visited places, the investment in the non-national roads network under the Local Infrastructure Sub-programme will provide part of the response to these challenges. A further part of the response will be to continue to provide an appropriate product base capable of supporting sustainable tourism development through enhancing and/or building up an interesting mix of tourism products, especially in underdeveloped tourist areas. Policy and financial support mechanisms will be designed to facilitate better tourism asset and visitor management, greater spatial development, with a bias towards thematic (e.g. heritage and cultural) programmes rather than individual project-based support.

8.40 Given the number of major attractors within the S&E Region and the resulting throughput of visitors, the more underdeveloped tourist areas are well positioned to benefit from investment in visitor facilities and to deliver significant returns both to local service providers and to the economy generally. In this context, the continuing growth of special-interest tourism, particularly in relation to cycling, trekking and water-based leisure pursuits, has the potential to deliver significant benefits to the communities living in these areas, provided the necessary infrastructure is in place.

8.41 Of the total allocation for the Measure, £65 million (€82.5 million) will be spent on the following three priorities in the S&E Region:

- support for suitable proposals to build up regional "clusters" of attractions and facilities in prioritised developing or undeveloped areas, based on co-ordinated plans agreed with public bodies in these areas, especially Local Authorities and the Regional Tourism Authorities;

- support for some special interest products, in particular, trekking and cycling routes, riding trails, health tourism. In addition, priority will be given to the development of facilities for disabled visitors;

- support for environmental initiatives designed to tackle congestion, traffic/visitor management, visitor flows to islands, innovative litter control, training and awareness, as well as area-based projects integrating tourism and the environment.

The balance of £10 million (€12.7 million) will be devoted to improving marine tourism and tourist-related angling facilities.

8.42 The development of the Tourism Industry by means of the above actions will facilitate spatially balanced economic growth in the S&E Region. It will also help many rural communities by providing employment opportunities and a viable alternative to agriculture as a source of income, thereby promoting rural development and social inclusion. Moreover, the development of special-interest tourist pursuits and a broader range of tourist destinations will result in reduced congestion in the more popular holiday locations while the newly-developed areas will benefit from improved spatial planning and infrastructure.

8.43 Micro-enterprises Measure: Total planned expenditure on this Measure is £96 million (€122.1 million).

8.44 The activities of City and County Enterprise Boards in promoting micro-enterprises are outlined in Paragraphs 7.45 to 7.49 of Chapter 7. As far as the S&E Region is concerned, the rapid growth of its economy and the concentration of larger companies there suggest that the Region has considerable potential internally to generate new micro-enterprises and to spur expansion in existing micro-enterprises. However, if this potential is to be realised, new business skills and enhanced management capabilities will be required. Consequently, funding by City and County Enterprise Boards in the Region will be focused increasingly on internal capacity building and new business and technology skills. A flexible approach will be taken to ensure that good opportunities are exploited. The changes in administration and focus set out in Paragraph 7.48 of Chapter 7 will also apply in the S&E Region.

8.45 Rural Development Measure: Total planned expenditure on this Measure is £78 million (€99 million).

8.46 Whilst the S&E Region as a whole is quite urbanised and has generally good farm structures, it also contains many disadvantaged rural areas, particularly in mountainous and more remote areas where structures are weak, soil poor and incomes low, with few, if any, off-farm employment opportunities. Consequently, rural development is an important element of the S&E Regional Operational Programme which aims to stimulate the rural economy, develop alternative income generating activities and encourage regionally balanced economic growth.

8.47 Chapter 11 deals with the approach to Rural Development to be taken in the Plan. This approach derives primarily from the recent White Paper on Rural Development. As regards the Operational Programme for the S&E Region, the allocation for rural development will be spent as follows:

- provision of support for diversification through the development of non-surplus products horticulture, market gardening, organic farming, and alternative enterprises such as equine breeding;

- provision of support for policy research, rural services and rural development programmes, including rural tourism;

- investment by the Western Investment Fund which will be operated by the Western Development Commission (County Clare only).

8.48 These, together with the broader infrastructural measures proposed throughout the NDP, will strengthen the economic base of fragile rural communities and help to underpin their future survival and prosperity.

8.49 **Forestry Measure:** Total planned expenditure on this Measure is £32 million (€40.6 million).

8.50 The forestry industry can assist in the realisation of more balanced regional development through providing off-farm sources of income and enhancing the recreation and tourism infrastructure. In the S&E Region, the focus will be on the development of forestry as a key regional and national resource. This will involve:

- improving structures in the area of primary productions; and

- the continued development of the primary forestry sector and the development of an efficient and competitive downstream processing sector.

8.51 The funding allocated will finance:

- funding for harvesting, forest roads, woodland improvement, publicity/education and technical assistance, including downstream development supports;

- funding for schemes which seek to maximise the beneficial externalities of the forestry infrastructure, in particular, the development of tourist activities within the forests, and more environmentally friendly forestry development.

8.52 Expanding the area under forestry will contribute to regionally balanced development by augmenting off-farm job opportunities for small farmers and providing an environmentally sound use for marginal land in remote rural areas. In this manner, it will reinforce other measures in the Operational Programmes aimed at rural development and social inclusion. The development of the forestry sector will also provide benefits for tourism infrastructure and recreational facilities for local communities. Expenditure on the Forestry Measure in the Regional Operational Programme will be additional to £125 million (€158.7 million) expended on forestry in the Region under the CAP Rural Development Programme.

8.53 **Fishery Harbours, Aquaculture Development & Gaeltacht/Islands Measure:** Total planned expenditure on this Measure is £55 million (€69.7 million) as follows:

Table 8.6:   Fishery Harbours, Aquaculture Development & Gaeltacht/Islands Measure Expenditure 2000-2006

Measures	€ million
Fishery Harbours	38.1
Aquaculture Development	11.4
Gaeltacht/Islands	20.2
Total	**69.7**

8.54   Many of the coastal regions of the S&E Region suffer the same economic disadvantages as those in the BMW Region. The S&E Region contains four of the principal bases for the fishing fleet, namely, Howth, Dunmore East, Castletownbere and Dingle. It also includes a large number of smaller but economically significant bases which are located predominantly on the south coast, notably Baltimore, Union Hall and Kilmore Quay. There are also a number of off-shore islands where fishing and tourism are the mainstays of economic activity.

8.55   The seafood industry in the S&E Region lacks adequate berthing and related on-shore infrastructure and facilities. An expenditure programme of £30 million (€38.1 million) will be undertaken to address this deficit by upgrading and developing the facilities at the key ports and landing places. New and improved facilities will also be provided in smaller harbours and landing places which will provide essential structures for the fishing and aquaculture industries. In this regard, the proposed investment in the road network will improve the efficiency with which these industries can access national and international markets. Particular attention will be paid to access infrastructure on off-shore islands and corresponding facilities on the mainland.

8.56   As regards aquaculture, the S&E Region has a high concentration of shell-fish farming. Investment in the aquaculture industry will enhance its contribution to the economy and promote the development of peripheral coastal areas. The focus of this investment will be on the balanced development of the sector, the achievement of critical mass in production, and cost and quality competitiveness. Priority areas for investment will be expansion of existing lines of production, new aquaculture species, infrastructural and technological development, quality and environmental sustainability.

8.57   The funding provided for the Gaeltacht/Islands under this measure will improve their accessibility as tourist destinations while also allowing greater mobility for their inhabitants. Expenditure in this area will also contribute to the fishing/aquaculture industry in the area, thereby promoting environmentally sustainable economic development in these more remote areas.

Social Inclusion Sub-programme

8.58   The Inter-regional and Regional Operational Programmes will contribute to the promotion of social inclusion which is a central objective of the NDP. Both the Regional Operational Programmes contain a Social Inclusion Sub-programme which will supplement spending under other headings in the Regional Operational Programmes designed to promote social inclusion. Chapter 10 sets out in detail the social inclusion measures across the Plan. The priorities for action under the Social Inclusion Sub-programme for the S&E Region reflects the nature and extent of the problem to be addressed in the Region.

8.59   The S&E Region has a mix of both relatively affluent and very deprived communities. The Region contains by far the greatest number of long-term unemployed and marginalised people. Areas of extreme deprivation are found in the large urban areas of Dublin, Cork, Limerick and

Waterford. Clusters of deprivation can also be found in other large urban centres in the Region such as Tralee, Ennis, Wexford, Kilkenny, Clonmel and Carlow.

8.60 In many of the Region's disadvantaged inner-city areas, less than 10% of the households derive their income from employment. Moreover, these areas are affected by long-term unemployment, poor education, skills deficits, one-parent families, drug addiction and homelessness. The communities in which they reside tend to be ghettoised and affected by low levels of self-esteem, early school leaving/youth unemployment, poor family support, lack of community support and infrastructure and high levels of crime. While the misuse of drugs is a nation-wide phenomenon, significant heroin abuse, with its very serious public health implications and close associations with crime, is confined mainly to the most disadvantaged areas in the Dublin region.

8.61 The weak capacity of these socially and economically marginalised groups to meet the increasingly sophisticated demands of modern employment creates the conditions in which, if no action is taken, the poverty gap in such areas will only widen. Consequently, the primary focus of the Social Inclusion Sub-programme in the S&E Region will be on alleviating social exclusion in urban areas where disadvantage and marginalisation is endemic and inter-generational, and where the effect of cohesive targeted programmes can have their greatest impact.

8.62 At the same time, many rural areas within the S&E Region continue to experience population decline, despite significant population growth in the Region as a whole. In the remoter areas, farmers are experiencing hardship due to poor infrastructure, poor land and difficult market access. Particular problems apply to the islands and peninsular areas of the Region. The measures in the S&E Regional Operational Programme on forestry, fisheries and rural development will address many of the problems of rural and coastal communities. Moreover, investment in non-national roads and public transport will alleviate the effects of peripherality in these communities. Nevertheless, there remain specific problems of social exclusion in rural areas which will need to be tackled under this Sub-programmme. In addition, targeted action will be required to meet the needs of people with disabilities, the elderly, travellers, and offenders who suffer the effects of social isolation by virtue of their particular circumstances.

8.63 Measures: As in the BMW Region, this Sub-programme will consist of measures in respect of Childcare, Equality, Community Development and Family Support, Crime Prevention, Youth Services and Services to the Unemployed. The planned total spending on these Measures in the S&E Region over the period 2000-2006 is £837 million (€1,063 million) broken down as follows:

Table 8.7:   Social Inclusion Sub-Programme Measures Expenditure 2000-2006

Measures	€ million
Childcare	229.8
Equality	21.7
Community Development/Family Support	259.5
Crime Prevention	62.6
Youth Services	326.8
Services to Unemployed	162.5
Total	**1,062.9**

8.64   In the S&E Region, there will be a particular focus on the following measures:

- Childcare Facilities and Community Development/Family Support, because of the high concentration in the urban areas of the Region of dysfunctional families and communities, and marginalised mothers both single and married, who need such facilities if they are to access education, training and employment opportunities;

- Crime Prevention and Youth Services, because crime and the associated problem of drugs are a major problem in the disadvantaged urban areas of the Region;

- Funding for Special Projects for Disadvantaged Youth, operated by the Department of Education and Science, aimed at facilitating the personal development and social education of youth at risk of drug abuse, juvenile crime, early school leaving, social exclusion, unemployment, welfare dependence, homelessness and marginalisation;

- Provision of resources for the Young People's Facilities and Services Fund in order to assist the targeted development of youth facilities and services in disadvantaged areas where a significant drug problem exists or has the potential to develop.

8.65   In addition to the above, the Measures in favour of Equality and Services to Unemployed will be implemented vigorously within the resources available and the EU funded Territorial Employment Pacts will also continue to be supported under this measure.

8.66   The foregoing Measures will be implemented by a number of different Departments and agencies. However, it will be necessary to have a sense of priority so that a focus is maintained on carrying through the actions that address the most pressing problems and that can have the greatest and most immediate beneficial impact in promoting social inclusion. Structures are in place at national level to ensure close co-operation in the formulation of policies on social inclusion. At local level, disadvantage and marginalisation will be combated in an integrated way. Such an approach will help to ensure that socially excluded groups receive optimal support for their re-integration into the community.

ERDF Assistance in 2006

8.67   Within the S&E Region, the South-East Region will qualify under the EU Structural Funds Regulations for ERDF support in 2006 in the order of £16 million (€20 million). A programme will be agreed with the European Commission on the allocation of this provision in due course.

Impact of Operational Programmes on Equality

8.68   The S&E Regional Operational Programme will have a positive impact on equality, particularly through the Social Inclusion Sub-programme which is specifically targeted at gender equality and marginalised groups. In relation to the latter, this sub-programme consists of a series of measures designed to integrate such groups, especially prisoners and drug-users into mainstream society. These measures encompass training, education and employment initiatives which also embrace long-term unemployed, early school-leavers and people, especially women, with young families. The initiatives aimed at people with young families are flanked by the provision of childcare and actions to support parental and family care.

8.69   These measures must also be seen in the broader context of the Operational Programme itself which has the objective of reinforcing the beneficial economic impact of the Inter-regional

Operational Programmes in promoting balanced development and creating job opportunities throughout the Region. Of themselves, the measures will make a significant contribution to equality but they will have the optimal impact when implemented against a background of continuing robust economic growth.

Impact on Poverty

8.70 In Ireland, the groups which suffer most from poverty are, to a large extent, the unemployed, single parents, people living in disadvantaged areas, prisoners and drug-users. Consequently, the measures in the Social Inclusion Sub-programme aimed at reducing inequality will also help to address the problem of poverty. In addition, the actions to assist the development of the Region (through, for example, the Urban and Village Renewal, Rural Development, Tourism, Forestry and Fisheries Measures) should make a substantial contribution to the fight against poverty.

Impact on the Environment

8.71 The Operational Programme will have a positive impact on the environment, notably via the Rural Water and Waste Management Measures. The former will improve water quality for beneficiaries. The latter will address the current over-reliance on landfill, in favour of an integrated waste management approach which utilises a range of waste treatment options to deliver ambitious recycling and recovery targets. There will also be positive environmental spin-offs from:

- the Urban and Village Renewal Measure, which will improve the quality of the built environment in the targeted areas;

- the Tourism Measure which will alleviate current pressures on popular tourist attractions and promote action to improve the visual environment in currently less-frequented areas; and

- the Forestry Measure which will improve the visual environment at local level and play an important role in achieving Ireland's CO_2 targets under the Kyoto protocol.

Rural Impact

8.72 The Rural Development Measure in the S&E Regional Programme will particularly benefit rural communities by supporting the development of rural services and rural enterprises. Rural Development will also be promoted by:

- the Non-National Roads Measure which will improve physical communication within and between rural communities and between them and urban areas, thus supporting the economic and social life of these communities;

- the Tourism Measure, which will open up additional rural areas for tourism, thereby creating additional potential sources of non-farm incomes for people living in these areas;

- the Forestry Measure which will provide employment opportunities in rural areas; and

- the Fisheries Measure which will strengthen the base of the fishing industry in remote coastal areas, thus helping to maintain the viability of local fishing and island communities.

9 Co-Operation with Northern Ireland

Background

9.1 The respective development Plans for Northern Ireland and Ireland for the 1994-1999 round of EU Structural Funds recognised the benefits which could be achieved for the whole of the island through closer economic co-operation. The importance of developing an agreed strategy for co-operation continues to be recognised by both administrations, which have again included a Common Chapter in their respective Plans covering the period 2000-2006 to develop the approach set out in the previous Plans, particularly in light of the extensive co-operation which has framed the 1994-1999 Programme period.

9.2 The creation of the Single European Market in 1992 removed many of the barriers to cross-border trade and business development in Europe. However, there is still considerable scope throughout Europe for further and enhanced co-operation to the mutual benefit of border economies. For the island of Ireland, cross-border co-operation has three key dimensions:

- co-operation along the Border Corridor and between Northern Ireland and the Border Counties of Ireland;

- co-operation North-South within the island of Ireland; and

- co-operation East-West between the island of Ireland and Great Britain, Europe and internationally.

9.3 This Chapter, which is common to the Structural Funds Plans North and South, seeks to set out a strategic framework for building on and developing co-operation in all its forms. This framework must be sufficiently flexible to take account of all dimensions of co-operation and be able to adjust to changing circumstances both in the short-term and long-term. This will include both economic and social change and, in particular, at this important time for the island of Ireland, the advent of political change.

9.4 There is clearly scope for co-operation within the context of the European Structural Funds and this Chapter lays the foundation for that co-operation. Arrangements will be made to implement this Chapter over the period of the Plan.

Political Context

9.5 North-South co-operation is to be placed on a new basis under the provisions of the Multi-party Agreement reached in Belfast on 10 April 1998. The 18 December 1998 Statement by the Office of the First Minister (Designate) and Deputy First Minister (Designate) sets out six agreed areas for Implementation Bodies and six areas for co-operation.

9.6 The Report on the 18 December 1998 Statement to the new Northern Ireland Assembly from the First Minister (Designate) and the Deputy First Minister (Designate) on 15 February 1999 was debated by the Northern Ireland Assembly on 15 and 16 February 1999. The Agreement subsequently done between the Government of the United Kingdom of Great Britain and Northern Ireland and the Government of Ireland establishing Implementation Bodies, at Dublin on 8 March 1999 ('the Implementation Bodies Agreement') will come into effect on the same date as the British-Irish Agreement. The North/South Co-operation (Implementation Bodies) (Northern Ireland) Order 1999, made on 10 March 1999, and the British-Irish Agreement Act 1999 enacted on 22 March 1999, will come into effect on the 'appointed day' (vis the date of devolution) as defined in section 3(1) of the Northern Ireland Act 1998.

9.7   The North-South provisions of the Agreement provided for the setting up of a North-South Ministerial Council (NSMC) and outlined a new institutional framework and context within which co-operation between the two parts of the island was to be taken forward. This provides a strategic focus for North-South co-operation and a foundation for this Common Chapter in the 2000-2006 Development Plans North and South.

9.8   The role of the NSMC will be 'to use best endeavours to reach agreement on the adoption of common policies, in areas where there is a mutual cross-border and all-island benefit, and which are within the competence of both Administrations, North and South, making determined efforts to overcome any disagreements'. The Council will also 'consider the European Union dimension of relevant matters, including the implementation of EU policies and programmes and proposals under consideration in the EU framework. Arrangements are to be made to ensure that the views of the Council are taken into account and represented appropriately at relevant EU meetings'.

9.9   The Agreement required a work programme on at least 12 matters, six being new Implementation Bodies and six being matters for co-operation. The six Bodies are as follows:

Trade and Business Development;

Inland Waterways;

Aquaculture and Marine Matters;

Special EU Programmes;

Food Safety;

Language (Irish and Ulster Scots).

9.10   The Implementation Bodies, when operational, will have an important, new role to play in economic development, particularly those with responsibility for the promotion and development of North-South co-operation on Trade and Business, Inland Waterways, Acquaculture and Marine Matters and Special EU Programmes.

9.11   The Trade and Business Development Body will exchange information and co-ordinate work on trade, business development and related matters. In close collaboration with existing agencies, it will develop co-operation on business development opportunities, North and South, devise new approaches to business development in a cross-border context and make recommendations to increase enterprise competitiveness in a North-South context in areas such as skills availability, telecoms, information technology and electronic commerce.

9.12   Waterways Ireland will be empowered to engage immediately in the promotion, including marketing and development, of the tourism and commercial potential of the Shannon Erne Waterway and, from 1 April 2000, of all of the island's currently navigable waterways. This work will include appropriate studies and appraisals on the possible restoration and development of the Ulster Canal.

9.13 The Loughs Agency of the Foyle, Carlingford and Irish Lights Commission will have, among its responsibilities, the development of marine tourism and aquaculture, including the preparation of strategic plans in these areas, with obvious benefit to the local economies.

9.14 The Special EU Programmes Body will be responsible for the administration of the new Peace Programme, INTERREG III, and the cross-border elements of the other Initiatives (LEADER III, EQUAL, URBAN). It will also be responsible for monitoring and promoting the implementation of the Common Chapter, which will have a specific budgetary allocation. The other areas agreed for co-operation through existing bodies in each jurisdiction are: Agriculture; Tourism; Transport; Environment and Health.

9.15 Whilst this Chapter deals mainly with North-South co-operation, the Belfast Agreement also makes provision for a British-Irish Council, which will be established to promote the harmonious and mutually beneficial development of the totality of relationships among the people of these islands. It is intended that enhanced North-South co-operation should be complemented by enhanced East-West co-operation on areas of mutual benefit and interest and that Northern Ireland should progressively develop and increase its degree of involvement in wider European and international networks of co-operation.

Aims and Objectives of Common Chapter

9.16 In setting out the opportunities and rationale for closer economic co-operation North and South, this Chapter puts in place a framework for increased co-operation between both economies and across all sectors over the period of this Plan from 2000-2006, where it is appropriate and mutually beneficial to do so. It identifies:

- the common challenges which face both economies;

- areas where co-operation has made a positive contribution to peace building and can do so in future; and

- areas in which common challenges can be more effectively addressed through co-operation within the island of Ireland, having due regard to the wider East-West and European context.

9.17 The Chapter highlights areas where co-operation already exists and identifies real examples of successful co-operation and the reasons for success. It considers in particular the potential for building on past experience to create new opportunities for co-operation in the future.

Economic and Social Context

9.18 The economies North and South have changed dramatically over the last decade. In particular, their improved economic performance is reflected in many of the headline labour market indicators. Unemployment has fallen rapidly with both economies now registering unemployment rates below the EU15 average. In turn, employment has increased rapidly in both regions, although in different ways.

9.19 Convergence to EU standards has been such that under the 2000-2006 round of Structural Funds, Northern Ireland and the Southern and Eastern Region of Ireland no longer qualify for full

Objective 1 status, but instead move to transitional status. The Border, Midlands and West Region of Ireland will retain Objective 1 status for 2000-2006. This region includes the Border Counties of Ireland which, together with Northern Ireland, have been the special focus of the INTERREG II and Peace Programmes. It is recognised that while the main economic indicators for the two economies have improved considerably in recent years, they mask sub-regional disparities within the two economies.

9.20   Within the overall context of North-South co-operation, it is generally recognised that the areas immediately adjacent to the border are some of the most disadvantaged areas of the North and South. Existing policies, such as new Targeting Social Need (TSN) in Northern Ireland and National Anti-Poverty Strategy (NAPs) in Ireland, allow for appropriate priority to be given to such disadvantaged areas and there is commitment to strengthen these policies. In addition, the immediate border areas suffer more directly from the effect which the border has had in limiting development opportunities. For both these reasons, a particular focus needs to be given to the needs of the areas immediately contiguous to the border and this will be provided mainly, but not exclusively, through the new INTERREG and Peace Programmes.

Opportunities for Future Co-operation

9.21   During the current round of Structural Funds, progress in cross-border co-operation has been significant and points up the potential for real inter-action between the two economies in the future. Significant developments have been effected at the level of local authorities, non-governmental organisations, the voluntary, community and business sectors and by central government and, in many cases, these sectors have been directly involved in implementing EU Programmes. Noteworthy examples include the establishment of the Centre for Cross-border Studies, based in Armagh, which has been set up using Peace Programme funding to research and develop co-operation across the border in education, business, public administration, communications and a range of other practical areas; and the development work carried out by the three cross-border networks, involving 18 local authorities, which have come together to propose a development strategy for the Border region as a whole. The main employer and trade union organisations North and South also have produced joint papers on developing North-South and East-West co-operation within a European context.

9.22   Other specific areas relevant to cross-border co-operation include:

Energy

9.23   There has been considerable progress by the European Union towards the achievement of the Internal Market for the energy sector and this will facilitate cross-border inter-action. Significant opening up of the respective energy markets will occur in the Plan period. It is recognised that there could be scope for considerable efficiencies through co-operation in the energy sector, where there is potential mutual benefit. Energy supply policies are under review in both parts of the island, pending, inter alia, full evaluation of the potential of the Corrib offshore gas field off the Mayo coast. In this context, the authorities in both jurisdictions will maintain close contact with a view to co-ordinating their approaches so as to exploit synergies in energy policies and in co-operative projects.

Communications and Electronic Commerce

9.24   The communications/electronic commerce sector is a key element for future economic development. It provides the basic infrastructure for the crucially important new information, communication and digital industries. Increasingly, inter-action between businesses and between consumers and businesses are taking place on the Internet. Thus North-South co-operation must be underpinned by the most advanced communications infrastructure. This is essential for the networking of key development and marketing agencies, industry, groups and community development actions North and South.

9.25   With a view to accelerating the necessary developments in this area:

- the relevant Departments in both jurisdictions have established a North-South Digital Corridor Working Group to examine all the elements necessary for the operation of such a corridor, including the necessary telecoms infrastructure;

- the North-West Region Cross-border Group has commissioned a study, with a view to developing an integrated, multi-sectoral cross-border information society; and

- a study is being undertaken of a proposed Digital Technology Corridor in the Armagh/Monaghan area.

Human Resource Development

9.26   Significant cross-border co-operation exists between the Training and Employment Agency (T&EA) in Northern Ireland and FAS, the training and employment authority in Ireland. At present, the two bodies are working together on a number of specific issues including the EURES cross-border partnerships and the Wider Horizons Programme. It is anticipated that this co-operation can and will be developed as the needs of trainees on both sides of the border evolve and opportunities for further joint working emerge.

9.27   These, together with a range of other sectoral areas have laid the foundation for co-operation and underpin the potential for expansion in the future. In addition, in accordance with the Belfast Agreement, the statement of 18 December 1998 highlights such potential by specifically identifying six such areas as suitable for initial consideration by the NSMC for co-operation through the mechanism of existing bodies in each separate jurisdiction. It will be open to the NSMC, by agreement between the two sides, to consider other matters. The six matters identified are considered in more detail in the following sections.

Agriculture

9.28   Agriculture and rural development continue to play a major role in the economies of both parts of the island, and make an essential contribution to maintaining the viability of rural communities. The two administrations remain committed to helping the sector adapt to the changes brought about by the further reform of the Common Agricultural Policy and changes in market conditions. Close co-operation already exists in a wide range of agriculture, fisheries, forestry and related activities. Under the direction of the NSMC, both administrations intend to seek ways to strengthen and enhance this co-operation in the future, particularly in areas such as CAP related issues, animal and plant health policy and research, rural development and agri-food research, education and technology transfer.

9.29   As indicated in the relevant chapters of the respective development plans, the two regions attach major importance to promoting and reinforcing vigorous measures to advance rural development. There is considerable scope for synergy and mutual learning across the border. This was recognised in 1991 when a cross-border steering committee on Rural Development was established to encourage and oversee progress on cross-border rural development and to co-ordinate official responses to joint plans developed by cross-border community groups. This steering committee has worked well and will continue to operate, henceforth in conjunction, as appropriate and under the direction of the NSMC, with the Special EU Programmes Body, which will be responsible for cross-border aspects of LEADER.

Tourism

9.30   Given the real social and economic benefits of tourism, particularly in terms of employment creation, foreign earnings and regional development, there are clear benefits to be derived from enhanced North-South co-operation in attracting visitors to the island of Ireland. The Departments of Economic Development in Belfast and Tourism, Sport and Recreation in Dublin are agreed that the continuation of all-island overseas co-operative marketing activities are essential to the continued success of the tourism industry in an increasingly competitive global marketplace. Under the direction of the NSMC, it is intended that the experience gained through North-South public-private partnership initiatives, such as the Overseas Tourism Marketing Initiative (OTMI), will be developed over the period 2000-2006 for the mutual benefit of all sectors of the industry in all parts of the island of Ireland.

9.31   In the context of the Belfast Agreement and building on the success of the OTMI, it has been agreed that a single company will be established to carry out overseas marketing and promotion activity for the respective tourist boards and that it will establish overseas offices for that purpose. The new company, which is to subsume the activities of OTMI, is also to plan and deliver international tourism marketing programmes; publish and disseminate in overseas markets information on the island of Ireland as a tourist destination; and provide market research and other support services for the tourism industry.

9.32   Other industry-led initiatives in North-South co-operation in tourism include the Hospitality Ireland Group, which has developed networks between those involved in tourism and hospitality education and training and promoted a tourism leadership development programme. There has also been significant co-operation in this area between local authorities, regional authorities and the private sector.

Transport

9.33   Efficient and competitive integrated public and private transport services are critical to the development of trade, inward investment and tourism and the provision of equality of access to employment opportunities through improved labour market mobility. They are particularly important in sustaining rural communities. Enhanced cross-border transport infrastructure offers the potential for major economic and social gains for the whole of the island, and for that reason, there is already very close cross-border co-operation in roads, rail and bus services. In the public transport sector, for example, Translink and Iarnrod Eireann have worked closely on the up-grading of the Belfast to Dublin railway line and jointly operate the successful cross-border Enterprise service. On that line, passenger numbers have increased by over a third in recent years to 900,000 annually following the upgrade and reflect the success of co-operation. There is a recognition that the value of proposed investments in roads infrastructure on either side of the Border can be enhanced significantly through co-ordination of planning and construction.

9.34   Consequently, a key aim of transport development policy during the period of this Plan will be to improve infrastructure and integration within and between road and public transport networks, in both jurisdictions, so as to provide a more coherent and sustainable strategic transport network for the island as a whole. The objective will be the generation of a co-ordinated transport and logistics plan for the island in the context of East-West linkages to Britain and Europe, including strategic cross-border roads and Trans European Networks (TENS) routes. To that end, under the direction of the NSMC, the authorities in both jurisdictions will be working together to identify and promote joint projects within this important area.

Environment

9.35 Both parts of the island of Ireland have inherited a shared heritage of a relatively unpolluted environment endowed with a diversity of natural and cultural assets. Many of these assets are a common resource, and co-operation to manage them sustainably is clearly in the interests of all. Research and monitoring are major requirements in managing the physical and biological environments. Joint strategies and planning are also beneficial where resources such as rivers, fish or migratory birds move across the border.

9.36 Under the direction of the NSMC, it is intended that authorities North and South will work together to review and co-ordinate activities across a range of environmental areas including:

- the establishment of a data base of environmental information;

- research into environmental protection and mutually beneficial ways to address this issue;

- identification of strategies and activities which would contribute to a coherent all-island approach to the achievement of sustainable development;

- the development of catchment-based strategies in relation to water quality;

- the environmental impact of agricultural activities and related issues;

- the scope for improved waste management in a cross-border context, taking account of waste policy in the EU, the UK and Ireland; and

- the management of shared bio-diversity resources.

Education

9.37 Considerable co-operation exists across all aspects of the education sectors North and South, ranging from primary to higher education and embracing libraries, youth, arts and sports. The valuable linkages which have been developed provide the basis to establish more closely integrated, coherent approaches in the future with clearer policy objectives and outcomes. The type of activities which will be promoted include:

- inter-active approaches at university and further education level, in areas such as R&D support for SMEs;

- the development of lifelong learning, adult guidance and counselling programmes;

- Information and Communications Technology in schools; and

- educational under-achievement.

9.38 Under the direction of the NSMC, both administrations intend to take forward and enhance co-operation in these and other agreed areas in the future.

Health

9.39 The Department of Health and Social Services (DHSS) and the Departments for Social Community and Family Affairs (DSCFA) and Health and Children have a close working relationship and have co-operated successfully in areas such as:

- the management of the "Achieving Better Community Development" initiative; and

- cross-border community development within the Peace Programme Cross-border Sub-programme.

9.40 Against the background of the peripheral nature of parts of the regions, there is considerable scope to co-operate in the provision of required services on a partnership basis, and these Departments are working together to identify the scope for enhancing co-operation across a range of areas. These will include extension and development of the existing mechanism (known as Co-operation and Working Together) for co-operation between the Western and Southern Health Boards in Northern Ireland and the North Western and North Eastern Health Boards in Ireland to improve co-ordination and co-operation in relation to ambulance cover and joint training; and the sharing of emergency admissions where hospitals are under pressure.

9.41 Other issues which, under the direction of the NSMC, may be taken forward in the future include planning for major emergencies; the procurement, funding and use of high technology equipment; collaboration on cancer and other research; participation in multi-centre trials; health promotion; and public information/education in the areas of heart disease, cancer and smoking.

European Support

9.42 The European dimension of cross-border co-operation within the island of Ireland has been of particular significance. The EU has provided valuable resources through the medium of INTERREG and the Special Support Programme for Peace and Reconciliation (the Peace Programme), which are targeted primarily at Northern Ireland and the Border Counties of Ireland. Co-operation developed under these Programmes will be further enhanced following the decision of the European Council at Berlin to continue the Peace Programme and to renew the INTERREG Community Initiative. These Programmes, which are managed jointly by the Department of Finance and the Department of Finance and Personnel, will have contributed in excess of 1.5 billion euro in public funding to the eligible areas over the 10 years 1995-2004 across a wide range of socio-economic sectors.

INTERREG

9.43 The INTERREG Initiative was the first European Programme specifically to promote cross-border co-operation. The underlying ethos of the Programme is that national borders should not be a barrier to the balanced development and integration of the European territory. The Single Market has been a strong catalyst for advancing cross-border co-operation, but the scope for strengthening it further remains enormous.

9.44 The 1994-1999 INTERREG II Programme developed co-operation through supporting a diverse range of activities across all sectors. The Programme saw a number of interesting developments, including the establishment of 3 cross-border networks of local authorities in the border region, representing 18 local authorities, which have developed strategic sub-regional Integrated Area Plans together with a Border Corridor strategy. Another notable initiative was the appointment of an INTERREG Development Officer (IDO) and the setting up of INTERREG Development offices in Armagh and Monaghan to actively promote and publicise the Programme.

9.45 The priority of cross-border, transnational and inter-regional co-operation proposed for INTERREG III, as reflected in the three separate strands of the new Programme, is a clear demonstration of the Commission's desire to concentrate its efforts on ensuring that regions on both internal and external Union borders build on cross-border and international co-operation to address their isolation. The Commission's proposals for INTERREG III should be particularly beneficial in terms of providing a framework for an integrated approach to common problems, which should create opportunities for genuine and practical benefits. The administrations North and South will seek to use the new Programme to build on the positive experiences of INTERREG II and to complement other cross-border proposals under other Programmes.

Peace Programme

9.46 Under the current Peace Programme, the cross-border dimension was specifically addressed through the Cross-border Development Sub-programme, to which some 15% of the available funding was allocated. The Sub-programme aimed to promote cross-border reconciliation and to exploit the opportunities for increased cross-border development arising from the ceasefire. Areas assisted included business and cultural links, infrastructure development, co-operation between public bodies and community reconciliation with particular reference to women, young people and the socially excluded.

9.47 More generally, the Peace Programme provided funding for a wide range of Measures in support of the peace process on both sides of the border. The Programme laid particular emphasis on the need to respond to the wishes of local interests and grassroots opinion throughout the eligible areas. A joint Consultative Forum, consisting of representatives drawn from the local government, social partners and community/voluntary sectors was set up to liaise directly with the Monitoring Committee.

9.48 The Peace Programme also involved the use of devolved delivery mechanisms, some of which played a part in the Cross-border Development Sub-programme. Co-operation Ireland, for example, in conjunction with the Joint Business Council of IBEC/CBI, was responsible for supporting cross-border linkages in business and cultural sectors. A unique cross-border partnership was also established by Area Development Management Limited and the Combat Poverty Agency in Ireland, in conjunction with the Northern Ireland Voluntary Trust. This intermediary funding arrangement brought in a range of other agencies such as the International Fund for Ireland, the Northern Ireland Community Relations Council, the Northern Ireland Rural Community Network as well as various local community organisations.

9.49 In March 1999, the Berlin Council 'in recognition of the special efforts for the peace process in Northern Ireland' decided that 'the Peace Programme will be continued for five years with an amount of 500 million euros of which 100 million will be allocated to Ireland.' The new Peace Programme will build on the work which was started under the first Programme, taking into account equality, equity and non-discrimination and developing initiatives for business, public bodies and voluntary and community sector co-operation. The overall objective will be to provide a strategic framework for support to cross-border co-operation strategies and projects for a variety of sectors and organisations.

IFI

9.50   The work of the International Fund for Ireland, to which the EU has been a significant contributor, is also of particular relevance to cross-border co-operation. The Fund has been very active since 1987 in promoting a wide range of collaborative ventures across a broad band of cross-border activities. Its work is of course entirely complementary to the overall objectives of the Structural Funds in promoting economic and social cohesion. In particular, however, its earlier success in creating cross-border networks and linkages has been helpful in shaping the implementation of Structural Funds operations North and South and in ensuring the maximum scope for the development of strategic partnerships between the Fund and specific EU Initiatives, including the Peace Programme.

9.51   For the future, the Fund has refocused its programmes under the three broad headings of Regeneration of Deprived Areas, Community Capacity Building and Economic Development. Within this framework, and in close co-ordination with EU Programmes, the Fund will continue to foster a distinctive range of community and economic interventions on a cross-border basis designed to build on earlier achievements in areas of real need.

Implementation of Common Chapter

9.52   Promotion and implementation of the Common Chapter will be fundamental to the impact of cross-border development in the European context over the period 2000-2006. The Special EU Programmes Body will be responsible for monitoring and promoting the implementation of the Common Chapter. It will have a specific budgetary allocation to enable it to identify and alleviate constraints which affect cross-border co-operation.

9.53   The Body will report to the NSMC and will have secretariat, monitoring, research, evaluation, technical assistance and development roles in respect of the new Peace Programme and the new Community Initiatives. It will also have grant-making and other managerial functions in respect of INTERREG III and of North-South elements of other Initiatives.

9.54   The Monitoring Committee for the new Peace Programme will be established under the chairmanship of the Implementation Body and will be managed jointly. The Body's operations will be overseen by the relevant Monitoring Committees established according to the EU Structural Funds Regulations.

9.55   The establishment of the Special EU Programmes Body is a significant development in the context of cross-border co-operation. It will, for the first time, ensure that the Common Chapter, and the potential identified within it for enhanced cross-border and wider co-operation, will receive structured, focused and on-going attention, and will be actively promoted within the CSF Monitoring Committees North and South, on which the Body will be represented. In this context, the strategic framework must be sufficiently flexible to enable it to adjust to changing circumstances, including developments in the political field. Pending the setting up of the Special EU Programmes Body, both Governments are committed to making arrangements to ensure that there will be a specific focus on the implementation of the Common Chapter during the next round of the Structural Funds.

10 Promoting Social Inclusion

Overview

10.1 Partnership 2000 defines social exclusion as cumulative marginalisation from production (unemployment), from consumption (poverty), from social networks (community, family and neighbours), from decision making and from an adequate quality of life. Creating a more inclusive society by alleviating social exclusion, poverty and deprivation is one of the major challenges facing Irish society over the course of the National Development Plan.

10.2 Table 10.1 provides a breakdown of the provisions which will promote social inclusion in each of the NDP Operational Programmes:

Table 10.1: Expenditure on Social Inclusion 2000-2006

Operational Programme	National € million	BMW Region € million	S&E Region € million
Economic and Social Infrastructure	10,157.9	2,451.9	7,706.0
Employment and Human Resources	7,576.7	2,154.7	5,422.0
Regional Programmes	1,343.1	280.1	1,063.0
Total	**19,077.7**	**4,886.7**	**14,191.0**
Expenditure Per Capita €	**5,261**	**5,062**	**5,333**

10.3 Social cohesion is an integral part of the partnership ethos which has developed in Ireland over the last twelve years and which has been the foundation of the State's economic success. As well as setting out objectives of increased employment and maintaining and enhancing national competitiveness, Partnership 2000 contained a specific commitment to pursue social inclusion as a strategic objective in its own right. Closely aligned with this commitment is the Government's undertaking to promote equality, involving the full integration into Irish society of women, people with disabilities, members of the Traveller Community and persons granted refugee status or permission to remain in Ireland. The National Development Plan contains a range of measures designed to promote social inclusion and the achievement of the Government's objectives in this regard.

10.4 The benefits of Ireland's rapid economic progress over the past few years are evident in the significant reduction in many of the key indicators of social exclusion. The National Anti-Poverty Strategy (NAPS) set a target in 1997 of reducing the number of people in consistent poverty over the period 1997-2007 from 9-15% of the population to less than 5-10% and set the goal of reducing unemployment from nearly 12% to 6.4%. The most recently available data from the ESRI and the CSO show that the NAPS targets set in 1997 have been substantially met. The number of people in consistent poverty has been reduced to 7-10%. By early 1999, overall unemployment had fallen to 5.8% with long-term unemployment dropping to 3%. In recognition of these developments, the Government has set a new target of reducing consistent poverty to 5% by 2004 and will draw up new social inclusion targets in consultation with the social partners.

10.5   However, it is clear that not everyone has benefited proportionately from this new-found prosperity — indeed, the disparity between higher income earners and the socially excluded may even have widened. In addition, concentration of poverty may be intensifying in certain areas for reasons such as the outward migration of previously socially-excluded persons who are now economically active, a factor which would also involve a loss of community leadership and beneficial role models. Indeed, in many disadvantaged communities, poverty, social deprivation and the effects of marginalisation are becoming, or may already have become, endemic and inter-generational.

10.6   Clearly, the outward manifestation of social exclusion and marginalisation is not limited to financial poverty or living in areas of social deprivation. Not only do disadvantaged people have greater reliance on the State for direct income support and housing, they also suffer from poorer health and lower educational achievement resulting in lower employability. Many marginalised areas are also disproportionately affected by crime and drug abuse, while a disproportionately large percentage of the prison population comes from them. As a result, society suffers in two ways. Firstly, social exclusion imposes additional costs, direct and indirect, on society and reduces the quality of life generally (e.g crime). Secondly, society is at the loss of the potential contribution — both economic and otherwise — which people who are affected by social exclusion could make to it. Thus, alleviating poverty and building an inclusive society will yield multiple benefits by reducing the direct cost of social exclusion, improving the quality of life generally and allowing people to contribute to the wealth of the nation and share in the benefits of economic and social development.

10.7   In summary, if the fruits of Ireland's recent economic progress are to be more widely spread, the promotion of social inclusion as a key objective of socio-economic development must form a central component of the Plan. Reducing social exclusion is crucial to maintaining and broadening social cohesion and thus consolidating the economic and social progress of recent years. Moreover, the continuation of the partnership ethos, which lies at the heart of Ireland's economic and social progress, requires a demonstration that all sections of the community have a stake in Ireland's future development. The pursuit of social inclusion is therefore a fundamental objective of the National Development Plan.

Regional Dimension

10.8   Both the BMW and the S&E Region contain areas of deprivation and poverty. The promotion of social inclusion will therefore be an objective in both regions which will be furthered through both the Inter-regional and the Regional Operational Programme. The implementation in both regions of education and training measures under the Human Resources and Employment Operational Programme will be of particular importance. In the Regional Operational Programme, the implementation of instruments aimed at promoting social inclusion will reflect the nature of deprivation in each Region. Thus, for example, the more urbanised S&E Region will see a special focus on urban disadvantage whilst the BMW Region will, reflecting its more rural and dispersed nature, benefit comparatively more from the rural development and local infrastructure measures.

Role of the Operational Programmes

10.9   More generally, each of the NDP Operational Programmes will contribute in its own way to promoting social inclusion. Their overall objective is to boost growth on a balanced basis throughout the country and their combined effect will be to generate employment opportunities for the socially disadvantaged and to create extra resources to enable the State to raise the living standards and the quality of life of the elderly and those who are incapable of work. In addition, four of the Operational Programmes will directly work to promote social inclusion. These are the Economic and Social Infrastructure Operational Programme, the Employment and Human Resources Development Operational Programme and the two Regional Operational Programmes.

10.10   The main direct contribution from the Economic and Social Infrastructure Operational Programme will be a £6 billion (€7.6 billion) investment in the provision of affordable housing by improving and significantly expanding the existing housing stock. In addition, there will be capital investment of £2 billion (€2.5 billion) in the public health services over the next seven years.

10.11   The Employment and Human Resources Development Operational Programme will include an extensive range of measures which will focus on particular aspects relevant to the promotion of social inclusion, especially educational disadvantage (including literacy), lifelong learning, work experience and equality of access to education, training and employment. A total allocation of nearly £6 billion (€7.6 billion) will be available for promoting social inclusion within this Operational Programme.

10.12   The Regional Operational Programmes will encompass a broad range of measures at regional level designed to combat poverty and promote equality and social inclusion. These measures, involving a total investment of over £1 billion (€1.3 billion), will:

- significantly boost childcare provision, thus enabling parents (particularly women), especially those from disadvantaged backgrounds, to combine family life with employment and education/training;

- support efforts at a local and community level, including a sustained effort to develop community leadership skills and capacity so as to support efforts towards greater social inclusion;

- enhance the capacity of the most disadvantaged families to improve their circumstances;

- directly address the needs and problems of young people (diverting them from drifting into unemployment, crime and substance abuse);

- assist the reintegration into the community of those who have been involved in crime;

- provide educational and training opportunities for the disadvantaged; and

- provide an outreach service to the long-term unemployed.

Economic and Social Infrastructure Priority

Affordable Housing

10.13   The NDP will provide £6 billion (€7.6 billion) essentially to assist in the provision of housing for those who cannot provide adequate and appropriate housing from their own resources. The provision of social and affordable housing is a concern not only with regard to its critical implications for social inclusion but also for its impact on potential economic growth and national competitiveness. With the smallest housing stock in relation to population in the EU, our recent economic success, coupled with increased employment and net immigration, together with growth in the key household formation age groups, has contributed to greatly increased demand for housing beyond current supply levels with resulting rapid increases in house prices and rents. These factors have also led to greatly increased pressure on the available social housing stock.

10.14   The proposed investment of £6 billion (€7.6 billion) is targeted particularly at increasing social housing output and the size of the social housing stock, both in the local authority and voluntary sectors. The provision of additional houses by local authorities under the Affordable Housing and Shared Ownership schemes is also a priority. Significant allocations will be provided for the redevelopment and refurbishment of the existing social housing stock, especially in run-down estates. Established communities will also benefit from area-based regeneration initiatives, for example, the redevelopment of Ballymun and other inner-city flat complexes. Special funding will also be available to provide and improve housing for the elderly, people with disabilities, travellers and the homeless.

Enhanced Access to Improved Health Services

10.15   Several studies have highlighted the higher rates of mortality and other illnesses amongst people from relatively disadvantaged backgrounds or low income groups. The NDP will address the problems of these groups by investing £2 billion (€2.5 billion) in capital projects in the public health services. The overall priority will be to replace old facilities or introduce new facilities, together with new and enhanced services to improve overall access and treatment and boost regional and local self-sufficiency. This investment in the health services will enhance the employability of the socially excluded by helping to improve their health and well-being and, thus, put them in a better position to escape from poverty.

Employment and Human Resources Development Operational Programme

Education and Training

10.16   Studies show that educational disadvantage can become ingrained at a very young age and can result in early school leaving and ultimately unemployment and long-term social marginalisation and its knock-on effects in terms of homelessness, substance abuse and crime. For this reason, the provision of comprehensive and diverse education and training facilities, which will cater for the needs of specific groups in society from early childhood through to adulthood, particularly those experiencing social disadvantage, is a priority of the National Development Plan. Such life-long learning supports are also essential, not alone to support reintegration of the socially excluded back into the labour market by equipping them with the necessary education and skills, but also to deal with emerging skills shortages and to cope with the ever-changing technological needs of the global economy.

10.17   The National Development Plan adheres to the definition of lifelong learning adopted by the National Employment Action Plan (NEAP) as "all purposeful learning activity, whether formal or informal, undertaken on an on-going basis with the aim of improving knowledge, skills and competence". Various measures under this priority, which are listed below, in effect, implement the commitment to life-long learning. In so doing, they also address many aspects of social inclusion such as literacy, early childhood education, reskilling, and second chance education. The individual initiatives in this area are:

- Active Support Measures for the Long-term Unemployed and Socially Excluded will assist entry or re-entry into the labour market by people in this category. £1.7 billion (€2.2

billion) will incorporate support for increased training and training allowances for the long-term unemployed. This will involve a range of services and programmes to assist the return to regular employment of the long-term unemployed, those on One Parent Family Payments and people with disabilities;

- The Back to Education Initiative, operated by the Department of Education and Science, will address the needs of those with minimal or no educational qualifications, and provide a re-entry route for those who wish to upgrade their skills. An allocation of over £1 billion (€1.3 billion) will support the initiative;

- With an allocation of £0.95 billion (€1.2 billion), the Employment Support Services Measure, operated by the Department of Social Community and Family Affairs, will fund the 'Back to Work' and 'Back to Education' Allowances Schemes for the long-term unemployed. These are supports for the most disadvantaged in the Community — those who are unable, without support, to re-enter the labour market;

- An Action Programme for the Unemployed will devote £663 million (€841.8 million) to identify those in, or drifting into, long-term unemployment, to guide them towards suitable educational/training options and labour market options and to assist them find employment;

- An allocation of £203 million (€257.8 million) under an Early School Leaver Progression measure will provide 6,000 places on training and assistance programmes for early school leavers which will build on the joint endeavours to date in this area by FAS and the Department of Education and Science;

- FAS will receive £179 million (€227.3 million) to allow its National Employment Service cater for job-seekers and those referred to it under the National Employment Action Plan (NEAP);

- A related measure, Sectoral Entry Training for Early School Leavers and Long-term Unemployed, will provide a cohort of new entrants to the tourism industry and ensure a basic training for school leavers entering the agricultural sector. Total spending on Sectoral Entry Training will amount to £229.2 million (€291.1 million);

- A Skills Training measure will provide £106 million (€134.6 million) for upgrading the skills of unemployed and redundant workers, thus enhancing their prospects for obtaining employment;

- An Educational Sector Social Inclusion Measure will provide £364 million (€462.3 million) for a range of initiatives aimed at retaining people in the education system from early childhood through to adulthood. These initiatives include, Early Education Initiative, Early Literacy Initiative, School Completion Initiative, Traveller Education, School Guidance Services and Third-Level Access;

- An allocation of £73.8 million (€93.7 million) under the National Adult Literacy Strategy will support increased access to literacy, numeracy and basic education for adults whose skills are inadequate in this regard;

- The Further Education Support Measure, will complement the Back to Education Initiative and the National Adult Literacy Strategy by providing an adult guidance and counselling service aimed at supporting participants in further education. An allocation of £35 million (€44.5 million) will underpin this measure.

Social Employment

10.18 A Social Economy Scheme will focus on developing innovative, locally-based, income-generating projects in disadvantaged communities. The objective is to create employment for 2,500 people by 2003. The NDP allocation for this scheme is £213 million (€270.5 million).

Promoting Equal Opportunities

10.19 Under the **Equality Measure** of the Employment and Human Resources Development Operational Programme, a range of measures will complement the allocations for the promotion of equality contained in the Regional Operational Programmes:

- Vocational Training and Pathways to Employment for People with Disabilities will be supported by an allocation of £175 million (€222.2 million);

- An Equal Opportunities measure, costing £21.5 million (€27.3 million), will embrace a wide ranging effort at administrative and technical level to ensure the maximum equality of access to education, training and other programmes of assistance;

- A Refugee Language Support Unit, costing £3.5 million (€4.5 million), will address the language difficulties of non-EU nationals who have acquired the right to reside in Ireland and thus ease their integration into Irish society.

Regional Operational Programmes

10.20 Very substantial provisions of over £1 billion (€1.3 billion) in total for social inclusion are included in both Regional Operational Programmes. These will finance a broad range of measures designed to alleviate the problems of people of all ages from disadvantaged backgrounds. The Regional Programmes will support community development generally, address the problems of equality, access to education and employment, and target some of the most persistent problems of social exclusion such as long-term unemployment, substance abuse and the rehabilitation of prisoners back into society. The following areas are covered in the Regional Operational Programmes.

Childcare

10.21 If the problems of social disadvantage are to be overcome, then it is necessary to improve skills and capacities of people in disadvantaged communities by enabling them to avail of labour market opportunities, including education and training. The lack of adequate childcare facilities has been identified as a significant contributor to exclusion from available education, training and employment opportunities. This impacts most severely on women, and in particular on disadvantaged women and single-parent families. The objectives of the childcare measure include reconciling work and family life and facilitating access for women to education, training and employment. It will have both an equal opportunities and a social inclusion focus. It will also address the needs of men and women generally in reconciling their childcare needs with their participation in the labour force.

10.22 With an allocation of £250 million (€317.4 million) the proposed actions under the Childcare measure in the Regional Operational Programmes are designed to support objectives such as providing diverse childcare which meets the needs of the child, increasing the number of trained personnel working in childcare and improving the co-ordination and delivery of childcare.

The Programme will also cater for the needs of disadvantaged children by initiating play and development opportunities for them.

Equality

10.23 While much progress has been made in the area of employment and human resources to improve equality as between men and women, much remains to be done. There is a need for measures to tackle attitudinal and cultural barriers both within the workplace, to participation by women in the work force and within the home, in relation to the balance to be struck between work and family responsibilities and the sharing of such responsibilities. There is also a need to support womens' access to education and training and to continue to develop the strategy to combat violence against women. Moreover, increasing womens' input to the decision-making process is a major priority. An allocation of £23.2 million (€29.5 million) is being provided to finance measures to promote equality including retraining and up-skilling for women employees, promoting greater sharing of family responsibilities, support for career development and entrepeneurship amongst women and the gender proofing of personnel practices in employment.

Community Development and Family Support

10.24 Support for community development, which enhances the capacity of disadvantaged local communities to participate in mainstream development initiatives, is an integral part of the Government's overall social and economic development strategy. Projects funded under this Measure will support a wide range of self-help activities designed to provide a first step for individuals to escape from poverty and to improve family life in disadvantaged communities. Resource projects that act as catalysts for development in disadvantaged communities will also be supported.

10.25 The Community Development and Family Support Measure, which will be supported by an allocation of £252.75 million (€321 million), will include:

- Provision of physical infrastructure for community, recreational and employment purposes particularly in deprived urban and rural areas, in particular, those with high youth populations;

- Provision of support for training, information exchange and local group networking for local community development groups and organisations to enhance the capacity of people living in disadvantaged communities to participate fully in local development opportunities;

- Funding for the Community Development Programme which is designed to enhance the capacity of disadvantaged communities to participate in mainstream local development, training and education, enterprise and employment opportunities;

- Provision of core funding to community and family support groups to assist the building of the capacity of particular target groups within disadvantaged communities;

- Provision of Family and Community Services Resource Centres to provide parenting skills training and to provide support and special services to lone parents and families at risk so as to improve the functioning of the family unit;

- Establishment of a Family Services Project which will involve working with people on an individual basis to enhance their capacity to improve their personal and family circumstances and to access opportunities for education and employment.

193

Crime Prevention

10.26 Research into the causal factors of crime conclusively demonstrates that offenders, both male and female, generally come from the most disadvantaged groups in society and, typically, that they are unemployed, unqualified, addicted and likely to re-offend. The label of having been in prison becomes a further layer of disadvantage in the community, as employers are less likely to employ someone who has been in prison. Offenders, therefore, experience multiple disadvantages which accumulate leading to economic and social exclusion and to an extreme form of marginalisation from the labour market. To counter this, an amount of £70.7 million (€89.8 million) will be expended as follows:

- Provision of work, vocational training and related education on an individual programme basis to custodial prisoners to enable them access employment opportunities on release from prison;

- Establishment of Probation and Development centres in high risk communities to provide services to offenders including ex-prisoners, juvenile offenders and young people at risk and to facilitate reintegration of prisoners/offenders into their communities;

- Provision within the community of work and skills training, work placement and personal development services including alcohol and drug abuse programmes to offenders so as to enhance the potential for reintegration into the community;

- Provision of services within the community to families at risk, in particular services to women and children whose lives are disrupted by crime and violence.

Youth Services

10.27 Lack of educational achievement and self-esteem are key factors leading to unemployment, crime and social deprivation. Low educational achievement, which generally is associated with early school leaving, means that people lack the skills necessary to access the employment market and the capacity to avail of opportunities for further skills training. This is a particular problem in today's increasingly sophisticated employment market where skill redundancy is accelerating. Inevitably, lack of skills, leading to economic deprivation, has knock-on implications for the community at large in that it can result in addiction, homelessness and criminal behaviour. Early intervention in this process is essential if these problems are to be avoided and the cycle of social disadvantage to be broken.

10.28 To support the personal and social development of young people so as to prevent them drifting into substance abuse, unemployment and crime, a sum of £302.4 million (€383.9 million) will be spent on the following proposals:

- Funding for National Voluntary Youth Work Organisations in relation to projects designed to develop young people as effective members of their communities;

- Provision of Youth Information Centres to provide easy access to information on youth services and welfare;

- Provision of funding to the Young People's Facilities and Services Fund to support the development of youth facilities and services in disadvantaged areas experiencing, or at risk of experiencing, significant drug problems;

- Funding for Special Projects for Disadvantaged Youth aimed at facilitating the development and social education of youth at risk of drug abuse, juvenile crime, homelessness, early school leaving and marginalisation;

- Establishment of early intervention programmes and substance abuse awareness programmes for young people who are at risk of early school leaving or have low educational achievements;

- Establishment of a number of projects in both urban and rural areas under the Garda Youth Diversion Programme which aims, through both intervention and prevention, to divert young people from becoming involved in criminal activity.

Services for the Unemployed

10.29 For the most marginalised who lack or have lost the capacity to access the mainstream employment services and training opportunities, there is a need for targeted interventions which are managed on an individual basis. Both Regional Operational Programmes will provide an outreach service for the target groups which will proactively identify, contact and engage with the most excluded and marginalised and will also support those wishing to start their own businesses. There will be a particular focus on the integration of ex-drug users and prisoners, both of which present particular challenges and require particularly intensive intervention. There will also be initiatives to support the relevant target groups through the provision of education and training. The EU funded Territorial Employment Pacts will also be supported under this measure.

10.30 A sum of £158.75 million (€201.6 million) will be spent under this heading as follows:

- Provision of a personalised employment outreach service for significantly marginalised groups in society including the provision of soft supports (e.g. business planning, training and mentoring) to assist those wishing to set up in self-employment;

- Provision of support for a tailored approach to identified local education and training needs, in particular, second chance education and training schemes targeted at disadvantaged people wishing to re-enter the labour market.

10.31 The initiatives under this Measure will complement the existing FÁS employment services and the Local Employment Service provided for under the Employment and Human Resources Development Operational Programme.

Indirect NDP Contributions Towards Greater Social Inclusion

10.32 Many of the other substantial investments proposed under the NDP will indirectly contribute to the promotion of social inclusion. The proposed spending under the Economic and Social Infrastructure and Productive Investment Priorities will expand the growth potential of the economy and provide new employment opportunities for all. Particular facets of this investment will also make a specific contribution to social inclusion. For instance, it is the poorer sectors of society which are almost exclusively reliant on public transport in their everyday life. Thus, the envisaged investment in public transport will facilitate the greater participation in economic and social life of those from disadvantaged backgrounds.

10.33 Under the Productive Investment Operational Programme, many of the agricultural development measures, including the substantial measures on income support for farmers contained in the CAP Rural Development Programme, will help to support incomes in poorer rural areas. Investment under the Regional Programmes in non-national roads, urban and village renewal, rural water supply, rural development and the development of tourism and forestry in the regions will also contribute markedly to tackling rural poverty. For example, investment in rural water supply will significantly improve the quality of life in rural areas and, by making the countryside a more attractive place for people to live in and boost the prospect of job and wealth creation in rural areas. These efforts will generate new and additional income generating activities and improve the quality of life in rural areas.

10.34   Investment in energy conservation for the needy and the elderly will reduce their energy costs. Moreover, training for the long-term unemployed in the installation of home insulation and the provision of energy conservation advisory services will provide them with skills which will enable them to re-enter the workforce.

10.35   The PEACE Programme (see Chapter 9) will also have a significant element designed to promote social inclusion.

Social Inclusion and the Implementation of the NDP

10.36   The overall objective of the many Social Inclusion measures contained in both the Inter-regional and the Regional Operational Programmes is to ensure that the socially excluded are enabled to fully participate in and contribute to the current and future progress of the Regions. Achieving this objective will require a comprehensive, holistic approach, involving the target communities and bringing together the services of a range of Departments, the Local Authorities, the relevant State agencies and the voluntary sector. Encouraging marginalised communities to help themselves by identifying their own problems and working towards their solution in a planned and integrated way with the agencies of the State, will be an essential element of the process. Moreover, prioritisation of projects will be essential if the significant resources, which are being set aside within the NDP to deal directly with social disadvantage, are to yield real material benefits for the disadvantaged of our society, their communities and society at large. Spreading the resources too thinly across a range of initiatives or putting in place a set of diverse programmes lacking integration and focus, will not address the real and acute needs of those suffering from social exclusion.

10.37   At national level, the current structures including the Cabinet Committee on Social Inclusion, the Senior Officials Social Inclusion Group, and the NAPS Inter-Departmental Policy Committee oversee and co-ordinate social inclusion policies. However, appropriate structures will need to be put in place at local level to co-ordinate overall planning and delivery of the wide range of social inclusion measures included in the Plan. The experience and expertise derived from the pilot Integrated Services Projects will inform future approaches by the State-funded sector in tackling disadvantage. The recommendations of the Task Force on the Integration of Local Government and Local Development Systems regarding the avoidance of duplication of effort, the filling of gaps and the provision of co-ordinated delivery at local level will also be especially important in this regard.

10.38   A senior officials working group, representative of all relevant Government Departments and reporting to the Task Force on the Integration of Local Government and Local Development Systems, is currently reviewing the planning and delivery mechanisms with a view to improved co-ordination in the delivery of social inclusion measures at local level. The recommendations of the working group in relation to an integrated approach will be reflected in the detailed arrangements to be set out in the Operational Programmes. In this regard, it is envisaged that the County and City Development Boards (CDBs), which are to be set up by 1 January, 2000, will have a key role to play in co-ordinating local delivery of social inclusion measures.

10.39 The CDBs will operate on the partnership principle with the Regional Assemblies and under the local government umbrella with membership drawn from local development organisations, social partners, local representation of State agencies and local government itself. The CDBs will:

- work towards and formulate an agreed county/city strategy for economic social and cultural development;

- develop a vision at local level to encompass the various local and sectoral plans;

- provide the focus for co-operation on a continuing basis at county/city level in the work of the various agencies, promote co-ordination and avoid overlap at this level; and

- by bringing together the various interests in this way, seek to maximise the effectiveness of spending on programmes and projects at local level.

10.40 All the relevant programmes and projects, and their delivery mechanisms, covered by the NDP will be expected to accord with this framework. Key underlying principles of the framework will be the use of common delivery areas (e.g county/city and, where appropriate, local electoral areas for community development/social exclusion) and of a single agency designated for delivery of specific components (e.g micro-enterprise) of local development in any one area so as to avoid overlap, confusion and competition between agencies.

11   Rural Development

Introduction

11.1   Ireland is still a predominantly rural country with 42% of the population living in villages below 1,500 in population or in the countryside. Outside of County Dublin 58% of the population live in rural areas. In the Border, Midland and Western Region, 68% of the population live in rural areas compared to 32% in the S&E Region. Population density in Ireland is among the lowest in Europe, with 52 persons per square kilometre (in 1996) compared with an EU average of 115. The overall rural population (as defined by the CSO) has been relatively stable at around 1.5 million in the most recent intercensal period, 1991-1996. Between 1971 and 1996, the rural population increased by 7%, while the urban population increased by 36%.

11.2   Urbanisation is a key influence on settlement patterns (NESC Report "Population Distribution and Economic Development Trends" (1997)). Counties with strong urban centres, predominately in the S&E Region, retain population whereas those with the lowest urbanisation rates, predominately in the BMW Region, experience large and persistent population decline. These areas have unfavourable age structures, fail to gain access to an adequate share of investment and frequently experience extreme forms of marginalisation. Rural areas also have higher than average dependency rates particularly in the western and border counties. The combination of a high dependence on agriculture, the lack of a diversified employment base to sustain off-farm income and employment opportunities and the out-migration of those with the higher levels of education has undermined the economic structure of many rural areas. The demographic situation has implications for public and private service delivery, with a trend towards service concentration in urban areas and increasing unit cost of service delivery in areas already sparsely populated.

11.3   **White Paper on Rural Development:** Against the above background the Government's White Paper on Rural Development articulates a vision of the long-term future of Irish rural society and an overall policy strategy to achieve this vision. The elements of the overall strategy for rural development which the White Paper emphasises are:

- a dedicated focus on rural development policy with the Department of Agriculture, Food and Rural Development as the lead Department;

- a regional approach to development;

- service and infrastructure provision;

- sustainable economic development;

- human resource development; and

- a determined focus on poverty and social exclusion.

The Government is committed to ensuring the economic and social well being of rural communities, to providing the conditions for a meaningful and fulfilling life for all people living in rural areas and to striving to achieve a rural Ireland in which there will be vibrant sustainable rural communities where individuals and families will have a real choice as to whether to stay in, leave or move to rural Ireland. The investment strategies in the NDP is supportive of this commitment.

11.4   The provisions in, and focus of, the NDP Operational Programmes for Economic and Social Infrastructure, Employment and Human Resources Development, the Productive Sector, and the two Regional Operational Programmes will address all of the elements of the strategy of the White Paper on Rural Development. Overall NDP Investment which will directly impact on Rural Development will be of the order of £6.7 billion (€ 8.5 billion) for the period of the Plan, and will be allocated between the broad categories set out in the table below:

Table 11.1: Rural Development Expenditure 2000-2006

Category	National € million	BMW Region € million	S&E Region € million
Agriculture & Fisheries Development	410	203	207
CAP Rural Development Accompanying Measures	4,324	2,474	1,850
Rural Enterprises (includes agriculture, forestry & fisheries)	495	285	210
Training in Agriculture, Food Forestry & Fisheries	152	72	80
Capital Investment for Food & Fisheries, Marketing and Research & Development for Agriculture, Food and Fisheries	479	200	279
Rural Infrastructure	2,694	1,303	1,391
Total	**8,554**	**4,537**	**4,017**

Regional Dimension

11.5   As table 11.1 indicates the instruments to promote rural development will be the same in both regions but a disproportionate amount of the expenditure will be expended in the BMW Region. This reflects the more rural character of the region and the consequent need for more resources to sustain and develop rural areas in the region. Provision is, however, made for the development needs of rural areas in the more urbanised S&E Region.

11.6   The strategy for rural development in the NDP, will pay particular attention to the natural resource industries (agriculture, forestry, fisheries and food) and the rural infrastructure which links the rural hinterland to the urban areas. Funding for agricultural and rural development will feature in the following component areas of the Plan;

- the CAP Rural Development Programme (Guarantee funded) — REPS, Early Retirement, Compensatory Allowances and Forestry;

- the Productive Sector Operational Programme covers Agricultural Development, the Food Sector and support for RTDI;

- Related Rural Development is covered in the two Regional Programmes;

- Training in all areas is covered under the Human Resources and Employment Inter-Regional Programme.

11.7   While efficient and productive agriculture, forestry and fisheries industries have an important role to play in rural development, the prosperity of rural areas will increasingly be determined by the success of businesses not directly involved in the natural resource sector. It is also recognised that there are synergies from the co-ordinated development of urban areas and their rural hinterlands. The importance of this is underlined in the Regional Development Policy framework set out in Chapter 3. In this context, the National Spatial Strategy to be prepared by the Department of Environment and Local Government will address rural-urban spatial development and planning needs.

11.8 The Regional Development Policy set out in Chapter 3 underlines the importance of a regional policy which fully recognises the potential and needs of rural areas. More generally the overall investment strategy in the NDP in the Inter-regional Operational Programmes is supportive of rural development. Whilst much of this investment is not included in the above table it will have an important influence. Under the Economic and Social Infrastructure Operational Programme, investment in roads and environmental services will make it more attractive for industry and services to locate away from larger urban centres thereby increasing the opportunities for rural people to find employment in their own areas. Public transport investment will also make it easier for rural people to commute to jobs in larger urban centres. Investment in Health capital will make health services more accessible. Under the Productive Sector Operational Programme, apart from investment in agriculture, the strategy for Foreign Direct Investment (FDI) and industrial investment generally will assist a greater regional spread of new jobs.

11.9 Under the Regional Operational Programmes, direct investment in a number of areas will assist rural development. Investment in village renewal will make rural villages more attractive places to live in and will also enhance their tourism potential. Specific investment in tourism will be in areas away from main urban centres which should be of benefit to rural areas whilst cultural and recreational investment will also make such areas more attractive places to live and work in. Investment in education and training will benefit rural and urban people alike. Investment to promote social inclusion will address pockets of rural deprivation as well as urban blackspots. The local development and community development measures under the Regional Programmes will have a particular focus on promoting enterprise in rural areas. Targeted investment in telecommunications and energy will also improve the accessibility of rural areas.

11.10 Agriculture, Fisheries and Forestry: While the majority of rural dwellers are neither farmers nor dependent on agriculture or other natural resource industries for their livelihood, agriculture, forestry and fisheries continue to be the most important sectors in the rural economy. Agriculture, forestry and fisheries account for 16.9% of employment and 8.7% of Gross Value Added in the BMW Region and 8% of employment and 3.9% of GVA in the Southern and Eastern region. A big element of rural development policy will therefore be continuing support for these sectors in both regions.

11.11 Agriculture: The agricultural sector, which is the dominant natural resource sector in the rural economy, suffers from a number of structural deficiencies. Many farmers require off-farm employment to ensure an adequate level of income. Teagasc estimate that only 30% of family farms are economically viable making off-farm employment necessary if the farm population is to be maintained. Based on the National Farm Survey results for 1997, it is estimated that on 43% of farms either the holder or the holder's spouse had an off-farm job. The farm population is relatively old, with 22% of farmers over 65 years old and only 12% under 35. This relatively old age structure militates against the improvement in farm productivity. Finally, environmental considerations necessitate increased investment in the management of farm waste and this will put further pressure on income margins in farming.

11.12   Marine: The seafood sector has the potential to make a substantial contribution to rural coastal communities in the less developed regions of the country. In particular it sustains remote coastal communities, including island and Gaeltacht areas, where there are few economic alternatives. At a national level, annual sales of marine food are worth over £330 million with 90% of output exported. The marine fishing, aquaculture, processing and ancillary sectors employ 16,000 people directly and an additional 9,000 people indirectly in supporting sectors. Including family dependants, nearly 60,000 people rely on the fisheries industry.

11.13   Forestry: Ireland has a relatively low percentage (8%) of its land area under forest, despite the fact that the potential for forestry production is quite high. In contrast the average area under forest in the EU is over 30%. Forestry is by nature a rural activity and is a valuable alternative to agricultural activity. Employment in the sector is about 16,000. Forestry has direct benefits for local communities:

- through the establishment of plantations;

- in spin-off effects in support services, through industries ranging from woodcraft to industrial processing;

- in rural tourism;

- by enhancing the environment through acting as carbon sinks thereby assisting in meeting the CO_2 obligations under the Kyoto Protocol.

Strategy for Agriculture

11.14   Irish agricultural policy is largely determined and constrained by the requirements of the Common Agricultural Policy and international agreements. The recent outcome of the Agenda 2000 negotiations sets the framework within which the agricultural industry will develop in the immediate future. That framework, which aims to enable farmers and other rural dwellers remain in rural areas with an acceptable standard of income and quality of life, is built around:

- the importance of improving the competitiveness of the European agricultural and agri-food sectors on internal and external markets, and

- the recognition of the need for an integrated rural policy, including the environment to accompany the reform process.

11.15   The Agenda 2000 Agreement in the area of agriculture includes reforms in the beef, milk and cereals sectors which essentially involve reductions in market supports and compensation by way of premia etc. Taking the period 2000-2006 as a whole, it has been calculated that there is a net gain from the Agreement of £395 million for farm incomes in Ireland.

11.16   The strategy for improving structures in the agriculture, food and related rural development areas in the National Development Plan will reflect in particular, the Council Regulation on Support for Rural Development agreed under Agenda 2000. Eight strategic areas have been highlighted for attention viz:

- improving agricultural structures at farm level;

- improving breeding, animal welfare, hygiene and quality;

- focusing on quality and food safety at processing level and assisting the further development of the food industry;

- developing non-surplus products;

- continuing direct income support for farmers in designated disadvantaged areas;

- improving the environment at farm level;

- developing rural services and rural enterprise support; and

- continuing to provide back up research, advice and training in the agriculture, food and rural development areas.

11.17   Improving Agricultural Structures: With a view to tackling the general structural aspects in the strategy above and addressing one of the overall NDP objectives of improving competitiveness, it is proposed to a Scheme of Installation Aid for Young Farmers and an Early Retirement Scheme for Farmers. These measures complement each other and their aim is to maintain as many viable farms as possible by encouraging the take-over of farms by the younger generation. These younger farmers are better able to adapt to the increasing challenge of competitiveness in the face of production constraints and the need on many farms to earn adequate off-farm income to supplement agricultural income. A provision of £27.5 million (€34.9 million) is being made available for the Installation Aid Scheme with indicative amounts of £11 million (€14 million) for the BMW Region and £16.5 million (€21 million) for the S&E Region. A provision of £565 million (€717.6 million) is being made available for the Early Retirement Scheme. This scheme will operate under a CAP Rural Development Programme throughout the country and financed by the FEOGA Guarantee Fund (and, therefore, outside of the Structural Funds). Expenditure between the Regions is difficult to predict — under the current scheme, the major expenditure has taken place in the S&E Region but improvements in the new Council Regulation related to the removal of the enlargement clause and the opening up of the scheme to part-time farmers are expected to result in increased numbers of farmers benefiting in the BMW Region. A provisional indicative 72% £407 million (€516.9 million) is provided for the BMW Region.

11.18   Improving the Quality of Products: The promotion of quality output will, along with measures aimed at improving consumer assurance and environment friendly production systems, be essential elements in securing the development of an efficient, competitive and modern agriculture. On the production side, it is proposed to operate measures which will improve breeding, animal welfare and general hygiene conditions and also enhance grain quality and safety. Funding will be of the order of £53.5 million (€67.9 million) for these measures, some of which, especially in relation to breeding will be expended at central level. It is expected that 54% of the expenditure will be in the BMW Region reflecting the weaker capacity of the farm sector there to carry out their own investment.

11.19   Food Quality and Safety: Food quality and safety is vital at every stage of the food chain. The industry must ensure that consumers have full confidence in the quality and safety of its products. Therefore, development in the food industry will be underpinned by attention to food safety and quality issues.

11.20   In line with the action plan proposed by the Food Industry Development Group, support will be provided towards capital investment, research/technology/innovation, marketing and promotion, and the development of human resources. The support measures will address particular sectoral issues — such as those identified by the Beef Task Force. They will also seek to maximise the added-value element of the overall industry. An allocation of £168 million (€213 million) is being provided in the NDP for capital investment, marketing and promotion in the food sector of which an indicative 45% will be invested in the BMW Region. The food industry will also receive support for training and R&D under the Employment and Human Resources Development Operational Programme and the Productive Sector Operational Programme respectively.

11.21   Non-surplus products: The pressure on margins in traditional products as well as changes in consumers tastes create opportunities for improving farm incomes through the development of non-surplus products. However in order to exploit these opportunities farmers will need selective support to upgrade their facilities to meet market and environmental requirements in the horticulture, potatoes and organic areas and also in housing and handling facilities for alternative enterprises such as horses and deer. An allocation of £38 million (€48.3 million) is being provided for this purpose of which £14 million (€17.8 million) (37%) will be in the BMW Region and £24 million (€30.5 million) (63%) in the S&E Region.

11.22   Compensatory Allowances in Disadvantaged Areas: Despite the many opportunities which may arise from diversification and off-farm work, there will remain considerable numbers of farmers in disadvantaged farming areas who cannot avail of these opportunities or who cannot secure enough extra income through this approach. This means that there will be a continuing need to provide such farmers with income support if the population in rural areas is to remain viable. This will be achieved through the continuation of the Compensatory Allowances Scheme, which operates horizontally across Member States in areas specifically designated by the European Union as disadvantaged in agricultural terms. Under Agenda 2000, major changes to this measure have been agreed — it moves to payment on a hectare rather than per head of animal basis and as a further move towards making it an environmentally orientated scheme, farmers must demonstrate that they are following accepted good agricultural practices. This measure will operate under the CAP Rural Development Programme (and, therefore, outside of the Structural Funds). A provision of £840 million (€1,066.8 million) is being made available in the NDP and given that the areas classified as more severely disadvantaged are generally in the BMW Region, expenditure in that Region is expected to be of the order of £546 million (€693.4 million) with possibly £294 million (€373.4 million) being expended in the S&E Region. However, these are broad indicative figures only.

11.23   Environmental Protection: Agenda 2000 makes provision for operating the measures outlined above but it also emphasises the more prominent role to be given to agri-environment instruments to support the sustainable development of rural areas and to respond to society's increasing demand for environmental services. Member States are, accordingly, obliged to offer farmers environmental programmes of aid and also they must ensure that all EU funded measures are operated in accordance with acknowledged good agricultural practices in relation to the environment. It is proposed to operate a Rural Environment Protection Scheme and a Scheme for Farm Waste Management. Funding for REPS, totalling £1,500 million (€1,905 million) will be made available under the CAP Rural Development Programme already referred to above. The scheme will operate throughout the country and rough forecasts of expenditure are likely to be of the order of £870 million (€1,105 million) in the BMW Region and £630 million (€800.1 million) in the S&E Region. As regards the Scheme for Farm Waste Management involving the provision of improved animal housing facilities and also farm waste storage, funding will be approximately £147 million (€186.7 million) and demand across both Regions is likely to be equally divided.

11.24   Development of Services and Enterprise Support: Agriculture will remain critical to the well-being of the rural economy and, indeed, in many areas it represents the main option for economic activity. Nevertheless, in the overall context, it continues to decline in economic importance and production controls ensure that many farmers cannot increase their income from farming. Therefore, alternative income generating opportunities from off-farm activities are vital if rural populations are to benefit from economic growth. This is fully recognised in the White Paper on Rural Development and takes effect in the Operational Programmes. In addition, some specific measures targeted essentially at local level, are proposed covering a number of areas such as:

- Rural Development Programme operating at local level and providing funding for local groups who are area-based and tripartite in structure and who submit local development plans for their areas covering administration, animation, training, rural tourism (in accordance with national policy), local crafts and services, alternative farm enterprises, including small food processing and small scale environmental activities. This proposal is essentially aimed at groups and collective bodies whose activities in the past were funded by LEADER. This Programme will have to be compatible with LEADER Plus and with any developments arising out of the Report of the Task Force on the Integration of the Local Government and Local Development Systems;

- Rural Development Fund, is being established with the objective of enabling an ongoing review of the rural development strategy outlined in the recent White Paper and to assist policy making in the future. The Fund will finance research, including collaboration in policy orientated rural research, by research organisations and third level institutions, evaluations and pilot actions, where appropriate. It will support specific assignments focused on important policy questions in order to provide information and advice to policy makers;

- Farm Relief Services will be assisted with the objective of further developing the farm relief services through better training for the operators, research and development and improved infrastructure. The Scheme will be operated through the National Co-operative Farm Relief Services Ltd., (NCFRS) which is the umbrella organisation for registered FRS Co-ops throughout Ireland on the basis of annual programmes to be agreed with the Department of Agriculture, Food and Rural Development;

- Western Investment Fund will operate with the objective of encouraging economic and social development within the Western Region as defined under the Western Development Commission Act, 1998. In relation to that Act, the coverage of the Fund relates to County Clare in the S&E Region and to Donegal, Leitrim, Sligo, Roscommon, Galway and Mayo in the BMW Region. The Fund will provide loans and take equity in a small number of strategically important investments, in business start-up and growth-orientated small and medium enterprises and in community based developments aimed at encouraging enterprise establishment.

Specific allocations between measures will be decided in the Operational Programme. The total allocation for rural enterprise development (i.e. the rural development measure of the Regional Operational Programmes) is £172 million (€218.4 million) of which an indicative £94 million (€119.4 million) (55%) is for the BMW Region.

11.25 Research, Advice and Training: Improvement in competitiveness and efficiency in the agricultural and food sector and compliance with relevant environmental standards require appropriate research, advisory and training support. In addition, all of these services will be required in identifying factors which influence the establishment and viability of alternative employment opportunities and enterprise. To address the research, advice and training needs of the agriculture and food sector an indicative provision of £226 million (€287 million) is being made in the Plan, £96 million (€121.9 million) (42%) of which will be in the BMW Region and

£130 million (€165.1 million) (58%) in the S&E Region. Teagasc will be the main body involved in delivering these services.

Forestry

11.26   In the NDP a total of £580 million (€736.4 million) has been provided for forestry of which £500 million (€634.9 million) will be co-funded under the CAP Rural Development (FEOGA Guarantee Fund). This latter investment will support a planting programme of 20,000 hectares per year over the period of the Plan. The focus will be on farm forestry with grants for planting and maintenance as well as income support premia. In addition to CAP supported measures an allocation of £80 million (€101.6 million) is being provided in the Regional Operational Programmes (of which 60% will be in the BMW Region) for investment in harvesting equipment, forest roads and general woodland improvement. Because of the relatively poor quality of land for agricultural purposes in the BMW Region and the consequent need to diversify, forestry has greater potential in that region. In order to exploit that potential an indicative £423 million (€537.2 million) (73%) of planned expenditure is being provided for the BMW Region.

Fisheries

11.27   A provision of £183 million (€232.4 million) is being made in the Plan for fisheries development (including fleet modernisation) acquaculture and harbours (both fisheries and other small harbours in the Gaeltacht and islands). Reflecting the greater dependence of the Region on this sector, 60% of this provision is for the BMW Region, and 40% for the S&E Region. In addition, the seafood industry will receive support under the RTD, Indigenous Industry, Marketing and training provisions. Development of the inland fisheries resource as an important recreational and tourism activity in the rural economy will also be supported.

Rural Infrastructure

11.28   The success of the rural economy is dependent on having an adequate transport and environmental infrastructure. Given the dispersed nature of rural population roads are the most critical component of transport infrastructure as far as rural dwellers are concerned and particularly regional and local roads that link rural communities to the national road network and to regional gateways. The Plan will provide £1,600 million (€2,031.6 million) for the improvement and maintenance of these roads. Because of the rural nature of the BMW Region and the need to provide better links between rural and urban areas in the Region non-national roads are relatively more important there and in reflection of this, 44% of the provision will be allocated to the region.

11.29   Good quality drinking water is a essential requirement for the public at large as well as for industrial and tourism development. Rural areas have a relatively high dependence on private water supply or private group schemes which tend to have poorer quality water than that supplied from public sources. In order to address this deficiency the Plan is providing £420 million (€533.3 million) for rural water schemes. £294 million (€373.3 million) (70%) of this is for the BMW Region reflecting the more rural character of the region.

11.30   The quality of the built environment in rural towns and villages is important to rural areas in terms of their attractiveness as places in which to live and work and as locations for industrial, services and tourism investment. An allocation of £103 million (€130.8 million) is being provided for village and urban renewal and this will be targeted on small towns and villages broken down by Region as follows: BMW Region £31 million (€39.4 million), S&E Region £72 million (€91.4 million).

Rural based industries

11.31 Small and medium sized enterprises (SMEs) and micro-enterprises are particularly important for rural development. The Plan provides £973 million (€1,235.7 million) for Indigenous industry and SME support and £150 million (€190.5 million) for micro enterprises. While all areas will benefit from these provisions, they should be of considerable assistance to rural areas. A particular focus of the micro-enterprises allocation will be to develop enterprises in or close to rural areas. Activity under this heading will compliment the rural enterprise measures referred to in Paragraph 11.24

Rural proofing

11.32 As agreed by the Government in relation to the White Paper on Rural Development, administrative procedures will be introduced for application by all Departments to ensure that policy makers are aware of the likely impact of all proposals on rural communities. The operation of these procedures will contribute significantly to integrating the strategy for the economic and social development of rural areas with the objectives and principles of other policy initiatives and, in particular, of the National Anti-Poverty Strategy.

Conclusion

11.33 The financial provisions in the Plan affecting Rural Development give real substance to the strategy set out in the White Paper on the subject. Particular attention will be paid in Plan implementation and monitoring to the effective delivery of these measures and more importantly to ensuring they have a tangible effect on the ground in rural areas.

12 Management and Implementation of Programmes

Management of Programmes

12.1   While the current NDP 1994-1999 treats Ireland as a single Region (Objective 1), the NDP in the programming period 2000-2006, arising from the division of Ireland into two regions for Structural Funds purposes, will see the country classified into two NUTS II Regions i.e. Objective 1 (Border, Midland and Western Region) and Objective 1 in transition (Southern and Eastern Region). As a result of this, new arrangements will be put in place regarding the management, implementation and monitoring of programmes in this Plan.

12.2   The National Development Plan will form the basis of discussions with the EU Commission which will result in agreement on a Community Support Framework (CSF) for the period 2000-2006. Structural Fund assistance will be channeled predominantly through the CSF. This will be complemented by further Structural Funds aid through Community Initiative programmes. Projects to be assisted by the Cohesion Fund and TENS will be approved separately by the Commission. The CAP accompanying measures which are co-funded by the FEOGA Guarantee Fund are not part of the Structural Funds and will not therefore be part of the CSF; they will be the subject of a separate EU programme. Unlike the current CSF, CSF 2000-2006 will have a very substantial element of non co-funded measures and expenditure. This expenditure will be included in the CSF tables and reported to Monitoring Committees for their information.

Structure of Operational Programmes

12.3   It is proposed to implement the Community Support Framework through 3 National (Inter-Regional) Operational Programmes — an Economic and Social Infrastructure Operational Programme, an Employment and Human Resources Development Operational Programme and a Productive Sector Operational Programme — and 2 Regional Operational Programmes for the Border, Midland and Western and Southern and Eastern Regions respectively. There will be a separate programme for the Peace and Reconciliation Programme which will be confined to the BMW Region. In addition to the Community Support Framework there will be four Community Initiative programmes — Interreg, Equal, Leader and Urban.

Programme Management

12.4   The Managing Authority for each Operational Programme will be as follows:

Operational Programme	Managing Authority
CSF (overall)	Department of Finance
Economic and Social Infrastructure	Department of Environment and Local Government
Employment and Human Resources Development	Department of Enterprise, Trade and Employment
Productive Investment	Department of Enterprise, Trade and Employment
BMW Regional Programme	BMW Regional Assembly
S&E Regional Programme	S&E Regional Assembly
Peace Programme	EU Programmes Body*
Cohesion Fund	Department of Finance

*As provided for in the Good Friday Agreement

209

12.5   With regard to the EU co-funded element of Operational Programmes, the principal responsibilities of the Managing Authority for each Operational Programme will be:

- chairing and providing the secretariat for the Monitoring Committee;

- assembling statistical and financial information required for monitoring the Operational Programme and supplying this information to the CSF Managing Authority (Department of Finance) in a computerised format to be determined by the Department of Finance in agreement with the European Commission;

- drawing up the annual implementation report for approval by the Monitoring Committee and submission to the Commission;

- submitting payment claims to the paying authorities for the Structural Funds in compliance with any instructions which these authorities may issue;

- ensuring that EU funded expenditure is properly accounted for and managed;

- ensuring compliance with EU policies, particularly regarding public procurement, publicity, the environment and equality.

Implementation of Measures

12.6   Measures will be generally implemented by existing implementing Departments and Agencies with functional responsibility for the service or policy area. However, over the course of NDP 2000-2006, delivery of measures will be subject to increased competition where appropriate. It is also intended to rationalise the number of agencies delivering schemes over the Plan period. The intended merging of existing measures may require a shifting of responsibility from one or more Departments or Agencies to a single entity. However, discussions will be held with the relevant Departments and other concerned Agencies before finally determining who the implementing agency will be in such instances. In the implementation of measures across all programmes account will have to be taken of national policies in relation to these measures. In the case of the rural water measure in the regional operational programmes, implementation will continue through the existing partnership structures at county, national and local level for the development and implementation of a sustained strategy to deal with rural water quality problems.

12.7   **Social Inclusion:** There will be a special Sub-Programme for Social Inclusion in each of the Regional Operational Programmes under the National Development Plan. The institutional and administrative arrangements which will be put in place to ensure efficient and coherent delivery of the measures under this sub-programme are described in Chapter 10.

Monitoring Committees

12.8   Each Operational Programme and the Community Support Framework will be supervised by Monitoring Committees. It is proposed that Irish membership of Monitoring Committees for the national (Inter-regional) Operational Programmes and Regional Operational Programmes will be broadly similar to existing arrangements for the current CSF (1994-1999). Accordingly there will be representatives from the Managing Authority, the Department of Finance, Government Departments and public bodies involved in implementation of programme measures. Additionally representatives from the Regional Assemblies and the four Social Partners Pillars will be included on all CSF and Operational Programme Monitoring Committees, not just selected committees. It is also proposed that all Monitoring Committees will include an appropriate member to represent equal opportunity and environmental interests to be drawn from a relevant Government

Department or an appropriate statutory body. The Commission services and the Central Evaluation Unit (see Paragraphs 12.18-12.21) will be represented on the Monitoring Committee in an observer capacity. The Monitoring Committees for Regional Operational Programmes will also include a representative (who will be a member of the Regional Assembly) from each of the existing NUTS III Regional Authorities in the Region. Gender balance will be promoted on all Monitoring Committees.

12.9 The Monitoring Committee will be responsible for decisions regarding EU co-funded measures in the Operational Programmes including decisions on the reallocation of co-funded expenditure between measures within an Operational Programme or between Operational Programmes in the case of the CSF Monitoring Committee. They will also be responsible for the mid-term review of the Operational Programmes in conjunction with the Department of Finance. The Monitoring Committees will be set up within three months after the decision on the contribution of the funds, with each Monitoring Committee being responsible for drawing up its own rules of procedure and agreeing them with the Managing Authority and the Department of Finance. The Monitoring Committee will be chaired by a representative of the Managing Authority. Details of the role and responsibilities of Monitoring Committees will be set out in a Department of Finance circular.

Non Co-financed Expenditure in Operational Programmes

12.10 All of the Operational Programmes will contain a substantial element of non co-financed (mainly Exchequer) expenditure and measures. Reports on all such expenditure and measures will be submitted to the relevant Monitoring Committees and the CSF Monitoring Committee. It will be open to the Monitoring Committees to consider the progress and impact of such expenditure and to make recommendations in this regard.

Monitoring Indicators

12.11 The Managing Authority and the Monitoring Committee will specify physical and financial indicators in the Operational Programme or programme complement for both co-financed and non co-financed expenditure. As provided for in the Regulations, these indicators will be used, inter alia, to assess performance at the mid-term stage in the context of decisions on the allocation of the performance reserve. It will be important therefore to ensure that a consistent approach is taken to the selection and quantification of these indicators.

12.12 The programme indicator system will be structured in line with the schema drawn up the CSF Evaluation Unit in its paper "CSF Performance Indicators: Proposals for 2000-2006 Programming Period". This paper essentially operationalises the requirements of the Regulations and takes account of the Commission's indicative methodology in this area. As regards the actual selection of indicators, account will be taken of the lists of examples published by the Commission and the categorisation of the fields of intervention. Where the nature of the assistance permits, the statistics will be broken down by gender and by the size of the recipients' undertakings. As recommended in the CSF Evaluation Unit's paper and in line with a proposal by the Commission in its methodological guidelines, it is also proposed to set up a small committee (to include the Central Evaluation Unit) which will review the selection of indicators and the quantification of targets prior to the submission of the programming complement documents to the Monitoring Committees. This should help promote objectivity and consistency in the establishment of the indicators.

Project Selection

12.13 Decisions in relation to project selection under the Operational Programmes will be a critical determinant of the socio-economic impact of this National Development Plan. For this reason and in the light of the various analyses which have been carried out in relation to current practice under the CSF 1994-1999[1], the general principles which will be applied to project selection under the NDP is set out here. This issue will also be explicitly addressed in more detail in the Operational Programme complements required under the general Structural Funds Regulations.

12.14 There are a number of criteria which will be explicitly incorporated into the project selection procedures of all implementing bodies under this Plan (while accepting the need to take account of additional specific Operational Programme or sectoral considerations). These criteria, which follow directly from the overall objectives underpinning this Plan, are as follows:

- programme and measure objectives;

- economic impact (as measured by an appropriate measure of additional economic activity or employment), taking particular account of the potential for deadweight and displacement effects;

- financial viability (in the case of productive sector projects and PPP projects);

- cost-effectiveness (i.e. overall benefits, as reflected in the above criteria, in relation to project costs);

- environmental impact;

- impact on equality of opportunity, particularly gender equality;

- impact on poverty;

- impact on rural development.

12.15 It is accepted that a degree of flexibility may be required in the translation of these considerations into individual programme contexts and that the weight to be attached to each will vary in the light of specific Operational Programme or measure/scheme objectives. However, in order to ensure objectivity and transparency, the programming complements will set out the specific criteria to be used in the case of individual measures and interventions and will indicate in general terms the relative priority to be attached in each case. Project selection criteria will apply to both co-funded and non co-funded projects.

12.16 The Government is also anxious to ensure that a much greater degree of competition is introduced into project selection under the Plan, especially in areas involving the provision of grant-aid to the private sector. Generally queue-based grant approval systems will be replaced by competitive processes, except where this is clearly inappropriate.[2] The programme complements will again set out how this general principle will be applied in each case.

12.17 In the case of infrastructural and large scale productive sector projects which are appraised using cost-benefit analysis, the approach and parameters set out in the CSF Evaluation

---

[1] These include (i) *Cost-Benefit Analysis in the CSF, A Critical Review* (CSF Evaluation Unit, June 1997) and (ii) *Review of Project Selection Procedures and Appraisal Techniques in the CSF* (Fitzpatrick Associates, May, 1999)

[2] This will not, for example, apply to certain measures in agriculture which are available to all farmers who meet specified criteria subject to funds being available.

Unit's report *Proposed Working Rules for Cost-Benefit Analysis* (June, 1999) will apply. In the case of once-off projects or where a cost-benefit analysis is required under Articles 25 and 26 of Council Regulation 1260/1999, the Central Evaluation Unit (referred to in Paragraph 12.18 below) will either carry out or commission the study under the direction of a steering committee.

Evaluation

12.18   Under the CSF 1994-1999, a high priority was attached to evaluation. Each of the nine main Operational Programmes were subject to ongoing evaluation at various stages in the form of either an internal independent evaluation unit or an external evaluator. As part of the mid-term review process completed in 1997, a mid-term evaluation was undertaken of the CSF and of each of the nine Operational Programmes, together with a mid-term evaluation of the regional impact of the CSF. These evaluations were all carried out by independent external evaluators. At CSF level, the CSF Evaluation Unit exercised a co-ordination and advisory role in relation to the evaluation process. Following a review in 1998 by the CSF Evaluation Unit of the ongoing evaluation process and its consideration by the CSF Monitoring Committee, the Department of Finance issued a circular setting out arrangements to apply to future evaluations on 23 July, 1999.

12.19   The evaluation arrangements for the next CSF will be designed to meet the challenges of the proposed programme structure and to take account of best-practice lessons drawn from the current programming period. The overall aim will be to ensure a more consistent, rigorous and cost-effective approach to evaluation in the future. The arrangements set out in the Department of Finance circular of 23 July, 1999 on the conduct of, and follow-up to, evaluations will apply. In addition, arrangements will be put in place to ensure that all evaluations are subject to quality control by small, tightly-focused steering committees.

12.20   Having regard to the Government's concern to ensure the best possible return to the resources committed to the Plan, the evaluation arrangements will apply to all expenditures under this Plan, regardless of funding source. To facilitate this, a Central Evaluation Unit will be established in the Department of Finance. It will be charged with the function of providing an ongoing evaluative input to the work of each of the Monitoring Committees and of carrying out or commissioning any evaluations which may be required at Operational Programme or CSF level. This will be done at the request of the Monitoring Committee and in accordance with terms of reference as set by the Steering Committee. It will also have a role in relation to project selection and appraisal under the Plan (see Paragraph 12.17 above). Given the significant ESF funding proposed in a number of Operational Programmes, particularly Education and Human Resources, a discrete ESF evaluation function will be included under the Central Evaluation Unit; this ESF evaluation function will be under the auspices of the Department of Enterprise Trade and Employment. Within this framework, a Steering Committee comprising the Department of Enterprise Trade and Employment, the Department of Finance and other relevant departments, as appropriate, will set the terms of reference and exercise quality control in relation to ESF evaluations. This evaluation unit, which will be co-funded under Technical Assistance, will comprise a small number of persons, generally recruited through open competition and appointed on a full-time contract basis, augmented by relevant external experts recruited on short-term contracts as required.

12.21   As provided for in the Structural Funds Regulations, the Operational Programmes will be the subject of mid-term evaluations in 2003 (to be updated in 2005). These will be commissioned from independent external experts and co-ordinated through the Central Evaluation Unit.

Financial Management of Funds

12.22 Under the current CSF the paying authorities with responsibility and authority for the administration of the Structural and Cohesion Funds have been assigned by Government to four Government Departments namely: the Department of Finance for the European Regional Development Fund and the Cohesion Fund; The Department of Enterprise, Trade and Employment for the European Social Fund; the Department of Agriculture and Food for the European Agriculture Guidance and Guarantee Fund (Guidance) and the Department of the Marine and Natural Resources for the Financial Instrument for Fisheries Guidance. The same arrangement will apply to CSF 2000-2006. Insofar as co-funded expenditure is concerned the paying authorities will have overall responsibility for ensuring that there is full compliance with the financial provisions of the Structural Funds regulations. Under the current CSF, the internal auditors for the paying Departments are signatories of financial protocols with the Commission's Financial Controller. It is proposed to continue this arrangement in the next round. The Department of Finance will issue a detailed circular on roles and responsibilities of paying authorities and implementing Departments and Agencies with respect to financial management and control.

Information and Publicity

12.23 The Member State is responsible for ensuring that information and publicity requirements of the Structural Funds are met. In the current CSF information and publicity for Structural Funds is co-ordinated and promoted by the CSF Information Office. There is also a separate information officer for ESF funded activities. In the CSF 2000-2006 it is proposed to continue the CSF Information Office and, in the interest of efficiency and more effective communication, to have information and publicity for all funds co-ordinated from that office. However, information and publicity for ESF funded activity will continue to operate from the Department of Enterprise, Trade and Employment under the auspices of the Structural Funds Information Office. While managing Departments and implementing Departments and Agencies will be responsible for publicity for programmes which they are managing or implementing, the CSF Information Office will be available to assist and advise them in this particular function.

Computerisation

12.24 The monitoring of financial and physical indicator information in the NDP and CSF 2000-2006 will be computerised. The Department of Finance in currently developing a computerised data management system for the NDP 2000-2006 and its constituent Operational Programmes which all Managing Authorities and implementing Departments will be required to use. This system is being designed to facilitate the electronic transfer of financial and indicator data for all measures and projects in the Plan into a central database which will be maintained by the Department of Finance. It will be an essential tool for monitoring, financial management and control, and for the provision of up-to-date and comprehensive information on the NDP and CSF 2000-2006.

13 Compliance with Community and National Policies

Introduction

13.1 The National Development Plan 2000-2006 was drafted having full regard to National and Community policies. In particular, the Plan reflects the following influences:

- *Irelands Stability and Growth Pact;*

- *National Action Employment Plan;*

- *Ireland's Objective 3 Policy Frame of Reference;*

- *National Anti Poverty Strategy;*

- *White Paper on Rural Development;*

- *Sustainable Development: A Strategy for Ireland;*

- *Structural Funds Regulations of 21 June, 1999;*

- *The Structural Funds and their co-ordination with the Cohesion Fund — Guidelines for Programmes in the period 2000-2006 (COM (1999) 344);*

- *Methodological Workings Papers: Vademecum for Structural Funds Plans and Programming Documents, the Ex- Ante Evaluation of the Structural Funds Interventions, Indicators for Monitoring and Evaluation, An Indicative Methodology and Implementation of the Performamce Reserve;*

- *1999 Employment Guidelines, Employment in Europe, Equal Opportunities for Men and Women — European Community Acts; and*

- *A Handbook on Environmental Assessment of the Regional Development Plans and EU Structural Funds Programmes.*

13.2 As a result of the decision to regionalise, Ireland comprises two NUTS II regions — the Objective 1 Region (Border, Midland and Western Region) and the Objective 1 Region in Transition (Southern and Eastern Region). Article 13 of the Structural Funds General Regulations affords Member States the discretion to determine the geographical coverage of their Plan, i.e. whether to cover a single region at NUTS II level or whether to submit a general plan covering some or all of their regions. A general plan may be submitted for Structural Funds purposes provided that all the requirements of Article 16 of the General Regulations are included in the plan. The Government decided that the National Development Plan should be an investment plan to address the country's economic and social development needs for the period 2000-2006, incorporating all relevant investment proposals to be cofinanced from Structural Funds and from public resources. Arising from the consultation on the Plan (Appendix 1 refers), there was consensus among the social partners and regional authorities that the Government's approach to the development of the Plan was the appropriate one. The Plan incorporates an integrated multisectoral strategy for securing balanced regional development which will address the development needs of both regions in Ireland.

13.3 The Commission have adopted indicative guidelines on relevant Community policies to help national and regional authorities to prepare programming strategies for the Objectives 1, 2 and 3 of the Structural Funds and their links with the Cohesion Funds. The guidelines set out the priorities of the Commission based on past experience in the implementation of programmes and on current Community policies for structural assistance. The approach to the application in the Plan of the Commission's guidelines has been to apply them having regard to the specific economic and social characteristics of the country and its two regions. Particular attention has been paid to Community policy priorities in proposing areas for cofinancing from Structural and Cohesion Funds.

13.4 The European Commission have identified **3 strategic priorities for Community Policies**:

- **Regional Competitiveness;**
- **Social Cohesion and Employment;**
- **Development of Urban and Rural areas.**

They recommend that these strategic priorities be pursued through integrated strategies for development of regions. The strategies are to be **underpinned by two horizontal principles, namely, sustainable development and equal opportunities**.

13.5 Under Regional Competitiveness the priorities identified by the Commission for consideration for assistance are investments in:

- transport (efficiency, multi modal, accessibility and sustainability);
- energy (efficiency and renewable);
- telecommunications infrastructure (towards the information society);
- infrastructure for a high Quality Environment (with the application of the Polluter Pays Principle);
- Research, Technological Development and Innovation (RTDI) (Modernising the productive base);
- where appropriate, partnership between public and private partners.

13.6 A key priority of the National Development Plan 2000-2006 is addressing Ireland's acknowledged infrastructural deficit (Chapter 4 refers). The need to provide good quality infrastructure is a priority in both regions, with the added dimension of relieving congestion in the larger urban areas, particularly in the S&E Region.

13.7 In line with the stated Community priorities in relation to transport, the Plan proposes €541 million Structural Funds and €220 million Cohesion Fund assistance towards the provision of National Roads in the Economic and Social Infrastructure Operational Programme, with the emphasis on the completion of TENs and major inter-urban routes. A small provision of €21 million is proposed for roads in the Regional Operational Programmes to support key links between gateways and their surrounding areas. Given the immediate infrastructural bottlenecks, the heavy reliance on roads for the transport of people and goods and the lack of alternative networks of real scale for inter- urban transport in Ireland, roads must continue to be the first priority for investment in transport. In recognition of the potential of public transport to relieve congestion and to contribute to more sustainable development, Structural Funds investment of €192 million under the Economic and Social Infrastructure Operational Programme is also proposed to support the development of an integrated public transport system in the Greater Dublin Area. The Cohesion Fund will contribute a proposed €57 million under this programme towards the renewal and upgrading of mainline rail, again with the emphasis on the completion of TENs. Table 13.1 over contains details of the areas proposed in the Plan for Structural and Cohesion Fund cofinancing.

Table 13.1 2000-2006 (€ millions)

	Total Cost	Total Public	Community Participation					National Public Participation				Private	Cohesion Fund	TENs and EFTA	EIB Loans
			Total	ERDF	ESF	EAGGF	FIFG	Total	Exchequer	Public Non-Exchequer	Non Co-financed Public				
Economic and Social Infrastructure															
National Roads	6,857	5,367	541	541				4,826	505		4,321	1,270*	220		
Dublin Transport	543	543	192	192				351	154		197				
Mainline Rail	186	129						129			129		57		
Urban Waste Water	965	609						609			609	76	280		
Coastal Protection/Catchment Protection	168	168	80	80				88	61		27				
Energy	186	186	43	43				143	47	48	48				
Productive Sector															
Agriculture	722	355	80			80		275	57		218	367			
Fisheries	163	57	26				26	32			32	106			
RTDI	3,381	2,473	313	313				2,160	172		1,988	908			
Employment and Human Resources Development															
Improving Employability	5,881	5,881	618		618			5,263	502		4,761				
Entrepreneurship	982	525	96		96			430	76		354	457			
Adaptability	5,918	5,918	179		179			5,740	124		5,616				
Equality	260	260	6		6			254	1.3		253.1				
Regional OPs															
Infrastructure															
Non-national Roads	1,524	1,524	21	21				1,503		9	1,494				
Waste Management	825	254	30	30				214		12	205	571*			
E-Commerce	382	98	50	50				48	48			284			
Rural Water	384	384	258	258				126	126						
Village and Urban Renewal	131	131	65	65				66	43		23				
Productive Sector															
Micro Enterprise	249	191	60	60				132	46		86	58			
Tourism	546	170	60	60				111			111	376			
Rural Development	414	238	60			60		178	38		140	176			
Forestry Development	130	102	40	40				62	25		37	28			
Aquaculture/Harbours	193	165	72	72				93	40		53	28			
Social Disadvantage															
Childcare	391	317	179	60	119			138	51		87	74			
Peace Programme	146	141	106	59	47			35	25	10		5			
Technical Assistance	10	10	5	5				5	5						
Total	31,536	26,195	3,172#	1,944	1,064	140	26	23,010	2,146	79	20,789	4,784	557	65†	
Objective 1 Region	10,403‡	8,557	1,359#	969	354	71	15	6,929	410	58	6,461	1,922			
Objective 1 Region in Transition	20,418‡	16,923	1,813#	975	710	69	11	15,323	1,736	12	13,575	2,862			

* Public Private Partnerships.

The Structural Funds Regulations require that 4% of each commitment be retained as a performance reserve. These figures exclude €55 million and €79 million respectively in respect of the Performance Reserve for the Objective 1 and the Region in Transition respectively which will be allocated following the Mid-Term Review.

† Proposal being developed for €60 million TENs and €5 million EFTA — Areas for allocation not yet known.

Structural Funds contribution is generally calculated at 75% of co-financed public expenditure in the Objective 1 Region and 50% in the Objective 1 Region in Transition.

‡ These amounts do not contain €557 million Cohesion Funding.

13.8   As regards investment in environmental infrastructure, the Plan proposes Cohesion Fund investment of €280 million towards a programme of €965 million of works to meet the requirements of Urban Waste Water Directive under the Economic and Social Infrastructure Programme. €80 million to support investment in Coastal Protection and Catchment Protection is also proposed under this programme. Structural Funds investment of €30 million is proposed to support investment in Waste Management in the Regional Operational Programmes which includes provision for Public Private Partnerships.

13.9   The Plan acknowledges that substantial investment is required in energy and information technology infrastructure to enhance national and regional competitiveness. However, the view taken is that the bulk of these investment needs will be provided by the market as a result of deregulation and increased competition in the sectors. In recognition of the potential that the development of alternative energies have to contribute to sustainable development and to achieving Kyoto limits and in line with Community Priorities, the Plan proposes Structural Funds expenditure of €43 million to support investment in respect of this in the Economic and Social Infrastructure Operational Programme. A similar provision is proposed to support investment in E-Commerce Infrastructure in the Regional Operational Programmes. It is envisaged that the market will largely deliver the investment in this area in the larger urban and more densely populated areas. Therefore the investment in the E-Commerce Infrastructure will be focused on the more remote areas, particularly in the BMW Region.

13.10   The Plan notes that RTDI is an area in which there has traditionally been under investment in Ireland (Chapter 6 on the Productive Sector Operational Programme refers). It acknowledges the priority accorded to this area in Community Policies in contributing to regional competitiveness by making this the single biggest area for investment in the Productive Sector. Public investment of €2.47 billion with Structural Funds cofinancing of €313 million is proposed for this purpose.

13.11   In the area of competitive enterprise, Community Policies emphasise support for SMEs with a shifting away from capital grants to alternative forms of assistance such as venture capital, loan capital and revolving funds etc. and improving the delivery. Areas with particular potential identified are the environment, tourism and culture, the social economy and fisheries.

13.12   The priority accorded and the strategy in relation to the development of SMEs in Community Policy will be pursued in the Productive Sector Programme. However, no Structural Funds assistance is proposed for this purpose. Rather the Plan proposes to focus the structural funds available for the productive sector on the areas identified in Community Policies as having particular potential. Accordingly, Structural Funds expenditure of €80 million and €26 million is proposed to support investment on Agriculture Development and Fisheries in the Productive Sector Operational Programme (Chapter 6 refers). The emphasis on the agriculture development investment will be on measures for improving on farm structures, namely farm waste management, animal welfare etc., complementing the substantial investment for REPS under the CAP FEOGA Guarantee funded Rural Development Programme. The fisheries investment will focus on the restructuring and modernisation of the means of production as required under the Common Fisheries Policy. Development of the Social Economy is addressed under the Entrepreneurship Priority in the Employment and Human Resources Development Operational Programme (Chapter 5 refers).

13.13   Structural Funds expenditure of €60 million is proposed in the Regional Operational Programmes to support investment in micro-enterprise. The Plan also provides for Structural Funds expenditure of €60 million to support investment in tourism under the Regional Operational

Programmes (Chapters 7 and 8 refer). The emphasis on this investment will be on developing the sector in rural and less developed areas as part of an integrated strategy of sustainable tourism and rural development. Also in the Regional Operational Programmes, €112 million in Structural Funds expenditure is proposed to support investment in Forestry Development and Aquaculture and Fishery Harbours. The Forestry investment will complement the investment in Forestry under the CAP Rural Development Programme and the investment in fisheries restructuring under the Productive Sector Priority.

13.14 In relation to human resources development the Commission highlight the European Employment Guidelines. They stress the role of the European Social Fund as the main financial instrument at EU level for supporting the implementation of the employment guidelines. The contextual framework for the implementation of European Employment Guidelines is the Member States National Employment Action Plans and the Objective 3 Policy Frame of Reference which guides the actions to be undertaken to fulfil these priorities including those supported under Objective 3. Specific areas of attention identified for support are:

- Active Labour Market Policies to promote employment;

- Promoting Employability, skills and mobility through lifelong learning;

- Developing adaptability and entrepreneurship;

- An inclusive society, open to all (special attention to be given to the needs of people with disabilities, ethnic minorities and other disadvantaged groups etc.)

13.15 The Plan fully supports the implementation of the EU Employment Guidelines. The structure and thrust of the strategy under the Employment and Human Resources Development Operational Programme (Chapter 5 refers) is based on the four pillars of the EU Employment Guidelines with appropriate linkages to Entrepreneurship Measures under the Productive Sector Operational Programme (Chapter 6) and to social inclusion measures under the Regional Operational Programmes (Chapters 7 and 8 refer). Total Structural Funds cofinancing of €618 million is proposed for Improving Employability to support lifelong learning and the development of employment services, €96 million for Entrepreneurship including in company training in SMEs and the social economy, €179 million for Adaptability to support skills development generally and €6 million for Equality. The emphasis in the proposed equality expenditure will, in particular, be on activities to monitor and document progress on gender mainstreaming.

13.16 Additional to this expenditure on Equality, the Plan proposes €179 million in Structural Funds cofinancing towards investment to support the provision of Childcare under social inclusion in the Regional Operational Programmes (Chapters 7 and 8 refer).

13.17 The Commission Guidelines view Urban and Rural Development as being critical to balanced territorial development:

- Urban Development within an integrated regional policy;

- Rural Development for modernisation, diversification and environmental protection.

13.18 The Plan proposes to promote balanced regional development through a combination of specific regional allocations of both Structural Funds cofinanced expenditure and National Public Expenditure and an integrated multi-sectoral strategy. Consistent with the principles of the European Spatial Development Strategy the Plan contains a commitment to develop a National Spatial Development Strategy. It also provides for a "gateways" approach to the development of urban and rural areas (Chapter 3 refers). It proposes Structural Funds expenditure of €65 million to support a programme of urban and village renewal and €258 million for the development of Rural Water Supplies in support of balanced regional development under the Regional Operational Programmes (Chapters 7 and 8 refer).

13.19 Chapter 15 contains financial tables setting out details of expenditure by priority and the source of the expenditure under the Plan. Full expenditure details by measure will be set out in the operational programmes. **The actual allocation of Structural Funds by priority will be a matter for negotiation with the European Commission in the context of agreeing a Community Support Framework (CSF) for Ireland on the basis of this Plan.**

13.20 Poverty and Rural Proofing are two national horizontal principles in addition to the principles of sustainable development and equal opportunities which are shared with the European Community. Each of the relevant chapters in the Plan on the Operational Programmes and the two Regional Operational Programmes contain sectoral analysis addressing, as appropriate, these horizontal issues. They also contain summaries of how the various policy interventions provided for in the Plan will impact on the environment, equal opportunities, poverty and rural development.

Environmental Impact (Sustainable Development)

13.21 Under the Treaty of Amsterdam, the Union's financial instruments are required to work, simultaneously and in the long term interest, towards economic growth, social cohesion and the protection of the environment; in other words, sustainable development. The European Council at Vienna confirmed the political priority of integrating the environment in structural and agricultural policies in the context of Agenda 2000. As indicated in the Commission's guidelines, this means that environmental considerations, and in particular, compliance with Community environmental and nature protection legislation must be incorporated into the definition and implementation of measures supported by the Structural Funds and the Cohesion Fund. This will help the Union to comply with its international commitments such as those concerning climate change at Kyoto. At the 1997 Kyoto conference, it was agreed that the EU Member States would reduce their collective emissions of greenhouse gases to 92% of their 1990 levels by 2010. Ireland's target has been set at an increase of not more than 13% over the reference period. Achieving this target will prove extremely difficult in the context of rapid economic growth.

13.22 The establishment of a system of eco-audit of policies is a key environmental priority in the Government's "An Action Programme for the Millenium". In addition, "Sustainable Development: A Strategy for Ireland" undertook to develop within three years, a Strategic Environmental Assessment (SEA) system for major sectoral plans and programmes. In June 1999, the Government approved:

- the introduction on a pilot basis of a procedure for the eco-auditing of policies in specific sectoral areas of Government Departments and in respect of national development plans; and

- the evaluation of the results of pilot exercises by the Departments concerned and the Green Network of Government Departments with a view to wider use of eco-audit after one year.

13.23 Eco-auditing (also known as environmental appraisal) involves the establishment of a formal procedure for identifying the environmental impacts of sectoral policies and programmes and for mitigating/eliminating their adverse impacts. This enables the environmental dimensions of policy to be considered in an integrated way, at the same time as the broad social, economic and other dimensions. Eco-audit will not apply to the carrying out of physical projects as these are already governed by Environmental Impact Assessment (EIA) legislation. Government Departments have been instructed to arrange for the introduction of eco-auditing of policies in accordance with the Government decision and on the basis of specific agreed guidelines. Pilot projects should be completed by the end of April 2000 and will then be evaluated by the Departments concerned and by the Green Network of Government Departments.

13.24 The National Development Plan 2000-2006 has been eco-audited on a pilot scale and the results are set out at Appendix 4.

13.25 Economic and social development should not be to the detriment of environmental quality. The Plan has been framed taking into account the need for balance between environment and development, embodied in the concept of sustainable development, so that economic and social activity will not undermine the long-term productivity of supporting ecosystems. Integration of environmental considerations into other policies is a key means of securing this balance, and environmental considerations associated with development proposals are addressed in the relevant chapters of the Plan. A National Spatial Strategy will be prepared to secure sustainable spatial development over the longer term. A new State of the Environment Report will be published by the Environmental Protection Agency in 2000.

13.26 While Ireland has retained a good environment, economic growth and changing lifestyles are placing greater pressure than ever before on environmental quality. Policies, including those in Sustainable Development: A Strategy for Ireland, and investments under previous NDPs have resulted in a number of improvements, for example in public drinking water quality, increased sewage treatment, reduced lead emissions from transport, increased packaging waste recycling, lower usage of phosphorus chemical fertiliser and growing participation by farmers in the Rural Environment Protection Scheme (REPS). However, with a growing population and trend towards smaller household sizes, and a doubling in industrial production in the period 1991 to 1998, there is increased demand for housing, services, infrastructure and energy. Greater consumption is placing pressure on resources and increasing waste generation, and increased urbanisation is focusing these pressures on certain areas.

13.27 The main environmental challenges which must be addressed by the NDP and other policy measures include:

- Halting the decline in the quality of rivers and lakes caused by excessive inputs of nutrients (eutrophication);

- Better management of solid waste;

- Meeting our Kyoto commitment to limit the growth of greenhouse gas emissions;

- Protecting the urban environment;

- Protecting flora and fauna in the countryside and along the coast.

13.28 A range of concerns are evident in these regards,[1] notably:

- The length of river classified as unpolluted has dropped by 10% over the past decade; although the percentage seriously polluted remains under 1%, slight to moderate pollution has increased to 32% of monitored river channel length;

---

[1] Source of key national environmental indicators Environment in Focus (Environmental Protection Agency EPA, 1999)

- While the quality of drinking water in group water schemes has been improving, it is still low in comparison to public supplies with only 64% of schemes at an acceptable standard compared to over 91% of public drinking water;

- At the end of 1997, some 22% of urban waste water received secondary treatment, and a substantial programme must be maintained to comply with Community legislation on urban waste water treatment;

- Household and commercial (collected) waste has grown at a compound rate of 4.5% since 1984; over 92% of waste is landfilled compared to the EU average of 66% and Ireland lacks a modern environmentally friendly waste management infrastructure;

- Although there has been some decoupling of growth in greenhouse gas emissions from growth in the economy, CO_2 emissions had increased by almost 20% over 1990 levels by end 1997. Ireland's Kyoto commitment is to limit the growth of a basket of 6 greenhouse gases to 13% above 1990 levels in the period 2008-12; on a business as usual basis net annual emission would increase by over 30% by 2010;

- Sulphur dioxide (SO_2), nitrogen oxides (NOx) and ammonia (NH_3) contribute to local and transboundary air pollution problems (acidification, eutrophication and ground-level ozone). Irish compliance with existing international obligations, particularly in the case of NOx, is under threat from rising emissions from transport. Future obligations, to apply from 2010, will require considerable reductions in emissions (76% reduction from 1990 levels in the case of SO_2, 42% reduction for NOx and 8% for NH_3). Meeting these targets will require significant action in the energy, industry, transport and agriculture sectors;

- Traffic growth has impacted in urban areas, especially in the cities, in terms of congestion, air pollution and noise; without more intensive traffic management, Ireland will face difficulty in meeting EU air quality standards for 2005 particularly in heavily trafficked urban areas;

- While over one third of farmers now participate in REPS, changes in farming practice have impacted on habitats and species; increasing tourist numbers are placing increasing pressures on environmental quality in sensitive areas; undisturbed peatlands, which are the last remaining habitats for many plant and animal species, now represent around 3% of the land area of the State.

Equal Opportunity

13.29 As the Commission's guidelines indicate equality for men and women is a basic democratic principle underpinned by the Treaty of Amsterdam. Its incorporation into all policies is therefore no longer an option but an obligation. Mainstreaming equal opportunities must therefore be introduced into all Structural Funds programming. This involves both efforts to promote equality and specific measures to help women and the mobilisation of all general policies by actively and openly taking into account at the planning stage their possible effects on the respective situation of women and men.

13.30 Ireland is developing a comprehensive legal framework for addressing inequality under the Employment Equality Act, 1998 and the Equal Status Bill, 1999. Under the new legislation discrimination both in employment and in the supply of goods and services on grounds of sex, marital status, family status, sexual orientation, religion, age, disability, race and membership of the travelling community will be unlawful. The new equality legislation gives a new emphasis to tackling inequalities including between men and women. The Equality Authority (replacing the Employment Equality Agency) will promote equal opportunities for the target groups covered by the legislation. The Authority will have an investigations arm to secure effective enforcement of the legislation.

13.31 The Plan provides for a number of specific actions designed to ensure that men and women share the benefits of the Plan. It contributes to the achievement of a more equal society for men and women through the mainstreaming of equal opportunities across all sectors.

Poverty Proofing

13.32 The 1997 National Anti-Poverty Strategy (NAPS) set a target of reducing the number of people in consistent poverty[2] over the period 1997-2007 from 9%-15% of the population to less than 5%-10%, as measured by the Economic and Social Research Institute (ESRI). The NAPS also set targets of reducing unemployment from 11.9% to 6% and long-term unemployment from 7% to 3.5% over the same period. The most recent data available from the ESRI and the Central Statistics Office show that these targets have been substantially met. The number of people in consistent poverty has been reduced to 7%-10%. Unemployment in early 1999 stood at 5.8% while long-term unemployment had fallen to 3%.

13.33 Having reviewed progress, the Government set new NAPS targets in the 1998/99 Annual Report of the Inter-Departmental Committee on Social Inclusion Strategy as follows:

- Consistent poverty to be reduced to below 5% by 2004;

- Unemployment to be reduced to below 5% by 2002;

- Long-term unemployment to be reduced to 2.5% by 2002.

13.34 Due to its unprecedented scale of investment in poverty and social inclusion, the National Development Plan 2000-2006 will play a major role in achieving these NAPS targets and the more ambitious employment targets in the revised National Employment Action Plan (NEAP) for 1999 of reducing unemployment and long-term unemployment to 5% and 2% respectively by the end of 2000. Chapter 10 on Social Inclusion sets out in detail the areas in which the Plan will impact on this issue.

13.35 However, the NAPS targets cannot be achieved exclusively through investments under the Plan. The Plan should therefore be viewed as but one, albeit a significant, element of the Government's wider NAPS strategy of tackling poverty and social exclusion through economic and social, fiscal and incomes policies generally.

---

[2] Consistent poverty is defined as being below 50%-60% of average household disposable income and experiencing enforced basic deprivation. Basic deprivation is the presence of at least one of a list of eight indicators determined by survey to be basic necessities by reference to the fact that they were both regarded as necessities by and possessed by a majority of those surveyed. Examples include having 2 pairs of strong shoes, having a warm waterproof overcoat and having a roast meal (or its equivalent) at least once a week.

Rural Impact

13.36 The White Paper on Rural Development provided that administrative procedures would be introduced for all Departments to ensure that policy makers are aware of the likely impact of all proposals on rural communities. The operation of these procedures will contribute significantly to integrating the strategy for the economic and social development of rural areas with the objectives and principles of other policy initiatives and, in particular, of the National Anti Poverty Strategy. The National Development Plan has been prepared in compliance with this requirement. Chapter 11 on Agriculture and Rural Development outlines the impact of the Plan on rural development.

Implementation of these horizontal principles at programme level

13.37 Operationally, these horizontal principles will be mainstreamed at programme level in the following manner:

- As indicated in Chapter 13 on the Implementation of Programmes, it will be mandatory to include the environment (sustainable development), equal opportunities, poverty and rural impact among the project selection criteria for all measures;

- These issues will feature as requirements in all evaluations to be undertaken under the Plan;

- Where appropriate and feasible, specific indicators to assess impact on these horizontal issues will be developed at programme and measure level;

- A monitoring unit is being established under the Department of Justice, Equality and Law Reform to monitor gender mainstreaming generally and to advise on the development of appropriate indicators in this regard. A dedicated unit in the Department of Education and Science will in co-operation with the main unit in the Department of Justice, Equality and Law Reform carry out similar work in relation to the education sector;

- All monitoring committees will include representatives from appropriate bodies responsible for environmental, equal opportunities, social inclusion and rural development policies;

- Three horizontal co-ordinating committees representative of all the management authorities for the programmes, the main implementing bodies and the appropriate bodies with overall policy responsibility for these areas will be established to promote and co-ordinate these horizontal principles; namely:
  - *Environment Co-ordinating Committee;*
  - *An Equal Opportunities and Social Inclusion Co-ordinating Committee (A joint committee for these two principles is considered appropriate having regard to common target groups); and*
  - *A Rural Development Co-ordinating Committee.*

In addition, there will be an Employment and Human Resources Co-ordinating Committee to co-ordinate employment policy across programmes.

13.38 The co-ordinating committees will monitor the situation across programmes and will report progress to the CSF monitoring Committee. The CSF and Operational Programme Monitoring Committees will have ultimate responsibility for securing the maximum application of these horizontal principles within their remit.

14 Community Initiatives

Review of Community Initiatives in operation in Ireland in the 1994-1999 period

14.1   Eleven Community Initiatives operated in Ireland in the period 1994-1999: SME (Small to Medium Enterprises), Employment, Adapt, Retex, Urban, Pesca, Leader II, Ireland/Wales Interreg, Interreg IIC (Transnational Spatial Planning), Ireland/Northern Ireland Interreg, and Peace. Apart from the latter two, this chapter reviews the operations and achievements of these initiatives. It briefly examines the proposed Community Initiatives for the period 2000-2006 and the prospects for Ireland's involvement in those initiatives. Arising from decisions taken at the Berlin summit, the Peace Initiative will be funded as a mainstream Structural Fund programme, and accordingly this initiative and the Ireland/Northern Ireland Interreg are reviewed in Chapter 9.

SME Community Initiative

14.2   The latest forecast of total expenditure under the SME initiative is €72.8 million. The Structural Funds contribution is expected to be €29.6 million consisting of ERDF €27.3 million, and ESF €2.3 million, with public expenditure of €13.2 million, and private expenditure of €30 million.

14.3   The aim of this initiative was to assist small to medium enterprises (SME's) in adapting to the Single Market, and in improving international competitiveness. In the Irish context, the focus was on small enterprises, which are estimated to represent in excess of 90% of the non-farming businesses in the country. A small enterprise was defined as one which employs less than 50 people or which has an annual turnover not exceeding €3.7 million.

14.4   The initiative contained six measures: (i) improving access to finance and credit (ii) improving access to public markets (iii) facilitating adaptation of service firms to the Single Market (iv) a programme of research to facilitate the dissemination of best practice (v) the fostering of pilot projects concerned with the improvement of business know-how and the business environment and (vi) technical assistance. The bulk of expenditure took place under the Access to Finance measure.

14.5   Under the Access to Finance measure, £208 million of loans were advanced by the four main commercial banks (AIB, Bank of Ireland, National Irish Bank and Ulster Bank) up to the end of 1998. The loans were advanced at a fixed interest rate of 6.5% over 7 years, with amounts ranging from £20,000 to £500,000, the average loan size being £150,000. Expenditure under the measure formed a subsidy to cover the difference between the commercial bank rate for loans, and the fixed interest rate granted on loans advanced. Up to the end of 1998, 1,414 firms received loans, with a projected job creation of 9,054. The Services Sector was the largest individual recipient at 39%, the Tourism and Manufacturing Sectors receiving 27% and 26% respectively, the Food Sector receiving 3% and the remaining 5% distributed between other firms.

14.6   Under Access to Public Markets, assistance was given by Public Procurement Specialists to 382 firms, and on 128 public sector tenders, generating an estimated £7.8 million of new business. Under the North/South Initiative, market opportunities in Northern Ireland were researched and published in a guide "Winning Business in the Northern Ireland Public Sector". An estimated £2 million plus of orders was generated up to end 1998 as a result of this activity, with a potential for £10 million in 1999. Similar research in the Scottish market was provided for in 1999.

14.7   Under the Adaptation of Service Firms measure, 10 studies were completed and 85 seminars held, researching the services sector, with a view to highlighting business opportunities. Seed support was given to 58 promoters, with 26 projects achieving sales. 15 firms received assistance on value-added electronic information services, with 4 SME's obtaining new electronic services. Overall, sales of £8.5 million were generated, giving employment to almost 200 persons.

14.8   Under the Best Practice Guides measure, 2 manuals, "Starting Your Own Business", and "How to Finance Your Business", were produced, 15,000 copies of which were distributed. Seminars were organised on "Starting Your Own Business" and on "How to Finance Your Business". A copy of "Starting Your Own Business" was also made available on the Internet, as was an Enterprise Link Database, providing information about state-backed enterprise support schemes for new and expanding small businesses. An Integrated Best Practice Solution for Year 2000 Compliance in SME's, drafted by Enterprise Ireland, was funded under this measure. It included a guide to Y2K compliance for SME's, a Y2K help-desk, a directory of Y2K consultants and service providers, a Y2K website, and a series of workshops and a targeted media campaign. Under the Improvement of Business Know-How measure, 11 pilot training projects on business know-how and improving the business environment were funded.

EMPLOYMENT Community Initiative

14.9   The latest forecast of expenditure under the EMPLOYMENT initiative is €123.2 million. The contribution from Structural Funds is expected to be €90.2 million consisting of ESF €86 million and ERDF €4.2 million, with public expenditure of €23.5 million, and private expenditure of €9.5 million.

14.10   This initiative aimed to contribute to the development of human resources and improve the workings of the labour market to enhance employment growth, to promote social solidarity, and to promote equal opportunities for women, through the piloting of innovative actions and projects. It was specifically targeted at socially excluded and marginalised groups. There were four strands to the initiative, each of which focused on a particular group, as follows:

- EMPLOYMENT Horizon was aimed at people with disabilities;

- EMPLOYMENT Integra was aimed at the socially excluded or those at risk of social exclusion, such as the long term unemployed, refugees, travellers, lone parents, prisoners, drug users, and disadvantaged urban and rural areas;

- EMPLOYMENT NOW (New Opportunities for Women) promoted equal opportunities for women;

- EMPLOYMENT Youthstart was aimed at young persons, particularly those without adequate training or qualifications.

14.11 Support was provided to promoting organisations to pilot innovative actions on behalf of their target groups over a defined time period. Under the initiative, particular emphasis was placed on the principle of *mainstreaming* — the transfer of lessons learned in the implementation of the EMPLOYMENT initiative to the mainstream of ESF policy and practice. Other significant criteria for project selection and approval were *transnationality* — the transfer and sharing of skills, information and experience between Member States in relation to particular projects, *innovation,* the use of *local partnerships/consortia,* and *complementarity* with other programmes and initiatives.

14.12 Three measures applied to each of the strands: (i) Delivery of Training (ii) Systems Development (guidance, training, counselling and employment systems) and (iii) Employment Creation. The organisations receiving support included education and training providers, statutory bodies, local community and voluntary groups, national representative organisations and employer organisations.

14.13 263 projects were supported under the initiative, 137 in the 1996 — 1997 phase and 126 in the 1998-1999 phase. A total of 772 transnational partners across Member States of the European Union were established for the various projects, significant numbers of partners being established in Great Britain, including Northern Ireland (187), Germany (96), France (90) and Spain (82). Up to the end of 1998, 13,241 trainers and trainees had participated in projects, with 5,259 (39.72%) completing courses, and 2,559 (19.33%) receiving accreditation. The breakdown over each of the strands, up to end 1998, was as follows:

Table 14.1: EMPLOYMENT Course Participation

Strand	Trainee & Trainers: Intake			Course Completion			Accreditation		
	Male	Female	Total	Male	Female	Total	Male	Female	Total
Horizon	1,403	1,453	2,856	543	605	1,148	219	295	514
Integra	1,156	1,264	2,420	532	524	1,056	186	292	478
NOW	528	5,023	5,551	294	2,112	2,406	48	1,148	1,196
Youthstart	1,259	1,155	2,414	324	325	649	201	170	371
Total	4,346	8,895	13,241	1,693	3,566	5,259	654	1,905	2,559

In addition to trainees and trainers, service users formed a third category of beneficiaries of EMPLOYMENT projects, i.e. persons who used the services of EMPLOYMENT projects, such as information and guidance services. An estimated 10,000 service users availed of EMPLOYMENT services in the 1996/98 phase, and a further 10,000 were expected in the 1998/99 phase. The total number of beneficiaries, i.e. trainees, trainers, and service users, is expected to be over 30,000 by the end of the programme.

14.14 Directories were produced for each of the four strands listing the projects in operation under the strands, and giving an overview of the projects, together with special studies and research reports. An Employment website was also developed. Activities undertaken to support mainstreaming included providing support to projects to increase their awareness and understanding of mainstreaming. The Department of Enterprise, Trade and Employment established a Policy Forum to promote mainstreaming from the Employment Initiative. The Forum included representatives from eight Government Departments, five State agencies, the Co-ordinating Structure for the Employment Initiative (the CSEI) and the National Support Structures.

14.15 Particular successes in mainstreaming were achieved as follows:

- learning from a Youthstart project on the value of individualised approaches to young people helped FÁS to introduce its Advocates programme into its mainstream Youthreach Centres; as part of efforts to address simultaneously skills shortages in the IT sector, and long-term unemployment;

- an Integra project developed effective employment-oriented training in IT skills for the long-term unemployed;

- project work under Youthstart on integrated local approaches to counter early school leaving assisted the definition of the Department of Education and Science's current 8-15 year old Initiative in using an integrated approach within a local context for the prevention of early school leaving;

- a Horizon project led to the establishment of a University accredited course in training and education in supported employment while another developed and piloted peer counselling training for the disabled which has been endorsed by many regional health authorities.

ADAPT Community Initiative

14.16 The latest forecast of expenditure under the ADAPT initiative is €39.3 million. The Structural Funds contribution is expected to be €28.5 million, with public expenditure of €3 million and private expenditure of €7.8 million.

14.17 The aims of the initiative were to adapt workers to change, improve the competitiveness of firms through training, prevent unemployment by improving qualifications, and create new jobs and activities. Approval of projects under the ADAPT initiative was informed by four strategic criteria:

- *innovation* — new ideas on retraining needs, and anticipation of retraining needs, and on partnerships/networks (between enterprises, and between enterprises and training providers) for individual and organisational development needs, arising from new technologies, and industrial change;

- *transnationality* — the transfer of knowledge, practices and technology between Member States, and the joint development between Member States of training programmes for new competencies; each approved project had to have at least one transnational partner in another Member State, the objectives and the tasks of the project being agreed between the partners;

- *consortia* — the formation of partnerships between companies, training institutions, local organisations etc. to co-operate in the development and implementation of projects;

- *multiplier effect* — demonstration that the benefits and impact of a project would accrue beyond the immediate participants, e.g. through the wider dissemination of skills and knowledge gained by participants in the project.

14.18 The initiative consisted of seven measures: (i) adaptation of the work force to industrial change, (ii) managing change for SME's, (iii) training systems development, (iv) accreditation of

228

continuing vocational training, (v) local development and micro-enterprise, (vi) SME-led technology transfer and (vii) Building the Information Society (BIS). ADAPT operated in two phases: ADAPT 1 from 1996 to 1997, and ADAPT 2 from 1998 to 1999, which had an added focus on Building the Information Society.

14.19 A total of 76 projects were approved under the initiative, 44 in ADAPT Phase 1, and 32 in ADAPT Phase 2. Participating organisations included companies, small to medium enterprises, micro-enterprises, education and training organisations, employer organisations, and trade unions and representative organisations. The largest single participating sector was the private sector with 36 projects approved for funding. Consortia/local partnerships were established with 318 organisations, 176 for the 44 projects in Phase 1, and 142 for the 32 projects in Phase 2. 264 transnational partnerships were established across EU member states, 159 for Phase 1 projects and 105 for Phase 2 projects.

14.20 Up to the end of 1998, 6,793 persons had completed courses and received accreditation, with 4,130 male participants, and 2,663 female participants. Measure 1, Adaptation of the Workforce to Industrial Change, had the largest number of participants, at 2,105, with 1,401 male and 704 female participants. The breakdown of participants over the seven measures was as follows:

	Male	Female	Total
1. Adaptation of the Workforce	1,401	704	2,105
2. Managing Change for SME's	637	369	1,006
3. Training Systems Development	1,019	725	1,744
4. Accreditation of Continuing Vocational Training	112	185	297
5. Local Development & Micro-Enterprise	414	181	595
6. SME-Led Technology Transfer	82	15	97
7. Building the Information Society	465	484	949
Overall totals	4,130	2,663	6,793

14.21 90% of Phase 1 projects, and 88% of Phase 2 projects were evaluated as having performed in the good to excellent range in terms of implementation of the criteria. A notable success in the multiplier effect/mainstreaming was achieved as follows:

- ADAPT Initiative projects focusing on new and flexible forms of work organisation, such as teleworking and job sharing highlighted potential in follow-through work to contribute to new ways of reconciling work and family life. Work on the take-up of teleworking informed the National Advisory Committee on Teleworking which reported on this area to Government.

RETEX Community Initiative

14.22 The latest forecast of total expenditure under the RETEX initiative is €23.12 million. The Structural Funds contribution is expected to be €11.6 million, consisting of ERDF €9.3 million, and ESF €2.3 million, with public expenditure of €0.02 million and private expenditure of €11.5 million.

14.23   The aim of the Retex initiative was to accelerate the diversification of economic activity in regions heavily dependent on the textile and clothing sectors, so as to render them less dependent, and to encourage the adjustment of commercially viable enterprises generally.

14.24   Six measures were implemented under the initiative: (i) improving know-how, (ii) co-operation schemes, (iii) temporary contributions towards engineers/technical staff/managers, (iv) vocational training schemes, (v) aid to reduce pollution, and (vi) technical assistance. The majority of expenditure was under Measure 1, Improving Know-How.

14.25   The bulk of activity under the Retex programme was related to the introduction of World Class Manufacturing (WCM) as a set of concepts and practices to Irish companies participating in the initiative. Through the Improving Know-How sub-measures Production Methods, and New Technology, and the Vocational Training Schemes measure, WCM received approximately 75% of the available ESF and ERDF funding. WCM is the pursuit of superior performance in quality, lead time, cost, and customer service through continuous improvement in just-in-time (JIT) manufacturing, total quality management (TQM) and employee management.

14.26   Under the Vocational Training Schemes measure, up to end 1998, assistance was provided for the training of a total of 2,593 employees (982 female, 1611 male) in WCM techniques, from 33 participating companies. Under the Improving Know-How measure, 45 companies, up to end 1998, received assistance towards the costs of hiring consultants in the introduction of WCM techniques, many of whom also sent employees for training in WCM. Up to the end of 1998, a total of 132 companies also received assistance under the Improving Know-How measure in the introduction of the new technologies of computer-aided design (CAD), computer-aided manufacture (CAM), management information systems (MIS), and electronic data interchange (EDS). Many of the companies also implemented WCM techniques and saw new technologies as an integral part of this strategy. Assistance provided for the introduction of World Class Manufacturing was not restricted to companies in the textile and clothing sectors, but included, among others, those in the engineering, food and manufacturing sectors also.

14.27   Under the Co-operation Schemes measure, the Irish Garment Technology Centre was set up as a mechanism to access international best practice for the Irish clothing and textile sector. Assistance was provided for the funding of a total of 14 projects up to end 1998 organised by the Centre. It included advising knitwear and weaving companies of best practices, the introduction of a computer-aided design programme in the fashion courses of the National College of Art and Design, and the promotion of CAD skills within the clothing sector.

14.28   Under the sub-measure Networks/Value Adding Partnerships, 8 networks were set up in sectors ranging from cheese making to mould making, with a brief to undertake joint research and development, marketing and procurement activities, to overcome the diseconomies of scale experienced by small companies so as to become credible suppliers to large multi-national customers. Additional sales of £16.7 million were achieved in 1997 by participating companies.

14.29   Under the Design sub-measure, assistance was provided for the hiring of design consultants, 14 companies receiving assistance up to end 1998. Assistance was also provided to 9 companies under the Temporary Contributions measure for the hiring of young designers to ensure that experience gained under consultant designers was retained within companies. Under the Aid to Reduce Pollution measure, 28 companies had received assistance up to end 1998 for the commissioning of studies on cleaner technologies and effluent treatment, and for the purchasing of effluent-treatment equipment with long-term viability.

URBAN Community Initiative

14.30 The latest forecast of expenditure for the URBAN initiative is €28.3 million. At an aid rate of 75%, the total Structural Funds contribution is expected to be €21.2 million consisting of ERDF €12.6 million, and ESF €8.6 million, with matching public expenditure of €7.1 million.

14.31 The URBAN initiative was developed to address a range of problems associated with socio-economic exclusion within deprived sections of inner city and peripheral urban areas. Under the initiative, community assistance was made available for integrated development programmes for a limited number of deprived urban areas in Dublin and Cork, namely Ballymun, Finglas and Darndale in North Dublin, West Tallaght and Clondalkin in South-West Dublin, and the Northside of Cork City. The integrated programme comprised a balanced and coherent set of economic development, social integration and environmental measures based on local partnership proposals. The initiative aimed to act as a catalyst in a broad-based approach, by undertaking key schemes to help deprived urban areas achieve a lasting improvement in the living standards of the people living there.

14.32 A particular concern was to ensure that the activities under URBAN complemented and were co-ordinated with the Operational Programme for Local, Urban and Rural Development (LURD), but had a focus distinct from LURD. In this context, a distinctive feature of the initiative was its focus on urban management, with explicit emphasis on equipping the institutions of urban governance, in particular the local urban authorities, to address more effectively the changing environment characteristic of disadvantaged urban neighbourhoods. It was seen as an opportunity to develop and test new approaches to the discharge of responsibility by local urban authorities, in particular through developing new consultative and participative structures.

14.33 Funding was available through the following six measures: (i) Employment/Enterprise Development (ii) Training and Education (iii) Community Infrastructure (iv) Children and Youth (v) Environment and (vi) Community Development. Each selected area had its own Steering Committee which had responsibility for implementing the programme within its area.

14.34 Significant achievements were made, with URBAN support, in the development of the social economy in Ireland. By 1999, over 30 Community Businesses had been assisted. The initiative included funding for capital projects, including the refurbishment of an industrial unit at St. Margaret's, Ballymun (URBAN contribution £0.5 m), the Ballymun Arts and Community Resource Centre (expected URBAN contribution £2.4 m) and the Darndale Village Centre (expected URBAN contribution £2.5 m). In Cork, capital projects funded included the Glen Resource Centre (expected URBAN contribution £1.1 m) and the Ballyvolane Enterprise Centre (expected URBAN contribution £0.9 m). The lessons learned in terms of the URBAN dimension and contribution to the development of integrated Enterprise Centres (such as the experience with the Brookfield Centre in Tallaght) and community facilities in Village Cores (such as the childcare complex in Clondalkin and the Village centre in Darndale) appeared likely to have an influence well beyond the three URBAN areas.

14.35 Allied to the programme of capital projects, a whole range of measures were implemented, designed to maximise local participation in the implementation of the plan, to address gaps in work-related and personal development skills and to meet the social needs of people requiring special support. The level and nature of interventions varied in light of the particular needs — from intensive support for a small group of young men who had few developmental options available to them, to the after-school activities for the large numbers of young people who had poor parental support at home.

14.36   Examples of URBAN-supported actions likely to be replicated and/or mainstreamed because of the achievements being reported were:

- the model of Community Planning/Consultation adopted by South Dublin URBAN (which attracted international recognition);

- the Training and Support Unit for early school leavers in Clondalkin;

- the preventative and education supports being offered to certain pupils in Cork (the Department of Education and Science introduced a pilot school testing similar provision over a wider area);

- North Dublin's experience of developing tailor-made training programmes geared to employment opportunities in the local economy and in the use of new technologies;

- Cork's support of ex-prisoners and their families.

PESCA Community Initiative

14.37   The latest forecast for expenditure under the PESCA initiative is €183.5 million. The Structural Funds contribution is expected to be €81 million consisting of FIFG €48.9 million, ERDF €25.9 million, and ESF €6.2 million, with public expenditure of €21.2 million, and private expenditure of €81.3 million.

14.38   The PESCA initiative aimed to alleviate difficulties associated with the fishing industry, such as stock depletion, reductions in fleet capacity and market difficulties. The initiative focused on fishing communities and remote coastal regions where these difficulties were more acute and impacted more severely on the socio-economic fabric of the areas. It aimed to enable the fisheries sector to cope with attendant socio-economic consequences of the difficulties facing the sector and to contribute to the diversification of the areas concerned by developing job-creating activities.

14.39   The initiative complemented the assistance for re-structuring and modernisation under the Operational Programme for Fisheries 1994-1999 and assistance from the ERDF and ESF for socio-economic conversion of coastal areas, and assistance for adjustment to industrial change. Accordingly, it sought to generate clearly-focused projects to help the fishing sector succeed in its adaptation and to diversify the socio-economic fabric of coastal areas. A key objective in ranking projects for assistance was to ensure as far as possible that they were of maximum benefit to coastal and island communities dependent on fisheries.

14.40   Under the initiative, the country was divided into four distinct coastal zones, (i) Louth to Waterford, (ii) Cork and Kerry, (iii) Clare, Galway and Mayo and (iv) Donegal, Sligo and Leitrim, containing the maritime rural districts, with a separate sub-programme for each zone. Funding was available in each of the sub-programmes through six measures: (i) Diversification of Activities (ii) Business Services (iii) Maintenance/Creation of Jobs (iv) Specific Projects (v) Productive Investment and (vi) Training.

14.41 The main types of projects approved under the PESCA Programme included shellfish cultivation, marine tourism, and training and feasibility studies. In coastal areas where fishing and tourism are the mainstays of economic activity, there was strong interest by fishermen and their families in developing marine tourism projects involving sea angling, island trips, dolphin and whale watching and marina facilities. PESCA was a particularly effective catalyst for diversification by inshore fishermen into extensive shellfish culture, notably mussels and scallops as well as lobster conservation programmes. The approach was designed to facilitate co-operatives and groups of fishermen to take ownership of their own economic future and to adapt stock management and aquaculture techniques to deliver sustainable development through their own community-based initiatives.

LEADER II Community Initiative

14.42 The latest forecast of expenditure under the LEADER II initiative is €198.9 million. The Structural Funds contribution is expected to be €85.5 million, consisting of ERDF €64.7 million, ESF €10.3 million, and EAGGF €10.5 million, with public expenditure of €36.7 million and private expenditure of €76.7 million.

14.43 The Leader II initiative was designed to involve rural communities in their own development, and to assist broadly based local rural groups in implementing development plans for their areas. 34 Local Action Groups and 3 collective bodies were selected to implement the programme. The selected Local Action Groups were provided with public funding to implement business plans which they themselves had drawn up for the development of their areas.

14.44 In accordance with the "bottom up" philosophy of the programme the local LEADER group was the decision authority in relation to approving actions falling within its business plan. There was a particular emphasis on community development in the programme and each of the groups was obliged to implement a programme in its area to encourage, support and facilitate the process of rural development, especially at community level. Two of the three collective bodies were funded to facilitate, promote and market the rural tourism concept, particularly through the local group or co-operative approach. The third collective body focused its effort on developing community council structures in several targeted areas.

14.45 The initiative was divided into the following sub-programmes: Acquisition of Skills; Rural Innovation Programmes — Local Action Groups; Rural Innovation Programmes — Other Collective Bodies; Transnational Co-operation; and Technical Assistance. The Rural Innovation Programmes consisted of six measures: (i) Technical Support (ii) Training and Recruitment Assistance (iii) Rural Tourism (iv) Small Firms, Craft Enterprises and Local Services (v) Exploitation and Marketing of Agricultural Forestry and Fishery Products, and (vi) Preservation and Improvement of the Environment and Living Conditions.

14.46 Some 2,703 full-time all year jobs were created up to 30 June 1999 (1,292 female, 1,411 male), with a further 4,041 seasonal or part-time jobs being created (female 1,982, male 2,059). In addition, 2,085 full-time all year positions were consolidated (835 female, 1,250 male), along with 2,200 seasonal or part-time positions (female 1,101, male 1,099). With regard to training, some 2,300 groups were improved as a result of training, and 667 projects emerged as a result of LEADER funded training. In addition 697 employment positions were gained by individuals as a result of their undertaking LEADER assisted training. In the same period, 1,468 new businesses were created, along with 504 new community associations/organisations (e.g. development

233

groups) and 632 sectoral/commercial associations (e.g. co-ops). Tourism capacity was increased by 2,326 bed-nights.

Ireland/Wales Joint INTERREG Maritime Programme

14.47   The latest forecast of expenditure under the Ireland/Wales Programme is €124.3 million. The contribution from Structural Funds is expected to be €71.2 million, consisting of ERDF €66.8 million, and ESF €4.4 million, with public expenditure of €50 million, and private expenditure of €3.1 million.

14.48   The aims of the programme were to contribute to the competitiveness of the Irish and Welsh economies through the upgrading of major transport linkages to the rest of the EU, to assist the internal maritime border between Wales and Ireland to overcome its special development problems which arose from its relative isolation particularly within the European Union, to promote the creation and development of networks of co-operation across the common maritime border and, where relevant, the linking of these networks to wider Community networks in the context of the completion of the Single European Market. The areas covered by the programme on the Irish Side were the regional authority areas of Dublin, Mid East and South East in Ireland (comprising the counties of Dublin, Kildare, Meath, Wicklow, Carlow, Kilkenny, South Tipperary, Waterford and Wexford), and on the Welsh Side the local authority areas of Anglesey, Gwynedd, and part of Conwy in North Wales, and Ceredigion, Pembrokeshire and Carmarthenshire in South West Wales. While the areas shared a significant historical and cultural heritage, they also shared problems, such as unemployment, structural weaknesses in regional economies and distance from the main European Centres.

14.49   The programme was divided into two sub-programmes: Maritime Development, and Economic Development Co-operation. The sub-programmes were divided into six measures: (i) Transport (ii) Transport Information Systems (iii) Marine Environment and Emergency Planning (iv) Economic Development (v) Tourism and Culture and (vi) Human Resources.

14.50   The Programme enabled significant additional investment to be made on Irish roads and ports essential for surface transport with the rest of the European Union, with 8 ports improved, and 11 roads built or improved. Despite a relatively short learning curve (compared with long-standing structures along land borders on mainland Europe) and the maritime barrier, the programme produced positive, tangible outcomes including new business opportunities, new products, market development and job creation. Networks and co-operation were developed in cross border projects, and between the authorities and agencies on both sides, leading to the setting up of 90 co-operative projects, with over 100 partners on both the Welsh and Irish sides. In the Marine Environment area, 27 full-time posts, and 36 part-time posts were created as a result of the projects. In the Economic Development and Tourism and Culture measures it was expected that substantial numbers of jobs and significant additional sales will be generated in the relevant sectors. Under the Human Resources measure, over 1,000 participants attended training courses.

INTERREG IIC — Transnational Programmes in Spatial Planning

14.51   In the 1994-99 period, Ireland participated in two programmes under the Initiative: the North West Metropolitan Area (NWMA, including Belgium, Ireland, Luxembourg, UK and Central regions of France, Germany, and the Netherlands) and the Atlantic Area (Ireland, Portugal, and Western regions of France, Spain, and the UK). Under the NWMA programme, Ireland's ERDF allocation was €2.7 million, with matching funding (mainly public) of €0.9 million. The ERDF allocation under the Atlantic Area Programme was €0.5 million, with matching funding (mainly public) of €0.2 million.

14.52   The aim of the INTERREG IIC initiative was, among other things, to encourage transnational co-operation in spatial planning. Funding was available under the Programmes for suitable joint pilot projects and studies, involving at least three Member States. Projects were selected by Joint Steering Committees representative of the participating Member States (supported by a Programme Secretariat) and funding was allocated to successful projects from the national allocation of the country of their lead partners. Priorities for funding under the NWMA were: Urban and Regional Systems; Infrastructure and Communications: and National and Cultural Heritage. The priorities under the Atlantic Area Programme were: Transport; Research and Technology Transfer; and Tourism and Environment.

14.53   Delays were experienced in implementing the Programmes because they were innovative in nature and in implementation structures. The Programmes were agreed after complex negotiations involving the Member States and regions concerned. The NWMA Programme became operational in June 1998, and by mid-1999, Ireland's allocation had been fully committed. This included allocations to 3 major projects in which Ireland had the lead partnership and Ireland's contribution to the administration of the Programme. In addition, Irish public and voluntary partnerships participated in a further 9 projects with lead partners from other Member States, including a Spatial Vision for the Area. Overall, by mid-1999, 40% of the Programme's total ERDF allocation of €30 million had been allocated to 22 projects, with a projected total 80% commitment by the end of 1999. Significant Irish participation in further projects, either lead by other Member States, or through the reallocation of unused ERDF from other Member States was projected. Some Irish partners were asked to join in the enlargement of projects which had already been approved. The Atlantic Area Programme was approved by the Commission in May 1999. Approximately 50 applications were lodged initially under the Programme, 7 of which were led by Irish partners. It was expected that when the selection procedure had been completed, the major part of the Irish and Programme allocations would be committed.

Community Initiatives 2000-2006

14.54   Arising from the Commission's Agenda 2000 proposals, and the outcome to the Berlin Summit, four Community Initiatives will operate in the period 2000-2006: INTERREG, LEADER plus, EQUAL and URBAN. Each initiative will be financed by a single Structural Fund. INTERREG will seek to promote transnational, cross-border, and inter-regional co-operation designed to stimulate balanced and harmonious spatial planning and development, and will be ERDF-funded. LEADER plus will seek to promote rural development through initiatives developed by local national groups, and will be financed by the EAGGF. EQUAL will focus on transnational co-operation designed to promote new means of fighting all types of discrimination and inequality with regard to the labour market, and will be financed by the ESF. URBAN will address the economic and social conversion of towns, cities and urban areas in crisis, in order to promote sustainable urban development, and will be ERDF-funded.

14.55   As a result of decisions taken at the Berlin Summit, the total amount allocated to Community Initiatives in the 2000-2006 programming round is 5.35% of the total Structural Funds budget of €195 billion, i.e. €10.4 billion. Included in the allocation of €10.4 billion is a provision of €155 million for the setting up of a Europe-wide network for each of the initiatives, to further facilitate the sharing of experience between Member States and regions. The indicative allocations for the implementation of the initiatives in Ireland are as follows: INTERREG €84 million, LEADER €45 million, EQUAL €32 million, and URBAN €5 million, giving a total of €166 million. The expenditure on URBAN will be in addition to substantial expenditure on urban poverty blackspots provided for in the NDP. The Commission's framework proposals for these new initiatives are awaited. The proposals are expected to contain new requirements such as more emphasis on innovation. The reduction in the number of initiatives, available funding and the new requirements will necessitate a rationalisation of the existing arrangements operated in Ireland. The general approach however, in relation to the development and implementation of the four Community Initiatives, will be to build upon and develop the positive actions and experiences of the previous programming period.

15 Financial Resources and Allocations

15.1 Proposed Public, EU and Public Private Partnership (PPP) expenditure under the NDP amounts to £40.588 billion (€50.536 billion) in 1999 prices over the 2000-2006 period. A profile of this expenditure is shown on the next page in Euros (€). This will be matched by an estimated additional £6.4 billion (€8.1 billion) of private funding bringing total Plan expenditure to an estimated £47 billion (€59.7 billion).

15.2 The tables in **Section A** set out total Plan expenditure by Operational Programme and by Sub-Programme showing the source of funding between public funding, proposed EU Funding and Private Funding over the Period 2000-2006, by year and by region. However, the Cohesion Fund figures are not required on a regional basis. The £6.4 billion private finance by way of matching additional expenditure is not shown in tables in Section A.

15.3 The table in **Section B** sets out, on an indicative basis, total Plan expenditure in respect of those priorities which are proposed for EU cofinancing from Structural Funds and the Cohesion Fund. As required under the Structural Funds Regulations, the tables show total expenditure for each priority broken down by Structural Funds, Cohesion Fund, other Community Financial Instruments, total national public cofinanced and non-cofinanced and related private expenditure. They also show the allocation of expenditure between the Objective 1 (BMW Region) and Objective 1 Region in Transition (S&E Region). Year by year tables in this format will be furnished to the European Commission.

15.4 The Structural Funds Regulations require that, in order to achieve a genuine economic impact, the appropriation of the Funds may not replace public or equivalent structural expenditure by the Member State. As a general rule, the level of relevant expenditure must be at least equal to the amount of the average annual expenditure in real terms achieved in the previous programming period, taking into account a number of factors including any reduction in Structural Fund expenditure when compared to the period 1994-1999. The table in **Section C** sets out on an indicative basis an ex-ante-verification of additionality as required under the regulations.

15.5 All monetary figures in the tables in **Sections A, B** and **C** are in EUROs (€) and in 1999 prices. In the tables in **Sections A, B** and **C** the expenditure under the CAP Rural Development Programme financed by the FEOGA Guarantee Fund is not included as this Programme is outside of the ambit of the Structural Funds. Total expenditure under this Programme, over the 2000-2006 period, will amount to £3.405 billion (€4.32 billion) of which the FEOGA Guarantee Fund will contribute £1.715 billion (€2.18 billion).

National Development Plan 2000-2006: Profile of Expenditure* (€ millions)

	2000-2006	2000	2001	2002	2003	2004	2005	2006
Economic and Social Infrastructure	22,360.1	2,552.6	3,125.8	3,279.9	3,310.7	3,346.1	3,336.4	3,408.6
Employment and Human Resources	12,562.7	1,967.3	1,841.2	1,837.9	1,753.2	1,721.4	1,721.3	1,721.1
Productive Sector	5,725.2	468.4	751.8	856.3	896.6	907.7	920.6	925.8
BMW Regional Operational Programme	2,646.1	336.5	370.6	366.4	390.6	407.1	442.2	332.4
S&E Regional Operational Programme	3,791.4	478.7	519.7	503.3	565.7	585.7	652.3	485.3
PEACE Programme	127.0	25.4	25.4	25.4	25.4	25.4	0.0	0.0
CAP Rural Development Programme	4,323.5	609.1	617.6	617.6	619.6	619.6	618.4	621.6
Total	51,535.9	6,438.0	7,252.2	7,486.8	7,561.8	7,613.2	7,691.1	7,494.8

*This table covers only public funding (Exchequer and EU) and PPP projects but excludes private finance.

SECTION A

Economic & Social Infrastructure Operational Programme
Expenditure: 2000-2006

TOTAL PLAN: 2000-2006 (€ million)	Total Public & Private Cost (State, EU, PPP & Private)	Total Public Cost (State, EU & PPP)	Total Public Funding		EU Funding		Private Funding	
			Exchequer	Other Public	Structural Funds	Cohesion Fund	PPP Projects	Private Finance
National Roads	**5,967.8**	**5,967.8**	3,938.0		540.0	220.0	1,269.7	
BMW Region	**2,229.7**	**2,229.7**	1,464.7		295.2		469.8	
S&E Region	**3,738.1**	**3,738.1**	2,693.4		244.8		799.9	
Public Transport	**2,836.6**	**2,836.6**	1,333.5	872.9	192.3	57.0	380.9	0.0
BMW Region	**299.3**	**299.3**	147.3	107.9	0.0	0.0	44.1	0.0
S&E Region	**2,537.4**	**2,537.4**	1,221.8	786.3	192.3	0.0	337.0	0.0
Environmental Protection	**3,212.4**	**3,212.4**	1,741.4	984.0	80.0	280.0	127.0	0.0
BMW Region	**887.5**	**887.5**	550.2	270.5	32.6	0.0	34.3	0.0
S&E Region	**2,324.9**	**2,324.9**	1,471.2	713.6	47.4	0.0	92.7	0.0
Energy	**185.4**	**185.4**	142.3	0.0	43.1	0.0	0.0	0.0
BMW Region	**90.2**	**90.2**	72.4	0.0	17.8	0.0	0.0	0.0
S&E Region	**95.2**	**95.2**	69.9	0.0	25.3	0.0	0.0	0.0
Housing	**7,618.4**	**7,618.4**	4,878.3	2,740.1	0.0	0.0	0.0	0.0
BMW Region	**1,651.9**	**1,651.9**	1,065.3	586.6	0.0	0.0	0.0	0.0
S&E Region	**5,966.5**	**5,966.5**	3,813.0	2,153.5	0.0	0.0	0.0	0.0
Health	**2,539.5**	**2,539.5**	2,539.5	0.0	0.0	0.0	0.0	0.0
BMW Region	**799.9**	**799.9**	799.9	0.0	0.0	0.0	0.0	0.0
S&E Region	**1,739.5**	**1,739.5**	1,739.5	0.0	0.0	0.0	0.0	0.0
TOTAL	**22,360.1**	**22,360.1**	14,573.0	4,597.0	855.0	557.0	1,778.0	0.0
BMW Region	**5,958.5**	**5,958.5**	4,100.0	965.0	346.0	0.0	548.0	0.0
S&E Region	**16,401.7**	**16,401.7**	11,009	3,653.0	510.0	0.0	1,230.0	0.0

Employment & Human Resources Development Operational Programme
Expenditure: 2000-2006

TOTAL PLAN: 2000-2006 (€ million)	Total Public & Private Cost (State, EU, PPP & Private)	Total Public Cost (State, EU & PPP)	Total Public Funding		EU Funding		Private Funding	
			Exchequer	Other Public	Structural Funds	Cohesion Fund	PPP Projects	Private Finance
Employability	**5,880.8**	**5,880.8**	5,263.2	0.0	617.6	0.0	0.0	0.0
BMW Region	**1,653.8**	**1,653.8**	1,400.4	0.0	253.4	0.0	0.0	0.0
S&E Region	**4,226.5**	**4,226.5**	3,862.3	0.0	364.2	0.0	0.0	0.0
Entrepreneurship	**981.4**	**524.4**	428.8	0.0	95.6	0.0	0.0	0.0
BMW Region	**157.4**	**157.4**	118.3	0.0	39.1	0.0	0.0	0.0
S&E Region	**367.0**	**367.0**	310.5	0.0	56.5	0.0	0.0	0.0
Adaptability	**5,900.2**	**5,900.2**	5,738.9	0.0	161.3	0.0	0.0	0.0
BMW Region	**1,713.9**	**1,713.9**	1,647.2	0.0	66.7	0.0	0.0	0.0
S&E Region	**4,186.3**	**4,186.3**	4,091.7	0.0	94.6	0.0	0.0	0.0
Equality	**257.2**	**257.2**	251.4	0.0	5.8	0.0	0.0	0.0
BMW Region	**69.8**	**69.8**	67.3	0.0	2.5	0.0	0.0	0.0
S&E Region	**187.4**	**187.4**	184.1	0.0	3.3	0.0	0.0	0.0
TOTAL	**12,563.0**	**12,563.0**	11,682.4	0.0	880.0	0.0	0.0	0.0
BMW Region	**3,595.0**	**3,595,5**	3,233.3	0.0	362.0	0.0	0.0	0.0
S&E Region	**8,967.1**	**8,967.1**	8,448.5	0.0	519.0	0.0	0.0	0.0

Economic & Social Infrastructure Operational Programme

Expenditure: 2000

PLAN EXPENDITURE: 2000 (€ million)	Total Public & Private Cost (State, EU, PPP & Private)	Total Public Cost (State, EU & PPP)	Total Public Funding		EU Funding		Private Funding	
			Exchequer	Other Public	Structural Funds	Cohesion Fund	PPP Projects	Private Finance
National Roads	**529.5**	**529.5**	349.7	0.0	121.0	55.0	3.8	0.0
BMW Region	**195.5**	**195.5**	131.7	0.0	63.8	0.0	0.0	0.0
S&E Region	**333.9**	**333.9**	272.9	0.0	57.2	0.0	3.8	0.0
Public Transport	**416.5**	**416.5**	274.4	74.8	53.0	14.2	0.0	0.0
BMW Region	**46.1**	**46.1**	34.4	11.7	0.0	0.0	0.0	0.0
S&E Region	**370.4**	**370.4**	248.9	68.5	53.0	0.0	0.0	0.0
Environmental Protection	**434.4**	**434.4**	209.0	138.4	17.0	70.0	0.0	0.0
BMW Region	**120.1**	**120.1**	75.8	38.1	6.2	0.0	0.0	0.0
S&E Region	**314.3**	**314.3**	203.2	100.3	10.8	0.0	0.0	0.0
Energy	**7.9**	**7.9**	3.9	0.0	4.0	0.0	0.0	0.0
BMW Region	**3.2**	**3.2**	1.7	0.0	1.5	0.0	0.0	0.0
S&E Region	**4.7**	**4.7**	2.2	0.0	2.5	0.0	0.0	0.0
Housing	**872.3**	**872.3**	542.2	330.1	0.0	0.0	0.0	0.0
BMW Region	**186.7**	**186.7**	113.0	73.6	0.0	0.0	0.0	0.0
S&E Region	**685.7**	**685.7**	429.2	256.5	0.0	0.0	0.0	0.0
Health	**292.0**	**292.0**	292.0	0.0	0.0	0.0	0.0	0.0
BMW Region	**83.8**	**83.8**	83.8	0.0	0.0	0.0	0.0	0.0
S&E Region	**208.2**	**208.2**	208.2	0.0	0.0	0.0	0.0	0.0
TOTAL	**2,551.8**	**2,551.8**	1,671.0	543.0	195.0	139.0	3.8	0.0
BMW Region	**635.0**	**635.0**	440.0	123.0	72.0	0.0	0.0	0.0
S&E Region	**1,917.8**	**1,917.8**	1,365.0	425.0	124.0	0.0	3.8	0.0

Employment & Human Resources Development Operational Programme

Expenditure: 2000

PLAN EXPENDITURE: 2000 (€ million)	Total Public & Private Cost (State, EU, PPP & Private)	Total Public Cost (State, EU & PPP)	Total Public Funding		EU Funding		Private Funding	
			Exchequer	Other Public	Structural Funds	Cohesion Fund	PPP Projects	Private Finance
Employability	**846.2**	**846.2**	721.2	0.0	125.0	0.0	0.0	0.0
BMW Region	**240.5**	**240.5**	194.7	0.0	45.8	0.0	0.0	0.0
S&E Region	**605.2**	**605.2**	526.0	0.0	79.2	0.0	0.0	0.0
Entrepreneurship	**49.0**	**49.0**	29.0	0.0	20.0	0.0	0.0	0.0
BMW Region	**14.7**	**14.7**	7.4	0.0	7.3	0.0	0.0	0.0
S&E Region	**34.3**	**34.3**	21.6	0.0	12.7	0.0	0.0	0.0
Adaptability	**1,035.3**	**1,035.3**	1,005.3	0.0	30.0	0.0	0.0	0.0
BMW Region	**294.3**	**294.3**	283.3	0.0	11.0	0.0	0.0	0.0
S&E Region	**741.0**	**741.0**	722.0	0.0	19.0	0.0	0.0	0.0
Equality	**36.7**	**36.7**	35.7	0.0	1.0	0.0	0.0	0.0
BMW Region	**10.0**	**10.0**	9.6	0.0	0.4	0.0	0.0	0.0
S&E Region	**26.8**	**26.8**	26.2	0.0	0.6	0.0	0.0	0.0
TOTAL	**1,967.2**	**1,967.2**	1,791.2	0.0	176.0	0.0	0.0	0.0
BMW Region	**559.6**	**559.6**	495.1	0.0	64.5	0.0	0.0	0.0
S&E Region	**1,407.3**	**1,407.3**	1,295.8	0.0	111.5	0.0	0.0	0.0

Economic & Social Infrastructure Operational Programme

Expenditure: 2001

PLAN EXPENDITURE: 2001 (€ million)	Total Public & Private Cost (State, EU, PPP & Private)	Total Public Cost (State, EU & PPP)	Total Public Funding		EU Funding		Private Funding	
			Exchequer	Other Public	Structural Funds	Cohesion Fund	PPP Projects	Private Finance
National Roads	**773.3**	**773.3**	568.8		131.7	55.0	17.8	
BMW Region	281.9	281.9	224.3		57.6		0.0	
S&E Region	491.4	491.4	399.5		74.1		17.8	
Public Transport	**447.1**	**447.1**	313.5	96.0	23.3	14.2	0.0	0.0
BMW Region	46.2	46.2	34.5	11.7	0.0	0.0	0.0	0.0
S&E Region	400.9	400.9	287.9	89.7	23.3	0.0	0.0	0.0
Environmental Protection	**433.1**	**433.1**	190.6	128.2	15.1	70.0	29.2	0.0
BMW Region	118.8	118.8	70.1	35.6	5.6	0.0	7.6	0.0
S&E Region	314.3	314.3	190.5	92.7	9.5	0.0	21.6	0.0
Energy	**24.9**	**24.9**	15.4	0.0	9.5	0.0	0.0	0.0
BMW Region	9.9	9.9	6.4	0.0	3.5	0.0	0.0	0.0
S&E Region	15.0	15.0	9.0	0.0	6.0	0.0	0.0	0.0
Housing	**1,104.7**	**1,104.7**	766.9	337.8	0.0	0.0	0.0	0.0
BMW Region	224.7	224.7	151.1	73.6	0.0	0.0	0.0	0.0
S&E Region	879.9	879.9	615.8	264.1	0.0	0.0	0.0	0.0
Health	**342.8**	**342.8**	342.8	0.0	0.0	0.0	0.0	0.0
BMW Region	104.1	104.1	104.1	0.0	0.0	0.0	0.0	0.0
S&E Region	238.7	238.7	238.7	0.0	0.0	0.0	0.0	0.0
TOTAL	**3,125.8**	**3,125.8**	2,198.0	562.0	180.0	139.0	47.0	0.0
BMW Region	785.7	785.7	591.0	121.0	67.0	0.0	8.0	0.0
S&E Region	2,340.1	2,340.1	1,741.0	446.0	113.0	0.0	39.0	0.0

Employment & Human Resources Development Operational Programme

Expenditure: 2001

PLAN EXPENDITURE: 2001 (€ million)	Total Public & Private Cost (State, EU, PPP & Private)	Total Public Cost (State, EU & PPP)	Total Public Funding		EU Funding		Private Funding	
			Exchequer	Other Public	Structural Funds	Cohesion Fund	PPP Projects	Private Finance
Employability	**888.8**	**888.8**	776.3	0.0	112.5	0.0	0.0	0.0
BMW Region	250.8	250.8	209.0	0.0	41.8	0.0	0.0	0.0
S&E Region	638.0	638.0	567.3	0.0	70.7	0.0	0.0	0.0
Entrepreneurship	**57.9**	**57.9**	39.9	0.0	18.0	0.0	0.0	0.0
BMW Region	17.4	17.4	10.7	0.0	6.7	0.0	0.0	0.0
S&E Region	40.5	40.5	29.2	0.0	11.3	0.0	0.0	0.0
Adaptability	**858.1**	**858.1**	830.7	0.0	27.4	0.0	0.0	0.0
BMW Region	250.0	250.0	239.8	0.0	10.2	0.0	0.0	0.0
S&E Region	608.0	608.0	590.8	0.0	17.2	0.0	0.0	0.0
Equality	**36.8**	**36.8**	35.9	0.0	0.9	0.0	0.0	0.0
BMW Region	10.0	10.0	9.7	0.0	0.3	0.0	0.0	0.0
S&E Region	26.8	26.8	26.2	0.0	0.6	0.0	0.0	0.0
TOTAL	**1,841.6**	**1,841.6**	1,682.8	0.0	158.8	0.0	0.0	0.0
BMW Region	528.2	528.2	469.2	0.0	59.0	0.0	0.0	0.0
S&E Region	1,313.3	1,313.3	1,213.5	0.0	99.8	0.0	0.0	0.0

Economic & Social Infrastructure Operational Programme
Expenditure: 2002

TOTAL PLAN: 2002 (€ million)	Total Public & Private Cost (State, EU, PPP & Private)	Total Public Cost (State, EU & PPP)	Total Public Funding		EU Funding		Private Funding	
			Exchequer	Other Public	Structural Funds	Cohesion Fund	PPP Projects	Private Finance
National Roads	**907.9**	**907.9**	680.6		108.8	55.0	63.5	
BMW Region	**339.0**	**339.0**	262.9		52.0		24.1	
S&E Region	**568.8**	**568.8**	472.7		56.8		39.4	
Public Transport	**447.1**	**447.1**	311.1	93.6	28.0	14.3	0.0	0.0
BMW Region	**46.2**	**46.2**	34.5	11.7	0.0	0.0	0.0	0.0
S&E Region	**400.9**	**400.9**	285.5	87.3	28.0	0.0	0.0	0.0
Environmental Protection	**411.8**	**411.8**	249.8	121.9	13.4	0.0	26.7	0.0
BMW Region	**113.9**	**113.9**	68.2	33.0	5.1	0.0	7.6	0.0
S&E Region	**297.9**	**297.9**	181.7	88.9	8.3	0.0	19.0	0.0
Energy	**32.3**	**32.3**	46.1	0.0	8.4	70.0	0.0	0.0
BMW Region	**13.0**	**13.0**	9.8	0.0	3.2	0.0	0.0	0.0
S&E Region	**19.4**	**19.4**	14.2	0.0	5.2	0.0	0.0	0.0
Housing	**1,112.3**	**1,112.3**	766.9	345.4	0.0	0.0	0.0	0.0
BMW Region	**231.1**	**231.1**	157.4	73.6	0.0	0.0	0.0	0.0
S&E Region	**881.2**	**881.2**	609.5	271.7	0.0	0.0	0.0	0.0
Health	**368.2**	**368.2**	368.2	0.0	0.0	0.0	0.0	0.0
BMW Region	**120.6**	**120.6**	120.6	0.0	0.0	0.0	0.0	0.0
S&E Region	**247.6**	**247.6**	247.6	0.0	0.0	0.0	0.0	0.0
TOTAL	**3,279.5**	**3,279.5**	2,331.0	561.0	159.0	139.0	90.0	0.0
BMW Region	**863.8**	**863.8**	653.0	118.0	60.0	0.0	32.0	0.0
S&E Region	**2,415.8**	**2,415.8**	1,811.0	448.0	98.0	0.0	58.0	0.0

Employment & Human Resources Development Operational Programme
Expenditure: 2002

TOTAL PLAN: 2002 (€ million)	Total Public & Private Cost (State, EU, PPP & Private)	Total Public Cost (State, EU & PPP)	Total Public Funding		EU Funding		Private Funding	
			Exchequer	Other Public	Structural Funds	Cohesion Fund	PPP Projects	Private Finance
Employability	**877.4**	**877.4**	778.0	0.0	99.4	0.0	0.0	0.0
BMW Region	**247.3**	**247.3**	209.5	0.0	37.8	0.0	0.0	0.0
S&E Region	**630.0**	**630.0**	568.4	0.0	61.6	0.0	0.0	0.0
Entrepreneurship	**64.2**	**64.2**	48.3	0.0	15.9	0.0	0.0	0.0
BMW Region	**19.3**	**19.3**	13.3	0.0	6.0	0.0	0.0	0.0
S&E Region	**45.1**	**45.1**	35.2	0.0	9.9	0.0	0.0	0.0
Adaptability	**859.4**	**859.4**	835.2	0.0	24.2	0.0	0.0	0.0
BMW Region	**250.0**	**250.0**	240.8	0.0	9.2	0.0	0.0	0.0
S&E Region	**609.3**	**609.3**	594.3	0.0	15.0	0.0	0.0	0.0
Equality	**36.8**	**36.8**	36.0	0.0	0.8	0.0	0.0	0.0
BMW Region	**10.0**	**10.0**	9.7	0.0	0.3	0.0	0.0	0.0
S&E Region	**26.8**	**26.8**	26.3	0.0	0.5	0.0	0.0	0.0
TOTAL	**1,837.8**	**1,837.8**	1,697.5	0.0	140.3	0.0	0.0	0.0
BMW Region	**526.7**	**526.7**	473.4	0.0	53.3	0.0	0.0	0.0
S&E Region	**1,311.3**	**1,311.3**	1,224.3	0.0	87.0	0.0	0.0	0.0

Economic & Social Infrastructure Operational Programme

Expenditure: 2003

TOTAL PLAN: 2003 (€ million)	Total Public & Private Cost (State, EU, PPP & Private)	Total Public Cost (State, EU & PPP)	Total Public Funding		EU Funding		Private Funding	
			Exchequer	Other Public	Structural Funds	Cohesion Fund	PPP Projects	Private Finance
National Roads	**909.1**	**909.1**	504.5		66.5	55.0	283.2	
BMW Region	**341.6**	**341.6**	195.2		39.7		106.7	
S&E Region	**567.6**	**567.6**	364.3		26.8		176.5	
Public Transport	**384.2**	**384.2**	94.4	176.0	36.0	14.3	63.5	0.0
BMW Region	**40.1**	**40.1**	10.8	22.0	0.0	0.0	7.4	0.0
S&E Region	**344.1**	**344.1**	92.6	159.4	36.0	0.0	56.1	0.0
Environmental Protection	**486.3**	**486.3**	234.7	148.6	11.5	70.0	21.6	0.0
BMW Region	**134.6**	**134.6**	83.2	40.6	4.4	0.0	6.3	0.0
S&E Region	**351.7**	**351.7**	221.5	107.9	7.1	0.0	15.2	0.0
Energy	**37.8**	**37.8**	30.6	0.0	7.2	0.0	0.0	0.0
BMW Region	**18.9**	**18.9**	16.1	0.0	2.8	0.0	0.0	0.0
S&E Region	**18.9**	**18.9**	14.5	0.0	4.4	0.0	0.0	0.0
Housing	**1,118.6**	**1,118.6**	744.1	374.6	0.0	0.0	0.0	0.0
BMW Region	**237.4**	**237.4**	154.9	82.5	0.0	0.0	0.0	0.0
S&E Region	**881.2**	**881.2**	589.2	292.0	0.0	0.0	0.0	0.0
Health	**374.6**	**374.6**	374.6	0.0	0.0	0.0	0.0	0.0
BMW Region	**119.4**	**119.4**	119.4	0.0	0.0	0.0	0.0	0.0
S&E Region	**255.2**	**255.2**	255.2	0.0	0.0	0.0	0.0	0.0
TOTAL	**3,310.7**	**3,310.7**	1,983.0	699.0	121.0	139.0	368.0	0.0
BMW Region	**892.0**	**892.0**	580.0	145.0	47.0	0.0	120.0	0.0
S&E Region	**2,418.7**	**2,418.7**	1,537.0	559.0	74.0	0.0	248.0	0.0

Employment & Human Resources Development Operational Programme

Expenditure: 2003

TOTAL PLAN: 2003 (€ million)	Total Public & Private Cost (State, EU, PPP & Private)	Total Public Cost (State, EU & PPP)	Total Public Funding		EU Funding		Private Funding	
			Exchequer	Other Public	Structural Funds	Cohesion Fund	PPP Projects	Private Finance
Employability	**840.9**	**840.9**	755.2	0.0	85.7	0.0	0.0	0.0
BMW Region	**235.0**	**235.0**	201.8	0.0	33.2	0.0	0.0	0.0
S&E Region	**605.2**	**605.2**	552.7	0.0	52.5	0.0	0.0	0.0
Entrepreneurship	**88.4**	**88.4**	74.7	0.0	13.7	0.0	0.0	0.0
BMW Region	**26.5**	**26.5**	21.2	0.0	5.3	0.0	0.0	0.0
S&E Region	**61.8**	**61.8**	53.4	0.0	8.4	0.0	0.0	0.0
Adaptability	**787.1**	**787.1**	773.4	0.0	13.7	0.0	0.0	0.0
BMW Region	**229.8**	**229.8**	224.5	0.0	5.3	0.0	0.0	0.0
S&E Region	**557.2**	**557.2**	548.8	0.0	8.4	0.0	0.0	0.0
Equality	**36.8**	**36.8**	36.1	0.0	0.7	0.0	0.0	0.0
BMW Region	**10.0**	**10.0**	9.7	0.0	0.3	0.0	0.0	0.0
S&E Region	**26.8**	**26.8**	26.4	0.0	0.4	0.0	0.0	0.0
TOTAL	**1,753.3**	**1,753.3**	1,639.5	0.0	113.8	0.0	0.0	0.0
BMW Region	**501.4**	**501.4**	457.3	0.0	44.1	0.0	0.0	0.0
S&E Region	**1,250.9**	**1,250.9**	1,181.2	0.0	69.7	0.0	0.0	0.0

Economic & Social Infrastructure Operational Programme

Expenditure: 2004

PLAN EXPENDITURE: 2004 (€ million)	Total Public & Private Cost (State, EU, PPP & Private)	Total Public Cost (State, EU & PPP)	Total Public Funding		EU Funding		Private Funding	
			Exchequer	Other Public	Structural Funds	Cohesion Fund	PPP Projects	Private Finance
National Roads	**910.4**	**910.4**	571.4	0.0	47.0	0.0	292.0	0.0
BMW Region	**342.8**	**342.8**	202.0	0.0	30.4	0.0	110.5	0.0
S&E Region	**567.6**	**567.6**	369.4	0.0	16.6	0.0	181.6	0.0
Public Transport	**388.5**	**388.5**	112.7	161.0	26.0	0.0	88.9	0.0
BMW Region	**40.8**	**40.8**	11.4	19.0	0.0	0.0	10.3	0.0
S&E Region	**347.8**	**347.8**	101.3	141.9	26.0	0.0	78.6	0.0
Environmental Protection	**484.7**	**484.7**	309.1	148.6	8.0	0.0	19.0	0.0
BMW Region	**133.7**	**133.7**	84.7	40.6	3.3	0.0	5.1	0.0
S&E Region	**351.0**	**351.0**	224.4	107.9	4.7	0.0	14.0	0.0
Energy	**31.2**	**31.2**	26.2	0.0	5.0	0.0	0.0	0.0
BMW Region	**16.3**	**16.3**	14.2	0.0	2.1	0.0	0.0	0.0
S&E Region	**15.0**	**15.0**	12.1	0.0	2.9	0.0	0.0	0.0
Housing	**1,150.4**	**1,150.4**	726.3	424.1	0.0	0.0	0.0	0.0
BMW Region	**253.9**	**253.9**	163.8	90.2	0.0	0.0	0.0	0.0
S&E Region	**896.4**	**896.4**	562.5	333.9	0.0	0.0	0.0	0.0
Health	**380.9**	**380.9**	380.9	0.0	0.0	0.0	0.0	0.0
BMW Region	**125.7**	**125.7**	125.7	0.0	0.0	0.0	0.0	0.0
S&E Region	**255.2**	**255.2**	255.2	0.0	0.0	0.0	0.0	0.0
TOTAL	**3,346.1**	**3,346.1**	2,127.0	734.0	86.0	0.0	400.0	0.0
BMW Region	**913.2**	**913.2**	602.0	150.0	36.0	0.0	126.0	0.0
S&E Region	**2,432.9**	**2,432.9**	1,525.0	584.0	50.0	0.0	274.0	0.0

Employment & Human Resources Development Operational Programme

Expenditure: 2004

PLAN EXPENDITURE: 2004 (€ million)	Total Public & Private Cost (State, EU, PPP & Private)	Total Public Cost (State, EU & PPP)	Total Public Funding		EU Funding		Private Funding	
			Exchequer	Other Public	Structural Funds	Cohesion Fund	PPP Projects	Private Finance
Employability	**809.2**	**809.2**	748.2	0.0	61.0	0.0	0.0	0.0
BMW Region	**226.1**	**226.1**	200.7	0.0	25.4	0.0	0.0	0.0
S&E Region	**582.9**	**582.9**	547.3	0.0	35.6	0.0	0.0	0.0
Entrepreneurship	**88.4**	**88.4**	78.4	0.0	10.0	0.0	0.0	0.0
BMW Region	**26.5**	**26.5**	22.3	0.0	4.2	0.0	0.0	0.0
S&E Region	**61.8**	**61.8**	56.0	0.0	5.8	0.0	0.0	0.0
Adaptability	**787.1**	**787.1**	777.1	0.0	10.0	0.0	0.0	0.0
BMW Region	**229.7**	**229.7**	225.5	0.0	4.2	0.0	0.0	0.0
S&E Region	**557.4**	**557.4**	551.6	0.0	5.8	0.0	0.0	0.0
Equality	**36.8**	**36.8**	35.8	0.0	1.0	0.0	0.0	0.0
BMW Region	**10.0**	**10.0**	9.6	0.0	0.4	0.0	0.0	0.0
S&E Region	**26.8**	**26.8**	26.2	0.0	0.6	0.0	0.0	0.0
TOTAL	**1,721.5**	**1,721.5**	1,639.5	0.0	82.0	0.0	0.0	0.0
BMW Region	**492.4**	**492.4**	458.2	0.0	34.2	0.0	0.0	0.0
S&E Region	**1,229.0**	**1,229.0**	1,181.2	0.0	47.8	0.0	0.0	0.0

Economic & Social Infrastructure Operational Programme

Expenditure: 2005

TOTAL PLAN: 2005 (€ million)	Total Public & Private Cost (State, EU, PPP & Private)	Total Public Cost (State, EU & PPP)	Total Public Funding		EU Funding		Private Funding	
			Exchequer	Other Public	Structural Funds	Cohesion Fund	PPP Projects	Private Finance
National Roads	**949.8**	**949.8**	596.0		49.0		304.7	
BMW Region	**356.8**	**356.8**	198.0		44.5		114.3	
S&E Region	**593.0**	**593.0**	398.0		4.5		190.5	
Public Transport	**380.9**	**380.9**	105.1	135.6	26.0	0.0	114.3	0.0
BMW Region	**39.9**	**39.9**	10.5	16.1	0.0	0.0	13.2	0.0
S&E Region	**341.1**	**341.1**	94.5	119.4	26.0	0.0	101.1	0.0
Environmental Protection	**480.0**	**480.0**	308.2	148.6	8.0	0.0	15.2	0.0
BMW Region	**132.6**	**132.6**	83.4	40.6	4.7	0.0	3.8	0.0
S&E Region	**347.4**	**347.4**	224.7	107.9	3.3	0.0	11.4	0.0
Energy	**27.4**	**27.4**	22.4	0.0	5.0	0.0	0.0	0.0
BMW Region	**14.7**	**14.7**	11.7	0.0	3.0	0.0	0.0	0.0
S&E Region	**12.7**	**12.7**	10.7	0.0	2.0	0.0	0.0	0.0
Housing	**1,111.0**	**1,111.0**	662.8	448.2	0.0	0.0	0.0	0.0
BMW Region	**251.4**	**251.4**	157.4	94.0	0.0	0.0	0.0	0.0
S&E Region	**859.6**	**859.6**	505.4	354.3	0.0	0.0	0.0	0.0
Health	**387.3**	**387.3**	387.3	0.0	0.0	0.0	0.0	0.0
BMW Region	**121.9**	**121.9**	121.9	0.0	0.0	0.0	0.0	0.0
S&E Region	**265.4**	**265.4**	265.4	0.0	0.0	0.0	0.0	0.0
TOTAL	**3,336.4**	**3,336.4**	2,082.0	732.0	88.0	0.0	434.0	0.0
BMW Region	**917.3**	**917.3**	583.0	151.0	52.0	0.0	131.0	0.0
S&E Region	**2,419.1**	**2,419.1**	1,499.0	582.0	36.0	0.0	303.0	0.0

Employment & Human Resources Development Operational Programme

Expenditure: 2005

TOTAL PLAN: 2005 (€ million)	Total Public & Private Cost (State, EU, PPP & Private)	Total Public Cost (State, EU & PPP)	Total Public Funding		EU Funding		Private Funding	
			Exchequer	Other Public	Structural Funds	Cohesion Fund	PPP Projects	Private Finance
Employability	**809.2**	**809.2**	748.2	0.0	61.0	0.0	0.0	0.0
BMW Region	**226.1**	**226.1**	189.9	0.0	36.2	0.0	0.0	0.0
S&E Region	**582.9**	**582.9**	558.1	0.0	24.8	0.0	0.0	0.0
Entrepreneurship	**88.4**	**88.4**	78.4	0.0	10.0	0.0	0.0	0.0
BMW Region	**26.5**	**26.5**	20.6	0.0	5.9	0.0	0.0	0.0
S&E Region	**61.8**	**61.8**	57.7	0.0	4.1	0.0	0.0	0.0
Adaptability	**786.9**	**786.9**	776.9	0.0	10.0	0.0	0.0	0.0
BMW Region	**229.6**	**229.6**	223.7	0.0	5.9	0.0	0.0	0.0
S&E Region	**557.3**	**557.3**	553.2	0.0	4.1	0.0	0.0	0.0
Equality	**36.8**	**36.8**	35.8	0.0	1.0	0.0	0.0	0.0
BMW Region	**10.0**	**10.0**	9.4	0.0	0.6	0.0	0.0	0.0
S&E Region	**26.8**	**26.8**	26.4	0.0	0.4	0.0	0.0	0.0
TOTAL	**1,721.3**	**1,721.3**	1,639.3	0.0	82.0	0.0	0.0	0.0
BMW Region	**492.3**	**492.3**	443.7	0.0	48.6	0.0	0.0	0.0
S&E Region	**1,228.9**	**1,228.9**	1,195.5	0.0	33.4	0.0	0.0	0.0

Economic & Social Infrastructure Operational Programme

Expenditure: 2006

TOTAL PLAN: 2006 (€ million)	Total Public & Private Cost (State, EU, PPP & Private)	Total Public Cost (State, EU & PPP)	Total Public Funding		EU Funding		Private Funding	
			Exchequer	Other Public	Structural Funds	Cohesion Fund	PPP Projects	Private Finance
National Roads	**987.9**	**987.9**	667.1		16.0		304.7	
BMW Region	372.0	372.0	250.5		7.3		114.3	
S&E Region	615.8	615.8	416.7		8.7		190.5	
Public Transport	**372.0**	**372.0**	121.9	135.9	0.0	0.0	114.3	0.0
BMW Region	39.0	39.0	11.0	14.7	0.0	0.0	13.2	0.0
S&E Region	333.2	333.2	110.8	121.3	0.0	0.0	101.1	0.0
Environmental Protection	**482.9**	**482.9**	310.8	149.8	7.0	0.0	15.2	0.0
BMW Region	134.0	134.0	85.0	41.9	3.2	0.0	3.8	0.0
S&E Region	348.9	348.9	225.8	107.9	3.8	0.0	11.4	0.0
Energy	**23.1**	**23.1**	19.1	0.0	4.0	0.0	0.0	0.0
BMW Region	13.1	13.1	11.3	0.0	1.8	0.0	0.0	0.0
S&E Region	10.0	10.0	7.8	0.0	2.2	0.0	0.0	0.0
Housing	**1,149.1**	**1,149.1**	669.2	480.0	0.0	0.0	0.0	0.0
BMW Region	266.6	266.6	167.6	99.0	0.0	0.0	0.0	0.0
S&E Region	882.5	882.5	501.5	380.9	0.0	0.0	0.0	0.0
Health	**393.6**	**393.6**	393.6	0.0	0.0	0.0	0.0	0.0
BMW Region	124.4	124.4	124.4	0.0	0.0	0.0	0.0	0.0
S&E Region	269.2	269.2	269.2	0.0	0.0	0.0	0.0	0.0
TOTAL	**3,408.6**	**3,408.6**	2,182.0	766.0	27.0	0.0	434.0	0.0
BMW Region	949.1	949.1	650.0	156.0	12.0	0.0	131.0	0.0
S&E Region	2,459.6	2,459.6	1,532.0	610.0	15.0	0.0	303.0	0.0

Employment & Human Resources Development Operational Programme

Expenditure: 2006

TOTAL PLAN: 2006 (€ million)	Total Public & Private Cost (State, EU, PPP & Private)	Total Public Cost (State, EU & PPP)	Total Public Funding		EU Funding		Private Funding	
			Exchequer	Other Public	Structural Funds	Cohesion Fund	PPP Projects	Private Finance
Employability	**809.2**	**809.2**	736.2	0.0	73.0	0.0	0.0	0.0
BMW Region	226.3	226.3	193.0	0.0	33.3	0.0	0.0	0.0
S&E Region	582.9	582.9	543.2	0.0	39.7	0.0	0.0	0.0
Entrepreneurship	**88.4**	**88.4**	80.4	0.0	8.0	0.0	0.0	0.0
BMW Region	26.5	26.5	22.9	0.0	3.6	0.0	0.0	0.0
S&E Region	61.8	61.8	57.4	0.0	4.4	0.0	0.0	0.0
Adaptability	**786.7**	**786.7**	740.7	0.0	46.0	0.0	0.0	0.0
BMW Region	229.6	229.6	208.6	0.0	21.0	0.0	0.0	0.0
S&E Region	557.2	557.2	532.2	0.0	25.0	0.0	0.0	0.0
Equality	**36.8**	**36.8**	36.4	0.0	0.4	0.0	0.0	0.0
BMW Region	10.0	10.0	9.8	0.0	0.2	0.0	0.0	0.0
S&E Region	26.8	26.8	26.6	0.0	0.2	0.0	0.0	0.0
TOTAL	**1,721.1**	**1,721.1**	1,593.7	0.0	127.4	0.0	0.0	0.0
BMW Region	492.4	492.4	434.3	0.0	58.1	0.0	0.0	0.0
S&E Region	1,228.7	1,228.7	1,159.4	0.0	69.3	0.0	0.0	0.0

Productive Sector Operational Programme Expenditure: 2000-2006

TOTAL PLAN: 2000-2006 (€ million)	Total Public & Private Cost (State, EU, PPP & Private)	Total Public Cost (State, EU & PPP)	Total Public Funding		EU Funding		Private Funding	
			Exchequer	Other Public	Structural Funds	Cohesion Fund	PPP Projects	Private Finance
Research, Technological Development & Innovation (RTDI)	2,471.0	2,471.0	2,158.0		313.0			
BMW Region	663.0	663.0	536.0		127.0			
S&E Region	1,808.0	1,808.0	1,623.0		185.0			
Industry	2,416.0	2,416.0	2,416.0					
BMW Region	1,092.0	1,092.0	1,092.0					
S&E Region	1,324.0	1,324.0	1,324.0					
Marketing	428.0	428.0	428.0					
BMW Region	141.0	141.0	141.0					
S&E Region	287.0	287.0	287.0					
Agricultural Development	353.0	353.0	273.0		80.0			
BMW Region	170.0	170.0	141.0		29.0			
S&E Region	183.0	183.0	132.0		51.0			
Fisheries	57.0	57.0	32.0		25.0			
BMW Region	33.0	33.0	24.0		9.0			
S&E Region	24.0	24.0	8.0		16.0			
TOTAL	5,725.0	5,725.0	5,307.2	0.0	418.0	0.0	0.0	0.0
BMW Region	2,100.0	2,100.0	1,933.9	0.0	166.0	0.0	0.0	0.0
S&E Region	3,626.0	3,626.0	3,374.3	0.0	252.0	0.0	0.0	0.0

Border, Midland & Western Regional Operational Programme Expenditure: 2000-2006

TOTAL PLAN: 2000-2006 (€ million)	Total Public & Private Cost (State, EU, PPP & Private)	Total Public Cost (State, EU & PPP)	Total Public Funding		EU Funding		Private Funding	
			Exchequer	Other Public	Structural Funds	Cohesion Fund	PPP Projects	Private Finance
Local Infrastructure	1,936.0	1,936.0	665.0	883.0	175.0		212.0	
Productive Sector	429.0	429.0	302.0		127.0			
Social Inclusion	281.0	281.0	208.0		73.0			
TOTAL	2,646.0	2,646.0	1,175.0	883.0	375.0	0.0	212.0	0.0

Southern & Eastern Regional Operational Programme Expenditure: 2000-2006

TOTAL PLAN: 2000-2006 (€ million)	Total Public & Private Cost (State, EU, PPP & Private)	Total Public Cost (State, EU & PPP)	Total Public Funding		EU Funding		Private Funding	
			Exchequer	Other Public	Structural Funds	Cohesion Fund	PPP Projects	Private Finance
Local Infrastructure	2,301.0	2,301.0	613.0	1,081.0	247.0		359.0	
Productive Sector	427.0	427.0	242.0		185.0			
Social Inclusion	1,063.0	1,063.0	957.0		106.0			
TOTAL	3,791.0	3,791.0	1,812.4	1,081.0	538.0	0.0	359.0	0.0

PEACE Programme Expenditure: 2000-2006

TOTAL PLAN: 2000-2006 (€ million)	Total Public & Private Cost (State, EU, PPP & Private)	Total Public Cost (State, EU & PPP)	Total Public Funding		EU Funding		Private Funding	
			Exchequer	Other Public	Structural Funds	Cohesion Fund	PPP Projects	Private Finance
TOTAL	127.0	127.0	21.0		106.0			

Productive Sector Operational Programme Expenditure: 2000

PLAN EXPENDITURE: 2000 (€ million)	Total Public & Private Cost (State, EU, PPP & Private)	Total Public Cost (State, EU & PPP)	Total Public Funding		EU Funding		Private Funding	
			Exchequer	Other Public	Structural Funds	Cohesion Fund	PPP Projects	Private Finance
Research, Technological Development & Innovation (RTDI)	**106.2**	**106.2**	39.0		67.2			
BMW Region	**28.1**	**28.1**	3.5		24.6			
S&E Region	**78.1**	**78.1**	35.5		42.6			
Industry	**280.7**	**280.7**	280.7					
BMW Region	**130.4**	**130.4**	130.4					
S&E Region	**150.3**	**150.3**	150.3					
Marketing	**31.3**	**31.3**	31.3					
BMW Region	**10.9**	**10.9**	10.9					
S&E Region	**20.4**	**20.4**	20.4					
Agricultural Development	**36.8**	**36.8**	20.0		16.8			
BMW Region	**17.7**	**17.7**	11.5		6.2			
S&E Region	**19.0**	**19.0**	8.3		10.7			
Fisheries	**12.7**	**12.7**	7.4		5.3			
BMW Region	**7.2**	**7.2**	5.3		1.9			
S&E Region	**5.5**	**5.5**	2.2		3.3			
TOTAL	**467.7**	**467.7**	378.4	0.0	89.3	0.0	0.0	0.0
BMW Region	**194.2**	**194.2**	161.5	0.0	32.7	0.0	0.0	0.0
S&E Region	**273.4**	**273.4**	216.8	0.0	56.6	0.0	0.0	0.0

Border, Midland & Western Regional Operational Programme Expenditure: 2000

PLAN EXPENDITURE: 2000 (€ million)	Total Public & Private Cost (State, EU, PPP & Private)	Total Public Cost (State, EU & PPP)	Total Public Funding		EU Funding		Private Funding	
			Exchequer	Other Public	Structural Funds	Cohesion Fund	PPP Projects	Private Finance
Local Infrastructure	242.7	242.7	86.1	128.4	25.7		2.5	
Productive Sector	59.2	59.2	32.0		27.2			
Social Inclusion	34.6	34.6	20.8		13.8			
TOTAL	**336.5**	**336.5**	138.9	128.4	66.7	0.0	2.5	0.0

Southern & Eastern Regional Operational Programme Expenditure: 2000

PLAN EXPENDITURE: 2000 (€ million)	Total Public & Private Cost (State, EU, PPP & Private)	Total Public Cost (State, EU & PPP)	Total Public Funding		EU Funding		Private Funding	
			Exchequer	Other Public	Structural Funds	Cohesion Fund	PPP Projects	Private Finance
Local Infrastructure	275.7	275.7	76.9	150.6	44.5		3.8	
Productive Sector	56.5	56.5	9.5		47.0			
Social Inclusion	146.9	146.9	122.9		24.0			
TOTAL	**479.1**	**479.1**	209.2	150.6	115.5	0.0	3.8	0.0

PEACE Programme Expenditure: 2000

PLAN EXPENDITURE: 2000 (€ million)	Total Public & Private Cost (State, EU, PPP & Private)	Total Public Cost (State, EU & PPP)	Total Public Funding		EU Funding		Private Funding	
			Exchequer	Other Public	Structural Funds	Cohesion Fund	PPP Projects	Private Finance
TOTAL	25.4	25.4	5.4		20.0			

Productive Sector Operational Programme Expenditure: 2001

PLAN EXPENDITURE: 2001 (€ million)	Total Public & Private Cost (State, EU, PPP & Private)	Total Public Cost (State, EU & PPP)	Total Public Funding		EU Funding		Private Funding	
			Exchequer	Other Public	Structural Funds	Cohesion Fund	PPP Projects	Private Finance
Research, Technological Development & Innovation (RTDI)	**290.0**	**290.0**	229.5		60.5			
BMW Region	77.9	77.9	55.5		22.4			
S&E Region	212.0	212.0	174.0		38.0			
Industry	**344.2**	**344.2**	344.2					
BMW Region	155.2	155.2	155.2					
S&E Region	189.0	189.0	189.0					
Marketing	**63.1**	**63.1**	63.1					
BMW Region	20.7	20.7	20.7					
S&E Region	42.4	42.4	42.4					
Agricultural Development	**47.0**	**47.0**	31.9		15.1			
BMW Region	22.6	22.6	17.0		5.6			
S&E Region	24.3	24.3	14.8		9.5			
Fisheries	**7.5**	**7.5**	2.8		4.7			
BMW Region	4.3	4.3	2.5		1.8			
S&E Region	3.2	3.2	0.2		3.0			
TOTAL	**751.8**	**751.8**	671.4	0.0	80.3	0.0	0.0	0.0
BMW Region	280.6	280.6	250.8	0.0	29.8	0.0	0.0	0.0
S&E Region	470.9	470.9	420.4	0.0	50.5	0.0	0.0	0.0

Border, Midland & Western Regional Operational Programme Expenditure: 2001

PLAN EXPENDITURE: 2001 (€ million)	Total Public & Private Cost (State, EU, PPP & Private)	Total Public Cost (State, EU & PPP)	Total Public Funding		EU Funding		Private Funding	
			Exchequer	Other Public	Structural Funds	Cohesion Fund	PPP Projects	Private Finance
Local Infrastructure	**261.9**	**261.9**	97.2	133.9	25.7		5.1	
Productive Sector	**68.4**	**68.4**	47.4		21.0			
Social Inclusion	**40.5**	**40.5**	27.9		12.6			
TOTAL	**370.8**	**370.8**	172.5	133.9	59.4	0.0	5.1	0.0

Southern & Eastern Regional Operational Programme Expenditure: 2001

PLAN EXPENDITURE: 2001 (€ million)	Total Public & Private Cost (State, EU, PPP & Private)	Total Public Cost (State, EU & PPP)	Total Public Funding		EU Funding		Private Funding	
			Exchequer	Other Public	Structural Funds	Cohesion Fund	PPP Projects	Private Finance
Local Infrastructure	**310.6**	**310.6**	97.6	161.8	43.6		7.6	
Productive Sector	**53.4**	**53.4**	17.7		35.7			
Social Inclusion	**155.2**	**155.2**	133.8		21.4			
TOTAL	**519.2**	**519.2**	249.1	161.8	100.6	0.0	7.6	0.0

PEACE Programme Expenditure: 2001

PLAN EXPENDITURE: 2001 (€ million)	Total Public & Private Cost (State, EU, PPP & Private)	Total Public Cost (State, EU & PPP)	Total Public Funding		EU Funding		Private Funding	
			Exchequer	Other Public	Structural Funds	Cohesion Fund	PPP Projects	Private Finance
TOTAL	**25.4**	**25.4**	4.4		21.0			

Productive Sector Operational Programme Expenditure: 2002

PLAN EXPENDITURE: 2002 (€ million)	Total Public & Private Cost (State, EU, PPP & Private)	Total Public Cost (State, EU & PPP)	Total Public Funding		EU Funding		Private Funding	
			Exchequer	Other Public	Structural Funds	Cohesion Fund	PPP Projects	Private Finance
Research, Technological Development & Innovation (RTDI)	**389.9**	**389.9**	336.5		53.4			
BMW Region	**104.4**	**104.4**	84.1		20.3			
S&E Region	**285.5**	**285.5**	252.4		33.1			
Industry	**345.5**	**345.5**	345.5					
BMW Region	**155.8**	**155.8**	155.8					
S&E Region	**189.7**	**189.7**	189.7					
Marketing	**63.6**	**63.6**	63.6					
BMW Region	**20.8**	**20.8**	20.8					
S&E Region	**42.8**	**42.8**	42.8					
Agricultural Development	**49.5**	**49.5**	36.1		13.4			
BMW Region	**23.9**	**23.9**	18.8		5.1			
S&E Region	**25.6**	**25.6**	17.3		8.3			
Fisheries	**7.7**	**7.7**	3.5		4.2			
BMW Region	**4.4**	**4.4**	2.8		1.6			
S&E Region	**3.3**	**3.3**	0.7		2.6			
TOTAL	**856.1**	**856.1**	785.1	0.0	71.0	0.0	0.0	0.0
BMW Region	**309.3**	**309.3**	282.3	0.0	27.0	0.0	0.0	0.0
S&E Region	**546.9**	**546.9**	502.8	0.0	44.0	0.0	0.0	0.0

Border, Midland & Western Regional Operational Programme Expenditure: 2002

PLAN EXPENDITURE: 2002 (€ million)	Total Public & Private Cost (State, EU, PPP & Private)	Total Public Cost (State, EU & PPP)	Total Public Funding		EU Funding		Private Funding	
			Exchequer	Other Public	Structural Funds	Cohesion Fund	PPP Projects	Private Finance
Local Infrastructure	**257.7**	**257.7**	94.1	134.7	26.4		2.5	
Productive Sector	**69.4**	**69.4**	50.4		19.0			
Social Inclusion	**39.4**	**39.4**	28.0		11.4			
TOTAL	**366.6**	**366.6**	172.5	134.7	56.8	0.0	2.5	0.0

Southern & Eastern Regional Operational Programme Expenditure: 2002

PLAN EXPENDITURE: 2002 (€ million)	Total Public & Private Cost (State, EU, PPP & Private)	Total Public Cost (State, EU & PPP)	Total Public Funding		EU Funding		Private Funding	
			Exchequer	Other Public	Structural Funds	Cohesion Fund	PPP Projects	Private Finance
Local Infrastructure	**305.4**	**305.4**	94.2	164.4	43.0		3.8	
Productive Sector	**57.8**	**57.8**	26.7		31.1			
Social Inclusion	**140.3**	**140.3**	121.7		18.6			
TOTAL	**503.5**	**503.5**	242.7	164.4	92.7	0.0	3.8	0.0

PEACE Programme Expenditure: 2002

PLAN EXPENDITURE: 2002 (€ million)	Total Public & Private Cost (State, EU, PPP & Private)	Total Public Cost (State, EU & PPP)	Total Public Funding		EU Funding		Private Funding	
			Exchequer	Other Public	Structural Funds	Cohesion Fund	PPP Projects	Private Finance
TOTAL	**25.4**	**25.4**	4.4		21.0			

Productive Sector Operational Programme Expenditure: 2003

PLAN EXPENDITURE: 2003 (€ million)	Total Public & Private Cost (State, EU, PPP & Private)	Total Public Cost (State, EU & PPP)	Total Public Funding		EU Funding		Private Funding	
			Exchequer	Other Public	Structural Funds	Cohesion Fund	PPP Projects	Private Finance
Research, Technological Development & Innovation (RTDI)	**410.5**	**410.5**	364.4		46.1			
BMW Region	**109.7**	**109.7**	91.9		17.8			
S&E Region	**300.8**	**300.8**	272.5		28.3			
Industry	**359.4**	**359.4**	359.4					
BMW Region	**162.0**	**162.0**	162.0					
S&E Region	**197.5**	**197.5**	197.5					
Marketing	**66.0**	**66.0**	66.0					
BMW Region	**21.6**	**21.6**	21.6					
S&E Region	**44.4**	**44.4**	44.4					
Agricultural Development	**53.3**	**53.3**	41.8		11.5			
BMW Region	**25.7**	**25.7**	21.2		4.5			
S&E Region	**27.6**	**27.6**	20.5		7.1			
Fisheries	**7.2**	**7.2**	3.6		3.6			
BMW Region	**4.1**	**4.1**	2.7		1.4			
S&E Region	**3.1**	**3.1**	0.9		2.2			
TOTAL	**896.0**	**896.0**	835.0	0.0	61.0	0.0	0.0	0.0
BMW Region	**323.0**	**323.0**	299.0	0.0	24.0	0.0	0.0	0.0
S&E Region	**573.0**	**573.0**	536.0	0.0	38.0	0.0	0.0	0.0

Border, Midland & Western Regional Operational Programme Expenditure: 2003

PLAN EXPENDITURE: 2003 (€ million)	Total Public & Private Cost (State, EU, PPP & Private)	Total Public Cost (State, EU & PPP)	Total Public Funding		EU Funding		Private Funding	
			Exchequer	Other Public	Structural Funds	Cohesion Fund	PPP Projects	Private Finance
Local Infrastructure	**291.6**	**291.6**	96.2	133.6	28.8		33.0	
Productive Sector	**57.0**	**57.0**	40.3		16.7			
Social Inclusion	**42.1**	**42.1**	32.1		10.0			
TOTAL	**390.7**	**390.7**	168.6	133.6	55.5	0.0	33.0	0.0

Southern & Eastern Regional Operational Programme Expenditure: 2003

PLAN EXPENDITURE: 2003 (€ million)	Total Public & Private Cost (State, EU, PPP & Private)	Total Public Cost (State, EU & PPP)	Total Public Funding		EU Funding		Private Funding	
			Exchequer	Other Public	Structural Funds	Cohesion Fund	PPP Projects	Private Finance
Local Infrastructure	**343.8**	**343.8**	82.9	159.5	45.6		55.9	
Productive Sector	**64.3**	**64.3**	37.8		26.5			
Social Inclusion	**157.9**	**157.9**	142.0		15.9			
TOTAL	**566.0**	**566.0**	262.7	159.5	87.9	0.0	55.9	0.0

PEACE Programme Expenditure: 2003

PLAN EXPENDITURE: 2003 (€ million)	Total Public & Private Cost (State, EU, PPP & Private)	Total Public Cost (State, EU & PPP)	Total Public Funding		EU Funding		Private Funding	
			Exchequer	Other Public	Structural Funds	Cohesion Fund	PPP Projects	Private Finance
TOTAL	**25.4**	**25.4**	3.4		22.0			

Productive Sector Operational Programme Expenditure: 2004

PLAN EXPENDITURE: 2004 (€ million)	Total Public & Private Cost (State, EU, PPP & Private)	Total Public Cost (State, EU & PPP)	Total Public Funding		EU Funding		Private Funding	
			Exchequer	Other Public	Structural Funds	Cohesion Fund	PPP Projects	Private Finance
Research, Technological Development & Innovation (RTDI)	**419.1**	**419.1**	386.5		32.6			
BMW Region	**112.5**	**112.5**	98.9		13.6			
S&E Region	**306.6**	**306.6**	287.3		19.3			
Industry	**360.7**	**360.7**	360.7					
BMW Region	**162.6**	**162.6**	162.6					
S&E Region	**198.1**	**198.1**	198.1					
Marketing	**67.2**	**67.2**	67.2					
BMW Region	**22.1**	**22.1**	22.1					
S&E Region	**45.3**	**45.3**	45.3					
Agricultural Development	**53.3**	**53.3**	45.1		8.2			
BMW Region	**25.7**	**25.7**	22.3		3.4			
S&E Region	**27.6**	**27.6**	22.8		4.8			
Fisheries	**7.2**	**7.2**	4.6		2.6			
BMW Region	**4.1**	**4.1**	3.0		1.1			
S&E Region	**3.1**	**3.1**	1.6		1.5			
TOTAL	**907.4**	**907.4**	864.1	0.0	43.3	0.0	0.0	0.0
BMW Region	**326.9**	**326.9**	308.8	0.0	18.1	0.0	0.0	0.0
S&E Region	**580.7**	**580.7**	555.1	0.0	25.6	0.0	0.0	0.0

Border, Midland & Western Regional Operational Programme Expenditure: 2004

PLAN EXPENDITURE: 2004 (€ million)	Total Public & Private Cost (State, EU, PPP & Private)	Total Public Cost (State, EU & PPP)	Total Public Funding		EU Funding		Private Funding	
			Exchequer	Other Public	Structural Funds	Cohesion Fund	PPP Projects	Private Finance
Local Infrastructure	**309.4**	**309.4**	98.9	136.5	22.0		52.1	
Productive Sector	**57.2**	**57.2**	44.4		12.8			
Social Inclusion	**40.5**	**40.5**	32.8		7.7			
TOTAL	**407.0**	**407.0**	176.1	136.5	42.4	0.0	52.1	0.0

Southern & Eastern Regional Operational Programme Expenditure: 2004

PLAN EXPENDITURE: 2004 (€ million)	Total Public & Private Cost (State, EU, PPP & Private)	Total Public Cost (State, EU & PPP)	Total Public Funding		EU Funding		Private Funding	
			Exchequer	Other Public	Structural Funds	Cohesion Fund	PPP Projects	Private Finance
Local Infrastructure	**369.2**	**369.2**	87.5	163.4	30.7		87.6	
Productive Sector	**64.4**	**64.4**	46.6		17.8			
Social Inclusion	**152.0**	**152.0**	141.3		10.7			
TOTAL	**585.6**	**585.6**	275.4	163.4	59.2	0.0	87.6	0.0

PEACE Programme Expenditure: 2004

PLAN EXPENDITURE: 2004 (€ million)	Total Public & Private Cost (State, EU, PPP & Private)	Total Public Cost (State, EU & PPP)	Total Public Funding		EU Funding		Private Funding	
			Exchequer	Other Public	Structural Funds	Cohesion Fund	PPP Projects	Private Finance
TOTAL	**25.4**	**25.4**	3.4		22.0			

Productive Sector Operational Programme Expenditure: 2005

PLAN EXPENDITURE: 2005 (€ million)	Total Public & Private Cost (State, EU, PPP & Private)	Total Public Cost (State, EU & PPP)	Total Public Funding		EU Funding		Private Funding	
			Exchequer	Other Public	Structural Funds	Cohesion Fund	PPP Projects	Private Finance
Research, Technological Development & Innovation (RTDI)	428.0	428.0	395.0		33.0			
BMW Region	116.0	116.0	96.4		19.6			
S&E Region	312.1	312.1	298.7		13.4			
Industry	362.0	362.0	362.0					
BMW Region	163.2	163.2	163.2					
S&E Region	198.7	198.7	198.7					
Marketing	68.5	68.5	68.5					
BMW Region	22.5	22.5	22.5					
S&E Region	46.0	46.0	46.0					
Agricultural Development	54.6	54.6	46.4		8.2			
BMW Region	26.3	26.3	21.4		4.9			
S&E Region	28.3	28.3	24.9		3.4			
Fisheries	7.4	7.4	4.8		2.6			
BMW Region	4.2	4.2	2.7		1.5			
S&E Region	3.2	3.2	2.1		1.1			
TOTAL	920.4	920.4	876.7	0.0	43.7	0.0	0.0	0.0
BMW Region	332.2	332.2	306.2	0.0	26.0	0.0	0.0	0.0
S&E Region	588.3	588.3	570.5	0.0	17.8	0.0	0.0	0.0

Border, Midland & Western Regional Operational Programme Expenditure: 2005

PLAN EXPENDITURE: 2005 (€ million)	Total Public & Private Cost (State, EU, PPP & Private)	Total Public Cost (State, EU & PPP)	Total Public Funding		EU Funding		Private Funding	
			Exchequer	Other Public	Structural Funds	Cohesion Fund	PPP Projects	Private Finance
Local Infrastructure	342.6	342.6	95.4	131.9	31.5		83.8	
Productive Sector	56.9	56.9	38.6		18.3			
Social Inclusion	42.8	42.8	31.8		11.0			
TOTAL	442.3	442.3	165.8	131.9	60.8	0.0	83.8	0.0

Southern & Eastern Regional Operational Programme Expenditure: 2005

PLAN EXPENDITURE: 2005 (€ million)	Total Public & Private Cost (State, EU, PPP & Private)	Total Public Cost (State, EU & PPP)	Total Public Funding		EU Funding		Private Funding	
			Exchequer	Other Public	Structural Funds	Cohesion Fund	PPP Projects	Private Finance
Local Infrastructure	430.4	430.4	90.7	173.3	21.6		144.8	
Productive Sector	65.2	65.2	52.6		12.6			
Social Inclusion	156.7	156.7	149.2		7.6			
TOTAL	652.3	652.3	292.5	173.3	41.8	0.0	144.8	0.0

PEACE Programme Expenditure: 2005

PLAN EXPENDITURE: 2005 (€ million)	Total Public & Private Cost (State, EU, PPP & Private)	Total Public Cost (State, EU & PPP)	Total Public Funding		EU Funding		Private Funding	
			Exchequer	Other Public	Structural Funds	Cohesion Fund	PPP Projects	Private Finance
TOTAL	0.0	0.0	0.0					

Productive Sector Operational Programme Expenditure: 2006

PLAN EXPENDITURE: 2006 (€ million)	Total Public & Private Cost (State, EU, PPP & Private)	Total Public Cost (State, EU & PPP)	Total Public Funding		EU Funding		Private Funding	
			Exchequer	Other Public	Structural Funds	Cohesion Fund	PPP Projects	Private Finance
Research, Technological Development & Innovation (RTDI)	427.6	427.6	407.6		20.0			
BMW Region	114.6	114.6	105.5		9.1			
S&E Region	313.0	313.0	302.1		10.9			
Industry	363.9	363.9	363.9					
BMW Region	164.2	164.2	164.2					
S&E Region	199.7	199.7	199.7					
Marketing	68.5	68.5	68.5					
BMW Region	22.5	22.5	22.5					
S&E Region	46.0	46.0	46.0					
Agricultural Development	58.4	58.4	51.6		6.8			
BMW Region	28.2	28.2	25.1		3.1			
S&E Region	30.3	30.3	26.6		3.7			
Fisheries	7.4	7.4	5.3		2.1			
BMW Region	4.2	4.2	3.2		1.0			
S&E Region	3.2	3.2	2.0		1.2			
TOTAL	925.8	925.8	896.9	0.0	28.9	0.0	0.0	0.0
BMW Region	333.6	333.6	320.4	0.0	13.2	0.0	0.0	0.0
S&E Region	592.2	592.2	576.5	0.0	15.7	0.0	0.0	0.0

Border, Midland & Western Regional Operational Programme Expenditure: 2006

PLAN EXPENDITURE: 2006 (€ million)	Total Public & Private Cost (State, EU, PPP & Private)	Total Public Cost (State, EU & PPP)	Total Public Funding		EU Funding		Private Funding	
			Exchequer	Other Public	Structural Funds	Cohesion Fund	PPP Projects	Private Finance
Local Infrastructure	230.7	230.7	98.6	83.6	15.5		33.0	
Productive Sector	60.5	60.5	48.9		11.6			
Social Inclusion	41.2	41.2	34.2		7.0			
TOTAL	332.4	332.4	181.8	83.6	34.1	0.0	33.0	0.0

Southern & Eastern Regional Operational Programme Expenditure: 2006

PLAN EXPENDITURE: 2006 (€ million)	Total Public & Private Cost (State, EU, PPP & Private)	Total Public Cost (State, EU & PPP)	Total Public Funding		EU Funding		Private Funding	
			Exchequer	Other Public	Structural Funds	Cohesion Fund	PPP Projects	Private Finance
Local Infrastructure	266.4	266.4	90.9	101.3	18.5		55.9	
Productive Sector	65.4	65.4	51.5		13.9			
Social Inclusion	153.5	153.5	145.2		8.3			
TOTAL	485.3	485.3	287.6	101.3	40.6	0.0	55.9	0.0

PEACE Programme Expenditure: 2006

PLAN EXPENDITURE: 2006 (€ million)	Total Public & Private Cost (State, EU, PPP & Private)	Total Public Cost (State, EU & PPP)	Total Public Funding		EU Funding		Private Funding	
			Exchequer	Other Public	Structural Funds	Cohesion Fund	PPP Projects	Private Finance
TOTAL	0.0	0.0	0.0					

255

SECTION B

Proposed Areas for Structural and Cohesion Fund Co-Financing (€ millions)

	Total Cost	Total Public	Public — Community Participation					Public — National Public Participation				Private	Cohesion Fund	TENs and EFTA	EIB Loans
			Total	ERDF	ESF	EAGGF	FIFG	Total	Exchequer	Public Non-Exchequer	Non Co-financed Public				
Economic and Social Infrastructure															
National Roads	6,857	5,367	541	541				4,826	505		4,321	1,270*	220		
Dublin Transport	543	543	192	192				351	154		197				
Mainline Rail	186	129						129			129		57		
Urban Waste Water	965	609	80	80				609			609	76	280		
Coastal Protection/Catchment Protection	168	168	43	43				88	61		27				
Energy	186	186						143	47	48	48				
Productive Sector															
Agriculture	722	355	80			80		275	57		218	367			
Fisheries	163	57	26				26	32			32	106			
RTDI	3,381	2,473	313	313				2,160	172		1,988	908			
Employment and Human Resources Development															
Improving Employability	5,881	5,881	618		618			5,263	502		4,761				
Entrepreneurship	982	525	96		96			430	76		354	457			
Adaptability	5,918	5,918	179		179			5,740	124		5,616				
Equality	260	260	6		6			254	1.3		253.1				
Regional OPs															
Infrastructure															
Non-national Roads	1,524	1,524	21	21				1,503		9	1,494				
Waste Management	825	254	30	30				214		12	205	571*			
E-Commerce	382	98	50	50				48	48			284			
Rural Water	384	384	258	258				126	126						
Village and Urban Renewal	131	131	65	65				66	43		23				
Productive Sector															
Micro Enterprise	249	191	60	60				132	46		86	58			
Tourism	546	170	60	60				111			111	376			
Rural Development	414	238	60			60		178	38		140	176			
Forestry Development	130	102	40	40				62	25		37	28			
Aquaculture/Harbours	193	165	72	72				93	40		53	28			
Social Disadvantage															
Childcare	391	317	179	60	119			138	51		87	74			
Peace Programme	146	141	106	59	47			35	25	10		5			
Technical Assistance	10	10	5	5				5	5						
Total	31,536	26,195	3,172#	1,944	1,064	140	26	23,010	2,146	79	20,789	4,784	557	65†	
Objective 1 Region	10,403‡	8,557	1,359#	969	354	71	15	6,929	410	58	6,461	1,922			
Objective 1 Region in Transition	20,418‡	16,923#	1,813#	975	710	69	11	15,323	1,736	12	13,575	2,862			

* Public Private Partnerships.
# The Structural Funds Regulations require that 4% of each commitment be retained as a performance reserve. These figures exclude €55 million and €79 million respectively in respect of the Performance Reserve for the Objective 1 and the Region in Transition respectively which will be allocated following the Mid-Term Review.
† Proposal being developed for €60 million TENs and €5 million EFTA – Areas for allocation not yet known.
Structural Funds contribution is generally calculated at 75% of co-financed public expenditure in the Objective 1 Region and 50% in the Objective 1 Region in Transition.
‡ These amounts do not contain €557 million Cohesion Funding.

SECTION C

Proposals for ex-ante Verification of Additionality
(in EURO millions – constant prices)
Member State – Ireland

(€ millions) 1999 prices	Annual average 1994-1999									Annual average 2000-2006								
	Public Total [2=3+4]	of which Budget [3]	of which Non-Budget [4]	Private [5]	CSF Structural Funds [6]	CSF National [7]	Total public net of SF Contribution [8=2-6]	EIB Loans and EFTA [9]	CF Contribution [10]	Public Total [2=3+4]	of which Budget [3]	of which Non-Budget [4]	Private [5]	CSF Structural Funds [6]	CSF National [7]	Total public net of SF Contribution [8=2-6]	EIB Loans [9]	CF Contribution +EFTA [10]
BASIC INFRASTRUCTURE	1,322.609	534.703	787.906	2.795	188.380	124.892	1,134.228	49.549	239.323	2,115.000	1,586.000	529.000	322.000	174.000	1,064.000	1,941.000		80.000
Transport (cap. exp.)	555.943	414.425	141.518		152.323	90.930	403.620	11.117	122.047	1,582.000	1,240.000	342.000	181.000	108.000	973.000	1,474.000		40.000
Communications (cap. exp.)	180.650	3.826	176.824	0.731	4.071	3.572	176.579	5.250	0.000	14.000	14.000	0.000	41.000	7.000	7.000	7.000		
Energy (cap. exp.)	467.199	7.981	459.218		7.520	4.938	459.680	29.017	0.000	21.000	14.000	7.000	0.000	6.000	20.000	15.000		
Water (cap. exp.)	82.289	75.777	6.512	2.064	12.721	6.456	69.569	4.165	115.412	429.000	295.000	134.000	18.000	37.000	18.000	392.000		40.000
Environment (cap. exp.)	5.978	4.314	1.664		4.228	0.561	1.750		1.864	69.000	23.000	46.000	82.000	16.000	46.000	53.000		
Health (cap. exp.)	30.550	28.380	2.169	0.000	7.519	18.435	23.031											
Miscellaneous																		
HUMAN RESOURCES	1,115.361	1,113.764	1.597	22.682	398.802	140.921	716.559	4.621		2,140.000	2,140.000	0.000	195.000	173.000	2,215.000	1,967.00		
Education (cap. exp.)	37.822	37.810	0.012	0.037	24.991	8.358	12.831	4.621		286.000	286.000	0.000	0.000	0.000	286.000	286.000		
Education (cur. exp.)	342.431	342.174	0.257	1.089	159.414	52.866	183.017			520.000	520.000	0.000	0.000	57.000	470.000	463.000		
Training (cap. exp.)	11.147	11.119	0.028	0.750	6.033	1.902	5.113			9.000	9.000	0.000	0.000	0.000		9.000		
Training (cur. exp.)	705.784	704.484	1.300	17.986	199.532	75.073	506.251			972.000	972.000	0.000	65.000	71.000	967.000	901.000		
R&TD (total)	18.178	18.178		2.821	8.831	2.722	9.347			353.000	353.000	0.000	130.000	45.000	483.000	308.000		
PRODUCTIVE ENVIRONMENT	786.066	758.894	27.172	760.398	426.360	138.087	359.706			594.286	589.286	5.000	155.000	58.000	127.000	536.286		
Industry & Services	411.797	411.797		602.216	183.655	55.608	228.142			434.000	434.000	0.000	n/a	9.000	19.000	425.000		
Agric + Rural Development	287.324	287.324		105.922	181.508	63.221	105.816			104.000	99.000	5.000	82.000	26.000	74.000	78.000		
Fisheries	20.887	20.186	0.701	10.460	11.565	3.504	9.322			32.000	32.000	0.000	19.000	14.000	18.000	18.000		
Tourism	66.058	39.587	26.471	41.799	49.633	15.754	16.426			24.286	24.286	0.000	54.000	9.000	16.000	15.286		
OTHER	125.564	100.817	24.747	13.801	77.839	28.823	47.725	0.000	0.573	94.429	85.429	9.000	11.700	50.714	34.714	43.714		
(Local urban & rural development)	125.564	100.817	24.747	13.801	77.839	28.823	47.725		0.573	71.000	64.000	7.000	11.000	35.000	29.000	36.000		
Peace programme										22.000	20.000	2.000	0.700	15.000	5.000	7.000		
Technical Assistance										1.429	1.429	0.000	0.000	0.714	0.714	0.714		
TOTAL	3,349.600	2,508.178	841.423	799.676	1,091.382	432.723	2,258.219	54.170	239.895	4,920.286	4,379.286	541.000	528.000	455.714	3,435.000	4,464.571	0.000	80.000
percentage of GDP	3.899%	2.920%	0.979%	0.931%	1.270%	0.504%	2.629%	0.063%	0.279%	6.763%	6.019%	0.744%	0.726%	0.626%	4.721%	6.136%		0.110%

Appendix 1 Preparation of the Plan and Consultation Process

1.1 Ireland's experience of social partnership has been very positive. The consensus approach to the development of economic and social policy which successive Governments have pursued since 1987 has been a significant contributory factor to Ireland's economic success. Under the 1994-1999 National Development Plan, the monitoring of the Structural Fund Operational Programmes at national level was carried out by committees which comprised representatives of the relevant Government Departments, the EU Commission, the implementing agencies, Regional Authorities and the Social Partners and, as appropriate, the community and voluntary interests.

1.2 The Government agreed in the Mid-Term Review of the 1994-1999 Community Support Framework (CSF) for Ireland that the partnership principle would be extended to provide for participation of the Social Partners and the Regional Authorities in the CSF Monitoring Committee. This afforded the Social Partners the opportunity, for the first time, to influence directly the implementation of policy in relation to the use of structural funds in Ireland at the highest level within the management and monitoring structure of the CSF. The partnership process has been deepened and strengthened in the course of the preparation of the National Development Plan 2000-2006 and has involved on-going and detailed consultations with the Social Partners, Regional Authorities and Government Departments.

1.3 In early 1998, the Minister for Finance invited the Regional Authorities and the Social Partners to make submissions on their investment priorities for the period 2000-2006. In order to ensure that the Regional Authority submissions and those of the Social Partners were given due consideration in the context of the determination of national priorities, the Department of Finance circulated their submissions to the relevant Government Departments for their consideration in the context of developing and refining their own sectoral proposals for the Plan.

1.4 Meetings to discuss these submissions and the views of the various interests on the Plan were held at both official level and Ministerial level. A number of informal meetings were also held at official level involving all the Departments and the European Commission. Submissions on the Plan were also received from the Western Development Commission and a number of interest groups.

1.5 The Department of Justice, Equality and Law Reform hosted a Conference on 29-30 March, 1999 on "Mainstreaming Equal Opportunities Between Women and Men in the next round of Structural Funds" at which the relevant Government Departments, the European Commission and the Social Partners were represented. The Department of Finance organised a Seminar on 13 May, 1999 involving a wide array of interests to hear presentations on, and to discuss priorities for, the Plan.

1.6 In an extension of the consultation process, an Overview of the draft National Development Plan was circulated to the Social Partners and the Regional Authorities. Meetings were subsequently held with these Groups at the highest political levels during which they responded to this Overview. This response was generally very positive as regards the structure and priorities of the National Development Plan.

1.7 Apart from political consultation at local level there was also political debate at national level on the Plan. In particular, Deputies and Senators were given an opportunity to highlight the areas that the Plan should address when the Minister for Finance addressed and answered questions from the Houses of the Oireachtas Joint Committee on Finance and the Public Service on 1 June, 1999. The Minister of State also addressed the Seanad on 20 October, 1999 on a motion before it endorsing the consultation process undertaken by Government in the preparation of the National Development Plan and the proposed broad priorities of the Plan.

1.8 There was on-going consultation with the Northern Ireland administration on a wide number of EU related fronts. The Department of Finance and the Department of Finance and Personnel in Northern Ireland, respectively, were responsible for drafting the new 'Common Chapter' of the National Development Plan. The Common Chapter sets out existing and proposed developments in North/South co-operation in the context of our respective Community Support Frameworks, including material on the proposed successor to the Special Programme for Peace and Reconciliation. The Chapter also includes a report on North/South co-operation in the Community Initiative area, in particular with respect to the Ireland/Northern Ireland INTERREG Programme, and on the EU Programmes Body, proposed as one of the North/South bodies under the Belfast (Good Friday) Agreement of April 1998.

Overview of the Social Partners priorities by Pillar:

Employers Priorities

1.9 The elimination of the infrastructure deficit was seen as the highest priority for the Employers Pillar. Stress was laid on the greater use of Public Private Partnerships (PPPs) in this regard. Tackling human resources and skills shortages, including social exclusion, was seen as the second most important priority by this Pillar. Among other priorities were greater concentration on addressing competitiveness, balanced regional development and a stronger North/South dimension.

1.10 Infrastructure: The Employers considered that an accelerated programme, with the target of eliminating Ireland's infrastructure deficit by 2006, had to be identified and planned for. A more streamlined planning process was needed to tackle the congestion in the system. Priority projects had to be fast tracked and the physical development process had to match the requirement of social and economic development. In the view of the Employers, the investment programme had to include social infrastructure, including housing and education facilities. The Employers stressed that PPPs should be introduced on a much wider scale and more rapidly.

1.11 Human Resources: The Employers supported the general thrust of the National Employment Action Plan. Eliminating Ireland's education and training deficit was viewed as the top priority. Other priorities included a national integrated programme to tackle the problem of labour and skills shortages; employer-led training programmes to improve in-company training capabilities, increased resourcing of primary and secondary education, particularly as regards language, science and technology teaching. Support was also sought for equal opportunities, labour mobility, childcare and measures to promote social inclusion in urban and rural areas. Innovative and active measures to improve the employability of the long-term unemployed were called for as well as the development of entrepreneurship among the potential self-employed.

1.12 Competitiveness: The Employer Pillar urged that, where eligible, EU co-financing should be concentrated on helping to put in place the measures identified by the Competitiveness Council to eliminate Ireland's competitiveness deficit. Sectoral initiatives of high national significance such as tourism, broadband technology and the information society should continue to receive EU co-financing in respect of the top priorities identified by those closest to the market place. New and more innovative ways to fund business development, including loan guarantee arrangements, revolving loan funds, and greater State intervention with the private venture capital industry needed to be encouraged. Another factor that had to be taken into account was the impact on the enterprise sector arising from the burden-sharing arrangements on greenhouse gases agreed as a consequence of the Kyoto Protocol.

1.13 Balanced Regional Development: In the view of the Employers, the National Development Plan should provide for Operational Programmes on regional development, covering both the Objective 1 Region and the Region in transition. Key economic sectors such as tourism, forestry and fisheries that had the potential to improve regional incomes and employment should be actively promoted. Emphasis was also put on the requirement for sustainable development, including the use of integrated spatial planning techniques, to drive the identification of priority investments. It was also pointed out by the Employers that the acute problems facing Dublin, including the need for a properly functioning public transport system, had to be tackled urgently.

1.14 North/South Co-operation: In a Joint Statement along with the CBI Joint Business Council in Northern Ireland and the Irish Congress of Trade Unions, the Employers stressed the need for greater cross-border co-operation. Given the potential and scale of cross-border joint endeavours, for example, in the area of public transport, a special case should be made for additional resources to underpin such initiatives.

The Irish Congress of Trade Unions (ICTU)

1.15   The National Development Plan 2000-2006, according to ICTU, should be a "National Partnership Programme" to further develop the Irish economy and Irish society for the next century. ICTU favoured moving away from the approach of promoting individual projects and programmes towards an integrated framework based on a select series of overriding planning goals. In its proposals, ICTU identified four key priorities:

1.16 An Integrated Investment Programme for Urban Living: The main emphasis here was to recognise the need to focus investment for urban living. An integrated planning approach was advocated which, according to ICTU, served a number of objectives. For example, a properly functioning transport system would link urban and suburban disadvantaged areas into the mainstream of city activity and, thereby, enable labour supply to respond to market demand. Social exclusion would be reduced, employment increased and growth improved. Major new investment was required in urban and suburban transport services, particularly in Dublin and Cork. Investment in the social infrastructure, particularly, supporting childcare and combating drug related crime was also required. ICTU stressed the role that third level education institutions had to play in economic competitiveness.

1.17 Investment Programme for Lifelong Learning: ICTU recommended that access to lifelong high quality education and training should constitute a central plank of Ireland's strategy to consolidate its success and build for the future. More emphasis would have to be put on the development of generic skills rather than job specific skills with access by all workers to the education system throughout their lives.

1.18   Investment in Infrastructure: In infrastructure, ICTU highlighted the need for investment in the environment, forestry, transport infrastructure, and the information, communications and telecommunications system. In the area of the environment, investment in waste water treatment facilities, the development of a national waste management system and recycling infrastructure were required. In forestry, ICTU called for the implementation of the Government's Strategic Plan for Forestry 1996-2035 in order to maximise the sector's contribution to the overall economy but particularly its contribution to the rural economy in Ireland. In the information, communications and telecommunications system, the emphasis should be on investment in broadband telecommunications infrastructure, digital parks and public institutions. ICTU pointed out that disadvantaged communities should be given financial assistance to ensure their access to technology and information networks.

1.19 Social Inclusion: ICTU considered social exclusion linked to long-term unemployment in urban areas as the biggest socio-economic problem facing the country and, consequently, investment in physical capital should be complemented by investment in human capital with the aim of community building. Particular importance had to be attached to eliminating long-term unemployment and individual "pathways back to work" plans should be introduced for the long-term unemployed. There should be greater integration between spatial planning and industrial development as part of a co-ordinated social inclusion programme that directly linked all employment policies.

1.20   North/South Cooperation: In a submission jointly prepared by ICTU and the IBEC-CBI Joint Business Council, ICTU pointed out that EU policy should be closely examined so that future policy and programmes contributed towards the completion of a single market on the island of Ireland. The next round of Structural Funds should contain a substantive Cross-Border Programme to replace the Common Chapter and should also provide for a restructuring of the Peace and Reconciliation and the Interreg Programmes. The submission advocated that the EU should provide significant funding for: improved cross-border co-operation on transport infrastructure and services; labour market issues like the delivery of lifelong learning programmes in the workplace and in local communities and preparing the island of Ireland for the information society by ensuring that the most modern information and communication technologies infrastructure was put in place throughout the island.

The Farming Group

1.21   The submission from the Farming Group was framed in the light of the challenges which the Group saw facing Irish agriculture in the coming years, namely, CAP Reform II (improving the efficiency of farms), increased environmental investment (to meet EU and national regulations), income requirements of farm families (to address low incomes in farming), structural change in the food processing industry (to address the negative impact of CAP II with the erosion of price guarantees) and halting decline in the rural economy (investing in rural infrastructure to attract investment and sustain employment). The Group's main priority programmes were as follows:

1.22   Agriculture, Rural Development and Forestry Programme: This programme should concentrate on: environmental investment on farms targeted at the control of farmyard pollution and dairy hygiene and animal welfare; on-farm investment to improve the sector's competitiveness, horticulture and potato modernisation (potato storage, grading and refrigeration), adaptation and development of rural areas concentrating on agri-tourism, services in rural areas and land reparcelling; human resources (training and education for farmers and their spouses), and installation aid for young farmers and forestry.

1.23 Industry Programme (Food): Under this programme, the Group sought investment for measures targeted at the restructuring of the beef processing industry, potato processing and marketing, horticulture and the upgrading of livestock marts.

1.24 Fisheries Programme: Under this programme, the emphasis was put on doubling the production of salmon, trout oysters and mussels, developing the production of new species and infrastructural development for handling, processing and packaging products.

1.25 CAP Accompanying Measures: Under this heading, the Group sought continued investment in the REPS, Early Retirement and Forestry Schemes (particularly as regards forestry headage payments to all farmers not in receipt of income on forestry plantations and training and advice on maintaining new forests). These schemes were aimed at strengthening the environmental role of agriculture, encouraging structural reform by facilitating retirement by elderly farmers and switching land from agriculture to forestry. It was emphasised also that disadvantaged areas payments made up a significant component of farm income on cattle and sheep farms and of total income where these farms had little or no off-farm income. These low-income farmers, according to the Group, had to be treated equitably in the switch from payments made on the basis of livestock headage to that of an area basis, as agreed in Agenda 2000.

1.26 Other Investment Programmes: In the broader context of rural development and the promotion of more balanced regional development, the farming group proposed investment in secondary and local roads, broadband telecommunications, water supply and treatment, waste management and transport. It was also suggested that a tourism programme be developed on a regional basis, a local urban and rural development programme targeted at the further development of the urban and village renewal scheme and a farm viability advisory service for low-income farmers.

1.27 In the context of regionalisation it was emphasised, in particular, that the Farming Group would be seeking the same level of grant assistance for farmers for structural improvements to their farms and for diversification grants in the Objective 1 Region and the Region in transition. They would be opposed to a "two-tier" scheme in operation whereby lower rates of EU co-financing for some sub-regions would be in operation. In this event, the Group stated that it would be seeking that the Exchequer made up any differences in aid rates in order for the structural schemes for agriculture to operate on a uniform basis throughout the country.

Community and Voluntary Sector Pillar

1.28 According to the Community and Voluntary Sector pillar, the primary objectives of the Plan should be to meet the National Anti Poverty Strategy and the National Employment Action Plan targets, reduce inequality and tackle poverty. With regard to inequality in particular, the Community and Voluntary Sector pillar emphasised that all actions in the Plan should be mainstreamed to combat inequality with the implementation of 'best practice' innovative projects carried out under the 1994-1999 National Development Plan. Gender proofing had to be transparent across all programmes with funding set aside for childcare measures in particular.

1.29 In specific terms, the Community and Voluntary Sector pillar indicated that the Plan should include measures on public transport, rural transport initiatives, social infrastructure including the areas of health, education, recreation and culture which would enhance the quality of life in disadvantaged communities. In addition, investment was needed in child care infrastructure and community infrastructure which would enhance the capacity of disadvantaged communities to organise and to develop effective responses to their situation. Emphasis was also put on the need for the Plan to provide for an equitable participation by women and equality organisations across all structures with responsibilities in relation to the management of the next round of Structural Funds.

1.30   The Plan needed to provide resources for local urban and rural development through an operational programme that focused on the twin goals of addressing the needs of the long-term unemployed and of the marginalised such as women, people with disabilities, ethnic groups, travellers, lone parents, ex-offenders and young and old people. The Community and Voluntary Sector pillar was particularly anxious that the Plan provide for the allocation of 1% of the European Social Fund for local social capital. It also sought a strengthening of the North/South dimension via a Common Chapter in the two plans, North and South, that built on and deepened the joint approach to combating mutual socio/economic problems.

The Border, Midland and Western Region and the Southern and Eastern Region Development Strategies 2000-2006

1.31   The development strategies for the Border, Midland and Western Region and the Southern and Eastern Region were prepared as an input to the National Development Plan on foot of the Government decision to divide the country into two new NUTS II regions and at the request of the Minister for Finance who asked the Regional Authorities to present a single prioritised strategic plan for each of the new Regions. The strategies had to contain a broad development plan for the new Regions and prioritise investment measures set out in the Regional Authority submissions on the Plan. The strategies were prepared by Fitzpatrick Associates, Economic Consultants and endorsed by a Steering Group comprising representatives of the constituent Regional Authorities and County/City Managers.

1.32   A key theme of the strategies was the need for integrated development in the Regions to be achieved by proper spatial planning. Cities were, and increasingly must be, the foci of regions which included large surrounding urban and rural areas. It was no longer a case of urban versus rural, but urban and rural each supporting each other. Modern economic growth was seen as generally heavily clustered around high quality infrastructure, third level and other education facilities, and a high quality workforce. This applied to both industry and services. In Ireland, the location of these facilities was strongly clustered around the established urban centres of Galway in the Border, Midland and Western Region and Dublin, Waterford, Cork and Limerick in the Southern and Eastern Region.

Characteristics of the Border, Midland and Western Region

1.33   The overall physical and spatial characteristics indicated for the Region are: a land area accounting for nearly 47% (33,276 square kilometres) of the state's land area and 27% (965,190 persons recorded in 1996) of its population, a predominance of rural areas with relatively poorly endowed agriculture resources and infrastructure and typical small town size; one major natural urban centre i.e. Galway city and surrounding areas, with two further ones located on its boundaries, i.e. Derry/Letterkenny and the Dublin-Belfast corridor including Dundalk. Other centres in the Region with an excess of 15,000 people were Sligo and Athlone.

1.34   After many decades of relative decline in much of the Region, recent years had seen considerable expansion. Between 1991 and 1996 output grew by about 7.5% per annum in current prices, population grew by 1.7% and numbers at work grew by nearly 44,000 people or

2.3% per annum. However, given the rapid pace of growth in the national economy, output per head in the Region had diverged from, rather than converged on the national average. Growth had also been heavily concentrated in the major urban centres. Excluding Galway city, population growth in the region was 1.1% between 1991 and 1996 against a national average of 3.2%.

Objectives and Strategy

1.35   The overall development objective for the Region was to maintain and improve the quality of life and to provide a reasonable living standard, in a sustainable manner, for all who wished to live and work in the Region. A reasonable living standard was one which continued recent convergence on EU average income per capita, and which halted divergence from and commenced convergence towards national average output per head. Other objectives included maintaining the pace of unemployment reduction, especially long-term unemployment, reducing social exclusion, promoting balanced spatial development within the Region, including integrated rural development, facilitating the presence in the region of key drivers of modern economic growth (for example, high quality infrastructure and services, highly skilled labour) and the promotion of North-South co-operation.

Spatial Strategy

1.36   The strategy proposed investment packages which were appropriate for different types of areas and the creation of realistic "counterpoles" to Dublin and the Southern and Eastern Region. It was recommended that a small number of urban centres be selected for additional investment to act as drivers of growth in the Region and that two new larger growth centres were needed in the North West and Midlands to spatially rebalance economic activity away from Dublin and the east coast. It was also suggested that the development of such centres would, through an appropriate urban/rural relationship, foster growth in rural and remote areas. In addition, specifically targeted urban and rural development programmes would provide appropriate infrastructure and support in other towns and villages in the Region.

Sectoral Strategy

1.37   Investment of the order of £7.7 billion (€9.7 billion) over the 2000-2006 period was recommended in the areas of agriculture, fisheries and forestry, industry, the services, tourism, transport, telecommunications and energy, water and sanitary services, human resources, research and technology, local development and social exclusion. Investment in these sectors, it was suggested, would contribute to: improving the quality of life in the Region, improving productivity and competitiveness, building on regional strength, promoting a more balanced spatial distribution of economic activity within the country, addressing social exclusion and expanding the productive capacity of the Region's economy.

Characteristics of the Southern and Eastern Region

1.38   It was indicated that the Region accounted for 53% (36,972 square kilometres) of the land area of the State and contained 73% (2.66 million persons recorded in 1996) of its population and was characterised by large built-up urban areas with other towns and attached rural areas on the one hand and weaker rural areas and remote disadvantaged areas on the other. The Region included the three largest cities in the State, Dublin, Cork and Limerick. It had five centres with a population in excess of 15,000 people, namely, Waterford, Kilkenny, Wexford, Carlow and Clonmel. The Region extended from just south of Drogheda to the islands of the coast of Kerry.

1.39 Overall, the Region had a high quality workforce but the pace of recent growth had brought about skill shortages in some areas. The region scored highly in Irish terms but not in European terms as regards research, technology and innovation with a city structure and third level education structure favourable to further development. A clustering of high-tech firms was now also emerging. In terms of infrastructure, the inter-urban road system was relatively well developed but the rapid increase in car ownership and freight traffic had meant that urban traffic systems were close to crisis proportions. The rapid growth of housing was exerting considerable pressure on sanitary services in cities and towns of all sizes. Water quality was under greatest threat in the eastern part of the Region. Energy and telecommunications infrastructure was in need of upgrading to make good existing deficiencies and to keep pace with rapidly expanding demand and to promote more dispersed development.

1.40 The Region offered a high quality of life in metropolitan Dublin and increasingly in other centres and the scenic areas which surrounded them. However, there had been a failure to address general issues of under-investment in the urban fabric, whereby cities and towns lacked a high environmental quality overall. There were also areas of multiple deprivation in larger urban areas, as well as in rural locations which continued to suffer from depopulation and loss of agricultural and non- agricultural employment. The high quality of the environment of the Region was a major attraction, although coastal erosion was a problem in many locations.

Objectives and Strategy

1.41 As in the case of the Border, Midland and Western Region, the overall objective of the strategy was to maintain and improve the quality of life, in a sustainable manner, for all who wished to live and work in the Region. Other objectives included: consolidating and building on the Region's economic performance especially in relation to reductions in employment and long-term unemployment, the development of Cork, Limerick and Waterford and other urban centres as a means of alleviating further congestion in Dublin, the targeting of social exclusion in urban and rural deprived areas, the distribution of economic growth and its benefits throughout the Region and the promotion of North/South co-operation.

Spatial Strategy

1.42 The strategy put forward a plan for sustainable planning development within the Region. It was centred around the development of the large urban growth centres of Dublin, Cork, Limerick and Waterford. It also dealt with appropriate development of other urban areas, towns and attached rural areas, disadvantaged rural areas and remote areas. Dublin would remain the primary national growth centre and a major international gateway as well as the southern node on the Dublin-Belfast economic corridor. It was in the interest of the State as a whole, as well as the Region, that the capital city functioned well and provided effective functions which it alone was capable of delivering. The preferred relationship of Dublin to its hinterland was one based on a corridor and node approach, using rail based links, and maximising the possibility of free standing towns in the sub-region developing economic activities of their own rather than being dormitories for Dublin. These larger towns, in turn, would relate to smaller catchments around them, generating employment and economic activity through retailing and indigenous manufacturing.

1.43 The urban centres of Cork, Limerick and Waterford would be central to regional growth and would be major gateways. These three proposed regional growth centres had significant potential to alleviate further congestion in Dublin and to provide an enhanced focus for inward investment, research and development and third level education. These centres were capable of handling a greater share of economic functions currently heavily concentrated in the capital. These included research, clustered high-tech investment, training and internationally traded services. It was recommended that the role of Limerick-Shannon-Ennis as a potential "growth triangle" should be fully exploited. The key to the sub-regional strategies were investment packages for radial routes into the regional centres, both road and rail, and the development of towns around each city which, whilst linked economically and socially, had a degree of independence which provided a rounded economic and social environment.

1.44 The strategy recommended that a cluster of urban centres in the South-East be developed as suitable locations for foreign direct investment and indigenous enterprise and that the necessary infrastructure be put in place to achieve this. The development of other towns and attached rural areas was also suggested in order to balance economic growth throughout the Region. As regards the development of disadvantaged rural areas, the strategy pointed out that in order to redress the low growth in these areas, measures with an agricultural adjustment function would have to play a part in the maintenance of rural communities. There would be a continuing requirement for measures with an income support dimension in view of the relatively low resource base, the small size structure and the scarcity of off-farm employment in many disadvantaged areas. For remote areas such as West Cork, South Kerry and West Clare, the development of aquaculture, fish processing, agricultural diversification into tourism and local community capacity building were recommended.

Sectoral Strategy

1.45 Investment of the order of £14.3 billion (€18.1 billion) over the 2000-2006 period was recommended in the areas of agriculture, fisheries and forestry, industry, the services, tourism, transport, telecommunications and energy, water and sanitary services, human resources, research and technology, local development/social exclusion and urban and village renewal. Investment in these sectors, it was suggested, would contribute to improving the quality of life in the region, improving productivity and competitiveness, building on regional strength, promoting a more balanced spatial distribution of economic activity within the country, addressing social exclusion and expanding the productive capacity of the Region's economy.

Findings of ESRI's ex-ante evaluation

1.46 As part of the preparations for the National Development Plan, the Department of Finance commissioned the Economic and Social Research Institute (ESRI) to carry out an assessment of the key priority areas for investment in the 2000-2006 period which would make the maximum contribution to Ireland's growth potential and sustainable employment growth. In choosing the investment priorities, the study had to have regard to factors which would:

- enhance Ireland's economic potential;

- contribute to continuing growth in sustainable employment;

- help the integration of the long-term unemployed and those at risk of becoming so into the economic mainstream;

- contribute to a balanced geographic distribution of economic activity which was consistent with maximising national economic growth; and

- identify the potential for cross-border investment in co-operation with Northern Ireland which would maximise the contribution of structural fund investment to economic and social progress for the mutual benefit of both parts of the Island.

In preparing their assessment, the ESRI as well as reviewing domestic and international economic developments and best practice, evaluated submissions on the Plan from the Regional Authorities, the Social Partners and Government Departments. Government Departments were asked for their comments on initial drafts of the ESRI's report and these comments were furnished to the ESRI for finalisation of their report.

1.47   The study pointed out that while public investment can play an important role in combating social exclusion, alleviating the difficulties of people with disabilities and promoting equal opportunities, it was not the only or even the most important instrument for tackling these challenges. The study stated that problems with the distribution of resources within society were most effectively dealt with through the tax and welfare system. The importance and role of public investment in promoting economic growth in Ireland and elsewhere in the EU was examined and the general experience indicated that investment in research and development, education and training and public physical infrastructure played a very important role in promoting high economic growth. Ireland, while having an income per head close to the EU average, had a smaller endowment of public capital than elsewhere.

1.48   The study found that in the absence of any external shock, the underlying competitiveness of the economy could allow a growth rate of around 5% per annum over the period of the Plan but in order for this growth rate to be achieved there would have to be a large expansion in public investment. However, there were a number of constraints on growth, most notably in the areas of the shortage of housing (and sanitary services), the road network and public transport. The shortages in these areas were now beginning to impact on the growth potential of the economy both directly and indirectly through their effect on the supply of labour. Demographics would lead to a slow down in the growth of labour supply implying that the priorities for industrial policy and an active labour market policy would change (for example, a reduction in the number of employment schemes).

Priorities

1.49   The study suggested investment in a number of priorities at a total cost of £47.2 billion (€59.9 billion) over the period of the Plan: Top priority was to be given to investment in public physical infrastructure, roads, public transport, sanitary services, social housing and social, cultural and recreational infrastructure. Investment in human capital, although not requiring a major increase in resources over the 2000-2006 period, would still play an important role in expanding the supply of skilled labour. Particular emphasis should be placed on improving the educational prospects of the disadvantaged. Increased investment in research and development was important for expanding the productive capacity of the economy. The study also recommended that there should be a scaling back in public resources devoted to promoting investment in industry, services, tourism, agriculture, energy and telecommunications and the freed up resources should be used to finance investment in physical infrastructure. The reason for this was that because of rapid economic growth, the justification for State intervention due to market failure was reduced in more developed regions.

1.50   The study recommended that the best strategy for promoting balanced regional development was to invest in a series of nodes which would provide a development focus for their surrounding hinterlands. The selected major regional centres for development were Dublin, Cork, Limerick/Shannon/Ennis, Galway, Waterford and Derry/Letterkenny. In addition, a limited number of smaller nodes would be needed to serve the widest population. Selection of these secondary nodes would require the undertaking of a National Spatial Strategy. It was recommended, also, that a special additional provision should be made to fund necessary development expenditure in the least developed regions of the country. Some innovative schemes to meet the very specific needs of certain severely disadvantaged communities was also justified.

1.51 In relation to North/South co-operation, a number of new possibilities were identified, most notably, the strengthening of the energy transmission system on the entire island. Secondly, the Belfast — Dublin road should be further developed as an economic corridor. It was also suggested that the economic development of the North West region hinged on the development of the Derry/ Letterkenny node. Investment in mainline rail to include a link to Dublin airport also held out the prospect for the greater integration of the transport systems North and South.

Outcome of the consultation process

1.52 The consultation process with the Social Partners, the Regional Authorities and the new Regional Assemblies culminated in a series of meetings at Ministerial level, in the context of Partnership 2000, to discuss the draft content of the National Development Plan. In accordance with a Government Decision, a copy of an Overview of the Plan provisions was forwarded to the Social Partners, the Regional Authorities and the new Regional Assemblies in advance of the meetings. The purpose of the meetings was to secure Social Partner consensus on the broad thrust of the investment proposals and the underlying strategy in the Plan. It was acknowledged that the Plan had to reflect the emerging consensus view of what the country's economic and social priorities ought to be for the Period 2000-2006 and the appropriate development policies and public investment proposals to address those development needs. In this regard, it was generally accepted that there had been a satisfactory outcome to the consultation process.

Appendix 2 Review of Programming Period, 1994 to 1999

Overview of the Community Support Framework, (CSF) 1994-1999

2.1 In line with the aims of the National Development Plan submitted to the European Commission in 1993, the central agreed objectives of the Community Support Framework (CSF) for Ireland, 1994-1999 were as follows:

- ensuring the best long-term return for the economy by increasing output, economic potential and long-term jobs;

- reintegrating the long-term unemployed and those at risk of becoming so into the economic mainstream.

2.2 The development strategy to achieve these objectives was built around four priorities as follows:

- to strengthen the overall productive capacity of the economy and identify and support the development of key sectors with the best long-term growth potential (productive sector priority);

- to improve competitiveness by investing in economic infrastructure (the economic infrastructure priority);

- to develop the skills and aptitudes of those in work and those seeking employment by both addressing the needs of the productive sectors and by integrating those who are marginalised and disadvantaged (human resources priority);

- to harness the potential of local initiatives to contribute to economic development (the local development priority).

2.3 The latest forecasts indicate that total expenditure under the CSF over the programming period (taking account of some expenditure overruns into 2000 and 2001) is projected to amount to just under £8.7 billion (€11 billion). Total co-financed public expenditure is projected at just over £6.4 billion (€8.1 billion) with an estimated contribution from the structural funds of just over £4.6 billion (€5.8 billion). Private expenditure under the CSF is projected to amount to £2.2 billion (€2.8 billion).

2.4 In terms of performance, it is clear that the central objectives of the CSF have been achieved. The quantified objectives set were considerably exceeded. As indicated above, real GDP expanded by an estimated average annual rate in excess of 8 per cent over the programming period, more than twice as fast as the target set. Total investment expanded at a rate of over 14 per cent per annum, compared to a target of 4 per cent. Net employment expanded by an annual average of over 74,000 in the five years to April 1999[1] compared to a target of 15,000 per annum over the period of the CSF. Reflecting this, the unemployment rate fell by some 9 percentage points in the five years to April 1999. This strong economic performance led to a rapid

---

[1] March to May Quarter as per the CSO Quarterly Household Survey.

273

convergence with the overall EU economy, with GDP per capita increasing from 85 per cent of the EU average in 1993 to an estimated 104 per cent by 1997. Increases well above the EU average are also projected for 1998 and 1999. In terms of performance in relation to the objective to reintegrate the long-term unemployed, the overall evidence points to substantial success on this front. On an International Labour Office (ILO) basis, total long-term unemployment fell to under 44,000 in the first quarter of 1999, compared to over 128,000 in April 1994, equivalent to a reduction in the long-term unemployment rate of some 6.4 percentage points.

2.5 The mid-term evaluation of the CSF, carried out by the Economic and Social Research Institute in 1997, included an assessment of the macroeconomic impact of the CSF. The short-run impact (i.e. in 1998/1999) of the CSF (structural funds element only) was estimated as an increase in the level of GNP of some 3 percentage points over what it would otherwise have been. The corresponding employment effect was estimated at some 33,000. These estimates capture the demand-side impacts of expenditures under the CSF on goods and services in the economy. The longer-term or permanent impact of the CSF, reflecting the supply-side impacts, is that GNP is projected to be almost one percentage point higher than it would otherwise have been. The combined long-run effect of the current CSF and the CSF for the 1989 to 1993 period will be to raise the level of GNP by about two percentage points.

2.6 In overall terms, the conclusions of the ESRI mid-term evaluation were positive, describing the CSF as representing *"a notable success story"*. It continued that *"funds have been deployed effectively to support and enhance what has been a remarkable economic recovery. Under the CSF process, medium-term planning of public expenditure has come more to the fore, allowing a more systematic and effective programming in many areas. Capacity and capability has been increased in the productive sectors; there has been a quantum-leap in the provision of public infrastructure; education and training attainment forges ahead; and experimental institutional arrangements have galvanised local initiatives"*.

2.7 The mid-term evaluation was an important input to the mid-term review of the CSF, which was completed by the CSF Monitoring Committee in 1997. In the light of the results of the evaluation and the policy priorities of the Government and the Commission, some €163 million of EU structural fund aid was reallocated within the CSF. Additional resources were allocated principally to Research and Development, National Roads, Broadband Technology, Control of Farmyard Pollution and actions to assist Early School Leavers, funded mainly from reductions in aid to Industry, Food Sector, Telecoms, Municipal and Hazardous Waste, Ports and Airports and Deflator Monies. These reallocations reflected the need to tackle growing infrastructural constraints in the economy and to address the difficulties facing the most disadvantaged groups in the labour market. They were also informed by a recognition that the rapid pace of economic growth meant that the necessity for certain types of aid to the productive or commercial sector of the economy had diminished.

2.8 Arising from a provision in the mid-term review for a review of progress of a number of major projects an additional major reallocation of €161 million of structural funds (mainly funds originally allocated to the Dublin Light Rail (LUAS) project) was agreed by the Monitoring Committee in mid-1998. Most of these resources were allocated to other public transport projects in the Dublin region and to improvements in the national roads network.

Productive Sector Priority

2.9 The productive sector priority accounted for just under €3,400 million of co-financed public expenditure (€2,569 million of EU aid) over the programming period (44 per cent of total EU aid). This priority comprised four Operational Programmes (OPs): the Operational Programmes for (i) Industrial Development, (ii) Agriculture, Forestry and Rural Development (iii) Fisheries and (iv) Tourism.

Industrial Development Operational Programme

2.10 The Industrial Development Operational Programme accounted for a projected €1,020 million or 18% of total EU aid under the CSF.

2.11 The principal objectives of the Operational Programme for Industrial Development were:

- the generation of sustainable employment in the industrial and services sectors;

- a greater integration of industrial activity with other sectors of the economy, thereby increasing the Irish value added share of industrial output;

- to develop our national resources, with particular emphasis on the food processing sector, to grow indigenous companies so that they could compete successfully on home and export markets and in technology based sectors;

- the achievement of a satisfactory regional balance in economic development.

2.12 The programme comprised seven sub-programmes. The Indigenous Industry Sub-Programme was composed of four broad measures under which €237 million of EU aid was provided for the development of industry's competitive capability as well as assisting firms to expand their productive capacity.

2.13 Under the Inward Investment Sub-Programme two measures were allocated €76 million of EU aid. The first measure covered fixed asset support under which projects received fixed asset grants or equity, as appropriate. The second measure covered employment and training grants.

2.14 The Research and Development Sub-Programme, which was allocated €311 million of EU aid, aimed at making the innovative capability of Irish firms and researchers commensurate with the competitive pressures facing Irish Industry. It comprised four measures covering industry research and development, industry/third level co-operation, human resource development and research support.

2.15 The purpose of the Marketing Sub-Programme was to promote and develop trade by indigenous industry through a market-led approach. €92 million was made available for guidance and assistance which was provided under three measures — market information and promotion, marketing expertise and advice and, marketing investment.

2.16 The Gaeltacht Development Sub-Programme was allocated €48 million of EU aid for measures covering finance for industry, training and recruitment initiatives and advisory support services.

2.17 The Food Industry Sub-Programme addressed a number of weaknesses in the food industry which had been identified in the early 1990s. The measures adopted covered capital investment grants, research and development, marketing and promotion, and human resources. €229 million of EU aid was made available under this Sub-Programme.

2.18   There was just one measure under the Land and Buildings Sub-Programme which accounts for €26 million of EU aid. Support was provided for site development, factory construction and upgrading/modification of existing buildings.

2.19   Over the period 1994 to 1997 gross job creation has averaged more than 26,000 jobs per annum, compared to a CSF target of 22,000. Net job creation (gross jobs created minus job losses) also performed significantly better than target, averaging over 11,000 jobs per annum compared to a target of just 5,000 per annum. Over the same time period the value of industrial exports has also climbed significantly, reaching a total of £35 billion in 1997. The 1999 target was £28.8 billion. There was also a marked increase in expenditure on research and development. By 1996, business expenditure on research and development is estimated to have reached 1.11% of GDP, compared to a 1999 target of just 0.82%. Similarly, by 1996 gross expenditure on research and development is estimated to have reached 1.59% of GDP, compared to a 1999 target of 1.3%.

Agriculture, Rural Development and Forestry Operational Programme

2.20   The Agriculture, Rural Development and Forestry Operational Programme accounted for a projected €998 million or 17% of total EU aid under the CSF.

2.21   The principal objectives of the Operational Programme for Agriculture, Rural Development and Forestry in the period 1994-1999 were:

- improved efficiency of agricultural production;
- promotion of farming in harmony with the environment;
- diversification of on and off farm activities;
- development of the forestry sector;
- income maintenance in less-favoured areas;
- effective education, training, advisory services and research in agriculture and forestry.

2.22   The Operational Programme comprised two main sub-programmes: (i) the Structural Improvement and Rural Development Sub-Programme and (ii) the Forestry Sub-Programme.

2.23   The Structural Improvement and Rural Development Sub-Programme contained 7 measures relating to On Farm Investment (€222 million); General Structural Improvement (€29 million); Farm Diversification (€28 million); Compensatory Headage Allowances (€467 million); Research (€30 million); Advisory Service for Farm Viability and Rural Enterprise (€36 million); and Human Resources.

2.24   The Forestry Sub-Programme comprised 3 measures covering Second Instalment Grants (€8 million); Forestry Development (€54 million); and Human Resources (€9 million).

2.25   29,000 farmers received support for on-farm investment (mainly related to environmental improvements but covering also dairy hygiene and animal welfare). The structural viability of almost 10,000 farms was enhanced through supporting the setting up of 3,700 young farmers and helping around 6,000 small to medium sized producers expand their Milk Quotas. 500 farmers received investment aid for horticulture and potato facilities. 4,000 farmers received investment aid for alternative enterprises (e.g. housing/handling facilities for horses, agri-tourism, etc.). About 120,000 farmers in designated disadvantaged areas received annual income support under the Compensatory Allowances Scheme. Around 4,000 young farmers were educated, about 10,000 adult farmers received training and about 40,000 farmers benefited from Teagasc's advisory services for conventional enterprises as well as alternative farm and rural enterprises.

2.26 Over the course of the operational programme, productivity, as measured by the net value added per annual work unit, has increased by over 50% compared to a target of approximately 14%. The ratio of total intervention to total output has also been substantially reduced. In 1998 only 4% of total output was bought into intervention compared to the CSF target of no more than 8% by 1999. In addition, serious pollution from agricultural waste has been reduced from 36 km of river in 1990 to 27 km of river in 1998 and the number of fish kills caused by agriculture has been reduced with 12 incidences in 1998 compared to 22 in 1991. The original CSF targets were 28 km of river and 15 incidences of fish kills respectively.

Fisheries Operational Programme

2.27 The Fisheries Operational Programme accounted for a projected €81 million or 1.4% of total EU aid under the CSF.

2.28 The overall objective of the Fisheries Operational Programme was to carefully target investment in order to maintain and strengthen the fishing industry's contribution to the national economy and in particular its contribution to growth and employment in the coastal communities.

2.29 The operational programme comprised 8 measures relating to Adjustment of Fishing Effort, Restructuring/Renewal of the Fishing Fleet, Marine and Land Based Aquaculture, Port Infrastructure and Facilities, Processing and Marketing, Promotion of Fish Products, Human Resources and Marine Research

2.30 The whitefish fleet has benefited from substantial investment support which has seen the introduction of 28 new state of the art fishing vessels and modern second hand vessels, the modernisation of vessels and the provision of safety equipment on vessels. There has been a substantial increase in fish landings with volumes increasing by more than 30% to 336,000 tonnes compared to a CSF target of only 18%. The value of landings increased by over 50% to £148 million over the same period, again exceeding the target set. Under the programme, 1,450 gross registered tonnage was removed from the Irish fishing fleet, facilitating the achievement of EU fleet targets. The Operational Programme has facilitated the improvement of existing landing facilities and related infrastructure and services and the provision of new infrastructure at a range of key fishery harbours. Works have also been undertaken at strategically important harbours to provide landing facilities to service the rapidly expanding aquaculture sectors. Sustainable development of the aquaculture industry (finfish and shellfish farming) has received targeted investment support to enhance its contribution to jobs and economic activity in coastal areas. Jobs have been maintained and competitiveness enhanced in the processing sector through investment required to meet mandatory EU Health and Hygiene standards together with a number of developmental projects.

Tourism Operational Programme

2.31 The Tourism Operational Programme accounted for a projected €470 million or 8% of total EU aid under the CSF.

2.32 The strategic objective of Ireland's tourism strategy over the period 1994-1999 was to maximise Ireland's tourism potential thereby increasing tourism revenue and tourism employment. The operational programme incorporated three key targets in relation to foreign exchange earnings, employment creation and the extension of the tourism season beyond the traditional summer and shoulder periods. Apart from these key targets, the programme also aimed to continue to expand, develop and market the Irish tourism product in accordance with identified market demand, having full regard to the need to conserve and protect the natural heritage. A further aim was to improve service and quality in the Irish tourism product, as well as value for money.

2.33 The operational programme comprised four main sub-programmes, each of which addressed a specific development need for the tourism sector. Under Sub-Programme for Natural and Cultural Tourism, €111 million of EU aid was allocated to the development of cultural, heritage and environmental sites. Projects varied in size from the development of the National Museum at Collins Barracks to small information developments on the canal services. A small part of the allocation was provided for the development of a regional programme of cultural facilities through the Cultural Development Incentive Scheme.

2.34 Under the Product Development Sub-Programme, €178 million of EU aid was provided towards the development of a broad range of tourism product through six measures. These include the development of major projects (such as the National Conference Centre); Tourism Information and Heritage; Tourism Angling; facilities for special interest holidays; improvements to hotel accommodation and the provision of accommodation related conference and leisure centres; and finally, the development of a greater base of information on the environmental impacts of tourism. Investment leverage exceeded expectations by more than 10 per cent under this sub-programme, resulting in an overall investment of nearly €400 million.

2.35 Under the Marketing Sub-Programme, ERDF support of some €72 million was made available to market Ireland abroad through a series of programmes including the Overseas Tourism Marketing Initiative. The sub-programme also supported a wide range of other marketing activities on the basis of selections made by the Marketing Management Board appointed under the programme. The Marketing Sub-Programme also attracted higher investment leverage than had been anticipated at the outset of the programme.

2.36 Almost €106 million of ESF support was allocated to the provision of training for the tourism sector under the Training Sub-Programme. Training was provided at three levels — to enable unemployed persons to re-enter the labour force; for school leavers entering the field; and finally to enhance the skills of those already employed within the industry.

2.37 Such has been the rate of growth of Irish tourism that most of the programme targets have been reached and tourism is now one of the fastest growing sectors in the Irish economy. Table 2.1 below reviews performance under each of the three key targets. The 1999 forecasts show that foreign exchange earnings are likely to exceed the programme targets by nearly 9 per cent to reach £2.45 billion. In fact, foreign exchange earnings from tourism reached £2.281 billion in 1998, exceeding the end programme target of £2.25 billion. Earnings have grown by some 66 per cent since 1993. Employment in the industry (which is calculated through the application of multipliers to tourism earnings data and includes employment both directly and indirectly supported) is projected to reach 133,000, again exceeding the target by some 8 per cent. The end-programme target was exceeded in 1998 and it is estimated that total direct and indirect tourism employment amounts to 126,700 whole time job equivalents. The third key target for the programme related to seasonality. It has proved difficult to attain the targets set in the programme particularly for the peak season in respect of which a target move from 30 to 25 per cent was set. Failure to meet the percentage based targets set within the programme with regard to shifts in visitors between the seasons should not, however, be viewed in a pessimistic light. An examination of the absolute numbers of visitors visiting in each season shows very positive and significant growth in the Shoulder and off-peak Seasons.

Table 2.1   Tourism in Ireland

	1993	1997 Actual	1998 Actual	1999 Target	1999 Forecast
Foreign Exchange Earnings £ million (in current prices)	1,367	2,105	2,281	2,250	2,450
Tourism Job Equivalents ('000) Targets	94	119	126	123	133
Seasonality (Overseas Tourist Numbers as % of Annual Total					
PEAK (July/August)	30	27.7	27.9	25	27
SHOULDER (May, June, September)	30	30	29.4	34	30
OFF PEAK (October-April)	40	42.3	42.6	41	43

Source: CSO/Bord Fáilte/Department of Tourism Sport and Recreation. 1998 Estimates are prepared by Bord Fáilte on the basis of CSO Tourism Statistics for three quarters, 1998.

Economic Infrastructure Priority

2.38   The economic infrastructure priority accounted for €1,755 million of co-financed public expenditure (€1125 million of EU aid) over the programming period (almost 20 per cent of total EU aid). This priority comprised three Operational Programmes (OPs), the Operational Programmes for (i) Transport, (ii) Economic Infrastructure and (iii) Environmental Services.

Operational Programme for Transport

2.39   The Operational Programme for Transport (OPTRANS) accounted for a projected €940 million or 16 per cent of EU aid under the CSF.

2.40   The fundamental objective of the programme was to provide essential infrastructural support for the development of the productive sectors of the economy and the creation of long-term sustainable employment. The primary transport objectives of the programme were to improve internal and access transport infrastructure and facilities on an integrated basis, thereby reducing transport costs and offsetting the negative effects of peripherality and to improve the reliability of the transport system by removing bottlenecks, remedying capacity deficiencies and reducing absolute journey times and journey time variance.

2.41   The programme comprised two sub-programmes. The National Economic Development Sub-Programme covered investment in strategic transport infrastructure and facilities, principally national roads, mainline rail, commercial seaports and the State airports. The Sub-Regional

Economic Development Sub-Programme dealt with investment in key sub-regional and local transport infrastructure and facilities, primarily non-national roads, the Dublin Transportation Initiative and regional ports.

2.42 The National Economic Development Sub-Programme comprised six main measures: 2 measures for National Primary Roads, Major Improvements and Integrated Network Improvement accounting for projected EU aid of €445 million; National Secondary Roads (EU aid of €97 million) Mainline Rail (EU aid of €53 million) State Airports (EU aid of €14 million) and Commercial Seaports (EU aid of €28 million)

2.43 The Sub-Regional Economic Development Sub-Programme contained four measures: Non-National Roads (EU aid of €145 million), DTI Public Transport (€93 million in EU aid), DTI Management (€49 million EU aid) and Regional Ports (€9 million EU aid).

2.44 The indications are that the main physical and investment impact targets for the operational programme, as revised in the course of the Mid-Term Review, will be achieved. At the end of 1998, 57% of the national primary road network had been up-graded to 'Mid D' standard (which represents an inter-urban travel speed of 80 kph). This compares with 35% at the start of the Operational Programme and the revised target for the end of 1999 of 58%. Time savings on the major road corridors as a result of major improvements, amounted to 124 minutes at the end of 1998 - the revised target for end 1999, arising from the Mid-Term Review, is 176 minutes. Indications now are that this figure is likely to be surpassed by the end of 1999.

2.45 As regards mainline rail, passenger numbers increased by 1.6 million, over the period 1994 to 1998, 0.3 million more than the revised target for 1999. The Operational Programme co-financed programme of improvements at State Airports was completed in 1997; passenger numbers and cargo throughput have been well ahead of the Operational Programme original projections and in line with the revised forecasts. There have been substantial increases in passenger numbers and RO/RO, LO/LO and bulk traffic at seaports and the Operational Programme target of reducing combined port and shipping costs to port users by 15% has been achieved.

2.46 In the case of non-national roads, 1,694 kilometres of roadway were improved in the five-year period to end 1998, corresponding to 85% of the target of 2000 kilometres for the period to end 1999. Under the DTI traffic management measure, a large number of projects have already been completed, including the provision of a number of Quality Bus Corridors (QBCs), cycleways, street improvements and improved facilities for the mobility impaired. A major programme of QBC (and associated cycleway) development, expedited through the assistance of the monies reallocated from the LUAS project, is underway.

Operational Programme for Economic Infrastructure

2.47 The Operational Programme for Economic Infrastructure accounted for €112 million or 2% of EU aid under the CSF.

2.48 The primary objectives of the Economic Infrastructure Operational Programme were to assist the cost-effective supply and consumption of fuel and to maintain and develop efficient postal and telecommunications services thereby improving the competitive position of Ireland's postal, energy and telecommunications sectors.

2.49 The Economic Infrastructure Operational Programme comprises two main sub-programmes: the Energy Sub-Programme (€59 million of EU aid) and the Communications Sub-Programme (€50 million of EU aid).

2.50 Under the Energy Sub-Programme, resources have been provided for a new Peat-Fired Power Station in the Midlands; the extension of mains electricity supply to the Aran Islands, Cape Clear, Inishbofin and Clare Island and reinforcement of the Connemara 38 kV network; energy efficiency audits and investments; investments in renewable and alternative energy; and the development of cutaway bogs. Over the period of the programme, overall energy intensity as measured by the ratio of total primary energy requirement to GDP (at constant 1990 prices) has been reduced from a 1993 value of 83 (Base Year 1980, value 100) to a 1998 estimate of 70, a reduction of over 15% in the ratio compared to a 1999 target value of 75. There has also been a positive impact in terms of the increase in installed electricity generating capacity from renewables from 8 MW in 1993 to 86 MW in 1998.

2.51 Grants were made available under the Communications Sub-Programme for telecommunications infrastructure including digitalisation of exchanges, improving fault clearance, reducing call failure rates, development of Synchronous Digital Hierarchy Cross Connect Systems, and increased telephone penetration; development of broadband technology and promotion of the development of the Information Society in Ireland; development of cost-effective e-commerce infrastructures; and postal measures including automation of rural post offices and the development of new regional mail centres in Athlone, Portlaoise and Sligo. Over the period of the programme the rate of exchange digitalisation has increased from 70% in 1993 to 95% in 1998, with a 1999 target of 100%. The rate of fault clearance within two working days has improved from 85% in 1993 to 94% in 1998. The 1999 target is for 97%. The 1999 targets for reductions in call failure rates for local, STD and international calls were all achieved by 1998, while the 1999 target for telephone penetration of 82% was achieved by 1996 and was 89% by 1998.

2.52 New broadband technology and the e-commerce infrastructures measures were developed on a small scale arising from the Mid-Term Review. As regards the postal measure, postal charges had been reduced from 113% per cent of the EU average in 1993 to 90% of the EU average by 1998.

Operational Programme for Environmental Services

2.53 The Environmental Services Operational Programme accounted for a projected €73 million or 1.3% of total EU aid under the CSF.

2.54 The primary objectives of the programme were the development and treatment of water supplies to meet development needs; the provision of systems for the collection, treatment and disposal of sewage and other water borne wastes; the development of waste disposal facilities, including appropriate provision for hazardous and non-hazardous waste management and disposal; coastal protection works, and environmental monitoring, research and development.

2.55 The programme was divided into four main sub-programmes. Under the Water Services Sub-Programme, €47 million of EU aid complemented substantial Cohesion and Exchequer funding in financing the completion of 163 major water and sewerage schemes between 1994 and 1999. By the end of 1998, a total of 128 schemes had been completed, increasing water treatment capacity by over 202,956 cubic metres per day, the equivalent of providing additional supply to over 812,000 persons. Water storage capacity had also been increased by 193,500 cubic metres and waste water treatment capacity had been increased by nearly 379,000 population equivalent.

2.56 €15 million of EU aid under the Waste Management Sub-Programme was directed to the provision of hazardous waste infrastructure, waste recovery and recycling infrastructure and the development of waste management strategy studies.

2.57 Some €10 million was allocated to 35 local authority waste recycling projects and 34 private sector projects. This supported total investment of over 3 times that amount and led to new recycling capacity exceeding 1.2 million tonnes, the provision of public access sites to recycling and provision of 8 large civic amenity sites by local authorities. It is estimated that these investments created direct employment of over 300 jobs.

2.58 Under the Coastal Protection Sub-Programme €5 million of EU aid was allocated to coastal protection. These works, which included one major protection scheme as well as a number of smaller priority locations around the coast have provided essential protection for public property, infrastructure and amenities at these locations.

2.59 €3 million in EU aid was allocated to two measures under the Environmental Monitoring/R & D Sub-Programme. The Environmentally Sustainable Resource Management measure focused on addressing priority environmental problems for which little information was available and where accurate data is essential for environmental assessment, decision-making and management of the environment. A total of 20 R&D projects were supported by the programme in the general areas of water quality, air quality, waste management, monitoring and environmental assessment techniques and methods. Data produced by the projects has been used in the development of national indicators of environmental performance and also to furnish environmental statistics to international bodies. The Cleaner Production Measure was aimed at encouraging manufacturing and service industries to introduce the environmental management approach to production. A demonstration programme involving 14 companies from a range of sectors and geographical locations implemented programmes resulting in significant environmental improvements including reduction in the use of solvents and hazardous materials and the use of energy and water, introduction of recycling and reuse, and reduction of emissions to air and water.

Human Resources Priority

2.60 The Human Resources Priority which comprised the Operational Programme for Human Resources Development accounted for €2.460 billion of co-financed public expenditure (€1.809 billion of EU aid) over the programming period (31 per cent of total EU aid). In addition, there were human resource development components in each of the four productive sector Operational Programmes and under the Operational Programme for Local, Urban and Rural Development.

Human Resources Development Operational Programme

2.61 The objectives underpinning this priority were to enhance education and skill levels and the employment prospects of the unemployed, particularly the long term unemployed, and persons excluded from the labour market.

2.62 The Operational Programme comprised 5 sub-programmes: Initial Training and Education (EU aid of €864 million) Continuing Training for the Unemployed (EU aid of €201 million), Objective 3-Social Exclusion, (EU aid of €425 million), Objective 4-Adaptation to Industrial Change (EU aid of €74 million), Improvement of the Quality of Training (including a technical assistance) (EU aid of €242 million).

2.63 The programme has directly provided training and education to a significant percentage of the population over the 1994-1999 period. The data below indicates the numbers of people who completed training or educational courses by sub-programme in each year of the programme. The reduction in recent years in the numbers completing under Social Exclusion — Objective 3 mirrors the same positive labour market trends that allowed for a reduction in expenditure. Even though over 90% of the Quality of Training completions relate to short in-service training courses provided for serving teachers, the numbers in the general population completing longer courses with support from the Operational Programme has been in excess of 125,000 annually.

Table 2.2   Course Completions

	1994	1995	1996	1997	1998	1999 Est.	Totals Est
Initial Education & Training	37,867	37,324	35,904	41,363	65,739	45,000	263,197
Cont Training for Unemployed (SP.2)	16,331	18,245	13,887	14,743	10,386	13,000	86,197
Social Exclusion Objective 3	48,933	68,045	67,143	68,286	49,804	49,000	307,211
Adaptation to Industrial Change	25,653	32,445	28,495	21,889	27,546	25,000	161,028
Quality of Training	56,289	68,709	134,940	131,764	139,88	132,000	663,579
Totals	185,073	224,768	280,369	278,045	293,877	264,000	1,481,607

2.64 The Operational Programme has clearly played an important role in providing trained people in sufficient numbers to cater for employment growth over the period. The overall indicators used to monitor the Operational Programme also point to considerable achievement. For example, total employed as a percentage of the working age population rose by 9 percentage points to 56.5 per cent between 1993 and 1998. The proportion of school leavers leaving without any qualification declined from 6.3 per cent in 1993 to 3.2 per cent in 1997. The pupil/teacher ratio at first level declined from 25.1:1 in 1993 to 22:1 in 1998. The education profile of population improved considerably with the proportion of the working age population with ISCED (International Standard Classification of Education) code 6-7 (third level) rising from under 7 per cent in 1993 to 11 per cent in 1998.

Local, Urban and Rural Development Priority

2.65 The Local, Urban and Rural Development Priority, which also comprised a single operational programme, accounted for €382 million of co-financed public expenditure (€269 million of EU aid) over the programming period (almost 5 per cent of total EU aid).

2.66 The Operational Programme was designed to bring about social and economic development at a local level, to involve and enable local communities to be involved in that development in a formal way, and to achieve physical improvements to the environment.

2.67   Arising from the Mid-Term Review the following strategic objectives were adopted.

- The provision of an effective framework for co-ordinated local development which embraces social, economic and environmental elements in an integrated manner;

- The maximisation of the number of sustainable new jobs and enterprises that can be created at local level;

- The provision of support systems which facilitate the maximum involvement of local individuals and groups in the development of their local area;

- The provision of a response to the urgent need to provide new channels of inclusion for the long-term unemployed and other marginalised groups in our society; and

- The provision of support for the physical and environmental improvement of Irish cities, towns and villages in a way that supports an inclusive and participative approach to such development.

2.68   There were three main sub-programmes. Under the Sub-Programme for Local Enterprise, EU aid of €77 million was made available through the mechanism of the County Enterprise Boards (CEBs) to provide a range of support services for local enterprise initiatives. The sub-programme provided support to enterprises through three measures with a fourth measure providing funding for the development of county enterprise plans and the promotion of enterprise.

2.69   In terms of the key job creation indicator, the sub-programme is expected to reach its revised target by the end of the programme with 13,100 new jobs having been created by end 1998 against the revised target of 17,175. (The original target for the entire programme, which was not broken down by sub-programme, was 16,900 jobs). The sub-programme is expected also to reach its revised target for Enterprise Creation and Development (9,800 enterprises to be assisted). The sub-programme also leveraged a higher level of investment than was originally envisaged.

2.70   The Sub-Programme on Integrated Development of Designated Disadvantaged and Other Areas, accounted for EU aid of €81 million. The programme provided support primarily to communities, especially disadvantaged communities. As provided for in the operational programme, in each of the 38 designated areas of disadvantage, Partnership companies (75-80% of funding) were set up to draw up and co-ordinate the delivery of a local action plan. Thirty-three Community Groups (17%-22% of funding) played a similar role for communities with significant needs outside the designated areas while a smaller number of Selected Organisations (3% of funding) complemented the work of the Partnerships and Community Groups. The sub-programme comprised two main measures (in addition to two smaller and fairly recent measures in respect of the Territorial Employment Pacts). Measure 1, co-financed by the ERDF, supported (i) Enterprise Creation and Development and (ii) Infrastructural and Environmental Actions. Measure 2, co-financed by the ESF, provided support to (i) Education and Training (Preventive Measures within the Education Sector and Complementary Education and Training), (ii) Services for the Unemployed and (iii) Community Development.

2.71   Significant achievements have been made under the sub-programme. For example, 12,744 people were assisted in setting up as self employed to end 1998. (These individuals would also have been in receipt of assistance from the Department of Social, Community and Family Affairs — through its Area Allowance and Back to Work schemes.) A further 11,417 people were placed in full-time work and another 2,900 were assisted in finding part-time work. Some 35,000 young people were assisted to end 1998 under Preventive Education measures.

2.72 The Urban and Village Renewal Sub-Programme accounted for EU aid of €78 million. Under this sub-programme funding was provided to finance a range of measures designed to rejuvenate the social and economic life of towns and villages, rehabilitate the built environment and restore and conserve important elements of Irish architecture and heritage.

2.73 Over the programme period a major urban renewal project was implemented in each of the five main cities: Cork, Dublin, Galway, Limerick and Waterford. In other urban areas over three hundred projects were implemented involving total expenditure in excess of €19 million. In village locations 1,000 environmental improvement projects were implemented supported with total funding of over €31 million. Over 150 conservation projects were assisted with total funding of some €9 million. In the Temple Bar area of Dublin, ten cultural projects were assisted involving expenditure of over €53 million, funded by both the EU and the Exchequer. While the population of the Temple Bar area had been in decline for many years prior to the commencement of the Temple Bar Programme, the population has increased from 200 to around 1,400. Retailing activity in the area has also increased and there are now over 340 new businesses in operation there.

Review of Cohesion Fund 1994-1999

2.74 One of the major innovations of the Treaty of Maastricht was the decision to establish a Cohesion Fund from 1 April 1993. The main aim of the European Union's cohesion policy is to reduce economic and social disparities between Member States. The Fund benefits Member States with a GNP per capita, of less than 90% of the Community average which have a programme leading to the fulfilment of conditions of economic convergence set out in Article 104c of the Treaty. The rate of Community assistance granted by the Fund is 80% to 85% of eligible expenditure. The Fund assists projects in the fields of environment and transport infrastructure forming part of the trans-European network. It focuses on the larger projects i.e. those costing more than €10 million .

2.75 Unlike the Structural Funds which are administered on a programme basis, assistance from the Cohesion Fund is approved exclusively on the basis of specific individual projects of which more than 100 have been approved in Ireland since 1993. The distribution of assistance in Ireland in the period 1994-1999 by infrastructural category was as follows:

Category	Total Investment (€ million)	Fund Contribution (€ million)
	Transport	
Roads	790	561
Rail	171	142
Ports	52	41
Airport	4	3
Sub-Total Transport	1,017	747
	Environment	
Water Supply	353	251
Waste Water	711	479
Solid Waste	12	10
Habitat	3	2
Technical Assistance	9	7
Sub Total Environment	1,088	749
Gross Total	2,105	1,496

2.76 The total costs of some of the more important developments co-financed by the Fund are: Balbriggan By-Pass (€59 million); Southern Cross Section of the Dublin Ring Road (€64 million): Dunleer — Dundalk Road (€80 million); Arklow By-Pass (€65 million) Portlaoise By-Pass (€44 million); Collooney — Sligo Road (€40 million); Rail Network Improvement (€69 million); Rail Network, Track and Signalling (€77 million); Dublin Region Water Supply Scheme, Stage 1 (€64 million); Tuam Regional Water Supply (€51 million); Dublin Region Waste Water Scheme (€58 million); Drogheda Main Drainage (€68 million); Dundalk Sewerage Scheme (€54 million); Wexford Main Drainage (€58 million) and Cork City Main Drainage (€80 million).

2.77 Roads investment co-financed by the Fund in the 1993-1999 period resulted in the provision of 71 km of motorway, 157 km of single carriageway, 47 km of dual carriageway and 5 km of three lane carriageway. The projected time savings associated with the foregoing is estimated to amount to 176 minutes.

2.78 The mainline track renewal programme has been concentrated on those sections of the network which are included in the trans-European networks of high speed , conventional rail and combined transport. The work involves the upgrading of the basic infrastructure to cater for increased operating speeds. The lines which have benefited from Cohesion Fund investment include the radial routes from Dublin to Belfast, Sligo, Galway, Limerick, Tralee, Cork and Waterford. The Dublin to Belfast route has been upgraded jointly by Iarnrod Eireann and Northern Ireland Railways. The track has been upgraded to Continuous Welded Rail (CWR) standard which involved the replacement of life-expired jointed rail on timber sleepers with CWR on concrete sleepers and other ancillary works e.g. installation of improved signalling systems.

2.79 Cohesion Fund investment is being supplemented by investment in mainline rail rolling stock co-financed by the European Regional Development Fund. Rail investment co-financed by the Cohesion Fund has resulted in the provision of 355 km of track renewal, 46 bridge renewals and the improvement/upgrading of 164 level crossings.

2.80 The development strategy for seaports focused on improving competitiveness and expanding the capacity of the internationally traded sectors of the Irish economy by overcoming selected deficiencies in port infrastructure and handling equipment and improving access. The type of works carried out include the installation of facilities to cater for unitised traffic — roll on/roll off operations at Dublin, Rosslare, Cork and Waterford.

2.81 While the growth in traffic through Irish Ports over the 1993 to 1997 period averaged 5% per annum, the most significant increase has been in unitised traffic with Ro/Ro (Freight Units) increasing from 221,059 in 1993 to 491,261 in 1997 (122%) and Lo/Lo (TEUs) increasing from 411,069 to 530,479 during the same period (29%) A cumulative real reduction of 15% in combined port and shipping charges was achieved between 1994 and 1997. This reduction has a significant positive impact on the productive sectors of the economy.

2.82 Investment was concentrated in a single development involving the construction of apron, warehouse and offices at Dublin Airport to provide expanded air freight facilities. The completion of the project has improved cargo facilities in the areas of sorting and forwarding freight. It has also upgraded infrastructure and provided enhanced freight handling facilities for wide-bodied aircraft. The development contributed to increased freight throughput at Dublin Airport which grew from 62,800 metric tonnes in 1992 to 90,000 metric tonnes in 1995 when the project was completed.

2.83   The Cohesion Fund, which co-financed environmental investment of €1,063 million (£837 million) in the 1993-1999 period, has mainly concentrated on projects that contribute to Community environmental policy and, in particular, to the priorities of the European Union's Environment Action Programmes. The main focus of Cohesion Fund investment has been on projects necessary to meet the requirements of Urban Waste Water Treatment Directive and the Drinking Water Directive. In addition, the Cohesion Fund has supported the development of waste water treatment, collection and phosphorous reduction facilities for the major river and lake catchments and also the development of water conservation schemes.

2.84   Over 50 projects were assisted, supporting more than one hundred individual schemes. Structural Funds assistance of about €122 million (£96 million) was also provided for these services in the period in question. Overall investment has allowed 128 major water and sewerage schemes to be completed by end 1998 with a further 35 scheduled for completion in 1999. This has facilitated an increase in water treatment capacity of almost 202,956 cubic metres (45 million gallons per day) and water storage capacity has increased by almost 193,500 cub metres (43 million gallons). It has also facilitated waste water treatment, collection and phosphorous reduction infrastructure to be provided in the major river and lake catchments including Lough Derg, Lough Ree, the rivers Suir and Liffey and the provision of water and sewerage services to open up land for residential development through the Serviced Land Initiative.

2.85   Cohesion Fund assistance of €9.4 million co-financed total investment of €12.0 million in two solid waste disposal facilities at Ballymount (Dublin) and Tralee. The Ballymount station contains waste reception and two waste baling halls, each with a design capacity to process 70 tonnes of refuse per hour, making the plant the largest of its kind in Europe. The Tralee project consists of a modern waste disposal site with a capacity of 20,000 tonnes per annum including facilities for the segregation of materials for recycling. This specially engineered landfill facility is designed so that leachate generated by rainfall cannot contaminate groundwater. The development has been fully completed and is operational.

2.86   The purpose of the habitat investment is to preserve the best examples of raised bog wetland habitat in Ireland. Work involves a programme of land acquisition followed by the blocking of drains to raise the water table and monitoring the condition of sites. All sites chosen have been selected as candidate Special Areas of Conservation under the Habitats Directive.

2.87   The Cohesion Fund also supported a number of key consultancies including the Greater Dublin Water Supply Strategic Study, the national water study, monitoring and management systems for some major catchment areas and the development of a computerised capital accounts system for local authorities for managing water services capital projects.

Appendix 3 Maps

Regions

New NUTS II Regions

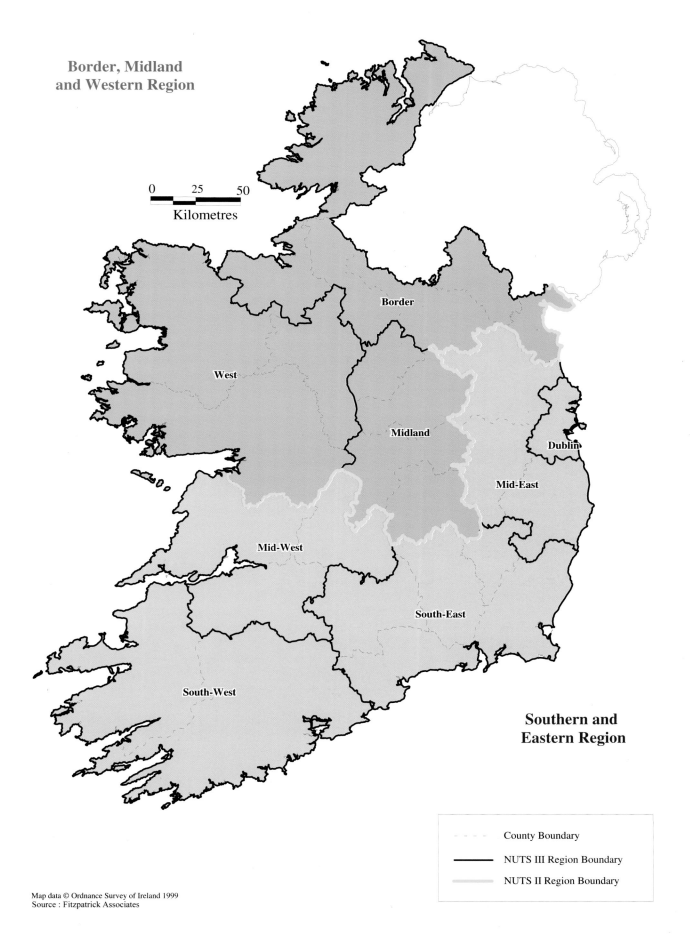

Border, Midland
and Western Region

0   25   50
Kilometres

Border

West

Midland

Dublin

Mid-East

Mid-West

South-East

South-West

Southern and
Eastern Region

County Boundary

NUTS III Region Boundary

NUTS II Region Boundary

Proposed Regional Aid Limits
Post 2000

PROPOSED REGIONAL AID LIMITS POST 2000

1 – NUTS II REGION – 'A' STATUS

5 – NUTS III REGION – 'C' STATUS

– IRELAND –

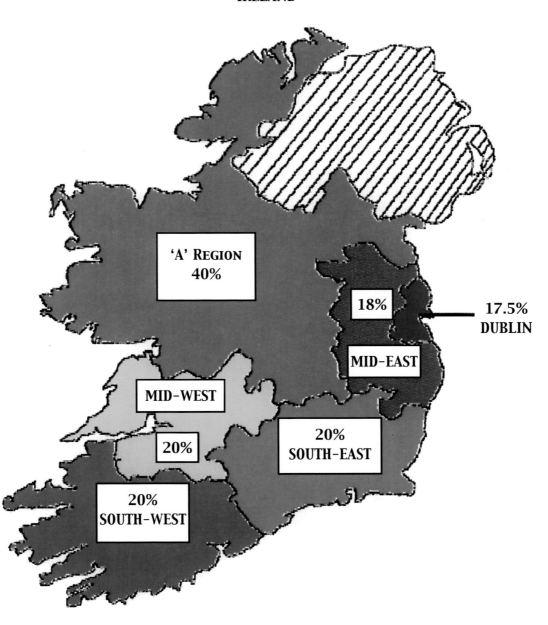

'A' REGION
40%

18%

17.5%
DUBLIN

MID-EAST

MID-WEST

20%

20%
SOUTH-EAST

20%
SOUTH-WEST

Road Improvements

INVESTMENT IN ROAD IMPROVEMENTS 2000 - 2006

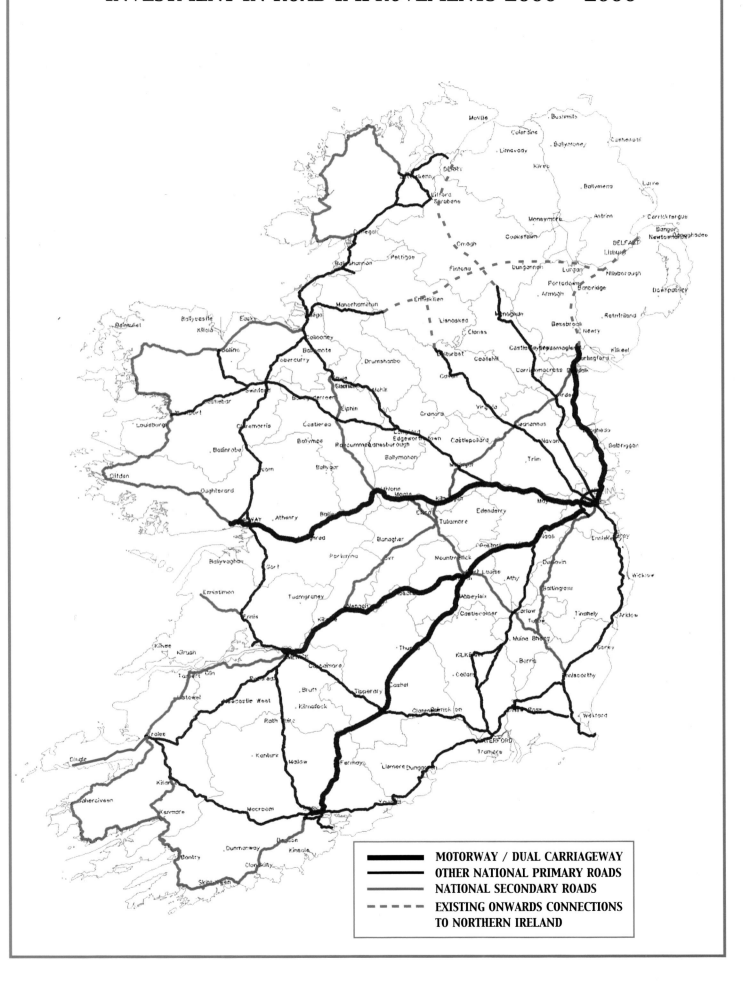

MOTORWAY / DUAL CARRIAGEWAY
OTHER NATIONAL PRIMARY ROADS
NATIONAL SECONDARY ROADS
EXISTING ONWARDS CONNECTIONS
TO NORTHERN IRELAND

Dublin Transportation Blueprint

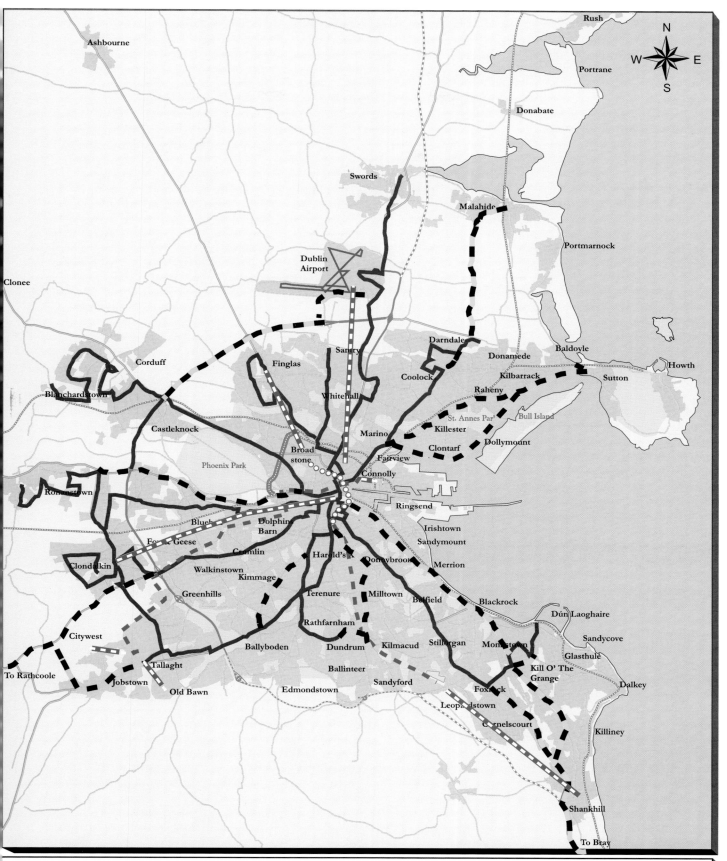

Dublin Transportation Blueprint
2000 - 2006 Main Projects

....	Upgrade of Heuston - Connolly Rail Line
———————————	QBCs in DTI
▬ ▬ ▬ ▬ ▬ ▬	QBCs in Transportation Blueprint
▬ ▬ ▬ ▬ ▬	LRT - work in progress
⊢ ⊣ ⊢ ⊣ :	LRT in Transportation Blueprint (Route to be chosen)
∘∘∘∘∘∘∘∘∘∘∘∘∘	Underground LRT section Harcourt St. - Broadstone

Blueprint lines shown are subject to further evaluation. Additional lines may also be required. (Subject to evaluation.)

dto

Dublin Transportation Office
Oifig Iompair Átha Cliath

Rail Improvements

RAILWAY ROUTE MAP

PORTRUSH
COLERAINE
DERRY
LARNE
ANTRIM
BANGOR
BELFAST
LISBURN
PORTADOWN LURGAN
NEWRY
DUNDALK

BALLINA SLIGO
COLLOONEY
BALLYMOTE
BOYLE CARRICK-ON-SHANNON
FOXFORD
DROMOD
CASTLEBAR MANULLA JUNCTION*
LONGFORD
WESTPORT
CLAREMORRIS CASTLEREA
DROGHEDA
BALLYHAUNIS EDGEWORTHSTOWN MOSNEY
ROSCOMMON MULLINGAR BALBRIGGAN
ENFIELD SKERRIES
GALWAY WOOD RUSH & LUSK
LAWN MALAHIDE
ATHLONE MAYNOOTH DUBLIN CONNOLLY STN.
ATHENRY CLARA DUBLIN PEARSE STN.
ATTYMON BALLINASLOE KILDARE DUBLIN DUN LAOGHAIRE
TULLAMORE HEUSTON
PORTARLINGTON NEWBRIDGE STN. BRAY
PORTLAOISE GREYSTONES
ROSCREA ATHY WICKLOW
CLOUGHJORDAN RATHDRUM
ENNIS BALLYBROPHY CARLOW
NENAGH TEMPLEMORE ARKLOW
BIRDHILL
CASTLE THURLES MUINE BHEAG GOREY
LIMERICK CONNELL KILKENNY THOMASTOWN ENNISCORTHY
LIMERICK JUNCTION
TRALEE CHARLEVILLE WEXFORD
FARRANFORE TIPPERARY CAHIR CAMPILE ROSSLARE STRAND
CLONMEL
MALLOW CARRICK-ON-SUIR BALLYCULLANE
KILLARNEY WATERFORD WELLINGTON BRIDGE BRIDGETOWN
RATHMORE COBH ROSSLARE HARBOUR
MILLSTREET JUNCTION
BANTEER
CORK COBH

* Passenger transfer point only

 Iarnród Éireann

intercity

Appendix 4 National Development Plan 2000-2006 Pilot Eco-Audit

4.1   The National Development Plan has been prepared within the overall framework of national environmental, as well as economic and social development, policy.

4.2   The overall aim of Sustainable Development: A Strategy for Ireland, as approved by Government, is to ensure that the economy and society can develop to their full potential within a well protected environment without compromising the quality of that environment, and with responsibility towards present and future generations and the wider international community.

4.3   Consistent with this strategic aim, the Government is committed to ensuring that concern for the environment is central to all policy decisions. In June 1999, the Government approved the introduction, on a pilot basis, of a procedure for the eco-auditing of policies in specific sectoral areas and of national development plans. This pilot eco-audit of the National Development Plan 2000-2006 takes into account guidelines on eco-auditing which have been developed to assist in giving effect to the Government decision.

4.4   The National Development Plan 2000-2006 envisages continued growth in the Irish economy over the medium term. The Plan is based on average annual growth in GNP of about 5% over the period and contains measures to secure and maintain that level of growth in the years ahead.

4.5   The Plan provides for expenditure of over £40 billion on the following priority areas:

- Economic and Social Infrastructure;
- Employment and Human Resources;
- Productive Sector;
- Rural Development;
- Social Inclusion;
- Social Capital (housing and health).

4.6   These priorities have been identified as areas for investment in order to support and maintain economic and employment growth. The Plan also addresses wider social issues by means of a commitment to a sharing of the fruits of economic activity, both across different sectors of society and in terms of spatial planning (through the designation of two regions at NUTS II level and the proposed National Spatial Strategy).

4.7   A broad overview of current trends in environmental quality, and of economic and social driving forces now exerting pressure on the environment, is contained in Environment in Focus, a discussion document produced by the Environmental Protection Agency (EPA) in 1999; this has informed preparation of the Plan. A new State of the Environment Report, being prepared by the EPA, will be available in 2000. Pending this comprehensive assessment, the EPA analysis indicates that the main threats to the environment arise in the areas of climate change, eutrophication, the urban environment (including transport) and waste.

4.8 Economic and social development, together with investment of the order contained in the Plan, has unavoidable implications for the environment. Without appropriate integration measures, there would be impacts, ranging from the insignificant to the significant, on among other things, water and air quality, biodiversity, patterns of land use, energy consumption and waste production. The Plan recognises this and aims to achieve a balance between environment and development.

4.9 The impact of the totality of proposed development on the environment as a whole places a premium on the pursuit of policies which promote economic efficiency, with less intensive resource use and less environmental stress.

4.10 For example, in the energy sector emphasis is placed on least cost approaches to achieving more sustainable energy systems. In the transport area, high importance is attached to increased efficiency which will reduce journey times, congestion and emissions and to the implementation of the integrated transport strategy for the Greater Dublin Area. Support for manufacturing industry will be linked to explicit commitments by firms to environmentally friendly production and appropriate waste management practices. Finally, in the tourism sector it is recognised that the future development of the industry is critically dependent on managing growth on an environmentally sustainable basis.

4.11 The Plan is a broad strategic document covering an extensive range of activities across most sectors of society. In a Plan of this nature, it is inevitable that detailed programmes remain to be worked out and that, at this stage, there is limited information on overall impact. It will be important that individual operational programmes are subject to eco-audit; these eco-audits will need to be built upon in the Plan and operational programme implementation, including by the use of appropriate indicators to measure the contribution to sustainable development. (Two reports, Environmental Evaluation of the Irish Community Support Framework 1994-99 and Environmental Indicators and Structural Funds Programmes in Ireland: A Guidance Document prepared by ERM Consultants for the Community Support Framework Environment Co-ordinating Committee, should be of assistance in these tasks).

4.12 The Plan incorporates a range of measures to address the environmental and social aspects of sustainable development. The environmental dimension is addressed, through measures to:

- Develop a National Spatial Strategy and promote balanced regional development (including through programmes for urban and village renewal);

- Secure better integration of land use and transport planning through, for example, adherence to the Strategic Planning Guidelines for the Greater Dublin Area;

- Enhance the eco-efficiency of transport through a more efficient road network, substantial investment in public transport, and other sustainable modes, and development of demand management measures;

- Support the meeting of climate change policy objectives, as a major test of sustainable development, through action across the Plan and in specific sectors, for example, in the energy and forestry areas (further measures in relation to climate change will be set out in the planned National Greenhouse Gas Abatement Strategy);

- Assist towards the achievement of sustainable agriculture through the Rural Environment Protection and Control of Farmyard Pollution Schemes;

- Improve water supply and waste water treatment facilities in accordance with the Drinking Water and Urban Waste Water Directives and national legislation;

- Implement integrated waste management strategies;

- Support a dedicated programme of environmental research.

4.13 The possibility of the emergence of some unsustainable patterns of development within the framework of the Plan cannot be excluded. This could arise from a number of factors, including the pace of current economic development, unforeseen interactions between measures, or unanticipated consequences of particular measures.

4.14 It will, therefore, be of critical importance to ensure that the environmental dimension is fully integrated into the further stages of programme planning and into implementation. This should be achieved through:

- Integration of environmental considerations into the preparation of Operational Programmes and specific policies and measures, with a view to maximising eco-efficiency and minimising adverse impacts;

- The use of environmental criteria in Operational Programme project selection;

- The inclusion of environmental representation on Operational Programme Monitoring Committees;

- The inclusion of the environmental dimension in all evaluations to be carried out under the Plan;

- The establishment of an Environment Co-ordinating Committee for the 2000-2006 Period.

4.15 Development and implementation of indicators of environmental performance at Operational Programme and measure levels will be key to demonstrating the proper integration of environmental considerations into Plan implementation.

4.16 Finally, projects implemented under the Plan will be required to comply with relevant planning and environmental legislation; all projects should aim to minimise their negative environmental impact and secure positive environmental gain.

Wt. PB00089. 3,000. 7/00. Cahill. (M64311). G. Spl.